Humanitarian Hypocrisy

Humanitarian Hypocrisy

*Civilian Protection and the
Design of Peace Operations*

ANDREA L. EVERETT

Cornell University Press

Ithaca and London

Copyright © 2017 by Cornell University

All rights reserved. Except for brief quotations in a review, this book, or parts thereof, must not be reproduced in any form without permission in writing from the publisher. For information, address Cornell University Press, Sage House, 512 East State Street, Ithaca, New York 14850.

First published 2017 by Cornell University Press
Printed in the United States of America

Library of Congress Cataloging-in-Publication Data

Names: Everett, Andrea L., 1982– author.
Title: Humanitarian hypocrisy : civilian protection and the design of peace operations / Andrea L. Everett.
Description: Ithaca : Cornell University Press, 2017. | Includes bibliographical references and index.
Identifiers: LCCN 2017028028 (print) | LCCN 2017028885 (ebook) | ISBN 9781501714818 (pdf) | ISBN 9781501714726 (r) | ISBN 9781501715471 | ISBN 9781501715471 (cloth : alk. paper)
Subjects: LCSH: War relief—Case studies. | Peacekeeping forces—Case studies. | Humanitarian assistance—Case studies. | International relief—Case studies.
Classification: LCC HV639 (ebook) | LCC HV639 .E94 2017 (print) | DDC 341.5/84—dc23
LC record available at https://lccn.loc.gov/2017028028

Cornell University Press strives to use environmentally responsible suppliers and materials to the fullest extent possible in the publishing of its books. Such materials include vegetable-based, low-VOC inks and acid-free papers that are recycled, totally chlorine-free, or partly composed of nonwood fibers. For further information, visit our website at cornellpress.cornell.edu.

Contents

List of Figures and Tables   *vii*

Acknowledgments   *ix*

Abbreviations   *xiii*

Introduction: Civilian Protection and the Design of
Peace Operations   *1*

1. Devil in the Details: Assessing Mission Design
   and State Policy   *21*

2. Political Will, Organized Hypocrisy, and
   Ambitions-Resources Gaps   *41*

3. Quantitative Evidence   *69*

4. France in Rwanda   *103*

5. The United States in Darfur   *137*

6. Australia in the Southwest Pacific   *169*

Conclusions and Implications   *199*

Appendix A: The Data   *213*

Appendix B: Statistical Tests   *219*

Notes   *223*

Index   *261*

Figures and Tables

Figures

1.1 Spectrum of protection goals 26
1.2 Representing protection 33
2.1 Predicting contribution types 62
3.1 Distribution of contributions 76
3.2 Contribution type by CE news coverage and operational environment 85
3.3 Predicted probabilities, model 1 90
3.4 Predicted probabilities, model 2 92
3.5 Predicted probabilities, model 3 93
4.1 Weekly *Le Monde* and *l'Humanité* coverage of Rwanda, March 6–July 2, 1994 119
5.1 Monthly U.S. newspaper coverage of Darfur, 2004–7 150
6.1 Monthly *SMH* coverage of East Timor, 1999 181
6.2 Daily *SMH* coverage of East Timor, September 1999 182
6.3 Monthly *SMH* coverage of Aceh, 1999–2004 194

Tables

1.1 A protection typology 35
3.1 Correlation coefficients—CE news coverage and political ties 80
3.2 Means of CE news coverage and operational environment, by contribution type 83

3.3	Effect of a change in CE news coverage, model 1	91
3.4	Effect of a change in CE news coverage, model 2	93
3.5	Effect of a change in CE news coverage, model 3	94
3.6	Effect of changes in control variables, model 2	96
3.7	Effect of changes in control variables, model 3	96
3.8	Effect of changes in contribution decade and CE news coverage, model 4	98
A.1	Post–Cold War complex humanitarian emergencies and peace operations	213
A.2	Components of operational environment	215
A.3	Control variables	216
B.1	Multinomial logits, contribution type	220
B.2	Summary statistics	222
B.3	Multinomial logit, contribution type (restricted sample)	222

Acknowledgments

The idea for this book first began to take shape in 2008. At the time it resembled a jigsaw puzzle: there were many interesting pieces, but it was hard to see how they would all fit together. Since then I have benefited from the guidance and advice of many generous people. To everyone who has supported me in the process of turning my early ideas into a cohesive project, it is a tremendous privilege to be able to say thank you.

This book would never have gotten off the ground without the patient mentoring and support of my outstanding advisers at Princeton. Bob Keohane consistently delivered feedback that was speedy, copious, and laser-focused on the central issues. For this, and for his enthusiastic help and encouragement, I am deeply grateful. Chris Achen once told me that if I took on this project, I would suffer. As with so many things, he was right. Yet despite clearly foreseeing the obstacles, Chris always supported what I wanted to do and made clear that he thought I could do it. Nothing was more important in giving me the confidence to persevere during difficult moments. For his steadfast support and friendship, I cannot thank him enough. Jay Lyall offered extremely helpful advice about conducting fieldwork, building a dataset, and finding relevant data sources. His input at the start of the project, when there were so many big decisions to be made, was especially critical.

Many others dedicated substantial time and energy to helping me improve this book. I received excellent advice at a manuscript workshop in 2014, hosted by Thomas Weiss and the Ralph Bunche Institute for International Studies at the City University of New York. Michael Barnett, Page Fortna, Michael Gilligan, Marina Henke, Bob Keohane, Paul Romita, and Taylor Seybolt each traveled to CUNY for the workshop and read the entire manuscript. Their detailed feedback inspired revisions that have made it far stronger.

I thank Roger Haydon, my editor at Cornell University Press, for his strong support of this book and for his valuable comments on several parts of the manuscript. Special appreciation also goes to Lamis Abdelaaty, Gary Bass, Sarah Bush, Alex Downes, David Hsu, Kris Johnson, Steve Krasner, and Ben Valentino for reading and offering helpful comments on major pieces and in some cases multiple iterations of the project. This group was also a tremendous source of mentorship, friendship, and support over many years. I am grateful, too, to the two anonymous reviewers whose suggestions inspired changes that improved the book in important ways. Additionally, Megan White and John Willingham provided helpful research assistance for chapter 4.

The book has also benefited from comments and questions at various talks and workshops, and from discussions with numerous friends and colleagues. In this respect I am particularly grateful to Ben Appel, Steve Brooks, John Carey, Tom Christensen, Chad Clay, Lynn Eden, Chris Gelpi, Kristen Harkness, Joanne Gowa, Emily Meierding, Jennie Miller, Daryl Press, Patricia Sullivan, and Emily Zackin. More broadly, I am indebted to everyone who attended seminars where I presented this work at Princeton, Stanford, Dartmouth, Duke, the University of Iowa, and the University of Georgia, and at conferences hosted by the American Political Science Association, the International Studies Association, the Midwest Political Science Association, and the Peace Science Society. I would also like to acknowledge Chip Blacker, my undergraduate adviser, who helped inspire my interest in foreign policy.

Assistance from several institutions helped enable the research and writing of this book. For financial support for fieldwork and data collection, I thank the Princeton Institute for International and Regional Studies, the Mamdouha S. Bobst Center for Peace and Justice, and the Lynde and Harry Bradley Foundation. I received a year of support from the Dickey Center for International Understanding at Dartmouth College, and am grateful to Chris Wohlforth and Daryl Press for the opportunity to participate in the center's outstanding fellowship program. I also thank the Center for International Security and Cooperation (CISAC) and the Freeman Spogli Institute for International Studies (FSI) at Stanford University—especially Lynn Eden and Steve Krasner—for providing me an institutional home during parts of the writing process. My fieldwork in Australia was greatly smoothed by an affiliation with the Research School of Pacific and Asian Studies at the Australian National University, kindly arranged by Chris Reus-Smit.

I am deeply indebted to the former policymakers, activists, and academic experts in Australia and the U.S. who so graciously allowed me to pick their brains about their foreign policy and advocacy work. I was repeatedly overwhelmed by their generosity as they welcomed me into their homes and offices, often giving me multiple hours of their time and submitting to repeated rounds of questioning. Special thanks goes to Hugh White, who not only patiently explained the ins and outs of nearly every actual or contemplated Australian use of military force over the past 30 years, but also used his own contacts to help me arrange many other interviews.

Some material in the introduction and chapters 1, 2, 4 and 5 previously appeared in my article "Mind the Gap: Civilian Protection and the Politics of Peace Operation Design," *Security Studies* 26, no.2 (2017): 213–48. The list of complex humanitarian emergencies described in chapter 3 was previously presented in "Post-Cold War Complex Humanitarian Emergencies: Introducing a New Dataset," *Conflict Management and Peace Science* 33, no.3 (2016): 311–39. I thank these journals and their publishers for their kind permission to use this content here.

My parents, sister, and dear friends outside of political science have provided consistent support and encouragement. I thank them for all the pep talks and for their enduring confidence that there would someday be a book for them to read. I am grateful above all to my partner, Andrew Narver, for pushing me to keep going, for cheering me on and hearing my complaints, for always offering the perfect synonym, and for supporting me in every possible way for longer than either of us anticipated.

Abbreviations

ACFOA	Australian Council for Overseas Aid
ADF	Australian Defence Force
AICF	International Action Against Hunger (France)
AMIB	African Union Mission in Burundi
AMIS	African Union Mission in Sudan
AU	African Union
CAVR	Commission for Reception, Truth and Reconciliation (East Timor)
CPA	Comprehensive Peace Agreement (Sudan)
DPA	Darfur Peace Agreement
DRC	Democratic Republic of Congo
ECOWAS	Economic Community of West African States
EU	European Union
FALINTIL	Armed Forces for the National Liberation of East Timor
FAR	Armed Forces of Rwanda
FDP	Forcibly Displaced Person
GAM	Free Aceh Movement
GI-Net	Genocide Intervention Network
ICG	International Crisis Group
ICRC	International Committee of the Red Cross
IDP	Internally Displaced Person
IMF	International Monetary Fund
INTERFET	International Force for East Timor
JEM	Justice and Equality Movement (Darfur)
MDM	Doctors of the World (France)

MONUC	United Nations Organization Mission in the Democratic Republic of the Congo
MRND	National Revolutionary Movement for Development (Rwanda)
MSF	Doctors Without Borders (France)
NATO	North Atlantic Treaty Organization
NGO	non-governmental organization
ONUSAL	United Nations Observer Mission in El Salvador
POC	Protection of Civilians in Armed Conflict
R2P	Responsibility to Protect
RPF	Rwandan Patriotic Front
ROE	Rules of Engagement
SHZ	Safe Humanitarian Zone (Rwanda)
SMH	Sydney Morning Herald (Australia)
SLM/A	Sudan Liberation Movement/Army (Darfur)
TNI	Armed Forces of Indonesia
UN	United Nations
UNAMET	United Nations Mission in East Timor
UNAMID	United Nations–African Union Mission in Darfur
UNAMIR	United Nations Assistance Mission for Rwanda
UNITAF	Unified Task Force (Somalia)
UNOMSIL	United Nations Observer Mission in Sierra Leone
UNOSOM (I & II)	United Nations Operation in Somalia
UNPROFOR	United Nations Protection Force (former Yugoslavia)
UNTAET	United Nations Transitional Administration in East Timor
USAID	United States Agency for International Development

Humanitarian Hypocrisy

Introduction

Civilian Protection and the Design of Peace Operations

> The question "to intervene or not?" gets answered every day, but with no sign that the judgments it requires are actually being made.
>
> —Michael Walzer, "The Politics of Rescue"

On January 13–14, 2005, residents of the village of Hamada in southern Darfur, Sudan, suffered a vicious assault by Sudanese government planes and government-supported Arab militia. The attack destroyed the town, displacing about 9,000 people and killing over 100, mostly women and children, in a pattern that had become all too familiar over two long years of war.[1] With the Sudanese government in Khartoum engaged in mass atrocities against the region's non-Arab population, some 2.5 million people required emergency assistance and between 63,000 and 380,000 had died by the time of the attack on Hamada.[2]

Although soldiers from the African Union Mission in Sudan (AMIS) were deployed in Darfur in early 2005, they did not reach Hamada in time to do more than document the destruction. AMIS was authorized, in part, to protect civilians it discovered in its immediate vicinity and to patrol to help deter expected attacks. Yet the mission faced extraordinary challenges. Insufficient numbers, unclear and restrictive rules of engagement, limited intelligence collection capacity, inadequate ground and air transport, and the inability to fly or patrol at night—among other limitations—left the force poorly prepared to meet Darfuris' most pressing security needs.[3] As a result, although AMIS did save some lives, its anemic response to the attack on Hamada was repeated in village after village, and it could not deliver even the limited amount of protection it was authorized to provide.

In Bosnia, from 1992 to 1995, Serbs, Croats, and Bosnian Muslims fought a devastating civil war in which all sides targeted civilians. Serb forces were the worst offenders, systematically beating, imprisoning, raping, and killing

Muslims and destroying their homes, all in their efforts to gain territory for their own ethnic brethren. By the end of the war, an estimated 1.3 million people were internally displaced, some 2.2 million were refugees in other regions, and an additional 1.4 million were "war affected."[4] At least 40,000 to 42,000 civilians had died.[5]

Starting in 1992, the United Nations Protection Force (UNPROFOR) deployed to Bosnia to help provide security for the delivery of humanitarian relief and to protect and oversee "safe areas" for civilians threatened by war and ethnic cleansing. It was a well-resourced force, with large troop contributions from wealthy European nations. Yet UNPROFOR operated under restrictive rules of engagement and with a traditional UN peacekeeping mandate that prevented soldiers from firing their weapons except in self-defense. These limitations undermined its ability to deliver on its promises of civilian protection. Highly trained, well-equipped soldiers were forced to stand by as the safe areas they were supposed to protect were attacked. Despite the help of NATO air strikes, Bosnian Serbs overran three of the six—Zepa, Bihac, and Srebrenica—in 1995. In Srebrenica, some 8,000 Muslim men and boys were murdered.[6]

The village of Com in the island territory of East Timor was lucky to escape the fates of Hamada and Srebrenica. On the night of September 27, 1999, a group of heavily armed militiamen herded several hundred frightened East Timorese civilians onto a dock. The militia intended to load their captives onto ships, probably to transport them against their will across the border into the Indonesian province of West Timor. Over the previous three weeks militia violence had destroyed nearly three-quarters of all buildings and houses in East Timor, killed perhaps 2,000 civilians, and forcibly displaced most of the territory's 800,000 inhabitants.[7] Thousands of East Timorese had been kidnapped and taken to West Timor. Under the circumstances, the militia seemed to have good reason to believe that the evening's abduction would go as planned.

Two hundred kilometers (125 miles) away, however, Australian soldiers with the International Force for East Timor (INTERFET) were busy examining recent air reconnaissance photos. Suspicious of the gathering at the wharf, Commander Peter Cosgrove ordered a Special Forces squadron to investigate. The Australians piled into their Blackhawk helicopters and flew off into the night. When they landed near Com, locals informed them of the hostage situation. The soldiers moved forward in the darkness and surrounded the militia, ordering them to surrender. When the latter sought to escape, the Australians' superior training and clear willingness to use force allowed them to capture and disarm the militia and free the terrified civilians, all without firing a single shot.[8] Over the next few months INTERFET continued to protect civilians and restore order in East Timor. Hundreds of thousands of people were able to return home and resume their lives.

As these and many other examples attest, peace operations—international military missions to promote peace and provide security during or after violent conflict—differ dramatically in the protection they afford to threatened civilians.[9] For victims of complex emergencies like those in Darfur, Bosnia, and East Timor, the difference between a force like AMIS or UNPROFOR and one like INTERFET can be the difference between a death sentence and a return to everyday life.[10] In this book I explore the reasons for this variation, focusing on the role of several great power democracies—the United States, the United Kingdom, France, and, in its own region, Australia—in contributing to these missions and determining how they are designed.

My central argument is that these powerful states support and contribute to missions like AMIS and UNPROFOR—missions defined by a gap between the protection that soldiers are asked to provide and the resources available for doing so—as a way to balance competing normative and material pressures both to protect civilians and to limit the costs and risks of any such efforts. In doing so, the policies they pursue represent a form of organized hypocrisy: leaders' attempts to reach a compromise between protecting civilians and controlling costs lead to disparities between the humanitarian principles they proclaim and the reality of what their actions are designed to accomplish. While domestic society and government are the main sources of these conflicting priorities, international partners can at times contribute as well. Whatever the source, the strength of competing political pressures related to civilian protection differs considerably both across conflicts and over time. This, in turn, leads to variation in the demand for and likelihood of compromise and of compromised peace operations. This demand peaks, and policies promoting such operations are most likely, I claim, when the tension between demands to protect civilians and limit costs is greatest, under conditions I enumerate below.

To test the argument I analyze original data on the four great power democracies' participation in peace operations in post–Cold War complex emergencies, as well as several in-depth examples of their responses to these conflicts. I also develop a new framework for conceiving and describing key distinctions in mission design as they relate to civilian protection. Though there has been much handwringing over peace operations' frequent failure to effectively protect civilians and the world's lack of political will for doing so, this book is the first major effort to clarify the politics behind this problem. Although it tackles only a piece of the puzzle, the evidence suggests that at least for the major liberal democracies, decisions about how to intervene are just as political as decisions about whether and when to do so. The book adds to our understanding of several aspects of international relations, including humanitarian intervention, peacekeeping, democratic foreign policy, and international norms. It also has practical and ethical implications for the challenge of protecting those threatened by devastating violence.

Describing Variation: Peace Operation Design, Great Power Democracies, and State-level Policy

How a peace operation performs in protecting civilians reflects both chance and planning. To understand why some missions turn out like AMIS and others like INTERFET, we must acknowledge that sometimes the best-laid plans go awry: intelligence is faulty, equipment malfunctions, or conditions change unexpectedly. Yet a peace operation's overall design determines the protection it can be reasonably expected to offer absent very good or very bad luck. Mission design thus represents a second layer of variation that is related to but distinct from the protection a force actually provides, and that more directly reflects its organizers' intentions and commitment.

In terms of protecting civilians I identify three basic types of peace operations, distinguished by the relationship between two core components. While details vary from case to case, missions that aim to provide effective protection for vulnerable civilians must do two key things. First, they must pursue appropriate political goals and military strategies, and second, they must deploy sufficient resources, including enough well-trained and properly equipped personnel. An operation's *ambitions* and *resources* for civilian protection, that is, must match both the needs on the ground and each other.

Unfortunately, few peace operations meet these standards, even in the worst conflicts. Many of these conflicts receive no peace operations at all. Among those that do, *robust* missions are least common. Like INTERFET, these missions involve both appropriate ambitions and a suitable level of resources. More often, *limited* missions are deployed, which have very little in the way of either ambitions or resources to address the key threats civilians face. Finally, as in Darfur and Bosnia, peace operations may display a gap between what soldiers are asked to do and what they are able to do. Such *ambitions-resources gaps* can emerge, as with AMIS, when a force aspires to provide more protection than it is able to deliver. Or, as with UNPROFOR, troops may have the resources and physical ability to deliver more protection than they are asked to provide.[11] Either way, such gaps run a significant risk of unintended consequences that can actually worsen civilians' plight.

Since most peace operations are multilateral, the form they take usually depends on a complex process of coordination among multiple states and, often, international bureaucrats. In particular, it is states that must contribute troops and other resources, and that must agree on mission goals and activities in international bodies like the UN Security Council, NATO, or the African Union (AU). Thus, ultimately, understanding operational design requires an account of policymaking at the state level. Seen in this light, state-level policy represents yet a third layer of variation, where the policies pursued by all states involved in authorizing and conducting a given mission together determine its basic type and overall capacity for civilian protection.

Still, while many countries and several international organizations regularly participate in peace operations, some are far more influential than others. In particular, the four great power democracies at the center of this book stand out both for the frequency of their involvement and for their unique ability to ensure that these missions are designed to meet civilians' needs by taking a lead role themselves. Indeed, in the worst conflicts few missions are conducted entirely without these states. Among the thirty-one post–Cold War complex emergencies that were ongoing between 1989 and 2009 and that received at least one peace operation, there were a total of sixty-six missions with distinct names and mandates. Only six (9%) had no financial or military involvement by any of these four states, and only two of the conflicts saw no peace operations involving them.[12] In part this reflects the permanent membership of the United States, the United Kingdom, and France on the UN Security Council, which gives each of these states tremendous influence over the landscape of UN action, even when its own troops do not deploy. Especially in Africa, they also regularly provide financial and logistical support that helps enable regional forces like AMIS.

Just as important, the United States, the United Kingdom, France, and Australia are the only states—aside from Nigeria—that have played the dominant leadership role in a force devoted substantially to protecting civilians. Major non-Western nations with at least some power projection capability—notably, Russia and China—have limited ability to deploy and sustain forces far from home, have focused mostly on regional security concerns, and have expressed serious reservations about civilian protection absent the full consent of the local government.[13] Meanwhile, the limitations of the five international organizations that have authorized and run post–Cold War peace operations—NATO, the EU, the AU, the Economic Community of West African States (ECOWAS), and the UN—are well documented. Neither NATO nor the EU has acted without significant direct involvement by the United States, the United Kingdom, or France. In Africa, missions led by the AU and ECOWAS have demonstrated serious holes in these organizations' capabilities.[14] Similarly, the UN lacks the logistics and command-and-control capabilities for more ambitious forms of civilian protection or war-fighting, and has struggled to find troops who are prepared for such missions.[15] Thus, it does not typically lead operations with a primary goal of civilian protection.[16]

Thanks to their unique influence, then, the United States, France, the United Kingdom, and Australia make policy decisions that are particularly crucial for explaining overall patterns of variation in peace operation design, and especially for understanding why missions like UNPROFOR and AMIS are more common than those like INTERFET. This justifies their role at the center of this book. At the same time, the characteristics that contribute to these states' influence—their extensive political clout and military capabilities—also allow them to contribute to peace operations in a wide variety of ways. As I explain further in chapter 1, for these states we can think about participating in these missions as an opportunity to promote any of the three key outcomes introduced above: limited protection, robust protection, or ambitions-resources gaps. This book, then, explores how leaders make these choices, concentrating on ambitions-resources gaps as the most puzzling—and simultaneously most troubling—outcome.

Ambitions-Resources Gaps: A Puzzle with High Moral Stakes

When it comes to protecting civilians from devastating violence, the design of peace operations is a high-stakes matter. Barring bad luck, robust missions can do a great deal of good, saving people from death at the barrel of a gun or from lack of access to international relief. Limited missions are not intended to address these threats but may help keep peace after war. In contrast, ambitions-resources gaps raise unique moral issues while also presenting a significant puzzle for traditional explanations of peace operations and individual states' participation.

First, these gaps run a particularly strong risk of creating or exacerbating problems of moral hazard related to military intervention, and may even increase risks to civilians. Although peace operations always create expectations among locals that the troops are there to assist them, ambitions-resources gaps are especially likely to generate expectations of protection that soldiers cannot meet.[17] Such unmet expectations, in turn, can threaten the credibility of the international community and civilian protection as an enterprise. More important, they can have the perverse effect of exacerbating suffering and death among the very people that peace operations are supposed to benefit. When civilians expect foreign troops to shield them from violence, they may change their behavior in ways that leave them even more vulnerable to attacks when adequate protection is absent.[18] The Srebrenica massacre in Bosnia, for example, was only possible because civilians had flocked to a UN "safe area" that was being manned by a Dutch UNPROFOR battalion. Similarly, during the Rwandan genocide in 1994, the arrival of French soldiers in an area known as Bisesero prompted some 1,000 people who had survived in hiding for the past two months to come out in hope of rescue. The French, lacking the trucks to take these people to safety, told them to wait until they could get proper transport. When the troops returned three days later, most of the people had been killed.[19] Similar issues have arisen in Darfur, the Democratic Republic of Congo (DRC), and beyond.

The prospect or reality of foreign military intervention may also affect the actions of violent actors in ways that make ambitions-resources gaps especially problematic. For example, the expectation of intervention may encourage rebels to engage in provocative behavior that will increase the risk of mass violence, and actual intervention may prolong war by giving them access to resources to sustain their insurrection.[20] Similarly, military action that punishes perpetrators of violence against civilians may increase the perceived threat represented by the victims and encourage an escalation in attacks. While these risks need not take intervention off the table they do imply an obligation to design peace operations robustly, with civilians' needs in mind. The alternative, as Benjamin Valentino has put it, is that intervention itself "can risk inciting a slaughter."[21]

Thus, peace operations' design and timing affect not only how many lives they can save but also whether they make things better or worse for vulnerable civilians. As a result, numerous policy practitioners and scholars of humanitarian action have bemoaned the frequent disconnect between needs, goals, and resources, and have argued—in the words of Thomas Weiss—that intervention in devastating conflicts "should be timely and robust or shunned altogether."[22] Yet while many scholars have sought to explain decisions to initiate and contribute to peace operations, our understanding of why these missions look as they do with respect to civilians' needs—and of ambitions-resources gaps in particular—remains surprisingly underdeveloped.

For the most part studies of the causes of peacekeeping and humanitarian intervention (or lack thereof) have not emphasized operational design. They focus mainly on why states or the UN act at all rather than why they deploy one type of mission and not another.[23] Still, when discussion does turn to peace operations' construction, shortcomings are often ascribed—as with international failures to prevent mass atrocities—to an absence of political will grounded in a seemingly pathological aversion to the costs and risks of more robust action.[24] A corollary is that, when peace operations are robust, it must be because sufficient political will is present.

As others have noted, however, to attribute inappropriately-designed peace operations to a simple lack of political will is to restate the problem of a spate of poorly-constructed missions without offering a clear account of the motives and constraints driving key decision-makers.[25] There are numerous reasons why states could be unwilling to bear the costs of robust action, but it is unlikely that they all matter equally. More fundamentally, framing the problem primarily in terms of cost-intolerance overlooks how non-robust missions come about at all. When peace operations are not designed to address civilians' key security needs, the problem is not just a lack of action, but rather insufficient action. There is enough political will to do something, but not enough to design a mission that fits the circumstances.

To understand ambitions-resources gaps in particular, we must explain why governments of powerful states aim to give the impression of trying to protect civilians, but do not follow through (or as Weiss has similarly put it in the context of UN action, why they aim "to appear to be doing something without really doing anything"[26]). Seen in this light, ambitions-resources gaps are puzzling indeed: not one of the three major explanations for states' involvement in peace operations identified by previous studies can explain them.

First, numerous scholars have argued that powerful states' strategic incentives account for their decisions to initiate and support peacekeeping missions and humanitarian interventions, or that certain strategic relationships—based on regional, colonial, or other ties—help explain their contributions to these operations.[27] Applied to civilian protection in complex emergencies, these arguments suggest that leaders typically want to achieve specific objectives in order to defend their state's strategic interests. These goals, in turn, might or might not require providing security and protection for vulnerable civilians. Either way, such arguments treat states as rational unitary actors. As such, they can be expected to choose political goals and military strategies commensurate with whatever level of civilian protection is consistent with their interests, and to provide the resources necessary to pursue them.[28] This, in turn, might yield either robust or limited military action (if any), but not a mismatch between means and goals.

Second, various observers have suggested that advocacy and media pressure can motivate humanitarian military action by generating domestic political costs for leaders who fail to respond.[29] Yet such studies do not explain how leaders might benefit politically with an attentive domestic audience from "doing something" that can at best accomplish little and may well make matters worse. Who would reward such policies, and what would lead them to do so? After all, recent research suggests that people tend to judge military operations according to the importance of the goals to be achieved and their success in achieving these goals.[30] Nor, as a general rule, do leaders expect to gain political favor by knowingly wasting resources and risking their credibility by appearing callous or incompetent. While supporting the UN or regional organizations might sometimes allow leaders of powerful states to escape responsibility for an operation's shortcomings, this is at best a partial answer since these states also lead missions that involve ambitions-resources gaps. Likewise, if leaders face pressure to act, why should the audience that creates those pressures accept such half-hearted gestures?

Third, even absent a direct and specific interest in a particular conflict, governments may perceive a general interest in participating in multilateral collective security efforts through the UN or regional organizations.

The most altruistic version of this argument is that they participate in peace operations to help secure the international public good of a more peaceful and humane world. Alternately, they may have more self-interested motives such as cultivating a reputation as a good international citizen that might prove useful down the road or pursuing immediate benefits like training and equipment for their troops.[31] A caveat here is that, in the absence of private domestic political or strategic motives for action, states may be tempted to freeride on the efforts of others and thus supply relatively few resources. Still, this alone does not account for ambitions-resources gaps, since it does not address the selection of mission objectives or military strategies, particularly why the states responsible for selecting them would choose ambitious protection goals in the knowledge that resources might prove insufficient.

In sum, it is hardly self-evident that ineffective or patently hypocritical operations should be attractive or risk-free for political leaders. To solve the puzzle of ambitions-resources gaps requires a more complete account of the political context surrounding the design of these missions than scholars have offered to date, particularly for the major democracies that can provide robust civilian protection instead. Such an account must recognize that political will for civilian protection is not just present or absent. As the International Commission on Intervention and State Sovereignty noted in its 2001 report, *The Responsibility to Protect*, "the trouble with most discussions of 'political will' is that more time is spent lamenting its absence than on analyzing its ingredients."[32] In practice, political will exists on a continuum and is affected by a complex mix of forces that can each work either to encourage or dissuade leaders from acting to protect civilians—to motivate or to constrain. What is needed is to clarify how these forces can interact to create a situation in which ambitions-resources gaps become acceptable policy, and when they are most likely to do so. I use the concept of organized hypocrisy developed in the literatures on organizations and international norms to frame this analysis.

The Argument

Organized hypocrisy occurs when leaders or large organizations respond to competing normative and material pressures in a given policy arena with "inconsistent rhetoric and action."[33] Specifically, "talk" is used to give the impression of living up to a normative standard despite actions that fall short.[34] This is an apt description of ambitions-resources gaps. States and international organizations regularly face conflicting normative and material demands to protect civilians on one hand, and to limit the costs and risks of doing so on the other. At the same time, the organizers of peace operations in complex emergencies often declare an intention to save the lives of vulnerable civilians. In doing so, they aim to give the impression of addressing civilians' most important needs and, by extension, of avoiding added harm to those they seek to help. In practice, however, norms of protection and of "do no harm" are belied when soldiers lack the capacity to fulfill their mandates or are forbidden from taking risks to shield civilians from ongoing attacks. Ambitions-resources gaps, that is, rest on a fundamental inconsistency between the commitment to life-saving humanitarian action that organizers hope to communicate and the reality of what their policies are designed to accomplish.

This depiction of ambitions-resources gaps as organized hypocrisy helps identify the basic structure of a problem that policymakers often confront during complex emergencies: How to balance simultaneous political pressures for strong action to protect civilians with competing imperatives to limit costs and risks. While Michael Lipson has applied this framework to UN peacekeeping, in this book I extend it to the policies of individual great power democracies when they create or promote ambitions-resources gaps.[35] For leaders of these states, these gaps represent a form of compromise between contradictory political impulses. Still, it is no surprise that leaders' words and actions sometimes diverge. Alone, describing ambitions-resources gaps as organized hypocrisy does not explain either when competing moral and material pressures are most likely to arise and pose challenges for leaders, or why these policies can be an acceptable, perhaps even desirable, response. Understanding the process by which ambitions-resources gaps occur requires moving beyond a simple acknowledgement that contradictory pressures may exist to a more detailed analysis of their origins and the interactions among them.

My argument focuses on the perspective of the top leaders, or national executives, who have ultimate authority over decisions about the use of military force in the great power democracies. I assume that these leaders seek to resolve competing pressures to protect civilians and limit costs in ways that are optimal for themselves—that help to keep them or their party in power and that do not distract from their other policy agendas. At the same time, I recognize the importance of the broader governmental decision-making context. In particular, the information top leaders receive and the ways it is presented reflect the preferences and identities of the bureaucracies and advisers they rely on for policy advice. These actors seek to persuade presidents and prime ministers to see things through their own eyes. Rarely, if ever, is there a single, objective interpretation of a given complex emergency or of possible responses to it, and so leaders' decisions inevitably reflect the environments in which they are made. In this sense, this book sees foreign policy decision making as a non-unitary, boundedly rational process: while leaders have interests they seek to pursue, their opportunities to do so also depend on the desires and influence of those who work for them.[36]

With this in mind, pressures for leaders of powerful democracies to protect civilians and limit the costs of doing so may each arise at three key levels: within domestic society, within government itself, and through international partners. At each level, in turn, significant tension between these pressures can help to encourage ambitions-resources gaps. This book focuses mainly on the first two: the third is more idiosyncratic, but merits at least brief discussion.

First, democratic society is regularly a source of competing attitudes about the importance of civilian protection and the acceptability of the costs required to provide it. On one hand, leaders typically face implicit (and sometimes explicit) expectations from citizens that any involvement in peace operations must remain relatively low-cost. Yet at times there can also be strong societal pressure to help protect civilians. This tends to reflect the explicit demands of activists, media, and other concerned citizens, but leaders may also perceive a form of broader, latent public pressure to act in order to avoid charges of shirking historical responsibility in a particular conflict. These contradictions can create a serious political dilemma about how to satisfy normative demands for action while avoiding backlash against expensive or unsuccessful policies. Ambitions-resources gaps can help resolve this dilemma. These gaps allow leaders to claim that they are making significant efforts to address civilians' protection needs and give concerned citizens some of what they want without all the costs and risks of more robust action. Concerned citizens, meanwhile, may accept these policies for several reasons, including failing to understand their limitations, judging them as the best available option when robust protection seems unlikely, and having psychological or organizational incentives to do so.

Second, governmental officials and agencies may also contribute to these contradictory pressures. Bureaucrats and key officials—especially in the military or defense establishment that must implement any direct involvement in a peace operation—often have good reason to worry about how the costs and risks will affect their own interests and those of their organizations and the nation. Yet the impulse to help endangered populations can also be powerful, especially for officials who are most exposed to information about their suffering. As with domestic society, some officials and agencies are likely to place greater emphasis on the importance of offering assistance while others will have lower tolerance for costs and risks. Thus these competing pressures can promote compromise and present executives with a different political dilemma: how to maintain the support and cooperation of the subordinates they need to implement their decisions. In such situations the process of intra-governmental bargaining through which competing priorities are resolved often leads to sub-par policies that no single actor would choose. Ambitions-resources gaps are an example, making at least some concessions to each perspective. Meanwhile, concerned officials are likely to accept them for most of the same reasons as other citizens and activists.

Third, international partners can also generate pressure to do either more or less than a government would on its own. As noted above, most peace operations are multilateral. Collaborating with other states, however, can induce yet a third sort of political dilemma when other governments' preferences differ from a leader's own: how to maintain strong relations and effective cooperation with key international partners while still respecting other constraints and priorities. When leaders choose to accept their coalition partners' political needs and constraints as the price of working together, promoting an ambitions-resources gap may provide an acceptable compromise. For instance, a leader might agree to limits on force goals or activities, but still send substantial resources to a mission with considerable physical capacity for protection in order to demonstrate his own commitment. Or, at his partners' urging, he could agree to more ambitious objectives than are warranted with the available resources.

Thus, ambitions-resources gaps may allow leaders to protect their own political fortunes, resolve intra-governmental conflict, or cooperate with key international partners. Still, leaders do not select these policies all the time. In most complex emergencies they are likely to perceive at least some pressure for action to protect civilians and some pressure to limit associated costs and risks. Yet the absolute and relative strength of these pressures varies significantly from one conflict to another and can even change dramatically over time during a single one. Sometimes leaders see little if any societal pressure to protect civilians, and sometimes it appears easier and less risky to do so than others. Sometimes the key bureaucracies and governmental players are on the same page, and sometimes there are no squabbling allies to confront. When multiple sources of pressure are in especially stark tension with one another, however, and neither can be easily ignored, the dilemma for a leader can be severe and the demand for compromise can be great. Under these circumstances policies that promote ambitions-resources gaps become particularly likely.

When does this tend to happen? Focusing empirically on the two domestic levels of society and government, I expect that the conditions under which contradictory pressures encourage leaders to promote and create ambitions-resources gaps will overlap and reinforce one another in predictable ways. On one hand, substantial pressure from ordinary citizens and activists to save lives can bolster the arguments of concerned officials, and vice versa. At the same time, while the perceived level of risk of public backlash against civilian protection efforts and the strength of bureaucratic opposition can depend on numerous factors, they are especially likely to vary with objective conditions on the ground. Specifically, while robust action is always more risky, costs and casualties also depend heavily on the *operational environment*, the various characteristics of a conflict that determine how difficult and dangerous any given contribution to a peace operation is likely to be. All else equal, a less hospitable operational environment should increase both the financial costs of deploying troops and the rate at which they may be injured or killed. It should thus both encourage bureaucratic opposition to risky military action and heighten the risk of eventual public backlash. In sum, then, leaders should be especially likely to promote ambitions-resources gaps when they face both strong societal or bureaucratic pressure to protect civilians and strong grounds for concern about costs and risks, especially as reflected in a formidable operational environment. More robust or more limited protection efforts, by implication, should be more likely when either more limited moral demands or a favorable operational environment reduce the pressure to compromise.

The conditions in which a leader might promote an ambitions-resources gap due to different preferences at the international level are more difficult to predict. A leader's own preferences about how (and perhaps even whether) to design and participate in a peace operation must differ from those of at least one potential international partner, and a concession to the partner's point of view must limit the leader's policy options. When these conditions are met, the key issue is the priority a leader places on the international partnership. The more important it is to ensure multilateral cooperation or maintain good relations with an ally who seeks his assistance in prosecuting a specific peace operation, the more likely a leader should be to give in.

Alternative Explanations

Although this book highlights multiple pathways by which great power democracies may come to promote or create ambitions-resources gaps, still there are distinct alternative explanations to my basic story about the politics of compromise. Two, in particular, imply that these gaps might not really be about political will at all, and merit careful consideration.

First, ambitions-resources gaps could emerge unintentionally: rather than knowingly compromising in response to a set of political pressures and opportunities, leaders may facilitate these gaps unwittingly. Perhaps they or their military advisers simply do not know how to design robust protection missions particularly well. They may misjudge the relationships between mission objectives, military strategies, and necessary resources. Alternately, they may lack the detailed understanding of a given complex emergency needed to gauge either the level of civilian protection it demands or the resources and troop capabilities needed to provide effective security.

This argument is worth taking seriously for several reasons. Notably, it has been offered as an explanation for some of the major peacekeeping debacles of the early 1990s—especially UNPROFOR, and UNAMIR in Rwanda. In their aftermath, the UN embarked on a period of soul searching, culminating in a 2000 report that laid out lessons learned for the future. The so-called Brahimi Report was used to inform a major overhaul of the UN's peacekeeping apparatus and practices. It emphasized, among other shortcomings, the failure of UN planners to fully grasp the importance of the relationship between resources and mandates, and of matching the latter to circumstances on the ground.[37] But it is not only the UN that has made such claims. In 1998 Bill Clinton memorably told Rwandans that, during the genocide there, he "did not fully appreciate the depth and the speed with which [they] were being engulfed by this unimaginable terror."[38] His statement seemed to suggest that if only he had understood the nature of the threat Rwanda faced and the protection required, the United States would have responded effectively.

More recently, the conviction that powerful countries continue to lack appropriate military doctrine for civilian protection inspired a 2010 military planning guide, the Mass Atrocity Response Operations (MARO) Handbook, to advise military and political actors on the unique challenges associated with military action in mass atrocity situations. As the authors note, "The MARO Project is based on the insight that the failure to act in the face of mass killings of civilians is not simply a function of political will or legal authority; the failure also reflects a lack of thinking about how military forces might respond."[39]

However, there are also reasons for skepticism that ambitions-resources gaps are usually unintentional. Indeed, the very fact that robust civilian protection missions do sometimes occur raises questions about this idea. More particularly, two of the most robust operations of the post–Cold War period were also launched in the early 1990s: Operation Provide Comfort, deployed in April 1991 to protect Iraqi Kurds from Saddam Hussein and the Iraqi army, and the U.S.-led UNITAF, which protected the delivery of emergency relief in Somalia starting in December 1992. The timing of these operations suggests that knowledge of how to design robust missions is not simply something learned over time in response to disasters like Bosnia and Rwanda. What is more, it indicates that any lack of understanding by the UN bureaucracy in the 1990s does not necessarily translate to the great power democracies: rather, there was a stark difference between these robust missions they led themselves, and those they chose to turn over to the UN.

This debate is not just semantic, but has important consequences for whether ambitions-resources gaps are avoidable. Certainly there are holes in the great power democracies' military planning for civilian protection, and certainly limited information has delayed their responses to complex emergencies at times. But to a considerable extent, avoiding ambitions-resources gaps comes down to basic principles that apply to any military operation, notably that resources and objectives must match one another. If the downsides of failing to apply these principles are not predictable, or if making appropriate inferences about civilians' protection needs is somehow more difficult than preparing for other types of military operations, the implications are serious. In particular, no amount of political will or commitment to effective protection could guarantee a robust mission or reliably guard against making things worse rather than better. If true, this should raise serious questions about the ethics of civilian protection efforts more broadly.

A second potential alternative explanation is that great power democracies facilitate or create ambitions-resources gaps when they have motives for intervening in a conflict that are unrelated to protecting civilians, but they feel compelled to hide this from a skeptical domestic or international audience. This is essentially a modified version of the interests-based explanation for contributing to peace operations mentioned above, and it has a long history in realist thought. As Hans Morgenthau once wrote, "All nations are tempted . . . to clothe their own particular aspirations and actions in the moral purposes of the universe."[40] In this story, international political interests are a leader's true motive for action and explain his involvement in a military operation. Yet the mission still fits the parameters of a peace operation: there is at least some humanitarian or peacekeeping element, even while the force also has other objectives. This allows the leader to offer a plausible humanitarian justification for his actions. Such a strategy might work in two ways. A leader could announce a primary intention of protecting civilians while employing military strategies or bringing troops and materiel more suited to other ends. Alternately, he might deploy troops capable of effectively protecting civilians, but assign them other primary objectives and leave protection as at best a minor part of the mission. Either way, claims of assisting at-risk civilians are mainly a fig leaf to conceal the intervener's true intent.

This second possibility deserves serious attention as well. If nothing else, given the prominence of arguments about strategic motivations in the peacekeeping and humanitarian intervention literatures, it is plausible. What is more, military interventions justified by their organizers primarily on humanitarian grounds regularly face charges that they are merely a cover for other interests and objectives: NATO's 2011 intervention in Libya is just the most prominent recent example.[41] More broadly, if this argument is true, it points to an even deeper disconnect between what leaders say and do than my own argument suggests.

Research Design

I use multiple methods to test my argument against these two alternatives, focusing mainly on my expectations about competing pressures from domestic society and government. First, extensive original data allow me to examine broad cross-national patterns in American, French, British, and Australian contributions to peace operations in the post–Cold War period. Using a unique dataset of 61 post–Cold War complex humanitarian emergencies comprising 495 emergency-years and ending in 2009, I recorded whether each of these states participated in at least one peace operation, and if so, whether its primary contribution was limited, robust, or promoted an ambitions-resources gap. I also developed original measures of the pressure leaders faced to help address the violence and of the relative difficulty of the operational environment.

Quantitative analysis of these data supports my expectations about the circumstances that make ambitions-resources gaps politically appealing: I find that leaders tend to create and promote these gaps when they face substantial pressure to protect civilians but a relatively unfavorable operational environment. Meanwhile, I find little or no evidence to support the alternative explanations. Ambitions-resources gaps are not more likely in the face of various political or strategic ties between the potential intervener and the state where the complex emergency occurs that might create an incentive for intervention. Nor were these gaps less likely in the 2000s than the 1990s, a pattern we would expect to see if they were initially unintentional but leaders later learned from their early mistakes. Finally, the data also provide evidence for a secondary implication of my argument about robust civilian protection. Namely, while leaders might have various motives for robust protection efforts, the combination of strong pressure for civilian protection and a favorable operational environment should create auspicious conditions for them. I find that these circumstances are associated with a greater likelihood of robust action.

Second, I conduct in-depth case studies of individual governments' responses to several complex emergencies. One covers France's Operation Turquoise, launched in response to the Rwandan genocide in June 1994. Operation Turquoise involved an ambitions-resources gap: it had a strong mandate to protect civilians and considerable resources, but the French government made several choices regarding military strategy that were inappropriate for its announced goals. As a result, the force did not act as efficiently to protect civilians as its resources could have allowed. A second case study examines U.S. policy toward war in Darfur, Sudan, between 2003 and 2007. Over this period the United States moved from doing nothing to address the security situation there to supporting two peace operations, AMIS and UNAMID. In supporting these missions, the United States also helped facilitate ambitions-resources gaps, but of a different type: here, the troops were unable to deliver the level of civilian protection they were asked to provide. Two further cases that did not involve ambitions-resources gaps compare Australia's responses to different complex emergencies in the Southwest Pacific: the violence in East Timor mentioned above and a separatist civil war in Aceh, Indonesia, from 1999 to 2004. Whereas Australia's leadership of INTERFET in East Timor was a robust and effective response to the attacks on civilians, Australia made no commitment to any peace operation in Aceh. Last, a much shorter analysis briefly illustrates how pressure from international allies encouraged Tony Blair's U.K. government to help create an ambitions-resources gap during NATO's Operation Allied Force in Kosovo in 1999.

These case studies build on the statistical analysis to support my argument in several additional ways. On one hand, they demonstrate that the overall trends observed in the quantitative data about when ambitions-resources gaps and robust civilian protection occur persist, even when examining a more diverse set of indicators for the pressures leaders face to protect civilians and to control associated costs. To assess the extent of these pressures, in the case studies I look at indicators such as the amount of civil society activism; the results of public opinion surveys; additional forces that affect the operational environment beyond those incorporated in the quantitative analysis; the positions of different governmental players; and leaders' own perceptions of these issues. In addition, the cases of ambitions-resources gaps allow me to confirm the key causal mechanisms of my argument that explain why leaders can benefit politically from these policies (and how they use what I call the rhetoric of organized hypocrisy to do so). To this end, I examine issues such as activists' and concerned officials' understanding of their states' policies; their psychological and professional incentives; and the statements leaders make when contributing to ambitions-resources gaps. Finally, the case studies allow for a more thorough assessment of the alternative explanations. While the statistical analysis examines various possible strategic incentives for military intervention that leaders might rather justify as humanitarian, the cases allow me to assess how leaders actually saw their nation's interests in specific conflicts. They also let me examine policymakers' understandings of the threats civilians faced and the actions needed to effectively counter these threats.

I selected the specific cases for several reasons. Collectively, they reflect variation across the great power democracies; complex emergencies in different regions; peace operations in different institutional contexts (UN, regional organizations, ad hoc coalitions); and the full range of policy outcomes. One limitation is that there is no full-length case study of a limited contribution to a peace operation. However, both the Rwanda and Darfur cases include brief periods of limited contributions before the ambitions-resources gaps that are the main focus. What is more, while there is clearly a distinction between making a limited contribution and not intervening at all, it is not central to my argument: I expect to observe these outcomes in largely similar circumstances, and this is confirmed in the quantitative analysis.

Both France in Rwanda and the United States in Darfur are "most likely" situations for contributing to ambitions-resources gaps: if we did not observe them here it would cast at least some doubt on my argument about the role of competing normative and material pressures in encouraging them, since such pressures were present in both cases.[42] In addition, since these two cases represent different styles of ambitions-resources gaps, they allow me to explore whether there may be further conditions—beyond those that generally encourage these gaps—that incline a leader toward one type or another (an issue I return to in chapter 2).

Operation Turquoise reflected a complex political compromise in which the key proponents of intervention—France's president and foreign minister—felt considerable pressure to act as a result of prominent NGO and media activism. On the other hand, the main opponents—the prime minister, defense minister, and top military officials—worried greatly about various serious physical and political perils related to the operational environment and French history in the country, and insisted on designing the mission to minimize these risks. The politics behind Operation Turquoise have been under-explored in the English-language international relations literature, and offer a chance to improve our understanding of an intervention that has received little attention from security scholars. This is also a strong case in which to assess my argument about ambitions-resources gaps because it offers a difficult test vis-à-vis one of the alternative explanations. Specifically, a long history of political and military involvement in Rwanda has inspired considerable controversy over France's 1994 intervention. Various observers have charged that the real motive behind Operation Turquoise was strategic: that it aimed to assist France's former allies, who were responsible for the genocide, or more broadly to further French interests in Africa. If true, this could also explain the ambitions-resources gap.

Meanwhile, in Darfur the United States moved from treating the conflict as a simple humanitarian problem to supporting AMIS and then UNAMID. The initial shift coincided with both growing concern in the State Department and the emergence of an influential advocacy movement devoted to "saving" Darfur. Yet Darfur also presented an extremely formidable operational environment for any potential peace operation, especially one involving Western troops. For this and several other reasons there was substantial bureaucratic opposition to direct U.S. military involvement. As a result, the Bush administration faced a serious political dilemma driven by the need to satisfy these competing demands and expectations. These tensions persisted for years and encouraged repeated compromises in the form of support to AMIS and UNAMID. The case is thus also an important one for my argument because it tests my theory's relevance for explaining temporal variation in policy as leaders adapt to changing pressures to protect civilians and control costs over the course of a single extended conflict.

The Australian cases represent circumstances in which ambitions-resources gaps should be unlikely, but for opposite reasons. INTERFET reflected tremendous pressure from a very large and influential group of concerned citizens, a dearth of bureaucratic opposition, and a fairly favorable operational environment. While an ambitions-resources gap was not impossible, it should have been less likely than in the above cases. What is more, this case provides a detailed example to support the quantitative findings on robust protection. By contrast, in Aceh there was virtually no pressure to intervene in any way from civil society or within the government. Here an ambitions-resources gap should have been very unlikely. These cases also help demonstrate my argument's applicability to governments beyond those of the United States, United Kingdom, and France, the focus of most studies of humanitarian military action.

Finally, British involvement with Operation Allied Force in Kosovo shows how international pressures can encourage ambitions-resources gaps. In brief, reluctance to deploy ground troops by key NATO members convinced Prime Minister Blair to accept an air operation in the interest of unanimity within the alliance, although he would have preferred a ground force in the interest of more robust civilian protection. Though not a rigorous test of this mechanism, this brief case does support the book's overall emphasis on competing normative and material pressures and the need for compromise as a key cause of ambitions-resources gaps.

Contributions

In focusing on the design of peace operations this book calls attention to a surprisingly under-studied issue with major consequences for the well-being of some of the world's most vulnerable people, and contributes theoretically and empirically to our understanding of these missions. Although many observers have highlighted the importance of mission design for what peace operations can accomplish, the related literature has mostly focused on general questions about whether and when international actors are willing to intervene in violent conflicts. I show, however, that decisions about how peace operations are designed and how individual states contribute to different outcomes are just as political as whether or not to intervene.

In the process I offer the first in-depth analysis of the politics of ambitions-resources gaps, a problem that has received much attention but little careful scrutiny. By doing so I fill an important hole in the literature on peace operations and civilian protection, which has long recognized that these gaps occur but has not adequately explained when or why leaders of powerful states who could do more would find them politically palatable. I also uncover new evidence about the conditions that promote especially robust civilian protection. At the same time, I conduct both the first quantitative test of peace operation design that goes beyond the number of troops deployed, and the first quantitative analysis to account for the domestic moral pressures that have featured prominently in qualitative work on humanitarian intervention. Through the use of interviews, detailed media analysis, and numerous primary and secondary sources, the case studies also add to our knowledge about several important peace operations.

Beyond this, the book has broader implications for our understanding of democratic foreign policy. First, it helps plug a gap in our knowledge about how society can affect leaders' policy incentives. Although the literature on bargaining has long recognized that competing bureaucratic priorities can give rise to policy compromises that differ from any single party's ideal outcome, studies of public opinion and NGO advocacy have given relatively little attention to how democratic society might promote similar results. Typically, these literatures treat society as either a motivator for positive international action or a constraining force. My argument, however, brings these roles together and highlights the way that competing pressures from within society can also create a demand for policy compromises.

Second, the book sheds light on the nature of compromise in morally tinged foreign policy issues, adding to a growing literature about how moral disagreements—and the hypocrisy they may encourage—can create foreign policy vulnerabilities for democracies. For instance, Gil Merom has argued that contradictions between liberal values held by society and espoused by government on the one hand, and the military brutality needed to defeat guerrilla insurgencies on the other, often lead to democratic defeat in small wars. Indeed, his logic is similar to mine in that the compromises governments adopt in response to societal pressure—less brutal counter-insurgency strategies—can also undermine their overall efforts. What is more, according to Kelly Greenhill, liberal democracies are the main targets of coercive engineered migration, the attempted blackmail of one state by another in which the initiator uses the threat of a large refugee flow from its territory into the target state as leverage. Democracies are vulnerable to these threats due to their susceptibility to potentially explosive domestic political controversy over how to handle such refugee influxes, between sympathetic citizens who want to live up to their government's international commitments and offer asylum, and others who do not.[43]

This book shows how such moral disputes can have yet another effect for democracies by encouraging leaders to adopt policy compromises that may actually be at odds with the values that underline normative pressures to act in the first place. This occurs because the policy is designed to address the political challenges associated with competing pressures on leaders, rather than the moral problem that motivates pro-intervention demands. In this sense, I highlight a potential dark side of political compromise as well as the sometimes-unintended ways that norm-driven actors can influence foreign policy and international cooperation. I also show how hypocrisy—a disconnect between talk and action—can help leaders succeed at managing complex political conflicts at home, while also creating risks for vulnerable civilians abroad. When it comes to the practical challenges of offering more effective civilian protection and avoiding unnecessary harm, all of this raises important questions for both leaders and those who aim to influence them.

Devil in the Details

Assessing Mission Design and State Policy

> There is a fantastic gap between the resolutions of the Security
> Council, the will to execute those resolutions, and the means available
> to commanders in the field.
>
> —Lieutenant General Francis Briquemont, UNPROFOR
> commander, *New York Times*, December 31, 1993

What do peace operations plagued by ambitions-resources gaps look like? How can we consistently distinguish them from more robust or limited missions despite variation among complex emergencies? And, given this book's focus on state-level policy, how can we assess the contributions of individual great power democracies to these different outcomes? By answering these questions, this chapter builds a conceptual framework for structuring the book's theoretical and empirical arguments. To do so, I build on studies of the military requirements for humanitarian military action and integrate them with an understanding of the security deficits that define complex emergencies and the unique capabilities of the great power democracies.

The chapter proceeds in three parts. First, I introduce definitions of three central concepts: complex emergencies, civilian protection, and peace operations. Because the policy and academic literatures do not always use these ideas consistently, it is important to be clear about how I use them in this book. Second, using the concepts of a peace operation's ambitions and resources, I develop a simple three-part typology that describes the key differences between limited and robust missions and ambitions-resources gaps. Finally, I translate this typology into a set of discrete policies available to leaders of the states I focus on in this book. The same qualities that make these states especially influential for understanding broad patterns in the design of peace operations—their ability to lead robust operations and their influence over many others—also give them unique flexibility and a wide range of options for whether and how to contribute. As a result, we can think about their participation in these missions as mimicking the basic distinctions between limited and robust civilian protection and ambitions-resources gaps.

Definitions

COMPLEX HUMANITARIAN EMERGENCIES

While war and atrocities always threaten innocent people, sometimes the violence simply must be stopped to avert catastrophe for the civilian population. When the local government cannot or will not do so, international help may offer civilians' best hope. Such help might involve diplomatic initiatives or targeted sanctions against perpetrators of violence. Yet this is also the type of security environment that creates the most compelling humanitarian case for military action to directly protect civilians and aid workers from ongoing violence, and, in the very worst instances, to compel human rights abusers to end their heinous crimes. It is in these conflicts that it makes the most sense to investigate such efforts.

To identify these situations, I rely on the concept of complex humanitarian emergencies, widely used by policymakers and the international humanitarian community to represent the conflicts of greatest concern to the UN, government agencies, and relief organizations. Most prominent definitions have been developed by and for this community and reflect its interests and prejudices, while sharing three key themes. First, complex emergencies result from political violence, not natural disasters. Second, they involve large-scale and intense civilian suffering, and a significantly heightened risk of death from the direct or indirect effects of violence. Third, this occurs at least in part because local authorities fail to meet the conflict-affected population's needs, either alone or with help from relief organizations. Drawing on these ideas, I define a complex emergency as an episode of political violence that severely and extensively disrupts civilian life, and in which the government responsible for public welfare is unable or unwilling to shield the population (or facilitate outside efforts to do so).[1]

Complex emergencies vary significantly in their political causes and characteristics, and may occur during various kinds of conflicts. First, both civil and interstate wars can be utterly devastating for civilians, even if they do not involve mass atrocity crimes like mass killing or ethnic cleansing.[2] When belligerents pursue military strategies that involve widespread theft of humanitarian aid or forced relocation of people away from homes and farms, for example, many thousands may die of starvation, disease, and exposure, as they have in places like Somalia and Mozambique.[3] Second, atrocity crimes and severe communal violence also occur outside of war. The Indonesian-supported militia violence in East Timor in 1999, for instance, faced no armed resistance. Likewise, mass violence in places like Indonesia, India, and Nigeria attests to the upheaval and suffering the worst communal conflicts can cause.

Complex emergencies, then, include the worst wars, atrocity crimes, and instances of communal violence. Civilians may be threatened directly by violence, by a security environment that creates widespread starvation and disease, or both. As a group, complex emergencies resemble the descriptions of conflicts sometimes identified as possible candidates for military action to protect civilians from grave harm, even without the local government's consent.[4] Still, in practice, even ambitious protection missions may be able to get this approval. Thus, the concept of complex emergencies is well suited to represent those conflicts where military action to physically protect civilians beyond traditional peacekeeping seems most plausible on humanitarian grounds, recognizing that potential interveners may or may not insist on local government consent. This, in turn, makes them ideal for exploring the sources of variation in these operations.[5]

Finally, despite their diversity, there are important similarities in the threats civilians consistently face in these conflicts. Hallmarks include large-scale forced displacement as well as attacks on humanitarian operations that threaten civilians' access to the basic necessities of life. Indeed, of the nearly 1000 major recorded attacks on aid workers between 1997 and 2009, at least 77% took place during conflicts I have identified as complex emergencies and an additional 11% occurred in places that later or previously experienced one.[6] Thus, at the very least these conflicts typically create the need for an improved security environment for international relief operations and, often, direct physical protection for civilians threatened by violent attacks.

CIVILIAN PROTECTION

Civilian protection means different things to different people and in different contexts.[7] In this book I use the term narrowly to refer to actions taken by military actors to shield civilians from physical threats created by others. These may include direct danger to people's physical integrity and disrupted access to basic necessities such as food and shelter. While many other activities can also help save lives threatened by armed conflict and mass violence, this book looks at how military missions are or are not designed to do so. Even as applied narrowly to military actors, however, civilian protection can span a range of activities with the potential to provide more or less protection relative to the major needs created by complex emergencies.

Used in this way, "civilian protection" is distinct from several related concepts, including the Responsibility to Protect (R2P) and the UN's agenda on the Protection of Civilians in Armed Conflict (POC). R2P deals with how international actors should respond to the most systematic and severe human rights abuses and can incorporate various diplomatic, economic, and military policies related to preventing, reacting to, and rebuilding in response to these situations.[8] By contrast, civilian protection as used here is both broader and narrower since it applies beyond the worst atrocity crimes where R2P is typically discussed, but focuses exclusively on military actors.

Similarly, the UN's POC framework is also much broader than my use of the term in this book. Since 1999 the UN has used it in reference to a wide variety of threats that may arise in virtually any conflict, and has advocated everything from sanctions to verbal shaming to address them.[9] A key part of this POC agenda does focus on UN peace operations, but many activities—such as assisting with security sector reform and ensuring the safe return of displaced persons—deal mainly with the needs of a post-conflict environment.[10] Still, the Security Council has also given increased emphasis to direct physical protection of civilians this century.

Military operations that respond to complex emergencies can vary dramatically, and range from forceful interventions to protect civilians from mass atrocities, on one end, to traditional consent-based peacekeeping, on the other. Yet although these missions may be, as Victoria Holt and Tobias Berkman point out, "fundamentally different" from one another, they do not always deploy in response to fundamentally different conflicts.[11] Indeed, for states with the capacity to provide robust civilian protection, very disparate kinds of policies are potential substitutes for one another depending on the costs and effort their leaders are willing to accept. Therefore, as discussed below, in the context of complex emergencies I treat missions designed to offer at best a little protection and those that are carefully tailored to civilians' primary needs as two ends of a single spectrum.

I use the term "peace operations" to refer to the full range of international military operations that may fall along this spectrum and that aim to promote peace, deliver aid, or provide security for civilians and aid workers. They range from small cease-fire monitoring forces to the most ambitious humanitarian interventions and coercive protection operations.[12] Missions deployed exclusively to evacuate foreign nationals, protect national assets, or intervene on behalf of one side in a conflict are excluded, as are civilian peace support missions. Peace operations may or may not have the consent of all parties to a conflict, and may or may not be authorized by the UN. They may be led by the UN, regional organizations, or individual states. Finally, while they may begin during a complex emergency they may also deploy shortly afterward to support a peace process, as an alternative to earlier action to shield civilians from ongoing violence.

In defining peace operations broadly, this book departs from much of the literature on peacekeeping and humanitarian intervention. Most studies of peacekeeping address questions such as when the UN chooses to deploy peacekeepers, when individual states contribute to these missions, and whether and under what conditions they are able to help build sustainable peace after war.[13] Understandably, such studies have focused narrowly on the missions most relevant to these questions. The humanitarian intervention literature, on the other hand, generally examines only missions that aim primarily to protect civilians and that lack the target state's consent, even though operations that offer little protection and that may have host state consent are often deployed in response to similarly severe conflicts.[14] While these literatures have good reasons to limit the missions they examine, my purpose here is different and justifies casting a wider net.

Ambitions, Resources, and a Protection Typology

Studies of the military requirements for humanitarian military action emphasize that robust protection requires political goals that match civilians' security needs, military strategies suited to achieving these goals, and sufficient resources to implement these strategies effectively. To organize and distill these guidelines into their most important elements, I break peace operations into two main components: their ambitions and their resources for civilian protection. First, a mission's ambitions reflect what the troops are told to do and how they are to do so, as defined by the force's goals and the military strategies it employs. In effect, these ambitions determine the extent to which troops attempt to meet civilians' security and protection needs, or the amount of protection they are asked to provide. Second, resources determine the level of protection that soldiers are physically able to deliver, which may be either more or less than the amount their ambitions imply. They reflect the number of troops deployed, the materiel and equipment at their disposal, and intangibles such as training and morale. Because civilians' security needs vary from conflict to conflict, the ambitions and resources needed to address them depend on the circumstances of the complex emergency. Still, research on the requirements for effective protection suggests several rules of thumb to guide our judgments on the suitability of various goals, military strategies, and resource levels in different situations.

AMBITIONS

Operational Goals: Do They Address the Threat? A peace operation's objectives are typically laid out in its authorizing mandate, if it has one. In order to offer the most protection possible these goals must address the key threats that civilians face in a complex emergency, but all too often they prove patently insufficient.[15] As Michael Walzer puts it, for example, "it isn't enough to wait until the tyrants, the zealots, and the bigots have done their filthy work and then rush food and medicine to the ragged survivors."[16] Similarly, deploying military observers during genocide or protecting aid operations when civilians are threatened by mass killing is clearly inappropriate.[17] Still, such judgments about the appropriateness of operational goals are often ad hoc, and a systematic assessment will require some consistent metrics for what constitute suitable objectives across varied conflict situations.

The concept of complex emergencies offers a useful starting point. As noted above, despite their diversity there are key similarities in the protection needs civilians consistently face in these conflicts. A secure environment for relief operations can help ensure access to food, medical care, and shelter, while direct physical protection is often necessary to prevent large-scale assaults of civilians. Given these needs, a few simple guidelines—summarized in figure 1.1—provide a foundation for assessing the goals of peace operations in these conflicts.

First, numerous missions pursue goals that simply do not address these needs. A distinguishing feature of these operations is that troops are not expected to provide security directly for anyone aside from mission

Goal

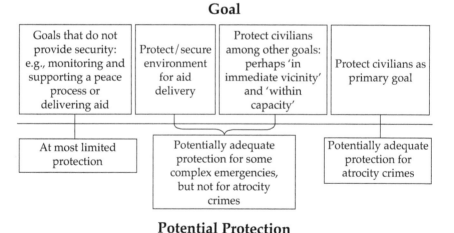

Potential Protection

Figure 1.1. Spectrum of protection goals

personnel. Many of these forces are UN-led and aim to help negotiate, observe, or keep a peace agreement or truce. Often this means deploying after the worst of the violence. For example, the UN Observer Mission in El Salvador (ONUSAL) aimed to verify implementation of a series of peace agreements but could not intercede if the parties violated them.

At other times these operations may arrive amid serious violence where there is no peace to keep; may be led by regional organizations or individual states; or may focus on humanitarian tasks such as the delivery of emergency relief. In 1998, for example, a small UN observer mission named UNOMSIL deployed to Sierra Leone in the midst of war, absent any peace agreement or ceasefire, to observe the security situation. Similarly, when AMIS first deployed to Darfur in 2004 it was only authorized to oversee a "humanitarian ceasefire" and to protect its own personnel. In practice, belligerents did not respect the ceasefire, and violence against civilians was rampant. Finally, after the Rwandan genocide in 1994, the United States launched Operation Support Hope to help deliver relief to the thousands of Rwandan refugees congregating in camps around Goma, Zaire. But while the genocide itself was over, the camps were far from safe and the United States made no effort to address the security situation.[18]

As such examples attest, when a force does not provide security except for itself it cannot credibly hope to ensure the efficient delivery of humanitarian relief in a dangerous environment, much less directly protect civilians from violence. Thus, although it may save lives by providing aid or helping prevent renewed violence, it can offer at best a little protection relative to the needs these conflicts create. In the first case, its goals are clearly too modest for the prevailing security environment. In the second, its goals may suit the circumstances on the ground at the time, but only because it deployed after the population's most pressing security needs are past.[19]

A second category of objectives may address the main security threats civilians face in certain complex emergencies, but not those that involve mass atrocity crimes. These include providing security for aid operations or directly protecting civilians as one part of a mission, but not as its central purpose. In the first case, operations that protect aid delivery do not shield civilians directly from large-scale violence, but can contribute to providing the humanitarian space aid agencies need to save lives. Soldiers may protect buildings where aid supplies are stored, escort humanitarian convoys, or guard safe areas where civilians are congregated. In Somalia, in the early 1990s, for example, three missions—the UN-led UNOSOM I and II and the U.S.-led Unified Task Force (UNITAF)—sought to protect aid delivery.[20]

Alternatively, peace operations may directly protect civilians as one of several objectives. As Holt and Berkman describe, tasks may include, inter alia, "providing support to law and order, escorting convoys, protecting camps, establishing safe havens, breaking up militias, demilitarizing refugee/IDP camps, organizing disarmament, and intervening on behalf of an individual or community under threat."[21] Such missions usually aim to support some kind of peace process and rely on the official acquiescence of the local government. Still, they recognize that the environment remains dangerous and that both peace processes and meaningful host government consent can be illusory. For instance, in Darfur after October 2004 AMIS's mandate fit this pattern, but, despite its official consent for the mission, the Sudanese government participated in attacking civilians.

In some complex emergencies, where violence directed against civilians is not widespread, an authorization to protect civilians as part of a broader mandate may be adequate to address the main threats civilians face. Where the population is the target of massive rights abuses, however, such missions can address at best some of civilians' protection needs and are clearly insufficient relative to the scope of the threat. What is more, language authorizing this kind of protection is often accompanied by substantial restrictions and caveats and must be evaluated within the broader context of the mission to determine whether soldiers are truly expected to engage directly in protecting civilians or aid operations at all.

Since 1999 in particular, it has become common for both UN and some non-UN force mandates to include language authorizing troops to protect civilians whom they encounter "under imminent threat" of violence, in their area of operations, and "within their resources and capabilities." Where such language is accompanied by explicit directives to engage in the kind of protection-related tasks laid out above, as with AMIS, it helps indicate an ambition to offer at least some meaningful protection relative to civilians' most pressing needs. Absent a clear expectation that soldiers engage in such tasks, however, and particularly when a mission begins at the end of a conflict in the expectation that the worst violence is past, such language may have little practical meaning. Not only are civilians' most pressing needs behind them, but, as Holt and Berkman point out, such restrictive instructions at best give force commanders the option to protect civilians and at worst can constrain them from doing so.[22]

For a third and final category of peace operations, protecting civilians is the primary goal. These missions seek to prevent or halt atrocity crimes such as mass killing, ethnic cleansing, and genocide, and in complex emergencies involving these crimes this is the only goal that is adequate to meet civilians' most pressing needs for an immediate end to the violence.[23]

In sum, goals that are too modest forestall robust civilian protection no matter how well a mission may stack up in other respects. In response to complex emergencies, peace operations should at minimum offer security for aid operations or include direct civilian protection among other goals, unless they follow an earlier mission that has successfully pursued these objectives. Where civilians are the targets of a major campaign of abuse, peace operations must make direct protection their primary aim if they hope to eliminate this threat.

Military Strategies: Suitable to Goals? To achieve its announced goals, a peace operation must also pursue activities and military strategies that are consistent with them. Otherwise, the message is muddled as inappropriate military strategies prevent soldiers from delivering the level of protection implied by their stated goals. Thus, in effect, a mission's ambitions reflect its goals *and* the means used to pursue them.

While many aspects of military strategy are relevant, two guidelines are crucial. First, rules about the use of deadly force must be consistent with the circumstances and with a mission's goals. Depending on its objectives, a peace operation may need to use strategies of deterrence, defense, compellence, or offense. These have clear implications for the operation's rules of engagement (ROE), which determine when troops may engage in hostile fire. Second, the choice of military activities and strategies cannot undercut the basic purpose of restoring stability and saving lives.

These criteria are generally easiest for the first operations discussed above, which do not expect troops to provide security or protection directly beyond their own personnel. In principle, missions to facilitate a peace process have at least the nominal consent of the violent parties and do not expect to regularly use or threaten deadly force. Similarly, delivering emergency aid does not interfere with the parties' objectives unless these include mass killing.[24] Thus, troops who can defend only themselves may still be able to maintain credibility and respond to challenges.

By comparison, missions that aim to protect aid operations and civilians directly must assume that at least one party to the violence will object to their presence: otherwise there would be no need for this kind of protection. In the first case, protecting relief operations involves stopping those who expect to benefit from stealing supplies or killing aid workers. This requires a strategy of deterrence to forestall attacks by local belligerents or, should this fail, defense in response to them. Thus, it may entail fighting and at least requires demonstrating the will to do so.[25]

Second, halting violence against civilians is similar, but focuses on the victims. Soldiers may guard camps and other areas where civilians are congregated, or offer safe passage to more secure locations. Establishing safe havens can allow people to gather without fear of assault. One successful example was Operation Provide Comfort, which protected Iraqi Kurds after the 1991 Gulf War. Like protecting aid operations, these activities involve strategies of deterrence and defense, but may also first require compellent action to "force the perpetrators to stop and possibly reverse actions they have already taken."[26] This tends to make direct protection of civilians even more challenging and risky, and troops should expect to use force, at least initially.

Any time a peace operation aims to protect civilians or aid operations directly, then, troops must be able to use force in defense of both themselves and others. In practice, though, ROE are often too restrictive, thus limiting soldiers' ability to pursue their supposed objectives and depriving the latter of meaning. For example, in Bosnia, UNPROFOR's rules of engagement assumed the consent of the warring parties where it did not exist and allowed soldiers to fire their weapons only in self-defense. They thus limited the mission's efforts to protect aid operations and civilians congregated in UN safe areas. Similarly, one reason the initial UN operation in Somalia, UNOSOM I, was relatively ineffective at protecting aid operations and led to the later deployment of UNITAF was that its ROE also permitted the use of force only in self-defense.[27]

In addition to overly cautious ROE, a second problem for missions that aim to protect aid operations or civilians directly is the selection of an inappropriate type of force. Notably, while ground, air, and naval activities can each contribute to civilian protection, it can be tempting for leaders hoping to limit risks to their soldiers to use air or, less commonly, naval forces in situations that call for ground troops. One way of defending a safe area, for example, is to establish a no-fly zone over the affected region. This strategy is dubious, however, if the threat to civilians is based on the ground. In these circumstances only ground forces can interpose themselves between civilians and those who threaten them.[28] Generally, then, a no-fly zone alone limits the protection a peace operation can offer, even if this is its primary goal, unless civilians are threatened only from the air. Even then, without the threat of ground troops, perpetrators may simply change tactics and begin attacking civilians from the ground.

Finally, while the above strategies focus on the victims of violence, another option for operations that aim primarily to protect civilians from atrocities is to focus on defeating the perpetrators. Although rescuing civilians is a reasonable approach for such a force, it does not resolve or eliminate the source of the threat. Defeating the killers is more dangerous and challenging, but may also offer a way to end the conflict and prevent future carnage. Doing so requires strategies of compellence and offense: fighting is a certainty, not a possibility, and success means military defeat for the perpetrators or a negotiated end to the conflict. In East Timor in 1999, for example, troops from INTERFET actively pursued and disarmed the militias responsible for targeting civilians, many of whom subsequently chose to leave the territory.[29]

Inappropriately narrow rules about when soldiers may fire their weapons do not seem to be a problem in these missions. Interveners do not select this strategy unless they are willing to engage in offensive action, which requires allowing troops to take the initiative in the use of force.[30] Still, not all approaches to offensive action are equally effective or equally consistent with the purpose of saving lives. Here again, the use of air power instead of ground troops can be a particular problem. Not only can air forces not place themselves between perpetrators on the ground and their victims, they may also have difficulty locating targets.[31] At the same time, the offensive use of air power heightens the risk of killing civilians and causing harm that is inconsistent with a humanitarian mission. Finally, without a ground component, it offers no remedy if those targeting civilians respond by increasing their attacks on the ground.[32]

In sum, the choice of military strategies can work to enhance or limit the protection a peace operation aims to provide, relative to what its announced goals alone imply. In particular, an inappropriate orientation to the use of force (especially as evidenced by restrictive ROE) and activities that are inconsistent with declared objectives have prevented a number of operations from achieving the potential represented by their ostensible goals.[33]

RESOURCES: PHYSICAL CAPACITY TO MEET THE NEED

Just as important as its ambitions are a peace operation's resources. I use this term to represent everything that affects a mission's physical capacity to provide protection. Thus, resources include materiel like troops, equipment, and funding; capabilities in areas such as communications, operational planning, and intelligence collection; and intangibles like soldiers' skills and morale.[34] The latter help determine how efficiently a force's physical assets can be translated into civilian protection.

As with its ambitions, to offer the most protection possible a force's resources must be suited to civilians' needs. In particular, they should be adequate to carry out whatever goals are most appropriate to the complex emergency, while employing suitable military strategies. Thus, to be clear, what constitutes adequate resources does not depend on the force's ambitions, since these may or may not be appropriate to the circumstances. Rather, it depends on the specific circumstances of the complex emergency itself.

When it comes to civilian protection, more troops are generally better than fewer. More soldiers can pursue more ambitious goals and more demanding military strategies and deploy in strength over a larger geographic area. Of course, the precise numbers required depend on the complex emergency. Two well-known rules of thumb for operations expecting to face resistance are based on the size of the population requiring protection and on the size of the potential armed opposition. The first suggests that a force requires at least 2 to 3 soldiers per 1,000 members of the civilian population. Alternatively, it should be at least as large as the strongest opponent it might face.[35] Such guidelines can lead to very large estimates of troop requirements: according to one analyst, 100,000 troops for an ambitious mission to enforce a cease-fire and maintain order in the DRC in the early 2000s; and according to the Pentagon, some 120,000 for a non-consensual rescue operation in Darfur in 2004.[36] Others, however, claim that even a relatively small force may be able to do a lot of good, depending on the nature of the threat to civilians.[37]

The latter argument notwithstanding, more soldiers can almost always be put to good use since most peace operations fall far short of the numbers suggested by these rules of thumb. The 1999 deployment of some 50,000 NATO troops to stabilize Kosovo—a small region of barely two million people—is the exception that proves the rule. All else equal, then, a larger force should be better able to handle the key protection challenges of complex emergencies, but a peace operation should have at least enough personnel to carry out the goals and strategies most suited to the conflict over an area containing a sizeable portion of the vulnerable population.

Troops' preparation and equipment also matter greatly. As discussed above, the objectives required to protect civilians in complex emergencies are challenging and require advanced skills and materiel. To achieve them, intervening forces should aim to dominate their areas of operation. This requires not only enough personnel, but also an adequate logistical support infrastructure.[38] These goals also demand considerable intelligence and surveillance capacity and effective command and control strategically, operationally, and tactically. Strong leadership and coordination are a must, and troops must be instructed in their objectives, understand their own role in achieving them, and have the motivation and morale to persist in the face of danger.[39] They must be not only authorized but also *able* to fight off any attackers. Finally, as Michael O'Hanlon notes, and especially where more aggressive or offensive action is required, they need the ability "to deploy quickly, to seal off potential enemy avenues of reinforcement, to locate and target opposition, and to attack in a coordinated and concentrated manner."[40]

Above all, these requirements suggest that in addition to sheer numbers, who deploys and how much outside help they receive to enhance their capabilities largely drives the protection a peace operation can hope to deliver. In particular, advanced-country militaries generally have a clear advantage in everything from training to access to advanced technologies that can assist in responding to attacks and pursuing perpetrators.[41] The key point here, though, is that troops with skills, planning capabilities, and equipment appropriate to addressing civilians' needs should be able to offer more protection than those who lack them.

PUTTING AMBITIONS AND RESOURCES TOGETHER: A PROTECTION TYPOLOGY

Thus far, I have described ambitions and resources individually in terms of their potential to address civilians' security needs. Next I use the relationships between them—as shown in figure 1.2 below—to define a protection typology that identifies missions as either limited, robust, or affected by an ambitions-resources gap.

In figure 1.2 the vertical axis represents a peace operation's ambitions. Moving from bottom to top, there is an increasingly better fit with civilians'

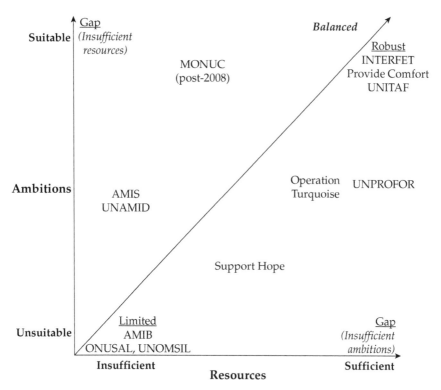

Figure 1.2. Representing protection

needs. At the top, soldiers pursue goals that are appropriate to the conflict and employ military strategies suited to achieving them. The horizontal axis represents resources. Moving from left to right these provide the physical capacity to pursue more ambitious goals and military strategies. At the far right an operation should be able to effectively pursue the goals and strategies most suited to the particular complex emergency, whether this means protecting aid workers or targeting perpetrators of violence.

The three categories in the typology reflect distinct areas in this two-dimensional space (though practical considerations may at times pose challenges for placing a specific mission in one or another). Two of the three types lie along the diagonal, which represents a balance between ambitions and resources. No gap exists between them, and a mission can expect to provide more protection as more suitable ambitions are matched with more resources.

First, then, I designate missions near the upper right as robust. With both appropriate ambitions and sufficient, well-prepared forces, they are designed to provide vigorous protection that is closely tailored to the circumstances of the complex emergency. Examples include INTER-FET in East Timor, Provide Comfort in Iraq, and the U.S.-led UNITAF in Somalia.[42]

Second, missions close to the bottom left I call limited. Here both ambitions and resources are inadequate to provide much if any security for civilians and aid workers, and thus these missions can offer only a little protection relative to civilians' most pressing needs. Typically they are monitoring operations such as ONUSAL and UNOMSIL, or smaller-scale peacekeeping forces like the African Union Mission in Burundi (AMIB). ONUSAL had fewer than 400 military observers and a similar number of civilian police for its monitoring and verification tasks, while UNOMSIL had barely 200 military personnel.[43] AMIB never reached more than 3,128 troops.[44]

Finally, peace operations that fall significantly off the diagonal are affected by an ambitions-resources gap. The key components of these missions are unbalanced, in that one is better suited to addressing civilians' protection needs than the other. In the upper left the troops lack the physical capacity to provide the level of protection they are asked to deliver. Examples include AMIS and UNAMID in Darfur, and MONUC in the DRC. Below the diagonal a mission has the resources to deliver more protection than it aims to provide. Such operations do not put their latent physical capabilities to meet civilians' security needs to the test. UNPROFOR is a classic example, as is Operation Turquoise, the French intervention in Rwanda I cover in chapter 4. Operation Support Hope, in which U.S. troops delivered relief supplies to Rwandan refugees in Zaire, is another. Although they saved lives, they were used less effectively than they might have been due to strict instructions only to deliver aid and not to deal with violence or insecurity.[45]

Operations above and below the diagonal are, of course, different in meaningful ways. Still, in terms of this book's core concerns they also share some key similarities. In both cases, a mission's less impressive component represents a hard constraint on what it can reasonably hope to accomplish, and thus determines what I call its overall protection capacity. Yet relative to a more limited force with the same overall capacity, an ambitions-resources gap creates additional problems. As described earlier it risks deceiving vulnerable civilians by creating the impression that troops are better prepared to provide protection than they actually are. To see this, we can think of a peace operation's more impressive component as representing what it might appear able to accomplish. That is, if vulnerable civilians see that thousands of well-equipped, seemingly competent soldiers are deployed to their region or if they hear that troops are being deployed to protect them, the limitations of these forces may not be as salient, at least initially. To the extent that this encourages civilians in unrealistic expectations of protection and that they act on these beliefs, it can have the

Table 1.1 A protection typology

Mission type	Component configuration	Protection
Limited	Ambitions unsuitable, resources insufficient	Little
Gap	Ambitions suitable, resources insufficient; OR Ambitions unsuitable, resources sufficient	Varies: little to some, but may also make things worse
Robust	Ambitions suitable, resources sufficient	Extensive

perverse consequence of increasing their suffering and may even add to the number of victims. As a result, as Alan Kuperman has noted, "half measures such as deploying inadequately sized intervention forces—or adequate forces with inadequate mandates—to high-risk peacekeeping situations may be worse than doing nothing."[46]

Given all of this, missions plagued by ambitions-resources gaps are in some respects qualitatively different from robust and limited ones. While the overall protection they can expect to provide is equally relevant, it is offset by the added risk of making things worse. Compared to robust missions, they are clearly inferior. Compared to limited ones, a blanket judgment is harder to make since the risks associated with a gap may or may not make up for a possible difference in overall protection capacity. Table 1.1 summarizes these arguments.

Describing Contributions: Great Power Democracies and Policy Design

Since most peace operations are multilateral, a complete account of why some are robust, others limited, and still others plagued by ambitions-resources gaps would need to deal with the decisions of numerous actors with varying input into the key decisions as well as their own motives for participating. Instead I focus on the roles of the United States, France, the United Kingdom, and, in its own region, Australia. Thanks to their ability to lead robust protection missions and their influence over many operations they do not lead, these four states' policies are vital to understanding overall patterns of civilian protection. Meanwhile, these attributes also afford the states' leaders a unique degree of choice over how to structure their involvement in these missions.

As noted above, providing robust protection in complex emergencies requires highly trained, well-equipped soldiers.[47] Yet while troops from numerous advanced democracies could perform the requisite activities, very few of these states can transport and maintain the necessary soldiers and equipment far from home. Across sizeable distances ambitious peace operations necessitate extensive strategic air and sealift and logistical capabilities.

The United States and to a lesser extent the United Kingdom and France have invested in these capabilities and have demonstrated their value by leading sizeable peace operations. As a result, military analysts have repeatedly singled out these states as having the greatest and most consistent capacity to deploy relatively quickly to halt serious threats to civilians.[48] Meanwhile, Australia's inclusion alongside these more powerful states is mainly a matter of geography. Like several nations that often contribute significant contingents to peace operations (e.g., Canada and the Netherlands), it has substantial military capacity for its size. Unlike them, however, Australia, with its proximity to a volatile region that has experienced several complex emergencies, has had a broad range of choices about how to respond to these conflicts, even with limited long-distance strategic lift capabilities. As a result it, too, has been able to lead multiple peace operations.

At the same time, the United States, United Kingdom, France, and Australia also enjoy extensive influence over the incidence and design of numerous missions they do not lead. For the United States, United Kingdom, and France this partly reflects their permanent membership and veto position on the UN Security Council, which approves the deployment and design of all UN-led missions, including details such as goals, ROE, and total troop numbers. To be sure, the Security Council does not dictate every feature of every UN mission. The UN's permanent bureaucracy, the Secretariat, offers extensive guidance, helping set the Security Council's agenda and often shaping the options it considers.[49] Ultimately, though, when key Security Council members are determined to avoid or pursue a particular course of action there is little the UN bureaucracy can do. At times these states prove immovable and override the Secretariat in order to forestall missions they oppose or dictate limits on those they approve.[50] Likewise, Security Council members have foisted operations on the UN bureaucracy that it had no interest in, including both UNPROFOR in Bosnia and UNAMID in Darfur.[51] The Secretariat itself has also repeatedly complained of a lack of input into the programs it is expected to implement.[52]

Still, many peace operations are not UN-led, and those that are require not only the help of the Secretariat but also the agreement of at least nine Security Council members, with no "no" votes among the Permanent Five. Thus, a second major source of the great power democracies' influence comes from their ability to affect the actions of other states. While they can by no means always convince other nations to do their bidding, they do have extensive political and economic leverage that they can often use to help bring about or shore up peace operations they care about, without having to lead them or even contribute any troops of their own. At the UN, for example, the expectation of repeated interaction between Security Council members—especially the Permanent Five—can create incentives to support each other's priorities. This, in turn, can help members to initiate UN missions when they do not want to intervene themselves.[53]

More broadly, great power democracies can often affect the incidence and design of peace operations through other states' contributions. Side payments of financial or non-monetary resources can help convince other countries to send troops.[54] Similarly, targeted financial and logistical support may help transport foreign troops or shore up the capabilities of an under-resourced force. Such assistance sometimes determines whether an operation can deploy at all, and at other times simply enhances its resources for civilian protection. In recent decades, the United States, United Kingdom, and France have played such supporting roles in UN, AU, and ECOWAS operations in Sudan, Côte d'Ivoire, Burundi, Somalia, Sierra Leone, and Liberia.[55] Similarly, Australia provided critical training, transport, and logistics for missions conducted by forces from the South Pacific in Papua New Guinea and Vanuatu and sponsored the contributions of other states while also deploying its own troops in East Timor, the Solomon Islands, and Tonga.[56]

With all this in mind, we can see how, in contributing to peace operations, American, French, British, and Australian leaders can choose between facilitating robust or limited protection or an ambitions-resources gap. In particular, their individual participation in these missions can be described in terms of the same two key components—ambitions and resources—and the relationship between them. First, when a great power democracy contributes to a peace operation, its leader makes a resource commitment that may go either a little or a long way toward providing the means for robust civilian protection. The amount depends on the nature and scope of the commitment. Because these states can often bring about or at least support peace operations run by others, they have regular opportunities to contribute to these missions purely financially or by providing logistical support. Still, this is not always a guaranteed option since it depends on others' willingness to contribute their own forces. As an alternative, leaders may deploy either a large or small contingent of their states' own military assets and personnel. Indeed, the ability to lead robust missions also provides these leaders with the flexibility to deploy their own troops even when others cannot or will not, or when taking charge is the only way to ensure a force meets their preferences for civilian protection.[57]

Generally speaking, the more leaders rely on providing financial or logistical assistance to support soldiers from other countries, the less they can expect their commitment to help provide for effective protection. Typically this kind of assistance goes to regional missions such as those led by the AU and ECOWAS described above, or to UN-led operations. Yet compared to highly-trained, well-equipped Western forces, these forces are much more likely to lack sufficient training, discipline, or equipment; or intelligence, communications, and planning capabilities.[58]

By contrast, because of their strengths in these same key areas, the more of their states' own troops leaders deploy, the greater the capacity this should create to deliver on the kind of protection goals commonly appropriate in complex emergencies. Indeed, if a leader sends a large enough contingent, this can ensure that a mission has adequate resources for robust protection, regardless of other states' participation. In practice, over the past two decades, major Western states have typically chosen to make significant troop contributions either to missions conducted entirely without the UN or to "hybrid" operations where their own troops are outside the UN command structure. These missions are usually led by one or more of the four states I examine in this book, and they can reflect either an inability to gain Security Council approval or the view that the UN is cumbersome or ineffective.[59] Hybrid operations often deploy in support of a UN mission. For example, the French-led Operation Artemis in 2003 supported MONUC and the United Kingdom's Operation Palliser in 2000 assisted UNAMSIL.[60] Still, both NATO's Operation Allied Force in Kosovo (conducted mainly by the United States, United Kingdom, and France) and the Australian-led Regional Assistance Mission in the Solomon Islands (RAMSI) lacked UN authorization.

Second, when a great power democracy contributes to a peace operation, we can also think about an "ambitions component." This reflects the combined goals and military strategies to be pursued by the soldiers the state helps to deploy, whether its own or contingents from other countries. Generally, they reflect the objectives and tasks laid out for the mission as a whole, but if troop contingents are affected by caveats or restrictions that limit their activities relative to those of other nations, they may reflect these as well. In particular, when leaders contribute their states' own troops and impose restrictions on them that do not apply to other contributors, this can affect the level of protection their soldiers are, in effect, asked to pursue.

As with opportunities to contribute resources to missions they do not lead, for powerful democracies influence over peace operations' ambitions varies from case to case. When they lead, they retain control over goals and military strategies. When they send troops but do not lead, they may have less overall influence but can still control how their own forces are used. Finally, when they do not send their own troops, they may retain some influence, but it may also be more tenuous. When the United States, United Kingdom, or France votes to authorize and fund a UN force, for example, it can exercise veto power over goals, tasks, and ROE, but cannot unilaterally make these more ambitious than other Security Council members will accept. Likewise, when offering financial or logistical support to regional actors, a leader can promote certain goals or military strategies but cannot guarantee they will be approved by the states directly in charge.

As this discussion suggests, the options open to even the most influential democracies can be limited by other states. They may not always be able to contribute to a peace operation without sending their own troops, and without leading they may not be able to ensure that a force's ambitions reflect civilians' needs. Still, because they can lead and send their own troops when sufficiently motivated, these states can pursue a variety of outcomes even when they do not wish to—or cannot—rely on others to do most of the work. For example, Alan Kuperman's assessment of U.S. options for intervention in Rwanda's genocide pointed to three possibilities—maximum, moderate, and minimal intervention—which could "be distinguished by the extent of their goals and the degree of cost and risk they would entail."[61] Similarly, according to a 2010 handbook on U.S. military planning for mass atrocity response, "Policymakers will usually want to explore options along the spectrum of 'doing nothing' and full-scale intervention."[62]

Finally, then, the basic decisions confronting these powerful democracies reflect the typology of protection laid out above. If sufficiently motivated, leaders can make a robust contribution that provides for appropriate goals and military strategies and enough of their states' own well-prepared troops to carry them out. This may require offering to lead the force, but ensures that both ambitions and resources reflect civilians' needs. Both Australia's leadership of INTERFET and U.S. leadership of UNITAF qualify, since they ensured these missions' overall robust protection capacity. Leaders can also make limited contributions. Here, ambitions are restrained: soldiers help deliver humanitarian relief or oversee a peace process but do not provide security beyond their own personnel. Meanwhile, the resources a leader provides are too limited to ensure any real capacity for civilian protection. Typically they involve financial or logistical assistance for a relatively small number of foreign troops that, in any case, may have limited ability to offer effective protection if asked. Alternatively, leaders may send too few of their states' own personnel to provide much protection. Examples include U.S., French, and British support for the limited missions discussed above—ONUSAL, UNOMSIL, and AMIB.

Last but not least, great power democracies can also contribute to peace operations in ways that create or facilitate ambitions-resources gaps. As above, such gap contributions can happen in two basic ways. One important difference for multilateral missions, though, is that they may or may not lead to a gap for the mission as a whole.

First, the resources a leader commits may generate the physical capacity to provide more protection than the mission aims to deliver. This involves a relatively significant deployment of the state's own troops along with restrictive goals or military strategies that apply either to the mission as a whole or, perhaps, only to the state's own personnel. Such contributions ensure at least some ambitions-resources gap for the mission as a whole, since at least there is a difference between capabilities and ambitions for the state's own contingent. Moreover, the more of the total force this contingent represents, the more this gap affects the mission as a whole. At the extreme are missions run almost or completely by the state itself, such as France's Turquoise and the United States' Support Hope. Still, these states also make such contributions in missions with many contributors. French and British decisions to send thousands of troops to UNPROFOR in Bosnia, but constrain them with modest objectives and restrictive ROE, are classic examples that had a profound impact on the mission as a whole.

Alternatively, a leader may provide fewer resources to a peace operation than are needed to pursue its key objectives. As with limited contributions, this typically involves offering financial or logistical support to troops from developing countries, who are instead asked to pursue relatively ambitious protection goals. In theory such a contribution could also involve sending too few of a state's own soldiers to accomplish the goals they are given. In practice, however, leaders have proved loath to do this, as it risks making the force an easy target and sets them up for failure. Such concern does not seem to apply to other states' troops. Examples of this type of gap include American, French, and British support to AMIS and UNAMID in Darfur, and especially after 2008, to MONUC in the DRC.

Finally, unlike when a state deploys and constrains its own military forces, when it instead supports foreign troops, there may be some ex ante uncertainty about their abilities. Sometimes it is obvious in advance whose troops will deploy and that they are not up to providing the protection they will be asked to deliver, even with international assistance. In these cases, the great power democracy runs the clearly foreseeable risk that the troops it is supporting will prove unable to deliver the level of protection they are mandated to provide. At other times, and especially with UN operations, the identity and limitations of the foreign troops who will deploy may not be clear beforehand. In these cases it may still be possible to predict that the likely troop contributors will not be up to the job at hand. At the least, though, relative to deploying one's own soldiers, supporting foreign troops with uncertain capabilities tasked with relatively ambitious protection goals increases the odds that the force will not achieve its objectives. Such contributions thus create a clear risk of an ambitions-resources gap at the overall mission level, and help to promote—but do not guarantee—this outcome.

Understanding when and how the international community uses peace operations to protect civilians in complex emergencies is challenging in part because it requires a way to describe and assess these efforts. In this chapter I have developed a simple framework for doing so, both at the overall mission level and at the level of policy choices by individual great power democracies. The same basic distinctions—between efforts that are robust or limited, or that involve creating or promoting ambitions-resources gaps—apply at both levels. Although they necessarily simplify a more complex reality, they also highlight the core concerns of observers who have long complained about peace operations that do not meet civilians' needs and even expose them to greater risks. The remainder of the book uses this framework to investigate when and why the great power democracies contribute to peace operations as they do.

Political Will, Organized Hypocrisy, and Ambitions-Resources Gaps

> The trouble with most discussions of "political will" is that more time is spent lamenting its absence than on analyzing its ingredients.
> —International Commission on Intervention and State Sovereignty,
> *The Responsibility to Protect*

This chapter turns to the nature of political will in the great power democracies and the politics of ambitions-resources gaps. The first section describes the basic problem that leads policymakers to create and promote these policies. Using the concept of organized hypocrisy, I explain how competing normative and material pressures to protect civilians and limit associated costs and risks create political dilemmas for leaders. These dilemmas generate demands for policy compromises that make concessions to each perspective, an apt description of ambitions-resources gaps.

The second and third sections expand on these ideas by first describing two key domestic sources of these competing pressures: society and the government itself. Specifically, leaders may face dilemmas about how to satisfy citizens and officials who want to help protect vulnerable civilians without creating an unacceptable risk of public backlash or alienating important subordinates or bureaucracies. I also explain just how ambitions-resources gaps can help leaders manage these dilemmas by earning the support (or at least acceptance) of those who favor action while limiting the risk of an adverse response. The second section focuses on these issues as they pertain to society, and the third deals with the governmental level.

I next develop the key empirical predictions I test in the coming chapters. The previous sections generate clear implications about why concerned citizens and officials are likely to accept ambitions-resources gaps and about how I expect leaders will promote them. Yet there is also the vital question of when leaders will be most attracted to them. To answer this, I argue that, although conflicting pressures within society and government may encourage ambitions-resources gaps for somewhat different reasons, they should coincide empirically in predictable ways. First, stronger societal pressure to protect civilians is likely to overlap with similar pressure from within government. In addition, while a leader may worry about the costs and risks of intervening to protect civilians for many reasons, the objective conditions on the ground in a conflict—the operational environment—can help him and his advisers anticipate how great these will be. An inhospitable operational environment that poses greater challenges and physical risks can add to leaders' worries about eventual public backlash against intervention and also inspire caution among key government officials and agencies. Thus, when leaders face strong pressure for action plus strong grounds for worry about such risks, especially due to a formidable operational environment, the need to help protect civilians and also limit costs will be intense, and ambitions-resources gaps will be particularly attractive.

The fourth section develops this argument, which also has interesting secondary implications for other policy outcomes aside from ambitions-resources gaps. Most notably, it suggests that a unique set of domestic political motives and opportunities may help explain some of the most robust and ambitious post–Cold War protection missions. I then summarize the chapter's chief empirical implications into a series of testable hypotheses.

Finally, the last section of the chapter outlines a separate, international-level argument that plays a smaller role in this book but that supports my overall emphasis on the need for compromise between competing normative and material pressures as a key cause of ambitions-resources gaps. In brief, I expect that when a great power democracy faces pressure from key allies or international partners to do more or less to protect civilians than its leaders would be inclined to do otherwise, the response may be to promote an ambitions-resources gap. Under the circumstances, this may help to balance a leader's other priorities and constraints against the need for effective cooperation and good relations with the relevant international partners.

Ambitions-Resources Gaps as Organized Hypocrisy

Organized hypocrisy refers to the disconnect between rhetoric and action that often results when policymakers are confronted with contradictory normative and material pressures about how to respond to a given situation or address a particular problem. There are at least two distinct versions of the concept.[1] As first formulated by the organization theorist Nils Brunsson, organized hypocrisy is a product of the complex operating environments in which large bureaucratic organizations function, and is committed by these organizations as collective units.[2] Organizations are responsible to multiple constituencies. They must secure funding and resources for their activities while efficiently carrying out the functions for which they were created. These roles are not always compatible. The norms an organization must espouse to retain legitimacy may be inconsistent with the competent performance of its core tasks or the resources available for doing so. As a result, words and actions may become decoupled from one another: the natural causal connection between them is snapped. At times, norm-consistent rhetoric may be used to compensate for inconsistent action, to give the impression of living up to normative standards that are being violated in practice. In this case there is an inverse relationship between words and action: they are counter-coupled rather than decoupled.[3] Either way, the organization says one thing but does another.

Second, among students of international relations, organized hypocrisy is best known through Stephen Krasner's analysis of the norm of sovereignty.[4] According to Krasner, states pay lip service to this norm but violate it regularly. Here, again, hypocrisy stems from the difference between words and action, but a key difference is that the actors who commit it are the individual rulers of states rather than formal organizations. Still, their hypocrisy is "organized" because it constitutes a regular pattern of behavior. Again, too, the cause of this disconnect is an environment defined by a clash between professed values and the practical requirements of effective governance, although for Krasner's leaders—unlike Brunsson's organizations—this conflict occurs at the international level. Sovereignty is a norm espoused by the rulers of states as a guide for their relations with other states, while the reality of anarchy in the international system imposes material incentives to maximize state power that contradict this norm.

The ambitions-resources gaps I analyze in this book represent yet another form of organized hypocrisy, which we can think about either as the product of large organizations à la Brunsson or—in line with Krasner—as policies pursued by the leaders or governments of individual great power democracies. Indeed, in the context of UN peacekeeping Michael Lipson has previously described these gaps—citing the problem of "divergence between mandates and capabilities" in UN-led missions—as a form of organized hypocrisy driven by competing pressures on the organization as a whole.[5] Within the UN system, normative demands for action conflict with member states' unwillingness to provide adequate resources. As discussed earlier, however, and as Lipson's own argument suggests, the politics of peace operation design occur largely at the state level, where leaders must decide what resources to contribute and what goals and military strategies the troops may pursue. What is more, as we have seen in chapter 1, ambitions-resources gaps occur not just in UN or regional missions, but in those led by powerful democracies as well. There are thus good reasons to explore the sources of these gaps through state-level policy-making in these countries.

I extend the notion of organized hypocrisy to describe the policies of individual great power democracies when they promote and create ambitions-resources gaps. Like Krasner, I recognize that leaders—specifically, national executives—bear ultimate responsibility for decisions about the use of military force, and that they aim to remain in power by catering to the needs and priorities of their constituents. At the same time, I also recognize that these leaders operate within the context of a broader government. The positions and influence of different officials and agencies affect the policy options presented to national leaders as well as the ways they are described. Leaders, then, make decisions, but these reflect not only their own political incentives but also the intragovernmental context in which options are debated.

As state-level policies, ambitions-resources gaps reflect the same sort of conflict between normative and material pressures described by Brunsson and Krasner, and the same disparity between talk and action. For almost any complex emergency it is possible to find at least some voices pushing to help protect vulnerable civilians. While this pressure can have important political consequences for leaders, its normative underpinnings are also central since they inform the image that leaders aim to project through their policies and the rhetoric they use to do so.[6] Yet, simultaneously, reluctance to accept significant costs and risks or to forego other priorities in an environment of limited resources is nearly universal. Indeed, individual officials and citizens often share both concerns, even if different actors ultimately diverge on their relative importance.

Ambitions-resources gaps, in turn, represent a particular sort of compromise between these positions. By contributing to peace operations with at least some resources or ambitions to protect civilians (that is, in ways that are not strictly "limited," as described in chapter 1), leaders can claim to be making a significant effort to meet vulnerable civilians' most pressing needs and that this effort can be expected to do substantial good. Casual or partly informed observers might even be forgiven for believing that such actions are well-tailored to the needs of the specific complex emergency. At the same time, the gap between ambitions and resources reduces the costs and risks the state must expect to bear compared with those that more robust action would require. Finally, talk and action are not merely decoupled; they are counter-coupled. As discussed earlier, such policies are designed to achieve at most some protection relative to civilians' needs and run a real risk of being worse than nothing. Thus, rhetoric is used to make up—and even cover up—for the deficiencies of actions taken.

The insight that ambitions-resources gaps represent a form of compromise between competing humanitarian values and material concerns suggests that the nature of political will for civilian protection is complex and multi-faceted. Contradictory demands for action and restraint can generate sufficient political will to do something, but not enough for robust action. Meanwhile, the risk of making a bad situation worse receives little consideration. Still, this alone does not explain where these pressures to protect civilians and limit costs come from or how ambitions-resources gaps can satisfy the various audiences responsible for them. I turn to these questions next.

Competing Societal Pressures

Democratic leaders generally have excellent grounds for concerning themselves with society's reactions to their foreign policies. Foreign policy influences people's views of political candidates, and thus potentially their voting decisions.[7] It also affects leaders' approval ratings, which in turn serve as a key source of political capital that affects not only leaders' prospects for survival in office, but also their ability to get things done.[8]

To be sure, leaders' incentives to pursue popular foreign policies vary somewhat across political systems and over their time in office. In all democracies this pressure tends to be strong just before elections.[9] Leaders in weak presidential systems like the United States are especially sensitive to their approval ratings.[10] Still, leaders in majority parliamentary systems like the United Kingdom and Australia or presidential-parliamentary systems like France also require consistent political support.[11] As Bruce Russett notes, they are "constantly under pressure to solve problems," and "popularity with the voters is a leader's most important resource for accomplishing any of his goals."[12] Thus, even well-insulated leaders and those not running for reelection have reason to husband political capital. Such leaders tend to care about both their own legacy and their party's electoral success, either of which can be threatened when unpopular foreign policies lead to low approval numbers or distract from their core policy agendas.[13]

Reflecting this logic, various studies have suggested that in democracies the public serves to constrain foreign policy decisions, its opinions setting the basic parameters within which leaders can safely work.[14] When it comes to protecting civilians from violence, though, leaders may confront two contradictory but simultaneous impulses from domestic society. First, while citizens often report that in principle they support military action to protect vulnerable civilians, in practice the low priority most people usually place on this goal translates into latent, if not explicit, pressure to strictly limit the costs of any such efforts. Second, sometimes leaders also perceive strong societal pressure to act to protect civilians. Together these conflicting demands can make it very difficult to design policies leaders can expect to be both popular and effective.

PRESSURE TO LIMIT COSTS: THE RISK OF PUBLIC BACKLASH

At first glance it may appear that leaders have little reason to worry about public backlash for trying to save civilian lives. In surveys, Western publics regularly approve of military action for humanitarian ends. In the United States, for example, five polls conducted between 2002 and 2010 by the Chicago Council on Global Affairs found large majorities for using U.S. troops "to stop a government from committing genocide and killing large numbers of its own people."[15] Similarly, in the 1990s, the French Ministry of Defence repeatedly found strong majorities for using French military force "to help a population in distress" (73–87%), and "to contribute to bring peace in a region of the world" (60–78%).[16] Indeed, every year from 1999 to 2006, over 90% of French respondents wanted delivering humanitarian relief to be a priority for the armed forces, a greater percentage than those who favored saving the lives of French nationals abroad or destroying terrorist hotbeds.[17] Cross-national polls like the German Marshall Fund's Transatlantic Trends series show similar views across the United States, United Kingdom, and France.[18] Finally, in 1993, 76.7% of Australian Election Study respondents thought military intervention could be justified "if the country oppresses its own citizens."[19] And, in 2005, Australians offered 91% support for using armed force "in support of United Nations or regionally endorsed peace-keeping missions," and 84% support "to prevent genocide and gross abuse of human rights on the scale of Rwanda, Kosovo or Sudan."[20]

Such polls appear to reveal strong latent support for the principle of civilian protection. Yet they do not probe two key, related dimensions of public attitudes: the intensity (or salience) of respondents' feelings and their sensitivity to potential casualties and other costs. Significantly, surveys that explicitly pose such tradeoffs often yield quite different results.[21] More broadly, numerous studies suggest that public approval of military operations depends only partly on people's views about their inherent merit or morality. Perceptions of success and costs, and the relationships between these factors, are also central.[22] By accounting for these additional aspects of public attitudes it is easier to understand the constraints that publics tend to place on leaders.

First, while they may see civilian protection as a worthy goal, for most citizens it is also a low-salience issue, and they tend to devote little if any attention to the particulars. According to one analysis of Australian attitudes, for example, "Generally, the community approves the basic idea of peacekeeping and then takes little interest in its operations."[23] As a result, most people lack the information about mission goals, strategies, and resources needed to reward their leaders for more robust protection efforts. Instead, as long as a mission is not obviously disastrous they may see it as successful even if it does little to address civilians' core security needs, and are likely to experience at best a sense of general satisfaction from supporting a good cause. As Russett has noted, "in many instances members of the public are willing to accept any of several alternative policies in pursuit of a general goal like 'peace and security.'"[24]

Second, when it comes to military operations there is ample evidence that, in general, "governments lose popularity in proportion to the . . . cost in blood and money."[25] At least in the United States, some recent research suggests that more financially expensive conflicts depress presidential approval ratings.[26] More significantly, numerous studies have identified a negative relationship between public support for military action and the number, rate, or trend of military casualties.[27] Indeed, the idea that costly or unsuccessful ventures lead to electoral defeat underpins several major findings in the international relations literature: notably, that democracies are more likely to initiate wars they can win and to target civilians to increase their odds of victory in protracted wars of attrition.[28] Thus, if a peace operation is longer or bloodier than expected, or if citizens otherwise judge that the costs exceed the value, there is real potential for a public backlash.

It follows that for a great power democracy, more robust efforts to protect civilians are unlikely to enhance a leader's standing with most of the public but increase the odds of being punished for the mistake of an excessively costly venture. As noted in chapter 1, troops that pursue more ambitious goals must be prepared for challenges to their presence and must employ more risky military strategies to be effective. Likewise, more troops cost more to support than fewer. More important, relative to supporting troops from other countries, deploying one's own forces—a hallmark of a relatively robust contribution—is expensive and risky.

All of this contributes to implicit, if not explicit, pressure on leaders not to do too much or accept too many risks to protect civilians. Even when citizens express early support for military action, they do not have the expert knowledge needed to assess the eventual costs and may not be thinking about how these would affect their views. Leaders, in contrast, have every reason to be closely attuned to these issues. What is more, even if worried leaders underestimate citizens' true cost tolerance, it does not follow that they are misreading their own incentives.[29] On the contrary, military operations are inherently uncertain, and costs and casualties can always exceed expectations. Thus, leaders can never be sure in advance how citizens will respond to actual developments or how well opposing politicians will be able to exploit potential setbacks.

PRESSURE TO PROTECT: CONCERN FROM DOMESTIC SOCIETY

While leaders always face pressure to control costs and avoid excessive risks, they may also perceive competing societal demands to save threatened civilians. Notably, explicit pressure may arise from a vocal minority of citizens who care strongly about a given conflict's civilian victims. Like other citizens, they might judge a peace operation negatively if it goes wrong, but they will also judge their leaders harshly for failing to do enough. The size, political influence, and membership of this "activist minority" can vary significantly from conflict to conflict. It may include NGOs and advocacy organizations, other groups like churches or diaspora communities, outspoken members of the media and public figures, and everyday concerned citizens. The latter may be followers of advocacy groups and participate in their activities, but individuals can also reach out on their own to contact their elected representatives, write letters-to-the-editor, or call in to political radio programs. NGOs, of course, also engage in these activities, in addition to others like staging demonstrations, sponsoring petitions, and fundraising for conflict victims.

Leaders may also have plenty of reasons to heed the wishes of these citizens. Their votes and readiness to contribute to political campaigns may well depend on their leaders' efforts to protect threatened civilians. Through their advocacy activities they may be able to gain attention and consideration from the media and opposition politicians, pull more and more citizens into their movement, and even derail a leader's focus on his other policy priorities. Ultimately, however, the amount of pressure they can create depends on their political position.

All else equal, the more vocal, better funded, better organized, larger, and more important to their leader's own key political coalition they are, the more pressure members of an activist minority should be able to exert on their leaders to respond to their demands. Yet in practice there are several possible pathways to significant influence. For instance, a group that is politically crucial to a particular leader or party's electoral hopes—part of the incumbent's winning coalition, in the language of the literature on selectorate theory—may be able to generate significant pressure for principled, moral policy goals even with relatively low numbers.[30] In the nineteenth century, a group of "Protestant dissenters" who sought to end Britain's participation in the international slave trade succeeded largely because they were positioned to determine the balance of power in parliament despite initially representing just 3–6% of the population.[31] More recently, U.S. evangelicals crucial to the election of George W. Bush in 2000 helped convince him to help broker an end to Sudan's long, devastating civil war.[32]

Alternatively, a particularly large or well-connected group of concerned citizens may be able to exert significant pressure on a leader even if they are not dominated by the leader's key supporters. If they are sufficient in number, and particularly if they are politically diverse and well organized, they may matter to any leader regardless of party. Such groups may be in a strong position to generate the kind of distractions from a leader's core agenda that all politicians hope to avoid. For example, members of the U.S. Darfur advocacy movement in the mid-2000s were not, by and large, Bush supporters. As Richard Williamson, who served as the president's special envoy on Sudan and met frequently with activists, recalled, "no one . . . was voting for George Bush!"[33] Yet Darfur activists were able to affect the Bush

Administration, as I detail in chapter 5. The height of this advocacy, moreover, was during the president's second term, when reelection was not an issue but when he was sensitive to how Darfur would affect his presidential legacy.

A large and diverse activist minority also includes many citizens who are not members or core followers of advocacy groups. Public expressions of concern from these people may signal to officials that a particular conflict has struck a chord with a significant segment of society and extends beyond a narrow activist constituency. Thus, elected officials often suggest that it makes a strong impression to hear from citizens who are not simply parroting advocacy talking points. According to the former U.S. Congressman Frank Wolf, for example, in today's era of mass-produced advocacy material and email, it stands out when a constituent writes something in his or her own words.[34] Similarly, according to the former Australian Foreign Minister Alexander Downer, when "the mainstream of the society" goes into the streets and calls political radio programs or an official's office in significant numbers, "then that's something you'd focus on."[35]

Finally, not all societal pressure to protect civilians is necessarily so explicit or so driven by overt activism. Instead, leaders might also perceive a form of latent pressure from the broader public that is similar to the threat of backlash against costly peace operations. Here, though, the risk is of broad-based public disapproval for not acting to protect civilians. Despite leaders' reasons to worry about how citizens will ultimately respond to the costs of military action, the surveys highlighted above suggest that on some level most people do share a moral concern to save vulnerable civilians. Thus, if political opponents or activists publicly criticize a leader for inaction, members of the broader public—lacking advance knowledge about the costs of intervention—could well judge him harshly, undermining his moral authority. This risk, in turn, seems greatest when critics can claim that their state has a particular obligation to a conflict's victims: for instance, if a complex emergency is in the vicinity or if their state is seen as having some historical responsibility for the affected population. Still, such broad public censure is likely to coincide with at least some explicit activist pressure.

THE COMPROMISE: AMBITIONS-RESOURCES GAPS

If leaders perceive substantial societal pressure for civilian protection—whether explicit, latent, or both—then they have a clear incentive both to respond to this pressure and to limit the costs of doing so in order to minimize the risk of later public backlash. This situation generates a political dilemma for leaders about how to balance these competing pressures. Ambitions-resources gaps can serve as an effective compromise by controlling military costs and risks while also helping leaders maintain the support of activists and other concerned citizens.

Compared with more robust action, ambitions-resources gaps can help leaders limit the risk of public backlash since they should involve fewer costs and lower risks for a leader's own state. If a leader deploys his state's capable soldiers but does not allow them to carry out ambitious protection tasks and activities, they will be exposed to fewer physical risks.[36] Alternatively, if a leader supports the deployment of less capable troops from other countries who are asked to carry out such ambitious tasks, this also saves on expected costs and risks for his state. On a per-person basis, Western soldiers cost more than those from developing countries, while supporting someone else's troops spares one's own soldiers from the dangers of deployment. Deaths among a state's own soldiers are likely to be most salient, and so deploying them creates the risk of casualties the public is likely to notice.

Yet ambitions-resources gaps also have important advantages for mollifying an activist minority. Notably, compared to non-military efforts to address civilians' needs, peace operations are easy even for concerned citizens with limited understanding of a complex situation to observe: the physical presence of boots on the ground or planes in the air is obvious, even if they are from other countries. Peace operations can also deploy and begin their work relatively quickly, whereas policies like diplomatic initiatives or economic sanctions may take a long time to achieve results. Further, compared to even more limited contributions, policies that promote ambitions-resources gaps gesture more clearly toward addressing threatened civilians' needs and are thus more easily connected to the goals of saving lives and alleviating security threats.

Still, why would activist groups and other concerned citizens give leaders credit for anything short of providing robust civilian protection, and especially for potentially harmful half-measures? That they should do so is not obvious. Thus, answering this question is central to accounting for ambitions-resources gaps, since these compromise policies would make little sense if they did not actually help leaders manage strong pressures to act. There are several reasons that members of an activist minority—and especially the broader public—are likely to accept these policies. First, they may not recognize ambitions-resources gaps or understand their limitations, especially the risk of making things worse rather than better. Just as these gaps may encourage vulnerable civilians on the ground to develop unrealistic expectations for a peace operation, citizens at home may come to believe their state is doing more to address civilians' security needs than it really is, or that its policies could be more easily fixed than they can.

For concerned citizens, the informational requirements to recognize ambitions-resources gaps, let alone determine whether and how they might be fixed, are high. In brief, they must be able to assess whether a peace operation meets the standards for robust protection laid out in chapter 1: whether its goals match civilians' needs, whether the military strategies it employs are suited to these goals, and whether the forces provided are sufficient in number and quality. This, in turn, necessitates access to extensive information about conditions on the ground, the details of operational goals and military strategies, and the kinds of activities that soldiers from other countries can realistically be expected to pursue. Meanwhile, properly interpreting this information requires a base of knowledge not only about the conflict itself, but also about the international political context in which peace operations are designed and about how details such as force objectives, ROE, and troop composition matter and interact.

The challenges to acquiring and sorting through all of this information are substantial. Conditions on the ground can be difficult to assess, especially early in a conflict or where journalists are absent, putting concerned citizens at a disadvantage vis-à-vis a reluctant leader.[37] Indeed, perpetrators of violence against civilians commonly seek to thwart NGOs' efforts to collect the relevant information themselves, attacking them physically or denying them entry to the conflict-affected area. Meanwhile, when it comes to peace operations, critical aspects of military strategy, such as ROE, are typically classified. As Holt and Berkman point out, "for missions not led by the United Nations, NATO, or nations with advanced militaries" such mission-wide rules may not even exist.[38] Confidential status of forces agreements and memoranda of understanding can restrict where forces from particular contingents deploy and what kinds of activities they engage in. Finally, even if they can acquire all of this information, few individuals or organizations have the combined military, foreign policy, and conflict-specific expertise needed to synthesize it effectively. Thus, key questions like whether foreign troops or regional organizations have the capacity to effectively run a complex, possibly dangerous mission can be difficult to answer.

Some NGOs may surmount these obstacles by devoting themselves to developing the relevant expertise. Others lack the required knowledge, however, perhaps especially if they are newly organized, have little experience with the particular society in conflict, or devote most of their energy to mobilizing followers rather than developing policy proficiency. For instance, societal groups concerned about a particular conflict may have an excellent understanding of the complex emergency itself, but lack broader contextual knowledge. In addition, the wider group of concerned citizens who may or may not be followers of advocacy groups generally have limited time for activism and even less expertise. The same certainly goes for the broader public, to the extent that leaders worry about latent pressure to respond to a given complex emergency.

Thanks to these challenges, activists—but perhaps especially their part-time followers and other concerned citizens—may fail to grasp the nuances of peace operation design, or even to focus on the issue at all. As Holt and Berkman note, advocates "often end their discussion at whether or not to 'send in the troops.'"[39] Alternatively, inexperienced activists might succumb to misperceptions such as perceiving some, but not all, of a mission's limitations, or interpreting a peace operation's use of civilian protection language as implying more extensive protection capacity than is actually intended.[40] The result can be unrealistically rosy expectations of what particular policies can reasonably achieve, and a level of support for them that concerned citizens might not otherwise offer. Leaders, in turn, may be able to help build this support through what I call the rhetoric of organized hypocrisy: by describing their policies in ways that are decoupled from the reality of what they are designed to accomplish.

Still, even activists and concerned citizens who clear these hurdles may have several reasons to accept policies that create and promote ambitions-resources gaps. For one, while they would presumably prefer more robust action, they may also concede that it is not immediately possible if confronted with firm resistance or strong arguments from leaders or other government officials. In such cases they may view an imperfect mission as the next best alternative. After all, it may succeed in doing some good and there may be opportunities to push for improvements later on. For members of the activist minority, moreover, the very act of pushing for government action may provide an expressive benefit, a sense of satisfaction created by publicly promoting personally held values or ideas.[41] Because such benefits arise through expression itself, for some people the precise form of a leader's response may be less important than the effort to move government policy in the first place. Such citizens might, like members of the broader public, be willing to accept any of several policies that reflect a response to their concerns.

Last, NGOs and activist groups may also have instrumental incentives to accept or even push for ambitions-resources gaps (or other imperfect policies). In recent years, scholars of the advocacy and NGO sector have emphasized that although these actors often proclaim principled objectives, they also pursue more material concerns: like other organizations, they aim to survive and grow. As a result, pressures related to their operating environments—the need to overcome collective action problems among potential followers and donors, and to compete with other groups in the same policy space for funding—can push them to behave in ways that are inconsistent with their professed principles. These needs may, for instance, drive them to prioritize publicity at the expense of effective service delivery; or to select causes at least partly on the basis of such instrumental incentives, rather than where needs are greatest.[42]

In the present context, advocacy groups seeking to survive, grow, and demonstrate their credibility need to build and maintain the enthusiasm of followers, and to elicit financial contributions. To achieve these goals they must be able to demonstrate tangible policy successes, to show that they can affect government policy. Otherwise, the supporters they need to donate money and time will not believe that their participation matters.

Groups that cannot point to concrete accomplishments, then, are likely to find their followers quitting, or simply never materializing. What is more, to the extent that the pool of potential followers and donors interested in any given complex emergency is limited, groups may find themselves not just collaborating on advocacy strategies, but also competing with each other for the same supporters.

This combination of competition and need to show results may create incentives for advocacy groups that are compatible with tolerating and perhaps even promoting ambitions-resources gaps. For instance, to increase their odds of appearing influential, activists may prefer to express support for such policies, at least for a time, even if they originally advocated more robust solutions or privately harbor doubts. After all, as Aseem Prakash and Mary Kay Gugerty put it, "publicity is the oxygen for advocacy organizational survival,"[43] and if activists can claim that they helped push their government to contribute to a peace operation, it may make more sense to highlight this than to call attention to the ways in which the force fails to reflect their recommendations. The same pressures may encourage activists to request policies they expect have a reasonable chance of adoption, rather than those they see as ideal. As Rebecca Hamilton has noted, "advocates may be tempted to seek 'quick wins' that demonstrate their own influence but do not necessarily improve the situation and may even be counterproductive."[44] For example, this might include asking their government to support less capable foreign troops if sending their own appears unlikely.

Competing Intragovernmental Pressures

Numerous government organs and bureaucracies usually participate in deciding whether and how to use a nation's military assets abroad. The major players include the foreign and defense ministries and the military itself, as well as the office of the executive and any related agencies within it, such as the National Security Agency in the United States. To varying degrees, the legislature may also have a say. As a result, as with most foreign policy issues, when it comes to responding to complex emergencies there are many cooks who help to stir the pot.

As with domestic society writ large, moreover, different agencies and officials within a government are likely to have different views on how to address these conflicts. While most may share a desire to prevent civilian suffering, there are also many reasons for individual officials or bureaucracies to worry about potential costs and risks of military action. Typically actors will place different emphasis on these considerations depending on the actors' different roles in policy implementation, organizational identities, or perceptions of which policies would be best for their own agencies, careers, or the nation. They may also operate under different assumptions or with different information that can affect how they frame the problems at hand. As a result, there may be some voices within government who favor robust action to protect civilians from violence, others who prefer a less ambitious approach, and still others who fear that the costs of any involvement in a peace operation will be too steep.

Such contradictory perspectives are often resolved through intragovernmental bargaining, as Graham Allison describes, "along regularized channels among players organized hierarchically within the government."[45] For many foreign policy issues and especially those that may involve military force, the national executive is at the top of the hierarchy and has primary responsibility for adjudicating disagreements. As a result, we can think about top leaders as facing competing pressures to protect civilians and limit costs not only from domestic society, but also from the advisers and agencies they rely on for expert advice and policy implementation. As with society, moreover, the strength of these pressures varies over time and across complex emergencies. Again, too, the pressure that different players can bring to bear on top leaders depends on who they are. Here, though, officials have different amounts of power to draw on depending largely on their position within the hierarchy but also on their own persuasive and negotiating skills, relevant expertise, and the quality of their arguments.[46] Officials try to influence policy to their liking by crafting arguments to appeal to the concerns of their superiors, and, ultimately, the national executive. Getting the right arguments to the people at the top of the hierarchy is crucial, but it is easier for those already higher up the ladder. As with domestic society, sufficient pressure both to protect civilians and to limit costs creates a demand for compromise that can encourage ambitions-resources gaps.

PRESSURE TO LIMIT COSTS

There is a long history of reluctance within government to help protect civilians threatened by violence abroad, in particular when it comes to any major use of a state's own military assets. A major reason is that while individual agencies and bureaucrats are unlikely to face serious consequences if their nation does not act to protect civilians or (in most cases) receive much credit for successful intervention, they may well find themselves criticized over any military deployments that go poorly. This imbalance, in turn, encourages a tendency to prominently emphasize the potential costs and risks of humanitarian military action. Indeed, as Samantha Power has reported about the United States, throughout the twentieth century officials who did not want to see their government pursue humanitarian intervention even manipulated information to make their case: they "overemphasized the ambiguity of the facts. They played up the likely futility, perversity, and jeopardy of any proposed intervention."[47]

Still, concerns about costs and risks are rarely distributed evenly across government. Players with other policy interests in a country affected by a complex emergency are likely to be especially attuned to how intervention there could affect their areas of emphasis. Even more significantly, those responsible for implementing any role in a peace operation have particularly strong reasons to focus on these issues. Thus, the military and civilian defense establishments often represent a main source of objections to ambitious civilian protection efforts. In any deployment of a state's own personnel they are likely to bear much of the blame for any mishaps, plus all of the physical risks. They may also see protecting civilians as inconsistent with, or at least a potential distraction from, their most important organizational responsibilities to defend the nation against potential threats. For instance, Jon Western has described U.S. officials who hold this attitude as "selective engagers" who believe "that U.S. military intervention should be reserved for those isolated cases when U.S. strategic material interests (are) directly threatened."[48] In perhaps the most infamous example of this logic, at the height of the Rwandan genocide in 1994 the U.S. Defense Department argued against using American transport planes to help deliver armored personnel carriers to UN troops in Rwanda, on the grounds that doing so "would sacrifice readiness to respond to some higher-priority crisis should one arise."[49]

Further, while other governmental players can also make a compelling case that military intervention in a complex emergency would be too costly or risky, the specialized knowledge and expertise of military actors gives them special advantages in this respect. Because the military is responsible for planning and conducting military operations, it is a primary authority, both within government and with society more broadly, on whether military action is a good idea in a given situation and on what it is likely to cost. Likewise, it is the military that estimates the resources needed to pursue different goals and provide different levels of civilian protection in any given complex emergency. These key roles in planning and implementation, in turn, allow military actors to be "disproportionately enfranchised" in the governmental bargaining process.[50] Their perspectives and recommendations tend to carry particular weight, and although these recommendations are not always accurate, they can be difficult to argue with or overcome. As the former U.S. National Security Advisor Anthony Lake recalled of a 1993 discussion about intervention in Bosnia, for instance, "When our senior military guys were saying, 'This mission can't be done,' it's hard to say, 'Listen, you professionals, here's an amateur's view of how and why it can be done.'"[51]

The same goes for the resources required for effective action. If outright opposition to a peace operation appears impolitic, military actors may resist and try to insulate themselves from blame for any problems that ensue by offering conservative estimates of the troops, materiel, or time needed to address civilians' protection needs.[52] Again, such assessments can be difficult to contradict. In another Bosnia-related example, during a June 1992 discussion on the potential use of U.S. military aircraft for a humanitarian airlift in Sarajevo, military planners announced that they would also need over 50,000 ground troops to secure the perimeter around the city's airport. President Bush's National Security Adviser Brent Scowcroft inferred that the Joint Chiefs "probably inflated the estimates of what it would take to accomplish some of these limited objectives, but once you have the Joint Chiefs making their estimates, it's pretty hard for armchair strategists to challenge them and say they are wrong."[53]

PRESSURE TO PROTECT

Still, governmental actors often also feel deep concern for the victims of complex emergencies. While for many this is insufficient to overcome worries about the costs and risks of military action, for some it can justify pressuring their superiors to protect civilians. Though such officials may not exist in every major democracy for every complex emergency, the phenomenon is a common one. As Samantha Power noted in her study of U.S. responses to genocide in the twentieth century, every single one "generated some activism within the U.S. foreign policy establishment."[54] In his study of nineteenth-century humanitarian interventions, Gary Bass, too, found at least some officials who worked hard to combat the era's worst atrocities.[55] These "liberal humanitarianists,"[56] as Western describes them, may push for non-military options like providing humanitarian aid or diplomatic efforts to halt a human rights crisis, but they may also push for peace operations.

Demands on leaders to protect civilians may come from throughout government. Proponents may be placed high or low, and work in the diplomatic corps, the defense establishment, the office of the executive, or anywhere else. At times militaries even see peace operations as opportunities to practice important skills and gain operational experience. Still, as Power also found, State Department desk officers responsible for the day-in and day-out of U.S. policy toward states experiencing genocide have often been among those most convinced of the need for stronger action. More broadly, the idea that low-level or diplomatic staff would often be the most vocal proponents of civilian protection makes sense, since they often have among the highest levels of daily exposure to information about atrocities and civilian suffering. At the same time, their position in the government hierarchy can make it difficult to transmit their concerns up the chain of command and affect the views of those in more influential positions. Similarly, for top officials, relative isolation from incoming information and broader policy portfolios may serve as obstacles to lobbying for humanitarian military action. Meanwhile, since diplomatic staff are not responsible for directly implementing peace operations they also have relatively little to fear professionally or for their own agency from the costs of military action.

THE COMPROMISE: AMBITIONS-RESOURCES GAPS

The process of bargaining to resolve competing views and priorities within government often results in a policy compromise that incorporates multiple perspectives, and that differs from what any one actor would choose. As Allison notes, "What the nation does is sometimes the result of the triumph of one group over others. More often, however, different groups pulling in different directions yield a result distinct from what any-one intended."[57] What is more, the policies that result from such compromises are often inelegant or suboptimal solutions to the problem. As the old saying goes, "A camel is a horse designed by a committee."

Ambitions-resources gaps can reflect just this type of imperfect intra-governmental compromise. As noted above, because contributing to peace operations may involve a state's military assets, the relevant bargaining process is typically resolved by the national executive. Much as with society, moreover, when these leaders face simultaneous pressure from their subordinates to protect civilians and limit costs they may also experience a significant—yet distinct—political dilemma. Executives both rely on their subordinates for sound advice and need their cooperation, if not full-throated support, to carry out the nation's foreign policies. Thus, there can be good reasons to try to accommodate both sides in these policy disagreements.

First, powerful players within the hierarchy may be able to make individually convincing yet opposing cases to their superiors. That is, depending on how they frame the relevant issues and the specific information they provide or withhold, they may persuade a national executive of both the desirability and the serious risks of acting to protect civilians. As a result, compromise may appear wise. Conversely, different framing or information might lead to another outcome. It is largely in this sense that the national executive's role in adjudicating competing governmental pressures is affected by the actions, preferences, and identities of those below him.

More instrumentally, for national executives compromise may help achieve policy buy-in from key subordinates by giving all players at least some of what they want. Such buy-in is highly desirable, if not an absolute necessity when it comes to the potential deployment of troops abroad. Certainly policy implementation is easier with the willing support and cooperation of the officials and agencies that must be involved. In addition, disgruntled officials may publicly undermine policy options or decisions they oppose. As Power noted of those who would see their government intervene for humanitarian reasons, "Bureaucrats within the system who grasp the stakes can patiently lobby or brazenly agitate in the hope of forcing their bosses to entertain a full range of options."[58] For instance, Western relates that when President Bush and many of his senior advisers were resisting growing pressure for military intervention in Somalia in the summer of 1992, a diplomatic cable describing the ongoing horror there "resonated with many liberal humanitarianists in the State Department who believed that the Bush administration needed to do more in Somalia, and the cable was immediately leaked to the press."[59]

Of course, policies that promote or create ambitions-resources gaps are not the only possible response to an absence of government consensus about how to handle a complex emergency.[60] Still, much as they can help strike a balance between competing priorities within society, they may provide a solution to a need for compromise within government as well. For those most worried about deploying their own state's troops, offering financial or logistical support to a mission run by other countries instead may be, if not exactly desirable, then at least an acceptable middle ground that can help alleviate their key concerns. Thus, when the military strenuously opposes taking action, a leader who still feels compelled to "do something" might go to considerable lengths to assist others to deploy instead. That those troops may not be able to do as they are asked, even with outside assistance, is a less pressing matter. Alternatively, though more expensive and risky, deploying a substantial number of a state's own personnel but restricting them to tasks like helping to deliver humanitarian aid is still far safer and more controlled than providing robust protection, especially in a mass atrocity environment.

Similarly, those who are most anxious to help protect civilians may accept these policies for at least some of the same reasons as the concerned citizens discussed above. If more robust action is ruled out over worries about costs and risks—worries at least some who favor civilian protection may also share—a less-than-ideal effort may seem better than nothing. Concerned officials may also hope that, once underway, such an effort may help pave the way for more ambitious action later on. After all, policy commonly develops over time through a sequence of bargaining decisions as governments deal with the most pressing aspect of a problem and leave other pieces for later. As a result, at any given time the policy options up for discussion may be affected by previous decisions or commitments.[61] Thus, pro-intervention proponents may be optimistic that even flawed steps toward protecting civilians in a given complex emergency could lead to escalation later on if the initial effort yields poor results.

Finally, for officials in government even policy initiatives that accomplish little can also have important symbolic and expressive value. Indeed, as James March has pointed out, "Studies of decision making suggest that the act of supporting a policy with appropriate symbolic meaning can be more important to decision makers than its adoption, and its adoption can be more important than its implementation."[62] Officials who favor action to protect civilians may thus be able to take comfort from helping to champion the cause and observing their government make a contribution to saving civilians' lives. Even if the effort is less ambitious than they would prefer, it may help support a sense of identity in which they and their nation strive to do the right thing and behave as good international citizens.

Empirical Expectations

The above arguments have implications for the conditions that encourage ambitions-resources gaps and other policy outcomes, for the responses of concerned citizens and officials when leaders facilitate these gaps, and for the rhetoric of leaders themselves. This section highlights my empirical predictions about these issues. The first part provides further context for the question of when leaders should tend to create and promote ambitions-resources gaps by stressing the likely overlap between moral and material pressures from society and government, and by considering when these pressures will be relatively strong or weak. By accounting for the overall relationship between these pressures I also identify conditions that should instead encourage robust, limited, or no protection efforts. The second part summarizes all of my expectations in a set of testable hypotheses that drive the analysis in the coming chapters.

MAPPING THE RELATIONSHIP BETWEEN COMPETING MORAL AND MATERIAL PRESSURES

If ambitions-resources gaps are indeed a promising way to manage political dilemmas caused by competing pressures to protect civilians and control associated costs and risks, then their appeal to leaders will depend on how these pressures vary empirically. On one hand, a leader may face anything from virtually no pressure to protect civilians up to a great deal, both from society and from within government. Meanwhile, though leaders are always likely to feel at least somewhat constrained by a risk of public backlash or by bureaucratic caution, these pressures can also be relatively weaker or stronger.

My arguments about domestic society and intragovernmental bargaining suggest that ambitions-resources gaps can emerge from distinct dilemmas that present leaders with different kinds of political problems. Leaders want to avoid future public backlash against their policies but also desire the approval of specific activist constituencies and other concerned citizens. Yet they also need the support and cooperation of subordinates who place different levels of emphasis on saving civilian lives, and on managing costs and risks. Despite the different logics underlying these dilemmas, in practice

I expect them to overlap and reinforce one another in predictable ways. First, pro-intervention arguments from within government should exert greater pressure on leaders when there is also considerable societal advocacy. Since part of what determines the pressure officials can put on their superiors is the arguments they are able to muster, and since leaders are likely to put strong weight on arguments that address their own political fortunes, related societal pressure may help bolster the case of officials who favor acting to protect civilians. In addition, while high-ranking officials have more power to put their views to the national executive, they also have little time for matters that are not already urgent national priorities. Thus, if concerned citizens can command the attention of potentially sympathetic top officials, they may increase pressure on the national executive from within government as well.

Similarly, this relationship should also work in the other direction. As pressure to protect civilians from within government trickles down through the media and through concerned officials' interactions with advocacy groups, it may enhance the level of pressure coming from society. By helping to publicize the horrors of a given complex emergency, officials may attract sympathetic citizens to join the activist minority. They may also provide concerned citizens and NGOs with information they can use to lobby more effectively. This, and the knowledge that their concerns are shared within government, may also work to encourage the ambitions of outside activists and fuel optimism about further advocacy efforts.

I also expect the extent of leaders' worries about public backlash to coincide with the strength of bureaucratic reluctance to act, and that the potency of these pressures should hinge at least in part on ex ante expectations about the physical costs and risks of contributing to a potential peace operation. Of course, numerous circumstances may influence a leader's concerns about public backlash. Likewise, bureaucratic reluctance to intervene can emerge at any time, since it may be rooted in general beliefs or concerns unrelated to conditions on the ground in a given conflict. Still, objective information about a conflict should be particularly relevant in helping officials assess the physical and political risks of any potential action to protect civilians. This information is reflected in the operational environment, the characteristics of the conflict that determine how difficult and dangerous it is to deploy and try to protect civilians. The greater the costs and difficulties a leader expects, the greater the risk he should perceive of a future public backlash. In addition, the more costs and risks that bureaucrats anticipate, the stronger the concerns they are likely to express about contributing military assets to a peace operation. And just as governmental proponents of civilian protection may gain influence by highlighting the political advantages of placating concerned citizens, higher expected costs and risks may play to the advantage of those arguing for caution.

Broadly speaking, we can think about the operational environment for intervention in a given complex emergency as ranging from relatively benign to extremely inhospitable. The less hospitable it is, the greater the expected costs and risks of contributing to peace operations. This applies to both financial expenses and to the rate at which troops may be injured or killed. Still, a better environment for foreign troops does not necessarily imply greater safety for the population or reduce local actors' ability to threaten civilians. As I discuss further in chapter 3, the operational environment for international forces tends to be more formidable when there are stronger and more motivated local forces to resist them, a more complicated and distant conflict, more challenging terrain, and a larger affected population and area. Crucially, the consequences of an operational environment also depend on a state's own contribution to a peace operation. The more of its own troops a state deploys and the more protection these troops are asked to deliver, the greater the exposure to whatever risks the operational environment poses.

For any given contribution to a peace operation, I expect a less hospitable operational environment to heighten a leader's worries about eventual public backlash and also to increase bureaucratic reluctance to act. This, in turn, puts pressure on leaders to control costs in other ways. While the surest solution would be not to contribute at all, other options include strictly limiting the resources they commit—especially their own troops—or the goals and military strategies their soldiers pursue. In other words, a more or less favorable operational environment can either expand or contract a leader's perceived room for policy maneuver.

With all this in mind, the relationship between the overall domestic pressures leaders face to protect civilians and to control associated costs and risks should help predict not just when great power democracies will facilitate ambitions-resources gaps but also when they will pursue more limited or robust civilian protection efforts (or none at all). Figure 2.1 summarizes my expectations, focusing on the operational environment as a consistently significant predictor of pressures to control costs and risks.

First, any political dilemmas about how to balance competing priorities should be minimal when domestic pressure to protect civilians is muted, regardless of the operational environment. In these circumstances leaders have little need to show they are making a significant effort to address civilians' protection needs. Thus, the risks inherent in the operational environment—even if it is relatively benign—should outweigh any consideration of potential benefits from helping to protect civilians. Leaders have little reason to promote or create ambitions-resources gaps, and these policies should be rare.

Still, this does not mean that leaders will not contribute to peace operations at all absent major domestic pressure for civilian protection. Rather, the reasons for doing so and the approaches they pursue are likely to differ.

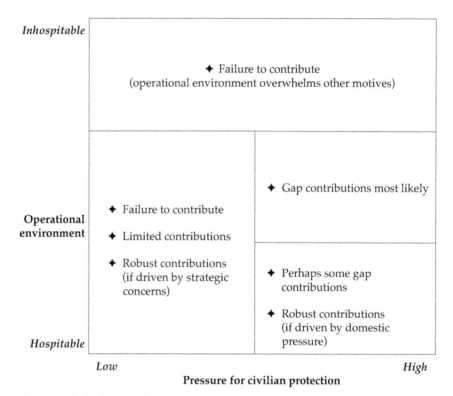

Figure 2.1. Predicting contribution types

As noted in the introduction, various strategic or broader international motives might inspire leaders to participate in peace operations in complex emergencies, even irrespective of moral concerns about vulnerable civilians. Thus, on the left in figure 2.1, leaders may not contribute to peace operations at all, but they may also make either limited or robust contributions. The latter, for instance, could occur if a leader saw a strong interest in protecting civilians to help restore stability in a strategically important country. Still, such motives for contributing to peace operations do not necessarily render the operational environment irrelevant: they may also run up against concerns about difficulties and costs. Likewise, powerful democracies may have fewer chances to support foreign troops in inhospitable operational environments, since other states may also be less inclined to send their own personnel. Thus, even absent substantial pressure for civilian protection, most contributions to peace operations should occur outside the least hospitable operational environments.

In contrast, when leaders do perceive significant pressure from concerned citizens or officials, the operational environment heavily informs the political dilemmas they face. As the operational environment becomes more formidable, in particular, these dilemmas grow more acute: it becomes more difficult for leaders to address pro-protection demands without running a serious risk of later public backlash and without garnering substantial bureaucratic opposition. Thus, while leaders have a clear imperative to make a demonstrable effort to protect civilians, doing so is increasingly risky. The tension between domestic demands to protect civilians and limit costs becomes intense, and a leader's incentive to compromise grows. Thus, ambitions-resources gaps become increasingly likely. Indeed, even if leaders have other reasons for contributing, the strength of combined societal and bureaucratic pressure for civilian protection should drive them to look for ways to accommodate these demands. Correspondingly, then, the odds of not contributing to a peace operation or of making a very limited contribution that will likely do little to satisfy concerned citizens and officials should fall as leaders feel increasingly compelled to make more than a token contribution. Still, even this argument likely works only to a point: due to the sheer challenges and risks, in the most inhospitable operational environments even extensive pressure may be insufficient motivation for action, and we should again see few contributions to peace operations at all.

Finally, when leaders perceive extensive pressure for civilian protection and the operational environment is favorable, the domestic political dilemmas they face should be more limited. Here, a leader's incentive to act is reinforced by what seems an opportunity to do so for a politically acceptable cost. Likewise, the odds of getting the military and other key agencies on board—or at least avoiding significant overt opposition—should be better. Of course, given the unavoidable uncertainty in military operations leaders will still worry about costs and the repercussions of any unforeseen problems: their political dilemmas do not disappear entirely. Still, overall, pressures to curb costs and risks through restrictive mission goals and military strategies or a minor commitment of resources are lower than with a less hospitable operational environment. Ambitions-resources gaps, therefore, should be less likely than above, though still more likely than when leaders face little or no pressure for civilian protection.

A significant implication of this last claim is that these final circumstances—strong pressure to protect civilians plus a hospitable operational environment—create auspicious conditions for robust protection efforts. Although concerned citizens and officials may accept ambitions-resources gaps or fail to notice them, this is no guarantee that they will always do so or that there are no political risks for leaders in these policies. On the contrary, if a leader helps create an ambitions-resources gap and concerned citizens or officials do judge it to be inadequate, they may withhold or rescind their support for the policy. In this case the leader will probably forfeit any political advantages from taking action in the first place. Alternatively, to avoid this, he may have to make improvements and pursue a more robust policy anyway. While these risks may seem well worth running in the face of an inhospitable operational environment, a favorable one may alter them considerably. Although moral pressure to save lives probably never truly dominates concerns about casualties and budgetary outlays, it is here that it comes closest to doing so. And because the odds of getting bureaucratic buy-in and maintaining the mass public's support for robust protection are relatively good, there is less to be gained in exchange for the risk of alienating influential concerned citizens and officials with an ambitions-resources gap.

Although secondary to this book's primary focus, this implication offers an interesting opportunity to compare arguments from the humanitarian intervention literature about the relative importance of strategic interests and domestic advocacy in driving the most ambitious civilian protection efforts. While my argument does not speak to whether one of these motives is more prevalent than the other, it does suggest that we should observe robust missions driven by these different logics under distinct circumstances. To the extent that robust protection reflects a reaction to normative pressures at the domestic level but relies on a relatively benign operational environment, we should mainly observe these contributions here, where pressures to protect civilians are strong. On the other hand, to the extent that robust contributions mainly reflect strategic or other international considerations, we should see them just as often—if not more so—in the scenario discussed above, where these pressures are fairly low.

HYPOTHESES

The arguments developed so far yield five distinct hypotheses that I test in the coming chapters. The basis for a sixth, more tentative one, is presented below.

Three of these hypotheses deal directly with the book's primary puzzle of when and why leaders facilitate ambitions-resources gaps. The first focuses on when these gaps are most likely. It should find empirical support if I am right that leaders use these policies to manage political dilemmas caused by starkly competing moral and material pressures surrounding civilian protection, and if I am right about the role of the operational environment:

- H1: Leaders will promote ambitions-resources gaps when they face strong pressure to protect civilians and strong bureaucratic opposition or reasons to worry about future public backlash, especially (but not only) as indicated by a relatively inhospitable operational environment

The next two hypotheses reflect key causal mechanisms that explain how leaders can maintain the support of core domestic audiences while facilitating ambitions-resources gaps. If leaders are able to benefit from these policies as I have suggested, then we should see evidence that concerned citizens and officials support or at least accept them for the reasons identified earlier.

- H2: Concerned citizens and bureaucrats will accept ambitions-resources gaps because they do not recognize key limitations of these policies, see them as acceptable alternatives to more robust action, experience expressive benefits from pushing for civilian protection, and/or have material incentives to accept these policies

Further, we should see leaders trying to facilitate this support by speaking about these policies in ways that aim to make up, or cover, for their limitations. This behavior will not surprise readers who accept the structure of ambitions-resources gaps as a form of organized hypocrisy. However, it is also a clear implication of the more specific claim that leaders use these gaps to help resolve particular kinds of political problems. As such, evidence of this rhetoric, especially combined with indications that leaders understand the compromises they are making, will further bolster the central argument.

- H3: Leaders who facilitate ambitions-resources gaps are likely to engage in the rhetoric of organized hypocrisy, as evidenced by statements that are counter-coupled from what their policies are designed to accomplish

The remaining hypotheses are ancillary to these three. Two deal with the prospects for policies aside from promoting ambitions-resources gaps. Support for them should increase confidence in my argument by confirming that leaders do not promote these gaps absent the political dilemmas highlighted above, while adding nuance to our understanding of the available alternatives:

- H4: Strong pressure for civilian protection plus a hospitable operational environment may promote robust protection efforts; to the extent that leaders make robust contributions to peace operations in these conditions, they are not drive by purely strategic considerations

- H5: Unless the operational environment is very inhospitable, low pressure to respond to civilians' needs should encourage limited or no contributions to peace operations, while strong pressure should discourage these outcomes

The final hypothesis deals with an issue not yet addressed, the distinction between the two ways that powerful democracies may facilitate ambitions-resources gaps: by deploying but restraining substantial numbers of their own high-quality troops, and by supporting underprepared forces from other countries who are asked to pursue ambitious protection goals. As this chapter has suggested, I expect both versions to serve the same basic political function and to be attractive to leaders in response to comparable political dilemmas. Still, the differences between them raise the question of how leaders select one approach or the other. Tentatively, I propose that the answer depends mainly on practicalities related to the speed with which a leader perceives a need to respond to a particular conflict and the availability of other actors to deploy in an acceptable timeframe. When possible, leaders probably prefer to assist someone else's troops, but this is not always feasible, especially on a tight schedule. It may take substantial time to recruit and deploy foreign soldiers, or it may be impossible to reach Security Council agreement on a UN force. In such cases deploying a state's own troops and limiting their goals, ROE, or other military strategies should prevail. This yields the last, exploratory hypothesis:

- H6: When leaders feel compelled to act quickly but lack a clear military option other than deploying their own troops, they will do so and restrain them. In contrast, when there is a ready chance to support a UN or regional operation or time to help make this an option, they will promote ambitions-resources gaps by supporting troops from developing countries.

Although I lack the data to subject this prediction to rigorous testing, the case studies in chapters 4 and 5 do at least allow for a plausibility probe of this interesting distinction.

Competing Pressures at Home and Abroad

As noted in the introduction, leaders may also come to promote ambitions-resources gaps through a distinct, international path. Although this mechanism is not as readily amenable to conventional hypothesis testing, it does reinforce the book's overall argument.

When great power democracies contribute to peace operations they typically prefer for these missions to be multilateral. Leaders want to ensure that other countries see their actions as legitimate, and the participation of other states and international organizations can help.[63] They also often want to share the burden, both financially and in terms of the military risks. In addition, multilateral missions may help to ensure broad public support at home. Surveys suggest that the public generally prefers multilateral operations, but whether this is because citizens see them as more legitimate or because of their burden-sharing advantages is less clear.[64]

Still, multilateral missions can pose numerous challenges in coordinating among all the participating states (and any relevant international bureaucracies). These states, in turn, each have their own reasons for participating and their own domestic constraints to account for. They may disagree on force objectives, and they may be willing to expose their soldiers to different levels of physical risk. Such differences are the source of the much-maligned caveats that have bedeviled numerous peace operations, in which some states restrict the tasks their soldiers may pursue or the areas where they may operate.[65] For leaders, then, the needs and priorities of potential international partners may differ from their own.

When such differences emerge, it may be possible to accommodate them without altering a state's own basic options for how to contribute to a shared mission. For instance, when Australia led INTERFET in East Timor, it recruited contributions to the force from a variety of states. Some of these were willing to deploy their soldiers only to the least dangerous parts of the territory and with strict limits on their use of deadly force, but these restrictions did not affect Australia's ability to pursue more ambitious tasks and military strategies with its own troops, and to make a highly robust contribution to the operation.[66] Yet at other times the preferences of international partners can create pressure to do either more or less than a leader would otherwise be inclined to do. Others might want soldiers to provide at least some direct protection for civilians when a leader himself would prefer a more limited objective of helping to deliver humanitarian aid. Alternatively, they might want to avoid more dangerous or risky military strategies, such as the use of ground troops, than those a leader would be willing to pursue.

Normative pressures to protect civilians and material pressures to limit costs may thus emerge internationally as well as domestically. Pressure to do more to protect civilians than a leader otherwise would may create political difficulties when it comes from core allies or other key states with which it is important to maintain close cooperative relationships. On the other hand, pressure to do less is a problem when a leader wants to provide robust protection but also wants any action he takes to be multilateral. Either way, such pressures can contribute to yet a third distinct type of political dilemma: how to achieve international cooperation and remain on good terms with important international partners while also safeguarding other important interests and values. As at the domestic level, ambitions-resources gaps may offer a compromise that can help leaders manage this predicament.

This can work in two different ways depending on a leader's own preferences and those of other relevant states. First, when leaders would otherwise favor robust protection, they may give in to restrictions imposed by partners whose participation in a mission they see as crucial for reasons of legitimacy or burden sharing. This translates to an ambitions-resources gap when a leader makes a major contribution of resources that help create considerable physical capacity for protection but that are then not put to use as effectively as they could be. In such cases, accepting the gap is simply the price of ensuring international cooperation. The case of British policy in Kosovo briefly considered in the conclusion is an example. Second, leaders may not be committed to doing very much, if anything, to address a particular complex emergency. Still, they may defer to pressure from states that are more committed. This can also translate into promoting an ambitions-resources gap when leaders accept outside pressure to approve relatively ambitious protection instructions for a mission but are not willing to make a commitment of resources that can help to carry them out.[67] In both cases, moreover, the disparity between talk and action works as above: the resources they contribute or the troops' ambitious protection goals can offer leaders cover for rhetoric about assisting civilians that is at odds with what their policies are actually designed to accomplish.

Quantitative Evidence

Policymakers will usually want to explore options along the spectrum of "doing nothing" and full-scale intervention.
—Sarah Sewall, Dwight Raymond, and Sally Chin,
"Mass Atrocity Response Operations"

Building on the conceptual framework from chapter 1, this chapter tests several key aspects of the argument laid out in chapter 2. In it, I use extensive original data to examine broad patterns in when great power democracies facilitate ambitions-resources gaps or instead make limited or robust civilian protection efforts—or do not contribute to a peace operation at all—in response to complex emergencies.

The chapter focuses on the three hypotheses from chapter 2 that relate most directly to these broad patterns: H1, H4, and H5. Each reflects the relationship between the domestic pressures leaders face to protect civilians and the contradictory material pressures they perceive to limit associated costs and risks. While material concerns about costs and risks may emerge for various reasons, as discussed in chapter 2 I expect their strength to be systematically related to the operational environment for intervention in a given complex emergency. In this chapter, therefore, I focus specifically on the relationship between domestic pressures for civilian protection and the nature of the operational environment. The case studies in chapters 4–6 look at this relationship as well, but also consider the role of other, more idiosyncratic factors that can further influence leaders' worries about the costs and risks of peace operations.

To review briefly from chapter 2, Hypothesis 1 predicts that leaders will typically pursue ambitions-resources gaps when they face extensive pressure to protect civilians as well as a relatively inhospitable operational environment. To be clear, though, I do not expect to regularly observe these policies when the operational environment is very inhospitable and leaders are likely to make few contributions to peace operations at all. Second, Hypothesis 4 notes that while robust civilian protection efforts may be driven by strategic motives, they may also be motivated in whole or in part by domestic, normative pressures for civilian protection. To the extent that the latter is a meaningful explanation for these policies, they should occur when leaders face strong domestic pressures for civilian protection but also a hospitable operational environment. Third, according to Hypothesis 5, as pressure to protect civilians increases and encourages leaders to pursue ambitions-resources gaps and perhaps robust protection efforts, decisions not to contribute to peace operations or to make only limited contributions should become less likely. Still, we may not observe this trend when the operational environment is extremely inhospitable since, again, gap and robust contributions will probably remain unlikely in those circumstances.

The chapter proceeds as follows. I begin by describing the unique data I collected to test these hypotheses. The following sections turn to the analysis, beginning with a look at the raw data. I then discuss my choice of statistical models and conduct a series of regressions. The results provide strong support for all three hypotheses, while also calling into question the major alternative explanations for ambitions-resources gaps.

Data

OBSERVATIONS

In this chapter I use three key sources of original data. The first is a unique dataset of post–Cold War complex humanitarian emergencies that defines the universe of conflicts I examine. In all my analyses, one observation is a combination of one complex emergency and one great power democracy with the potential to intervene—the United States, United Kingdom, France, or Australia.

As discussed in chapter 1, complex emergencies describe the set of conflicts in which severe violence might most reasonably prompt peace operations to protect civilians, based on the severity of the threats they face. This concept allows us to distinguish between the many conflicts that are bad for civilians and those that are the most devastating, where it makes the most sense to study variation in civilian protection efforts. Unfortunately, however, existing sources of data on these conflicts suffer from major limitations. Thus, I developed the Post–Cold War Complex Humanitarian Emergencies Dataset, which consists of 61 severe conflicts that were ongoing between 1989 and 2009, comprising a total of 495 emergency-years.[1] Nine complex emergencies (15%) were still ongoing at the end of 2009 and 43 (70%) began in 1989 or later.[2] Since I define complex emergencies with respect to a government's responsibility toward its own citizens, moreover, each reflects the effects of a conflict within a single state.

I use two main quantitative indicators—civilian deaths and forcible displacement—to help identify the complex emergencies. In particular, each complex emergency killed at least 20,000 civilians or displaced at least 500,000 within a five-year period. While there is necessarily some arbitrariness in these numbers, they are intended to strike a balance between the goals of clarity and inclusiveness. On one hand, following Benjamin Valentino's definition of mass killing as at least 50,000 intentional deaths within five or fewer years, I aim to set a high bar for civilian suffering in order to encourage agreement that the cases I identify as complex emergencies are truly both extensive and severe. This is in keeping with the idea that they represent the very worst conflicts for civilians.[3] At the same time, these thresholds necessarily exclude some serious but smaller conflicts. As Nicholas Sambanis points out in the context of civil war, this runs the risk of discounting devastating conflicts in small societies.[4] To limit this problem and include more conflicts that most people would likely recognize as severely disruptive to civilian life, I use the lower fatality threshold of 20,000 in the same five-year period used by Valentino. Finally, since relatively few people who are displaced typically die as a result, the threshold for displacement must be substantially higher than for deaths. Comparing the two is complicated, but drawing loosely on guidelines used by international organizations and relief agencies for identifying humanitarian emergencies, I use the figure of 500,000, which also seems likely to meet with broad acceptance as extensive disruption to civilian life.[5]

Next, annual proportions of these thresholds determine the onset, continuation, and termination of each event. To qualify as the start of a complex emergency a single year of conflict should produce at least 10% of the overall threshold (2,000 deaths or 50,000 displaced persons). All subsequent years should reach at least a majority of this (thus, 6% of the total) to count as part of the same complex emergency. These requirements aim to ensure that complex emergencies are characterized by persistent, sustained violence, while allowing for variation in intensity over time.

Still, such measures do not incorporate information about governments' willingness and ability to respond to civilians' needs or about uncertainty in death and displacement estimates. Thus, drawing on various other qualitative and quantitative indicators I also developed an additional schema to reflect my confidence—from 1 (less) to 3 (more)—in the extent to which each complex emergency fully reflects both my definition and the quantitative thresholds. Fully 84% (51) meet the highest standard. In the ten others there is some uncertainty, typically due to mitigating evidence suggesting that a government made a serious effort to provide for civilians' basic needs or that even massive displacement did not severely threaten large numbers of lives.

The complex emergencies occurred in 39 countries, with Indonesia, Iraq, Afghanistan, Sudan, Angola, and the DRC (formerly Zaire) each experiencing at least three. While most affected an entire country, some were limited to a sub-national region, as in Indian-controlled Kashmir or Aceh, Indonesia. Still, while they serve as the basis for identifying the universe of observations, not all are relevant for each potential intervener. As discussed earlier, I treat Australia as a potential intervener only for complex emergencies in its region but operate on the assumption that the other three states could, with varying degrees of difficulty, lead a peace operation in response to any of the complex emergencies. In addition, I exclude situations where the potential intervener's military actions directly helped create the complex emergency (Afghanistan after 2001 for the United States, United Kingdom, and France; Iraq after 2003 for the United States and United Kingdom; and Pakistan after 2004 for the United States). These restrictions help ensure that the potential intervener is consistently facing a foreign crisis not of its own making and can substitute among various responses, including in how it contributes to any peace operations. After accounting for them, there are 181 observations: 57 for the United States, 58 for the United Kingdom, 59 for France, and 7 for Australia.[6]

DEPENDENT VARIABLE

The dependent variable, *contribution type*, reflects whether a great power democracy participated in a peace operation, and if so, the primary type of contribution it made. Using the typology from chapter 1, there are four categories: no contribution, limited, gap, and robust.

To code *contribution type*, I first identified all the military missions that meet the definition of a peace operation from chapter 1 and that deployed no later than the year after the end of a complex emergency.[7] As noted earlier, half the complex emergencies (31 out of 61) saw at least one peace operation, and among these I identify 66 missions with distinct names and mandates. They were led by the UN and by regional organizations, ad hoc coalitions, and individual countries. These missions need not deploy to the territory where a complex emergency occurred as long as they responded to its effects. For example, because it was deployed largely to help protect refugees from Darfur, the EU's 2008–9 mission in Chad and the Central African Republic (EUFOR Chad/CAR) counts as a response to that complex emergency. Finally, a few operations were already deployed at the start of a complex emergency, in response to previous violence. I included these as long as they continued to encourage peace and security in response to the changing circumstances. For each complex emergency, table A.1 in appendix A lists the start and end date, my certainty that it meets the definition and coding guidelines, and all peace operations to which at least one potential intervener contributed.

Next, I collected detailed data on contributions to these operations. Specifically, for each contribution a great power democracy made I began by coding its ambitions and resources on separate scales of 1 to 3. A number of complex emergencies involved multiple operations and contributions by certain potential interveners. I coded each such contribution separately, but as discussed below, I use only one per observation in the statistical tests. Where there was no contribution, I coded both components as 0.

To code ambitions I drew on the guidelines developed in chapter 1 as well as specific information about the complex emergency to assess the suitability both of operational objectives and the military strategies used to pursue them. For the former I examined operational mandates and, where these were unavailable or inconclusive, case study accounts for evidence about the tasks soldiers actually pursued. To assess military strategies I considered available information about the kinds of forces that were deployed and how they were used.

First, type 1 ambitions can offer at most a little protection relative to the security needs created by a complex emergency. I coded ambitions as 1 for any mission with goals that fall at the far left on the "spectrum of protection goals" (fig. 1.1) from chapter 1: those that do not involve providing security or protection for either civilians or aid workers. They are typically observer missions or traditional peacekeeping operations, or involve delivering emergency relief. As discussed in chapter 1, I also coded ambitions as 1 in some cases where language in the mandate allows troops to protect civilians "in the immediate vicinity" or "within capabilities," but where they are not clearly expected to do so during serious ongoing violence.

Type 2 ambitions imply that soldiers are expected to provide somewhat more protection, and may take one of two forms. First, they may involve goals that aim to offer at least some security, but that are still insufficient to address civilians' most pressing needs. This could include pursuing goals in the middle two boxes in the "spectrum of protection goals," such as protecting aid operations or including direct protection of civilians among other goals in an environment of mass killing. Alternatively, they may involve ambitious goals but military strategies that are inadequate for meeting them, such as when UNPROFOR's restrictive ROE were inconsistent with its announced goal of protecting Bosnian civilians.

Finally, type 3 ambitions involve goals tailored to meet civilians' most pressing security needs given conditions on the ground, and no evidence of military strategies that restrict soldiers' ability to pursue them. Typically this requires that protecting civilians directly or defeating the perpetrators of violence be a main goal, and that soldiers be authorized to pursue tasks and military strategies appropriate to these outcomes. Still, in some instances where civilians are not the primary targets of a campaign of atrocity crimes and their main security needs revolve around access to humanitarian relief, other objectives also meet this standard. For example, the U.S.-led UNITAF that deployed to Somalia in 1992 pursued a primary goal of providing security for aid operations, a perfectly sensible choice given the prevailing conditions at the time.

For resource commitments I developed three categories to reflect, as far as possible, comparable protection capacity as the corresponding level of ambitions. I coded a resource commitment as type 1 if it involved at most logistical or financial support to troops from other countries or a token contribution of up to 50 military observers or liaison officers; type 2 if it involved up to 1,000 of the potential intervener's personnel; and type 3 if it involved 1,000 or more personnel. These distinctions, though somewhat rough, reflect important differences in the physical capacity for protection that great power democracies can anticipate helping to provide.

First, as noted in chapter 1, when these states offer at most financial or logistical support or a few observers, the high quality of their own soldiers can do relatively little to enhance the capabilities of under-prepared foreign troops. Certainly this is true if they provide financial support alone. Such support—though it may be used to purchase equipment, pay soldiers, or for other important purposes—can typically only marginally alter foreign troops' preparedness for ambitious protection tasks, command and control capabilities, and operational planning and intelligence proficiency, if at all. The same applies to logistical support, such as aid with transport. Training and technical advice may achieve more, but it is difficult to make significant changes in a short time. For all these reasons, assistance that does not engage a great power democracy's own personnel directly in a peace operation's core tasks usually has little ability to overcome major limitations of the troops it is intended to help.

In contrast, by contributing a limited number—identified here as up to 1,000—of its own forces to participate in a peace operation, a great power democracy can expect to substantially enhance the mission's capacity to provide at least some security. Units of this size can help to protect narrowly defined geographic areas or humanitarian relief facilities. They can also augment the capabilities of a larger number of foreign troops in several ways, including by playing critical roles that other force contributors cannot in areas such as intelligence and communications. They are, however, typically too few to implement the most ambitious protection strategies, such as the creation and defense of safe zones or the defeat of the perpetrators of violence against civilians.[8]

Finally, when a potential intervener contributes over 1,000 of its own personnel this indicates an even greater capacity to contribute to ambitious protection. Although far more than 1,000 troops would be needed in many complex emergencies, this seems a reasonable minimum for the top contribution level for two reasons. First, as above, 1,000 highly capable troops can play a major role in augmenting the abilities of a larger force. Second, on their own or alongside a small number of similarly well-prepared troops, they may be able to pursue even the most ambitious protection tasks, even if only in a limited geographic area. On multiple occasions, contingents of about this size—such as the United Kingdom's Operation Palliser in Sierra

Leone and France's commitment to Operation Artemis in the DRC—have indeed represented the minimum for leading an operation entrusted with fairly ambitious goals and military strategies. Still, in most contributions with a type 3 resource commitment, the number of personnel is much larger.[9]

Next, I used these coding schemas to identify a single primary contribution type for each observation. To do so, I first labeled each contribution individually as limited, gap, or robust. Where both resources and ambitions are of type 1, a contribution is limited: it neither seeks to address civilians' most pressing protection needs nor provides resources that would substantially contribute to the capacity to do so. Similarly, contributions are robust if both components are of type 3: soldiers aim to provide a level of protection appropriate to the complex emergency and the state offers enough of its own military resources to do so, although perhaps only in a limited geographic area. Last, gap contributions occur when the two components are coded differently.[10] One important exception is when a state provides support to a robust contribution by another great power democracy (typically the lead state on the mission). Such support can be expected to augment a force that already has considerable protection capacity, rather than facilitate an ambitions-resources gap at the mission level. For example, the hundreds of ground troops, seamen, and medical personnel that France and the United Kingdom sent to INTERFET supported the efforts of the highly capable lead Australian force. Thus, instead of gaps I coded eight such contributions as limited or robust, depending on the scale of the resource commitment.[11]

Finally, the great power democracies often contributed to more than one peace operation in the same complex emergency. Indeed, of 86 observations involving at least one contribution to a peace operation, 51 (59%) saw more than one. This occurred in various ways. Sometimes a state supported multiple successive UN operations. In other cases it sent its own troops as part of a non-UN mission (such as the United Kingdom's Operation Palliser or France's Operation Licorne in Côte d'Ivoire) but also supported a UN or regional mission that deployed before, after, or alongside its own force. In these cases a state's contributions might be similar (such as two limited ones) or they might differ (such as a gap contribution followed by a robust one). This variation in the number, timing, and type of contributions by the same state in the same conflict presents a challenge about how to assess a government's overall commitment to civilian protection, but also creates an opportunity to study the dynamics of how this commitment may change over time.

While I explore these dynamics in the upcoming case studies, here I focus on one main type of contribution per observation. Where all of a state's contributions in a given conflict are of the same type, I code that type for the observation as a whole. Where a state made both a limited contribution and one that was robust or promoted an ambitions-resources gap, I use the latter as the main contribution to ensure that the data reflect all commitments of a state's own personnel. For example, in Croatia, the United States, United Kingdom, and France sent troops to UNPROFOR/ UNCRO and then financially supported two later UN missions. The primary contribution for each is to UNPROFOR/UNCRO. Last, where a state made both a gap and a robust contribution, I use the one that came first. For example, in Kosovo these states participated in Operation Allied Force (gap) and then KFOR (robust). The primary contribution for each is Allied Force.

With these rules in mind, figure 3.1 shows the distribution of *contribution type* for each of the four potential interveners. In total, 95 observations (52%) involve no contribution to a peace operation, 43 (24%) are limited, 27 (15%) are gap contributions, and 16 (9%) are robust. Thus, among the 86 observations that do involve some contribution to a peace operation, half are limited while gaps occur 31% of the time, about 1.7 times as often as robust contributions. In other words, gap contributions represent fully 63% of observations involving more than the most limited resources or ambitions for civilian protection.

For the most part there are no dramatic differences in the distribution of these outcomes across the four democracies. With far fewer observations, Australia contributed to peace operations relatively less often and made no limited contributions. The remaining countries, though, were similarly likely to contribute to peace operations and to make the three types of contributions, though the conflicts in which they did so varied. Limited contributions

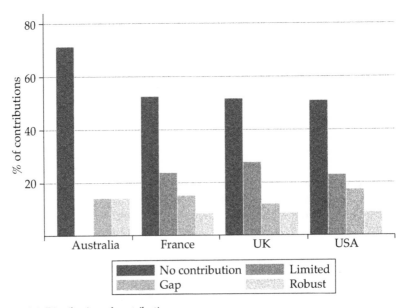

Figure 3.1. Distribution of contributions

were slightly more common for the United Kingdom and gap contributions somewhat more frequent for the United States. Variation in the institutional context of these contributions is also consistent with the discussion from chapter 1 about great power democracies' opportunities to select different venues depending on how they wish to participate. While 37 of the 43 limited contributions were to UN-led missions, 13 of the 16 robust ones were unilateral or involved an ad hoc coalition. Meanwhile, the gap contributions were more evenly distributed. While 8 were in UN missions, 19 involved a mission led by an ad hoc coalition or a regional organization. Of these, 10 were also accompanied by a second "gap" contribution to a related UN mission.

INDEPENDENT VARIABLES

CE News Coverage. I harness changes in elite news coverage about each complex emergency in each great power democracy to proxy for the pressure leaders face to help address the violence. This measure, *CE news coverage,* seeks to overcome a key limitation of the existing literature: to date, quantitative studies of peacekeeping have generally neglected the influence of the domestic pressures that are central to this book and that have featured prominently in qualitative work on humanitarian intervention.[12] One reason for this oversight, presumably, has been a lack of appropriate data, as there are serious obstacles to identifying direct measures of pressure to protect civilians—whether from activists, the broader concerned public, or within government—that can be compared across the full range of complex emergencies. For instance, while groups like the Pew Research Center conduct polls on attitudes toward the use of force in particular conflicts, such polls are only taken for conflicts that attract considerable public and media attention. Similarly, advocacy efforts are difficult to measure directly because of variation in the numbers, identities, and influence of interested groups across different conflicts. The need to make these comparisons across different states only amplifies these problems.

A measure based on media coverage represents a promising alternative, but requires attention to some important methodological concerns. In brief, the literature on media, public opinion, and the use of force emphasizes that the volume and tenor of media reporting on foreign conflicts can reflect either of two main influences. First, it may echo official policy. In the present context, a key concern would be if such coverage reflected a leader's efforts to generate public support for a peace operation he already plans to pursue. Second and in contrast, groups and individuals—whether private citizens or public officials—can use the media to promote alternatives to current policy. Opportunities to do so, in turn, tend to be greatest when journalists are able to frame the issue in a compelling and culturally resonant way, such as when the policy issue is ambiguous and opponents of official policy are motivated and politically influential.[13]

For a complex emergency where a leader is otherwise reluctant to intervene, this second pattern suggests that activists, journalists, and concerned officials may use the media to argue for a vigorous response, and should be especially effective in doing so when they are strong politically. Gary Bass has documented this pattern in some of the nineteenth and early twentieth centuries' worst humanitarian crises.[14] More recently, growth in U.S. media coverage of Darfur tracked the development of the Darfur advocacy movement rather than the severity of the violence.[15] And, according to Robert Entman, such conflicts (he cites Somalia, Haiti, Bosnia, and Kosovo as examples) often reflect ambiguities about how to respond that present especially good opportunities for those who would oppose official policy through the media.[16] Finally, these findings also resonate with various claims that media coverage is an important indicator of interest in foreign conflicts, and that leaders see it as such.[17] As Natalie La Balme concluded based on extensive interviews with French politicians and their advisers, for instance, "French foreign policy officials are indeed very receptive to [the media] and consider it to be the main operational source of public opinion, far more than opinion surveys, elites, or elected officials."[18]

In sum, where a government already plans to contribute to a peace operation, media coverage is likely to reflect its efforts to generate public support. But when activists, journalists, and other concerned citizens or officials believe their government is not doing enough to respond to a complex emergency, we should see more media coverage that reflects pressure on a reluctant executive. As suggested in chapter 2, moreover, in addition to signaling current demands from activists or within government, such coverage could also help fuel leaders' concerns about the potential for even broader-based public disapproval of government inaction. Thus, media coverage can serve as a promising proxy for the humanitarian pressures leaders are likely to perceive, if we can separate these two basic patterns of coverage. To do so, I isolate news coverage during periods when it is likely to reflect these concerns about a complex emergency and not an executive's efforts to generate support for interventionist policies.

Specifically, I used full-text news searches from one major elite newspaper in each potential intervener to measure the natural log of the ratio of average annual news coverage during a complex emergency (but before intervention) to average coverage of the same place over the five years before the start of the complex emergency. That is,

$$CE\ news\ coverage = ln\left(\frac{average\ annual\ news\ hits\ during\ CE}{average\ annual\ news\ hits\ during\ 5\ years\ before\ CE}\right)^{19}$$

I then transformed these values to range from 0 (least concern) to 1 (most). Insofar as it is possible to do so I exclude coverage during the lead-up to a decision about contributing to a peace operation in order to eliminate active discussion of anticipated military action. At the same time, I seek to include coverage from key periods in a complex emergency that might influence societal and bureaucratic activism and concern.

CE news coverage thus reflects the relative increase in coverage of places that experience complex emergencies in response to the outbreak of these conflicts. Although not all of the coverage it captures directly concerns the violence itself, it seems reasonable to infer that when a place receives substantially more attention during a severe conflict than it did beforehand, that conflict has generated greater concern than if it sees no, or only a small, increase. What is more, the measure takes precautions against reflecting the influence of leaders' efforts to sway public opinion and coverage of ongoing or upcoming operations. In addition, the ratio format eliminates the potential problem of more geopolitically significant conflicts appearing to generate more concern simply because they occur in places that typically receive more attention.

To make this more concrete, it is helpful to consider a few examples of observations that fall at high, middle, and low values on *CE news coverage*, or about the 10th, 50th, and 90th percentiles. First, at .33, is the United States during the Afghan civil war that began in 1992. Here, average annual references to Afghanistan as measured in *CE news coverage* declined by about a third when compared with the immediately preceding years of Soviet occupation, withdrawal, and violence (falling from 492 to 326). Second, the median observation (.5) is the United Kingdom during the war in Burma that began in 1988. Relative to the mid-1980s, annual media references to Burma during the conflict increased by about 65% (from 103 to 169). Finally, the 90th percentile falls at .79, the approximate value for the United Kingdom during the war in Bosnia. Here, elite British media references to Bosnia rose nearly seven-fold, from an average of 53 in 1987–91 up to an annual rate of 391 during the first five months of 1992 (before UNPROFOR's mandate was first extended from Croatia to Bosnia in June).[20]

A brief investigation suggests that *CE news coverage* does a good job of reflecting the forces it is intended to capture while excluding those it is not. First, like Bosnia, many of the other complex emergencies known for attracting extensive interest and generating pressure on leaders in certain great power democracies to respond—including in Darfur, Kosovo, East Timor, and Northern Iraq in 1991—take on some of the highest values. Second, as shown in table 3.1, the correlation between my measure and various indicators of strategic or political relationships that might plausibly encourage intervention in a particular complex emergency, discussed at greater length below, are consistently low and in several cases negative. This suggests that such connections are not responsible for the changes in press attention captured in *CE news coverage*.

Table 3.1 includes indicators for whether the potential intervener and the state where a complex emergency occurs (1) shared a colonial relationship,

Table 3.1 Correlation coefficients—*CE news coverage* and political ties

	Former colony	Region	Alliance	Contiguous ally	Trade	Affinity	Pre-CE coverage
CE news coverage	−.1003	.2913	−.0469	.2528	.0452	.1044	−.1812

(2) are in the same region, or (3) are allies, or whether (4) the potential intervener has an ally contiguous to the complex emergency. Measures of trade and the similarity of the two states' votes at the UN General Assembly (*affinity*) serve as more general indicators of their economic and political ties. *CE news coverage* also correlates negatively with its own denominator, the average annual coverage before a complex emergency (*pre-CE coverage*). Thus, if more geopolitically significant locales do attract more coverage in general, we can be confident that *CE news coverage* is not picking up this relationship.

Operational Environment. Next, to represent the challenges of deploying a peace operation in a given complex emergency I created an index, *operational environment*, based on various conflict characteristics the literature identifies as particularly relevant to the dangers and challenges that intervening troops must expect to face. Like *CE news coverage*, this measure is not perfect. Any number of issues may affect the operational environment for a peace operation in a particular complex emergency, and they may change over time within it. As a result, it is impossible to account quantitatively for all of the potentially relevant factors. In particular, the consent of the target state's government can be especially important, but is not possible to observe unless a peace operation is proposed.

Still, a number of conflict characteristics appear to consistently influence the difficulties and dangers that potential interveners must expect to face, and can be measured for all complex emergencies whether or not a peace operation is ever actively considered. Together they should account for a large portion of the variation in operational environments across conflicts and can be used to construct an informative, if incomplete, measure of the dangers and challenges they pose. It is useful, in turn, to think about these characteristics as falling into two basic categories.

First, various aspects of a complex emergency relate directly to the risk of confrontation between a potential intervention force and indigenous armed groups, and are thus especially relevant for anticipating likely casualties to foreign troops. Like the issue of local government consent, these characteristics largely reflect local actors' will and capacity to resist a peace operation. As Michael O'Hanlon points out, casualties are likely to be greater where the indigenous armed groups that might resist foreign troops are stronger and more dedicated. These might include governments with large, well-equipped military forces or highly motivated and capable rebel groups, especially revolutions or guerrilla movements with extensive popular support. Such actors should generally be able to put up a stronger and longer fight if they choose to oppose foreign interveners.[21] They may also be more likely to object to outside intervention. Strong states, for instance, are often especially unwilling to countenance interference within their borders or in their spheres of influence. Meanwhile, rebellions with the popular support and resources to present a potentially serious military threat are often highly committed to particular political goals. If they expect foreign intervention to interfere with these, they can be expected to resist and may also be willing to tolerate high casualties among their own forces to do so.

Two further factors also influence the casualties that foreign troops should expect to face. First, difficult terrain that favors local actors can add to the dangers foreign troops face when local armed groups decide to oppose their presence. It can also pose a host of other difficulties for transportation, troop movement, and communications.[22] Second, a larger number of violent parties in a complex emergency complicates the challenge of intervening. As Michael Doyle and Nicholas Sambanis point out in their study of post-conflict peace-building success and failure, a larger number of factions can make it more difficult to negotiate a lasting resolution to civil wars because it implies "a larger pool of potentially divergent preferences."[23] Yet both in civil wars and more broadly in complex emergencies, the number of parties to the violence can also be relevant for interveners while it is still raging. Notably, on average more parties should increase the risk that at least one will perceive foreign troops as a threat to its interests, especially since interveners may thus be seen as partial to some groups over others. More parties can also make the job of civilian protection harder. A more complex political situation, with the possibility of shifting alliances among belligerents, can make it difficult for interveners to identify those who represent the greatest threats to civilians. Finally, a larger number of violent parties may create hurdles to establishing the kind of working relationships with belligerents that can help peace operations avoid attacks against aid operations and themselves.

While often contributing little to the risk of confrontation with local parties, a second group of conflict characteristics still affects the general challenges and financial costs of deploying a peace operation. In particular, a larger population affected by a complex emergency, a larger conflict-affected geographic area, poor infrastructure, and even a remote location can all add up to greater difficulties and higher financial—and potentially human—costs.[24]

Drawing on these arguments, my *operational environment* index includes nine components that reflect the relative difficulty and anticipated costliness of deploying a peace operation. Two aim to capture situations where strong states represent potentially serious obstacles for interveners. These include the size of the army in the state where the complex emergency occurs and an indicator for whether it occurs either in or next door to Russia or China. These measures reflect the findings of several studies that conflicts in states with stronger militaries or in or near major powers (especially the Security Council P5) are less likely to receive peacekeepers.[25] The third component aims to capture the presence of a strong and motivated rebellion by recording whether the complex emergency involves either a guerrilla or revolutionary war. The fourth element reflects the number of unique parties to the violence. The fifth component aims to capture difficult terrain by recording the proportion of territory in the state where the complex emergency occurs that is mountainous.

The other pieces of the index aim to capture the most important conflict characteristics that relate less directly to the risk of confrontation with local parties. They include the size of the affected population and the affected area. The proportion of roads that are paved reflects the state of infrastructure in the nation where the complex emergency occurs. Finally, to capture remoteness I include the distance between the capital cities of the potential intervener and the affected country.

To construct the index I placed each component on a 0–1 scale ranging from the least to the most challenging conditions.[26] A description of all nine components, along with the sources for each, is included in table A.2 in appendix A. For the main version of *operational environment* used below, I weighted all components equally and again arranged the results on a 0–1 scale, with 0 representing the most favorable operational environment and 1 the most challenging. However, to assess the robustness of my findings I also created and tested various alternative versions of this index. As I discuss below, these do not affect any of my conclusions.

To illustrate the variation in the main version of *operational environment*, we can again consider a few examples. As I highlight below, leaders are likely to perceive complex emergencies that fall at approximately its 10th, 50th, and 90th percentiles as representing fairly hospitable, somewhat inhospitable, and extremely inhospitable circumstances for military intervention respectively. The 10th percentile falls at .23. While the values for the same complex emergency vary slightly across potential interveners because of differences in distance to the affected state, one conflict that falls close to this is Iraq's victimization of its Kurdish population after the Gulf War, starting in 1991. Despite Iraq's relatively large army, most other components of the index helped keep *operational environment* fairly low. These include the relatively small area and population in Iraqi Kurdistan, the fact that there were more paved roads than for almost all other complex emergencies, and the fact that Iraq is not contiguous to either Russia or China. Just as important, since this was a case of one-sided violence against civilians committed by the Iraqi government, there was only one main party committing the violence and it was not a case of guerrilla or revolutionary war. Next, the 50th percentile of *operational environment* occurs at .49. Here a representative complex emergency is the civil war in Aceh, Indonesia, from 1999 to 2004 that I discuss in chapter 6. It involved few extreme values on the components of the index, except that it was among the conflicts furthest from the United States, United Kingdom, and France. Otherwise, its population and affected area were somewhat below average while the size of Indonesia's army was somewhat above. Indonesia is not contiguous to Russia or China and while this was a guerrilla conflict, it was less complex than some, since there were only two belligerents. Finally, the 90th percentile of *operational environment* falls at .83, which is near the values for all observations associated with Ethiopia's civil war (a complex emergency through 1992). This conflict scored highly on six of nine components: the war affected a large area and population, the terrain was very mountainous, Ethiopia had a fairly large army, the conflict was a guerrilla war, and there were numerous belligerent parties.

Testing the Argument: A First Cut

For an initial look at how *CE news coverage* and *operational environment* influence leaders' policy decisions, I examine how their average values vary across the four categories of *contribution type*. This information is presented in table 3.2.

As the data show, policies designed to provide greater civilian protection are associated with higher values on *CE news coverage*. The major distinction occurs between observations that involve either no contribution or a limited one, and those that involve either a gap or robust contribution. The differences in means between no contribution and limited, and between gap and robust, are both small and statistically insignificant. In contrast, the jump from limited to gap is much larger (nearly .16), and the mean values for both no contribution and limited are each statistically different from

Table 3.2 Means of *CE news coverage* and *operational environment*, by contribution type

Contribution type	Observations	Mean, CE news coverage	Mean, operational environment
No contribution	95	.478	.604
Limited	43	.499	.507
Gap	27	.657	.392
Robust	16	.669	.274
Total	181	.526	.52

those for gap and robust (p < .001 in each case, calculated using Tukey-Kramer pairwise comparisons). This suggests that on average, both gap and robust contributions occur in situations where leaders face greater societal or intragovernmental concern about a complex emergency than either limited contributions or decisions not to contribute to a peace operation.[27]

For *operational environment* we again see sizeable differences across values of *contribution type*. On average, observations involving no contribution to a peace operation have more formidable (less hospitable) operational environments than limited contributions, which have more formidable operational environments than gap contributions, which in turn have more challenging operational environments than robust contributions. All but the last of these differences (between gap and robust contributions) is statistically significant at the 10% level or better (p < .10 in Tukey-Kramer pairwise comparisons).[28]

These results provide reason for confidence that, despite their limitations, *CE news coverage* and *operational environment* are reasonable measures of the concepts they aim to represent. The data also support my expectation about the conditions that encourage ambitions-resources gaps, since these observations are concentrated at relatively high values of *CE news coverage* and at values of *operational environment* that are neither very high (very inhospitable) nor very low (hospitable). It also appears that on average robust contributions fit the pattern described in hypothesis 4, since they occur at relatively high values of *CE news coverage* and at values of *operational environment* that are more hospitable than any other outcome.

Figure 3.2 presents this information another way, showing how the percentage of observations represented by each outcome of *contribution type* varies with changes in *CE news coverage* and *operational environment*. To simplify, I break both *CE news coverage* and *operational environment* into groups representing their bottom, second, third, and top quartiles.

Again, the data appear consistent with my expectations. First, when *operational environment* takes on very high values contributions to peace operations are infrequent. Among the quarter of observations with the least hospitable operational environments leaders contribute to peace operations in any way only 15% of the time. Second, in the lower left-hand part of the figure represented by the bottom three quartiles of *operational environment* and the bottom two quartiles of *CE news coverage*, the vast majority of observations involve either no contribution (52%) or a limited one (35%). As I would expect, there are few gap contributions. Moreover, the small number of robust contributions offers little support for the realist view that the most ambitious civilian protection efforts are usually driven mainly by strategic considerations.

Next, at the right *CE news coverage* is in its top two quartiles, while *operational environment* is either in its lowest quartile (bottom) or its middle two quartiles (above this). The bottom right-hand space includes 39% robust contributions, which represent 69% of those in the data (11 of 16). That these

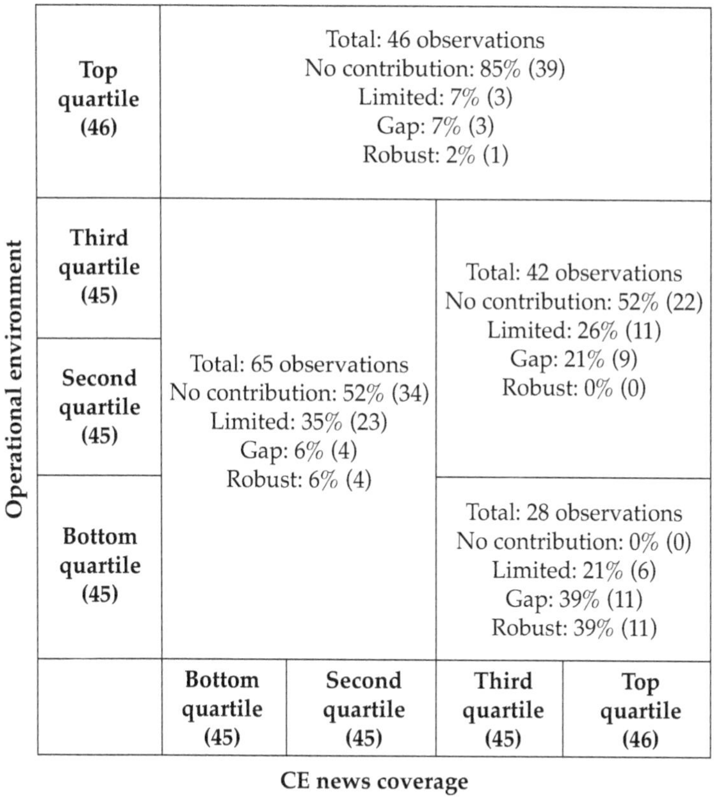

		Total: 46 observations No contribution: 85% (39) Limited: 7% (3) Gap: 7% (3) Robust: 2% (1)			
	Top **quartile** **(46)**				

Figure 3.2. *Contribution type* by *CE news coverage* and *operational environment*

contributions are concentrated so heavily here suggests the empirical importance of hypothesis 4: domestic pressure for civilian protection together with an auspicious operational environment indeed seems to promote the most ambitious civilian protection efforts.

As I would expect, gap contributions are also more common in these regions than elsewhere. Although they represent 39% of observations in the bottom right and only 21% above this, the division of *operational environment* into quartiles is largely arbitrary and leaders may perceive important variation within them. Indeed, in the lower right-hand corner the mean value of *operational environment* among gap contributions is .07 higher than among robust contributions (about one third of a standard deviation), and this difference is statistically significant ($p < .02$ in a one-tailed t-test). This, combined with the fact that there are no robust contributions in the region above this (the middle two quartiles of *operational environment*) is consistent with my expectations in that it suggests there is a clear difference between the most favorable operational environments that promote robust contributions and the less hospitable ones that encourage ambitions-resources gaps. Finally, also consistent with my expectations, below the top quartile of *operational environment*, limited and no contributions to peace operations are less common at higher values of *CE news coverage*. In the case of not contributing at all, this effect is due to the complete absence of such observations in the bottom quartile of *operational environment*.

Testing the Theory: Regression Analysis

Next, regression analysis allows me to examine these patterns in the data while accounting for other factors that might affect leaders' contributions to peace operations. In particular, insofar as it is possible, it is important to account for the potential influence of strategic or other international political motives for these contributions. If such factors help promote ambitions-resources gaps, this could provide evidence of the alternative explanation that leaders' claims of assisting vulnerable civilians serve mainly as a fig leaf to hide other reasons for military action. To test this possibility I run a series of regressions that use the full dataset of 181 observations. Separately, I also analyze a restricted sample of only those observations involving contributions to peace operations. This permits a limited test of the other alternative explanation for ambitions-resources gaps, that leaders promote them unknowingly and unintentionally.

MODEL SPECIFICATION

The statistical tests I present below use multinomial logistic regression, which is appropriate for a discrete, categorical dependent variable such as *contribution type*.[29] This model assumes that for each observation, the potential intervener may not participate in a peace operation at all or may make a limited, gap, or robust contribution. As discussed earlier there are various reasons to think this assumption is reasonable for the great power democracies considered here, although the same would not be true for less influential and capable states.

The models include both *CE news coverage* and *operational environment* as covariates. They also include *CE news coverage*operational environment*, an interaction term that is the product of these two variables. Such interactions are standard when there are theoretical reasons to believe that the effect of one covariate depends on the value of another, which is exactly what my argument predicts. Namely, hypotheses 1, 4, and 5 suggest that the effect of an increase in *CE news coverage* on *contribution type* depends on the value of *operational environment*.

First, according to hypothesis 5, when *operational environment* takes on low and medium values, an increase in *CE news coverage* should discourage no and limited contributions, since leaders will be more likely to promote an ambitions-resources gap or perhaps make a robust contribution. Yet when *operational environment* takes on high values and is very inhospitable, even a large increase in *CE news coverage* may not have these effects since leaders usually will not contribute to peace operations in this case. I also expect meaningful differences in the effect of *CE news coverage* when *operational environment* is low (most hospitable) compared with its middle range, where it is somewhat but not highly inhospitable. If hypothesis 4 is correct and strong pressure to protect civilians plus a hospitable operational environment promotes robust protection, then an increase in *CE news coverage* should increase the chance of robust contributions when *operational environment* is low, but not necessarily at mid-level values. Finally, from hypothesis 1, since ambitions-resources gaps should be most likely in the middle range of *operational environment*, an increase in *CE news coverage* should increase the odds of these policies by more here than when *operational environment* is lower and more hospitable.

CONTROL VARIABLES

The regressions also include various control variables to reflect the influence of possible strategic and political incentives for intervention, plus other factors that might influence leaders' decisions. Detailed descriptions and data sources are provided in table A.3 in appendix A.

First, the existing literature employs various measures to represent the kinds of strategic relationships that might promote peace operations. I focus on several that seem likely to generate an interest in stability and thus potentially provide a motive for helping to promote peace or provide civilian protection. *Former colony* indicates whether the country where the complex emergency occurs received its independence from the potential intervener. *Region* indicates whether a complex emergency occurs in the same region as the potential intervener. *Contiguous ally* indicates whether the potential intervener has an ally contiguous to the complex emergency. *Alliance* reflects whether the potential intervener is an ally of the state experiencing the complex emergency. Although it is shown above in table 3.1, however, I exclude *alliance* from the regressions due to limited variation on the dependent variable: the value of *alliance* never equals one when there is a gap or robust contribution, and it equals one in only a single instance for a limited contribution.[30]

Two additional variables represent more general political and economic ties between the potential intervener and the state experiencing the complex emergency. *Affinity* measures the similarity of the two states' voting positions at the UN General Assembly the year before the complex emergency begins and thus reflects shared political interests. *Trade* reflects the share of the potential intervener's total trade that is with the country affected by the complex emergency, averaged over the two years before it begins. As shown above, the correlation between these variables and *CE news coverage* is quite low or even negative.

Next, three other controls reflect potential political incentives for contributing to peace operations that do not rely on direct relationships with the state where the complex emergency occurs, or its neighbors. Several scholars claim that states contribute to peace operations to promote democratization in unstable, conflict-ridden countries.[31] To represent this possibility, *democracy* reflects how democratic or autocratic the government is in the state affected by the complex emergency the year before it begins. Larger values represent more democratic countries, so if states do intervene to promote democracy they should do so more often when *democracy* is low. *Pre-1989 complex emergency* indicates complex emergencies that began during the Cold War (before 1989). It reflects the possibility that lingering Cold War concerns may affect states' willingness to contribute to peace operations or protect civilians in these conflicts. Still, I have no clear expectations about this variable's likely effects. Conflicts that began during the Cold War may be less likely to see contributions to peace operations because these missions became generally more common thereafter. Alternately, Cold War conflicts that persisted into the 1990s might have been especially likely to merit such contributions as the UN Security Council sought to wrap up earlier sources of superpower tension.[32] Next, *mass killing* indicates whether a complex emergency was part of an episode of mass killing involving the intentional killing of at least 50,000 civilians within 5 years. It serves as a blunt indicator of where civilians' protection needs may be greatest, and where powerful democracies should be likely to contribute to peace operations—and particularly, to make robust contributions—to the extent that their responses reflect the variation in severity even among the worst conflicts.[33]

Finally, the kind of violence that generates a complex emergency might influence contributions, although I have no particular expectations about how it might do so. Thus, I also include indicator variables for different categories of complex emergencies. *Civil conflict*, the most common, involves the state and at least one organized opposition group, without external military intervention. *Internationalized civil conflict* is otherwise similar, but there is international military intervention in a non–peace operation capacity. Finally, *non-civil conflict* is a composite of several other types of complex emergencies. In international conflicts, the violence is either interstate war or a dispute between two actors in different states; in communal conflicts, the primary fault line reflects intercommunal tension and the government is not a main party to the violence; and in one-sided violence, large-scale violence against civilians occurs without sustained concurrent hostilities between at least two organized parties. Unfortunately there were relatively few observations in these categories and too little variation on *contribution type* to include them in the models independently. However, I am still able to test for systematic differences between civil conflicts and, collectively, other kind of complex emergencies.

RESULTS

I focus first on the results of three regressions. Model 1 includes *CE news coverage, operational environment*, and their interaction. Model 2 adds the controls except for the indicators of complex emergency type. Model 3 includes five controls from model 2 that have statistically significant effects and adds indicators for *internationalized civil conflict* and *non-civil conflict*, leaving *civil conflict* as the reference category.[34] Model 3 also uses an alternative version of *operational environment* based on only seven components. It excludes information about whether there is a strong and motivated rebellion (guerrilla or revolutionary war) and about the number of violent parties. Because these elements of the index reflect information about the type of conflict that prompts a complex emergency (for instance, an interstate war or communal conflict is by definition not a guerrilla or revolutionary war), it is inappropriate to include them in *operational environment* while also controlling for the type of complex emergency.

The regression table is included as table B.1 in appendix B, and table B.2 provides summary statistics for the covariates. These models produce separate coefficients for limited, gap, and robust contributions, which are interpreted individually as compared to no contribution. The results show that a number of covariates appear to have statistically significant effects on at least certain types of contributions, including *CE news coverage, operational environment*, and their interaction. What is more, various measures of model fit suggest that these key variables improve the models' predictive power and should be included, including the interaction term.[35]

However, in logistic regression the magnitude and statistical significance of each covariate's effect depends on both its own value and those of the other variables. The interaction term further complicates the interpretation of *CE news coverage* and *operational environment* because each variable's total effect is reflected in both its own coefficient and the interaction. Indeed, to interpret the effect of these variables we cannot rely on either the significance or even the sign of their coefficients.[36] Together these issues make the results very difficult to interpret from the regression table. Thus, I use predicted probabilities for each value of *contribution type*, calculated at different values of the independent variables, to describe the results.

First, for model 1, figure 3.3 presents predicted probabilities (solid lines) for all four outcomes, with 95% confidence intervals (dashed lines) as they vary over the range of *CE news coverage*.[37] To capture the relationship between *CE news coverage* and *operational environment* I generated these probabilities for three separate values of the latter. In the left-hand column

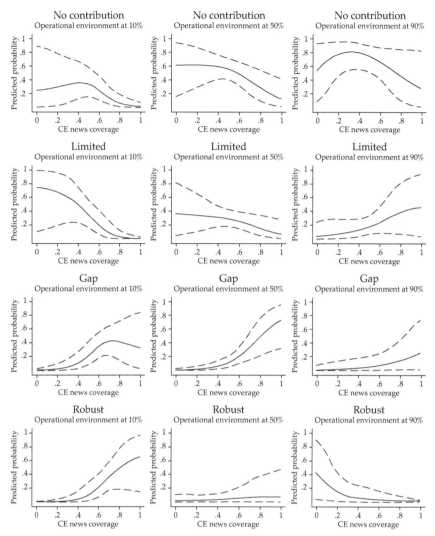

Figure 3.3. Predicted probabilities, model 1

operational environment is set at its 10th percentile, where we can reasonably expect leaders to consider it fairly hospitable. In the middle column *operational environment* is set at its 50th percentile. Here it is notably less hospitable than at its 10th percentile, but still not extremely inhospitable. Finally, in the right-hand column *operational environment* is set at its 90th percentile, where I expect leaders would consider it very inhospitable.

Table 3.3 summarizes these same results, listing the predicted probabilities for each of the 12 cases when *CE news coverage* equals 0 (its lowest

Table 3.3 Effect of a change in *CE news coverage*, model 1

	Operational environment								
	10th percentile			50th percentile			90th percentile		
	CE news coverage			CE news coverage			CE news coverage		
	0	1	Change	0	1	Change	0	1	Change
No contribution	.26	.01	−.25	.62	.12	−.50	.54	.27	−.27
Limited	.73	.00	−.73**	.36	.07	−.29	.04	.45	.41
Gap	.00	.34	.34**	.00	.75	.75**	.01	.27	.26*
Robust	.00	.64	.64**	.02	.06	.04	.41	.00	−.41**

** $p < .05$, * $p < .10$

value) and 1 (its highest value), and the difference between them. I also indicate where these differences are statistically significant. Slightly changing the values for hospitable and highly inhospitable operational environments to the 20th and 80th percentiles has only minor effects on these results. Finally, figure 3.4 and table 3.4 provide the same information for model 2, as do figure 3.5 and table 3.5 for model 3. For these latter models the control variables are set to their means (for the continuous ones) or modes (the dichotomous ones). For model 3 the type of complex emergency is *civil conflict*.

Examination of these results reveals important support for each of the hypotheses. First and most importantly, they are consistent with my expectations about ambitions-resources gaps. Across all three models gap contributions are extremely unlikely when *CE news coverage* is low, with predicted probabilities that round to 0 whenever *operational environment* is at its 10th or 50th percentile. However, as *CE news coverage* increases, gap contributions become much more likely when *operational environment* is at its 50th percentile, where it is relatively but not extremely inhospitable. The size of this increase ranges from .75 (model 1) to .87 (model 2) and is statistically significant: there would be less than a 5% chance of observing these results by chance if the increase in *CE news coverage* had no effect on leaders' decisions.

By comparison, when *operational environment* is at its 10th percentile there is also a statistically significant increase in the probability of gap contributions, but it is much smaller (.34 in models 1 and 3, and .13 in model 2). Thus, at high values of *CE news coverage* gap contributions are more likely when *operational environment* is relatively inhospitable than when it is most hospitable, just as I would expect. In two of the three models this comparison is also statistically significant. In model 1, when *CE news coverage* equals 1,

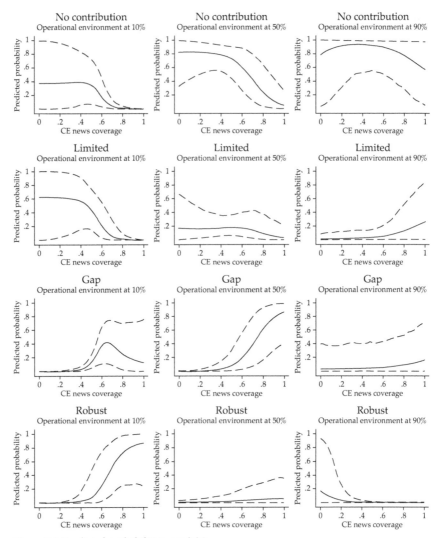

Figure 3.4. Predicted probabilities, model 2

a change from the 10th to the 50th percentile of *operational environment* increases the probability of a gap contribution by .41 (from .34 to .75), and there is less than a 10% chance of observing this outcome by chance. In model 2 the probability of a gap contribution goes up even more—by .74 (from .13 to .87)—and the probability of observing this by chance is less than 5%. Finally, in model 3 the same probability increases by .47 (from .34 to .81). Here this increase narrowly misses conventional statistical significance, but the odds are still less than 12% of observing it by chance.

Table 3.4 Effect of a change in *CE news coverage*, model 2

	Operational environment								
	10th percentile			50th percentile			90th percentile		
	CE news coverage			CE news coverage			CE news coverage		
	0	1	Change	0	1	Change	0	1	Change
No contribution	.37	.00	−.37*	.83	.05	−.78**	.79	.57	−.22
Limited	.62	.00	−.62**	.17	.03	−.14	.01	.26	.25
Gap	.00	.13	.13**	.00	.87	.87**	.03	.16	.13
Robust	.00	.87	.87**	.00	.05	.05*	.17	.00	−.17**

** $p < .05$, * $p < .10$

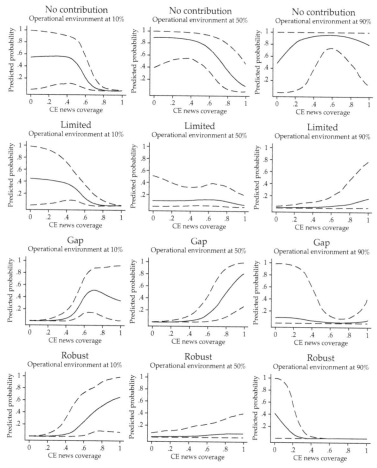

Figure 3.5. Predicted probabilities, model 3

Table 3.5 Effect of a change in *CE news coverage*, model 3

	10th percentile			50th percentile			90th percentile		
Operational environment									
	CE news coverage			CE news coverage			CE news coverage		
	0	1	Change	0	1	Change	0	1	Change
No contribution	.55	.00	−.55**	.89	.10	−.79**	.49	.79	.30
Limited	.45	.00	−.45**	.10	.03	−.07	.00	.15	.15*
Gap	.00	.34	.34**	.00	.81	.81**	.09	.05	−.04
Robust	.00	.66	.66**	.01	.06	.05	.42	.00	−.42**

** $p < .05$, * $p < .10$

When *operational environment* is at its 90th percentile we do not see these same trends, again as I would expect. In model 1 there is a smaller increase in the probability of gap contributions by .26 that is statistically significant at the 10% level (the odds of observing this by chance are less than 10%) but this does not show up in either model 2 or 3.

Second, there is clear support for hypothesis 4: the combination of a high value on *CE news coverage* and a hospitable operational environment provides fertile ground for robust protection efforts. We can see this in the bottom left-hand corners of these tables and figures. In each model, when *operational environment* is at its 10th percentile, there is a large increase in the probability of a robust contribution as *CE news coverage* increases (ranging from .64 in model 1 to .87 in model 2). Moreover, at the high end of *CE news coverage* robust contributions are more likely than gaps (by .30 in model 1, .74 in model 2, and .32 in model 3), the only other outcome that regularly occurs here. In contrast, when *operational environment* is at its 50th percentile the probability of robust contributions grows by only .04-.05 as *CE news coverage* increases, and this is only statistically significant in model 2.

Meanwhile, at *operational environment*'s 90th percentile there is a very different pattern. Here there is a notable chance of a robust contribution when *CE news coverage* equals 0, ranging from .17 (model 2) to .42 (model 3). However, as *CE news coverage* increases, this probability soon drops to effectively 0. These decreases are also significant at the 5% level. Taken together, the results suggest that while robust contributions do not occur only in the face of strong pressure for civilian protection and a hospitable operational environment, these circumstances do indeed promote them and they are more likely here than in other scenarios. Thus, this secondary implication of my argument appears empirically quite meaningful.

Third, given the above, the results also support hypothesis 5: that limited contributions and no contribution will become less likely as *CE news coverage* increases, at least for low and mid-level values of *operational environment*. In each model the probability of these outcomes does exactly this, although the precise amounts vary. In models 2 and 3, these effects are statistically significant for no and limited contributions when *operational environment* is at its 10th percentile, and for no contribution when *operational environment* is at its 50th percentile. When *operational environment* is at its 50th percentile, limited contributions become only a little less likely (by -.14 in model 2 and -.07 in model 3), evidently because leaders are quite unlikely to contribute to peace operations at all when *CE news coverage* is low and are very likely to promote an ambitions-resources gap when it is high. Still, in model 2 if we consider a change in *CE news coverage* only over the top half of its range—from .5 to 1, where the confidence intervals are smaller— the probability of limited contributions also falls by .14, and this is statistically significant at the 5% level. Similarly, in model 1, as *CE news coverage* increases, the only one of these four effects that is statistically significant is for limited contributions when *operational environment* is at its 10th percentile. Yet if we look at what happens as *CE news coverage* moves from .5 to 1 instead, the probability of both no and limited contributions falls at both the low and middle values of *operational environment*. In each case this would occur less than 5% of the time by chance if the increase in *CE news coverage* did not affect leaders' decisions.

When *operational environment* is very inhospitable, these patterns again look different and on the whole are less consistently significant. In each model the probability of making no contribution briefly increases as *CE news coverage* rises, reflecting the drop in robust contributions. Soon, though, not contributing to a peace operation becomes less common, mainly because limited contributions are more likely at high values of *CE news coverage*. Only in model 3 is the increase in limited contributions statistically significant, however, and in no case is there a significant change in the probability of no contribution as *CE news coverage* moves from 0 to 1. In model 1 the probability of no contribution drops by .47 as *CE news coverage* moves from .5 to 1, and this is significant at the 10% level. Overall, the less consistent and significant results at *operational environment*'s 90th percentile are not surprising given the relative infrequency of contributions to peace operations in these circumstances.

Finally, the results provide important evidence against the alternative explanation that ambitions-resources gaps are just a cover for leaders' strategic or economic goals. The key point is that not a single measure of the potential interveners' possible strategic, economic, or more general political interests has a significant positive effect on the probability of gap contributions.

Tables 3.6 (model 2) and 3.7 (model 3) show the effects of changing the value of each control while holding all other variables at their means or

Table 3.6 Effect of changes in control variables, model 2

	Former colony	Contiguous ally	Region	Trade	Affinity	Democracy	Pre-1989 CE	Mass killing
No contribution	−.08	.16*	.10	.39**	−.01	.00	−.19	−.64**
Limited	−.08	−.11**	−.11	−.20**	.02	.05	−.05	.70**
Gap	.14	−.04	.02	−.19**	−.02	−.04	−.03	−.05
Robust	.02	−.01	−.01**	.00	.01*	−.02	.26**	−.01

** p < .05, * p < .10

Table 3.7 Effect of changes in control variables, model 3

	Contiguous ally	Region	Trade	Pre-1989 CE	Mass killing	Int'l civil conflict	Non-civil conflict
No contribution	.13**	.10	.24**	.01	−.67**	−.34	−.29
Limited	−.07**	−.06	−.15**	−.04	.65**	.08	.18
Gap	−.04	−.03	−.11**	.02	−.01	.26	.10*
Robust	−.02*	−.02**	.01	.05	.03	.01	.01

** p < .05, * p < .10

modes. The effect of the dichotomous variables reflects a change from 0 to 1, and for the continuous variables—*trade, affinity,* and *democracy*—it reflects a change from the 25th to the 75th percentile (using the minimum and maximum values does not substantively change any results).

Considering first the five variables that represent direct strategic and political relationships between a potential intervener and the state where a complex emergency occurs—*former colony, contiguous ally, region, trade,* and *affinity*—there is almost no statistically significant evidence of a positive effect on any type of contribution to peace operations. *Former colony* has no significant effects at all, and both *region* and *affinity* have only very minor ones for robust contributions. For *region* this effect is significant but negative. A higher level of *affinity* has a positive effect on robust contributions, but the increase is only .01. The other variables, meanwhile, act as statistically and substantively meaningful deterrents to contributing to peace operations. In models 2 and 3 having an ally contiguous to a complex emergency makes a leader more likely not to contribute to a peace operation (by .16 and .13 respectively). All types of contributions become less likely, but the effect is largest—and significant in both models—for limited contributions. In model 3 the probability of a robust contribution also drops by .02.

In addition, a stronger trade relationship with a state experiencing a complex emergency substantially increases the chance that a potential intervener will do nothing and discourages limited and gap contributions. These effects are larger in model 2 than model 3, but in each case there is less than a 5% chance of observing them if trade had no effect on leaders' policy choices.

Next are the variables I would expect might reflect more general political incentives for contributing to peace operations, *democracy* and *pre-1989 complex emergency*. The level of democracy in a state experiencing a complex emergency appears to have no meaningful impact on leaders' policy choices in these data. Meanwhile, in model 2, *pre-1989 complex emergency* increases the probability of robust contributions by .26, but this effect disappears in model 3. It may be, for instance, that the effect of beginning during the Cold War is less meaningful among civil wars that did not see outside intervention than among other complex emergencies.

The indicator of *mass killing* has very similar effects in both models, which are substantively larger than those any of the other controls. A complex emergency that also involves mass killing sees the probability of no contribution drop by .64 and the probability of a limited contribution increase by .70 in model 2; in model 3 these numbers are .67 and .65. It is interesting that mass killing encourages limited contributions, which as we have seen are inappropriate for such circumstances, but has no notable effect on gap or robust contributions.[38]

Finally, the indicators of the different types of complex emergencies reveal that *non-civil conflicts* are more likely to receive gap contributions than *civil conflicts* are. The difference in predicted probabilities is .10 and is significant at the 10% level. Otherwise, although the potential interveners appear more inclined to contribute to peace operations in *internationalized civil conflicts* and in *non-civil conflicts*, these effects are not statistically significant. On the whole, it appears that the type of complex emergency has some limited impact on leaders' decisions, but it is difficult to say more because of the need to combine several types of complex emergencies under *non-civil conflict*.

RESTRICTING THE SAMPLE

When using the full dataset I cannot investigate whether leaders promote ambitions-resources gaps unknowingly and unintentionally. However, by limiting my analysis to observations in which potential interveners contribute to at least one peace operation, it is possible to conduct at least a crude test of this possibility. In brief, if ambitions-resources gaps are unintentional, they should have become less common over the course of the post–Cold War period as leaders learned from past mistakes. In particular, if leaders learned lessons from the debacles of the 1990s we should see relatively fewer ambitions-resources gaps in the 2000s. Thus, for each observation in which a potential intervener contributed to a peace operation I coded the decade in which the primary contribution began. A glance at the results is instructive: while 28% of contributions starting in the 1990s promoted ambitions-resources gaps, 44% of those from the 2000s did so. Still, to test this idea more thoroughly I include this variable, *contribution decade*, in a model that looks only at this restricted sample of observations. This also allows for another check on my expectation that the conditions that promote ambitions-resources gaps will differ from those for other types of contributions.

Because model 4 uses fewer than half the observations of models 1–3, aside from *contribution decade* I include only *CE news coverage, operational environment*, and their interaction. The regression is presented as table B.3 in appendix B, and I again focus on the results in terms of predicted probabilities. These are shown in table 3.8 below. First, in the left-hand column I examine the effect of changing *contribution decade* from the 1990s to the 2000s while holding *CE news coverage* and *operational environment* at their mean values (within this reduced sample). Making this change yields a .28 increase in the probability of gap contributions, and there is less than a 10% chance of this result occurring by chance. While this finding is sensitive to model specification, it still provides at least some evidence against the notion that leaders promote ambitions-resources gaps unknowingly.[39]

Next, the right-hand side of table 3.8 is similar to the results presented above, but with some important differences. Here I examine the effect of *CE news coverage* as it ranges from .3 to 1, as there are no contributions to peace operations at lower values. In addition, I look at two values of *operational environment*, which I selected to represent fairly hospitable conditions and relatively (but not very) inhospitable conditions comparable to those from models 1–3. Respectively, these represent the 20th and 80th percentiles of *operational environment* in this restricted sample of the data.[40]

Table 3.8 Effect of changes in *contribution decade* and *CE news coverage*, model 4

	Change in contribution decade from 1990s to 2000s	Operational environment					
		20th percentile			80th percentile		
		CE news coverage			CE news coverage		
		.3	1	Change	.3	1	Change
Limited	−.22	.93	.00	−.93**	.63	.09	−.54**
Gap	.28*	.05	.33	.28	.03	.90	.87**
Robust	−.06	.02	.67	.65**	.33	.01	−.32**

** p < .05, * p < .10

The results here help confirm the earlier findings. When the operational environment is quite hospitable, an increase from the minimum to the maximum value of *CE news coverage* leads to a dramatic drop in the probability of limited contributions by .93 and a large increase in the probability of robust ones, by .65. Gap contributions also become more likely, but this effect is not significant and they remain much less likely than robust contributions when *CE news coverage* equals 1. Meanwhile, when the operational environment is relatively inhospitable the same increase in *CE news coverage* yields a .87 increase in the probability of gap contributions. When *CE news coverage* equals 1, gaps are much more likely—by .59—when *operational environment* is relatively inhospitable than when it is highly hospitable, and this difference is significant at the 95% level. Also when the operational environment is relatively inhospitable the probability of limited contributions drops by .54 as *CE news coverage* increases, again as I would expect. Finally, when *CE news coverage* is at its low end, the predicted probability of robust contributions is .33. While this again suggests that robust protection efforts do occur under various conditions, they are nearly twice as likely when *CE news coverage* equals 1 and the operational environment is hospitable. This further supports the idea that normative pressures for civilian protection play an important role in promoting these policies.

ROBUSTNESS TESTS

While the results presented so far strongly support my hypotheses, it is also important to test the robustness of my findings to variations in model specification. Thus, the models discussed above represent only a small sample of the many regressions I ran, focusing on the full-sample results from models 1–3, to check their reliability.[41]

First, one concern is the coding of the core independent variables, *CE news coverage* and *operational environment*. As discussed above, in coding these variables I made a number of important decisions about issues such as how to measure changes in news coverage as compared with earlier periods and how to assess the likely costs and risks of intervention in particular conflicts. My findings will be more credible to the extent that they do not hinge on any single one of these decisions. Thus, I conducted a series of tests that examine how well my results hold up in response to minor changes to these variables. Focusing on *CE news coverage*, I repeated model 2 with four additional versions of this variable. These involved changing how I constructed the ratio of coverage during a complex emergency relative to beforehand, and using headline news searches rather than full-text searches to measure the volume of coverage. I also made a number of changes to *operational environment*. As we have already seen in model 3, dropping the components of the index that reflect a strong and motivated rebellion and the number of violent parties yields results that are consistent with my argument. To further ensure that no single aspect of the index is driving my findings, I repeated model 2 with ten further versions of *operational environment*. Nine of these separately drop each different component. For the tenth, reasoning that interveners may care more about the factors that most directly affect the risk of confrontation and casualties, I included all nine components but weighted the five that I would expect to be more closely associated with these risks twice as heavily as the others.

Next, considering the categorical structure of the dependent variable there are relatively few observations in the dataset. I also examine many controls, most of which are dichotomous. Yet in such cases too many covariates can lead to incorrect inferences about their true effects, especially if there are nonlinearities in the data.[42] I thus ran a series of models that includes each control separately alongside *CE news coverage, operational environment*, and their interaction.

Finally, a series of tests dropped different combinations of observations from the analysis. In separate regressions I dropped all observations for each potential intervener to examine whether the results hinged on any particular great power democracy. Because they involved dropping nearly one third of the observations, for the United States, United Kingdom, and France I performed these tests without the control variables. In addition, as noted above, for a few observations there was some uncertainty as to how I should code the dependent variable, *contribution type*. I thus ran the models without these.[43] Separately, I also dropped all observations where there was any doubt about whether the conflict met the definition and full set of operational criteria for a complex emergency (where it was not coded at the highest level of certainty, as discussed above). I further ran one model that excluded all complex emergencies that had not yet ended by the end of 2009, the final year in the data.

In total I conducted more than thirty of these robustness checks. Concerning *CE news coverage* and *operational environment* the results were overwhelmingly consistent with those shown above. In every case, the broad trends in the predicted probabilities were in line with those from models 1–3, and the changes in predicted probabilities discussed above usually remained statistically significant. Gap contributions become more likely as *CE news coverage* increases at both low and mid-level values of *operational environment*, but this effect is larger and more consistently significant at mid-level values. Thus, gap contributions remain reliably more likely in relatively inhospitable operational environments than in more hospitable ones, and this effect is statistically significant at the 10% level or better in nearly 80% of the robustness tests. Robust contributions also become much more likely as *CE news coverage* increases when *operational environment* is fairly hospitable. When *CE news coverage* equals one, they remain more likely than gap contributions in all but one test. They usually also become somewhat less likely at very high values of *operational environment*. Reduced probabilities of no and limited contributions as *CE news coverage* increases also persist in these tests.

Finally, with fewer variables in the models two of the controls—*former colony* and *contiguous ally*—achieve further statistically significant results. While the former discourages limited contributions, the latter significantly reduces the probability of both limited and gap contributions. Both of these results affirm my conclusion above that the measures of strategic and political ties between the potential interveners and states experiencing complex emergencies do not appear to promote contributions to peace operations, including ambitions-resources gaps.

This chapter has provided important support for my central argument. Despite the challenges of quantifying many of its core concepts and the limits of some of the data, the statistical evidence aligns closely with my expectations. Great power democracies are highly likely to create and promote ambitions-resources gaps when substantial news coverage of a complex emergency indicates strong normative domestic pressure to respond, and when the operational environment for intervention is relatively (but not extremely) inhospitable. Further, robust contributions are most likely when *CE news coverage* is also high, but the operational environment is more hospitable. This not only supports my expectation that these conditions may promote robust action, but also suggests that empirically they are quite important for understanding the most ambitious civilian protection efforts. These findings are both substantively and statistically significant, and hold across a variety of model specifications.

Still, there are limits to these statistical tests, and the next three chapters supplement them in several key ways through in-depth investigation of specific cases. First, leaders and their advisers certainly assess normative pressures to protect civilians and the operational environment for intervention in more nuanced ways than my data can capture. Likewise, other considerations beyond the operational environment can inform the strength of their concerns about the costs and risks of intervention. The case studies should thus bolster my arguments about when leaders will turn to ambitions-resources gaps and other policies by confirming the patterns observed here even while accounting for more indicators of the moral and material pressures highlighted by my theory, and for leaders' actual perceptions of them. As we will see especially with U.S. policy on Darfur, they also show that my argument can explain temporal variation in states' responses to particular conflicts, in addition to the cross-case variation examined in this chapter.

Second, as highlighted in chapter 2, my argument generates several predictions that are not amenable to statistical testing. Primarily they focus on how leaders can benefit politically from ambitions-resources gaps by gaining the support of domestic audiences for these policies, as summarized in hypotheses 2 and 3. In addition, hypothesis 6 represents an extension of my main argument that focuses on potential differences between the two versions of ambitions-resources gaps. The case studies are vital to investigating these expectations and confirming that ambitions-resources gaps indeed serve the political purposes I claim.

Finally, concerning alternative explanations, the measures I used in this chapter to capture potential international political motives for contributing to peace operations probably do not reflect all the ways such considerations affect leaders' calculations. Leaders' perceptions of geopolitical interests are complex and multifaceted, and therefore difficult to measure quantitatively. Thus, the statistical tests offer only a partial check on the possibility that ambitions-resources gaps are really a fig leaf for interventions motivated by strategic or economic interests. Similarly, comparing the relative frequency of gap contributions in the 1990s and the 2000s is a rough test of the idea that leaders promote ambitions-resources gaps unknowingly. While the results are encouraging, it could be that even if leaders recognized the problems these gaps created in the 1990s, they might not have learned how to correct them. The case studies more fully test these alternative explanations by examining both how leaders and their advisers actually saw their states' geopolitical interests in several complex emergencies and also what they understood about the requirements of effective civilian protection in these conflicts.

France in Rwanda

> We have stopped the violence, cared for the victims, and prepared the
> way for those who deserve the beautiful name of humanitarians.
> —François Léotard, French minister of defense,
> *Libération*, July 22, 1994

The 1994 Rwandan genocide stands out as one of the most appalling and
devastating crises of the twentieth century. In less than four months, hundreds of thousands of people were brutally murdered. Millions more—
including many of the perpetrators—fled the country, setting the stage for a
tremendous humanitarian emergency centered in neighboring Zaire. The
international response to these events has rightfully faced stinging criticism
for being too little, too late. In this chapter, I examine one piece of this
response, the French military intervention known as Operation Turquoise
that deployed to help protect civilians from June through August.

Of the several peace operations that deployed during or immediately
after the genocide, Operation Turquoise was the most ambitious in that it
had a clear mandate to use force to protect civilians and well-trained, well-
equipped troops who were capable of doing so. Still, its ability to offer
effective protection was limited in several ways, including by an ambitions-
resources gap. In particular, despite its appropriate mandate, several key
decisions about military strategy prevented the French force from operating as efficiently to save lives as it might have.

Operation Turquoise has received relatively little in-depth attention in
the English-language international relations literature and thus represents
an opportunity to improve our understanding of an important and controversial intervention. It is also a strong case on which to test my argument
about ambitions-resources gaps in part because it offers a difficult test. Specifically, the case is complicated by a history of French political and military
involvement in Rwanda. This history is the reason that the French government was more vulnerable to moral pressure to halt the genocide than the

other major democracies with the capacity to intervene, as we will see. However, it has also inspired considerable controversy over France's motives. A number of observers have charged that the real objective of Operation Turquoise was strategic: that it aimed either to assist France's former allies, who were responsible for the genocide, or more broadly to further French interests in Africa. If true, this could also explain the ambitions-resources gap, and provide support for one of the key alternative explanations to my own theory.

The other most common explanation for Operation Turquoise, however, is that moral pressure from NGOs and the media pushed France's leaders to intervene by convincing them that their public image would suffer otherwise. As I demonstrate, this pressure was indeed crucial for the instigators of the decision—President François Mitterrand and foreign minister Alain Juppé—but was also offset by great concern to limit the costs and risks of the operation by the officials most involved in designing it—defense minister François Léotard and military leaders—as well as prime minister Édouard Balladur. These material concerns were directly related to the operational environment, but also to legitimacy issues stemming from France's history in Rwanda. For all the key politicians, these issues were also magnified by France's upcoming 1995 presidential election. Thus, competing normative and material pressures were not only present, but front and center in the deployment and design of Operation Turquoise. Consistent with my argument, French leaders responded by compromising on a mission that, despite its humanitarian mandate, placed a premium on risk management and thus displayed an ambitions-resources gap. What is more, ample evidence suggests that the French public, NGOs, and concerned French officials supported this outcome for the reasons laid out in chapter 2, and that French leaders engaged vigorously in the rhetoric of organized hypocrisy.

My analysis relies on a broad range of primary and secondary sources. The former include recently released material from the archives of the renowned humanitarian medical group Médecins Sans Frontières (MSF) and the firsthand written accounts of French military leaders, as well as contemporary polling data. I also conducted an in-depth analysis of both the volume and content of French media coverage of the genocide and the French government's reactions to it.

The chapter proceeds as follows. I first briefly describe the domestic institutional context in which France intervened in Rwanda. Next I discuss the background to and course of the genocide itself. I then outline France's involvement, briefly describing its role in Rwanda's 1990–93 civil war and its initial responses to the genocide before offering a detailed account of Operation Turquoise. The next section shows how the mission reflected both societal pressure and firm efforts from within government to limit physical and political risks. Finally, I discuss two alternative explanations for ambitions-resources gaps: that Turquoise's protection mandate was a cover for other interests and that French leaders may not have understood its limitations.

Foreign Policy Making and *Cohabitation* in France

The institutional context surrounding France's intervention in Rwanda differed from the norm in French foreign policy making. As we will see, this significantly affected how Operation Turquoise was designed by promoting intragovernmental bargaining and compromise.

In France, executive power is shared between a directly elected president, the prime minister, and the cabinet. The latter are responsible to the legislature, the National Assembly. Under typical conditions, when the president and parliamentary majority are of the same party, foreign and military policy are treated as a *domaine réservé* (reserved area) for the president, who has ultimate decision-making authority. Between 1993 and 1995, however, France was operating under an unusual balance of executive power known as *cohabitation*. While President Mitterrand belonged to the left-leaning Socialist Party, a conservative coalition held the parliamentary majority. As a result, the Balladur government was led by conservatives, including the prime minister, defense minister Léotard, and foreign minister Juppé.

Under *cohabitation*, foreign policy becomes a *domaine partagé*, or shared area, between the president and the prime minister and cabinet. Most relevant here, with a split executive any decision to deploy the armed forces abroad becomes a joint decision. Although the president is chief of the armed forces, the prime minister's government is responsible for national defense and controls the essential means of action in the defense department. Thus, the president cannot declare a military intervention without approval from the prime minister and cabinet. What is more, both parties must agree on the goals as well as the implementation of any such operations.[1]

The Complex Emergency

The Rwandan genocide lasted over three months, from April to July 1994, but followed a civil war in 1990–93 and a long history of ethnic tension and violence. Other authors have discussed these events in detail.[2] Briefly, during several decades as a Belgian colony until 1962, Rwanda saw relations between its two main ethnic groups sour as the Belgians favored the Tutsi minority over the Hutu majority. Hutu resentment led to a 1959 uprising and anti-Tutsi violence. From 1959 to 1973 several hundred thousand Tutsi fled to neighboring countries, where many became long-term refugees.[3]

Then, in 1973, a Hutu army officer named Juvénal Habyarimana seized power in a military coup. Under Habyarimana and his ruling party, the Mouvement Révolutionnaire National pour le Développement (MRND), Rwanda experienced economic growth and an end to ethnic violence. Still, the Tutsi remained largely politically marginalized, and Habyarimana would not let the many refugees scattered around the region return to Rwanda.

It was this last issue that eventually led to civil war. In the late 1980s, international and domestic pressure on the MRND to democratize and permit the return of the refugees made little headway. In October 1990 a group of refugees in Uganda, fed up with poor treatment and discrimination, launched an invasion of Rwanda. Many had military experience in the Ugandan army, and they organized under the banner of the Rwandan Patriotic Front (RPF). Although their initial offensive failed, they soon regrouped, and the war dragged on intermittently for three years.

Meanwhile, the pressure on Habyarimana continued. Yet despite some reforms and the formation of new political parties, the MRND retained a tight grip on power and organized violent reprisals against Tutsi in Rwanda.[4] To facilitate this violence, Hutu extremist parties fostered and deployed youth militias. The largest and best organized, the Interahamwe, received training, weapons, and equipment.[5]

At the same time, the RPF became a legitimate contender for political power by taking territory and allying with some of Rwanda's new opposition parties. International pressure for a political resolution to the conflict intensified. After a year of on-and-off negotiations and a February 1993 RPF offensive that revealed the weakness of the Rwandan army (Forces Armées Rwandaises, or FAR), in August 1993 Habyarimana agreed to sign the Arusha Accords. These agreements provided for the MRND, RPF, and domestic opposition groups to share power in a transitional government pending democratic elections, and for the integration of the RPF and FAR. The terms were highly favorable to the RPF and opposition parties and provoked strong hostility among Hutu hardliners in or allied with the government.[6] These extremists immediately set out to undermine the accords and began preparing for the genocide of the Tutsi population.

Fearing violence, moderates in the major Rwandan parties requested a UN peacekeeping force. In October the Security Council approved the United Nations Assistance Mission for Rwanda (UNAMIR), a traditional peacekeeping operation intended to help provide security and reassure the parties that it was safe to implement the Arusha Accords. In terms of the typology from chapter 1, UNAMIR was a limited mission, deployed in what the UN saw as a benign post-conflict environment without either the ambitions or resources for meaningful civilian protection. Still, the force was undersized and lacked the basic provisions it needed to do its job.[7]

UNAMIR commander Roméo Dallaire found circumstances in Rwanda to be far more complex and dangerous than expected. Thanks to Habyarimana's obstructionism, UNAMIR's weakness, and the extremists' preparations for genocide, political conditions deteriorated drastically. The inauguration of the transitional government was postponed several times. Meanwhile, violence increased and UNAMIR was unable to respond effectively.[8]

The event that precipitated the genocide was President Habyarimana's death in a plane crash on April 6, 1994, as he returned from a conference in Tanzania, where he had agreed to install the transitional government on April 8. Instead, his plane was shot down as it approached the Rwandan capital of Kigali. Immediately, Hutu extremists blamed the RPF and used the crash as a pretext to initiate their murderous plans.[9] That night, the presidential guard and militia began slaughtering Tutsi and moderate Hutu politicians. Over the following days, focusing in and around Kigali, they eliminated their political opposition and on April 8 announced the formation of a new interim government.

The killing spread quickly around the country. At the urging of the ringleaders, Hutu peasants joined in killing their neighbors, and they, along with the militia, were at various times aided by elements of the FAR and the local police.[10] Tutsi citizens abandoned their homes in droves, often seeking shelter in public places such as stadiums and churches. Soon most Tutsi were congregated at these locations, which quickly became targets for the killers. Indeed, most of these sites were attacked within two weeks of Habyarimana's death, and more than half of the genocide's Tutsi victims died at such sites.[11] While UNAMIR tried to assist where it could, it had too few personnel and too conservative a mandate to prevent the vast majority of attacks.

The genocide was extremely fast moving. Some 80% of victims were killed in the first six weeks, by the third week of May.[12] In July it was brought to an end by the RPF, for the genocide also sparked renewed civil war. On April 8, an RPF battalion stationed in Kigali under the Arusha Accords began engaging the FAR. The next day the main RPF force, led by Major-General Paul Kagame and located in the north of the country, set off for the capital. While it took until July 4 for the RPF to take Kigali, in the meantime they gradually gained control of most of the rest of the country.[13] Most observers date the end of the genocide as July 18, when the RPF declared a new government after taking the final extremist holdouts in northwest Rwanda.

The total number of Rwandans who died during these months is of course impossible to establish with certainty. Numerous sources estimate the total at somewhere between 800,000 and 1.1 million, including those who were killed in the genocide itself as well as those killed in the renewed civil war, by the RPF, in opportunistic violence, or by disease.[14] There is disagreement as to how many were Tutsi: most estimates suggest that the number is at least 500,000, and 800,000 is the figure most commonly cited in media and popular reports.[15]

The end of the genocide did not, unfortunately, mean the end of Rwanda's suffering. As the RPF victory approached, a massive Hutu exodus began. In the days after the RPF captured Kigali, about 1.5 million people headed either for the northwest and the last FAR and interim government holdouts, or for the southwest where the French force was then operating. Then, in the week before July 18, over a million people crossed into Zaire.[16] By the fall, nearly two million people had fled to nearby countries, with Zaire—especially the border city of Goma—the top destination. Another 1.3 to 1.8 million people were internally displaced in Rwanda.[17]

The refugees' reasons for fleeing included both genuine fear of the RPF and duress. Among them were the organizers of the genocide, who hoped to maintain political control of the Hutu population by forcing them out of Rwanda and beyond the RPF's reach. Their chaotic departure took a heavy toll, as people crowded together in hastily constructed camps without adequate food, water, shelter, or medical care. Disease soon ran rampant. Within a week, a cholera epidemic in Goma that began July 20 was killing 600 people each day, and within two weeks the daily toll climbed to 3,000. Before it was over the epidemic took an estimated 30,000 lives, while thousands more died of other diseases and related causes. Meanwhile, Hutu leaders used violence to control the population and limit access to humanitarian aid, which they extracted from relief agencies in order to support preparations for a new invasion of Rwanda.[18]

The French Response

BEFORE TURQUOISE

Thanks to a 1975 military cooperation agreement between France and Rwanda, when the RPF invaded in 1990 France sent troops to assist the FAR. Over the next three years, France—led by Mitterrand and the Africa Bureau in the Elysée (the French president's official residence)—would play the role of patron and supporter to the Habyarimana regime. Military assistance included advising and training the FAR, helping maintain order in Kigali, collecting intelligence on the RPF, and offering logistical and combat support against the RPF. France also delivered extensive arms and materiel for FAR use.[19] Publicly, however, the French government tried to avoid drawing attention to this support and spoke little about it.[20]

Although Paris also encouraged Habyarimana to improve human rights and move toward democracy, French military aid was not contingent on progress in these areas. Yet by 1993, the French government was looking for a way out of the Rwandan morass. With the advent of *cohabitation* that spring, Mitterrand's Rwanda policy was subject to new scrutiny by Prime Minister Balladur and Foreign Minister Juppé. At the same time, the RPF's February 1993 offensive highlighted the failings of France's support for the FAR. Thus, Paris pushed harder for democratic reforms and urged Habyarimana to sign the Arusha Accords. It also pressed the UN to deploy UNAMIR, hoping this would help end the war and the need for continued French military involvement in Rwanda.[21] With UNAMIR in place, in December 1993 France removed the last of its military personnel except for a twenty-member military cooperation team.[22]

When the genocide began, neither France, the UN Secretariat, nor other relatively well-informed countries initially saw it for the campaign of extermination it was. Instead, Rwanda's recent civil war sowed confusion among foreign observers. The prevailing interpretation when the violence began was that it merely reflected a known risk: the resumption of war, including deplorable but not unexpected ethnic violence. The renewal of the war alongside the genocide encouraged this impression. Other explanations include confused media reports and a dearth of international journalists in Rwanda in April; inaccurate intelligence; a failure to anticipate Habyarimana's assassination; and a simple failure of imagination.[23] In Paris, French leaders saw the violence as the result of "ancient hatreds" and ethnic conflict that was "inherent to Africa."[24]

In this environment, the French government at first tried to distance itself from the situation. Its main policies in April included delivering humanitarian aid to refugees and helping lead a military evacuation of French and other foreign nationals (known as Operation Amaryllis) from April 8 to 14. At this time the French also evacuated various MRND notables including President Habyarimana's wife, Agathe, and her family.[25] Meanwhile, at the UN the focus on the renewed civil war led to an emphasis on getting a new ceasefire between the interim government and the RPF, rather than ending the massacres of civilians. It also encouraged the impression that without a ceasefire there was little the UN or UNAMIR could achieve in Rwanda. Far from disagreeing with this assessment, in an April 13 cabinet meeting both Mitterrand and Juppé approved of the possibility of withdrawing UNAMIR altogether. Ultimately, eight days later, the Security Council voted to reduce UNAMIR from over 2,500 to a mere 270 troops.[26]

Within a week of this decision, however, France's position began to shift. By the last week of April numerous human rights groups and journalists were referring to genocide and calling attention to the UN's inaction. Privately the Security Council members soon came to agree on this interpretation and began looking for a new approach to address the violence.[27] On April 28 the French government announced its desire to see UNAMIR reinforced. Then, led by Juppé, over the next few weeks it repeatedly asserted this position—albeit on the unlikely condition of a ceasefire between the parties—and made clear France's willingness to participate in a reinforced UNAMIR. On May 16 Juppé went further, publicly referring to genocide and declaring that reinforcing UNAMIR should not require an improbable ceasefire.[28]

The next day the Security Council indeed authorized an expanded "UNAMIR II," with 5,500 personnel to help protect displaced and at-risk Rwandans.[29] Yet, at U.S. insistence, most of the troops were to deploy only after clear progress toward a ceasefire between the warring parties, a possibility ruled out by the RPF's refusal to negotiate with the perpetrators of genocide (*génocidaires*) and growing confidence in its own victory. The force also faced extended delays while the UN negotiated with Western powers over the details of equipping and supporting the African countries that volunteered troops. Thus, as Michael Barnett points out, "The next month was an extended waiting period created by the absence of both a cease-fire and troops."[30]

The French government hoped to see UNAMIR II deploy as soon as possible, although its own offer to contribute was ruled out because the RPF objected. On June 1, therefore, Juppé announced France's willingness to help equip the African contingents, but the UN did not move quickly on this offer.[31] Still, until just a few days before their decision to launch Operation Turquoise French officials repeatedly denied any intention of intervening outside UN auspices. On May 10, for instance, Mitterrand noted that while France wanted "to be good peacekeepers for the United Nations," it was not its role to serve as a substitute.[32] Similarly, at a May 31 breakfast with German chancellor Helmut Kohl, Mitterrand indicated it was up to the UN to act.[33] On June 10, pressed by journalists, Juppé added: "What would we do there? One thousand five hundred men would not be able to stop the killings, especially since one party, the RPF, rejects us."[34]

FRANCE INTERVENES—OPERATION TURQUOISE

In a June 15 meeting France's split executive reached an agreement to intervene in Rwanda. While Mitterrand and Juppé pushed for action, Balladur and defense minister Léotard were reluctant but ultimately consented. There is some debate over who was the main instigator. According to some observers, Turquoise was the president's initiative.[35] Yet both Léotard and Mitterrand's chief of staff Hubert Védrine have claimed that it was Juppé who first raised and pushed the idea of intervention. Indeed, according to Védrine there were intense discussions in the cabinet for two weeks before Mitterrand came around to Juppé's point of view, evidently on June 13.[36] Regardless, a comprehensive understanding of the mission requires accounting for the motives of both Mitterrand and Juppé, as well as of Balladur and Léotard.

Against Mitterrand's wishes, Juppé publicly announced the decision later on June 15. An official joint declaration from the president and prime minister followed three days later.[37] Meanwhile, the government sought UN authorization for the force, which it received in Resolution 929 on June 22. The idea was for Turquoise to fill in only until UNAMIR II could deploy, so it was authorized for at most two months. It would not interpose itself between the RPF and FAR, but would otherwise have the same objectives as UNAMIR II: to "contribute to the security and protection of displaced persons, refugees and civilians at risk in Rwanda, including through the establishment and maintenance, where feasible, of secure humanitarian areas" and to "provide security and support for the distribution of relief supplies and humanitarian relief operations."[38] At France's request, it would operate under UN Chapter VII.

Operation Turquoise's primary goal was to end the massacres wherever possible, using force if necessary. It was also to facilitate humanitarian operations and prepare for the transfer to UNAMIR II when the time came.[39] For these purposes the ROE were quite permissive. The troops could use force in situations involving a threat to themselves or their mission (whether directed against the troops or threatened civilians). With the agreement of force commander Jean-Claude Lafourcade, they could also use force in case of efforts to obstruct the execution of their mission.[40] Meanwhile, a set of "behavior rules" (*règles de comportement*) accompanied the ROE, directing the troops to adopt an attitude of strict neutrality between the warring factions.[41]

Turquoise comprised some 2,900 soldiers including about 2,500 from France and several hundred from seven African countries, mainly Senegal.[42] The troops came mostly from units stationed at French bases in Africa, allowing for the quickest possible projection of force.[43] They also included an elite contingent from France's joint Special Operations Command (Commandement des Opérations Spéciales), whose deployment was also aimed at ensuring all possible speed.[44] These special forces were the first to arrive in theater on June 20, and acted as a vanguard for the rest of the troops. On June 23 they began making forays into western Rwanda from the Zairean border towns of Goma and Bukavu with the goals of gathering information, affirming their humanitarian role, and protecting as many people as possible.[45]

One of the most remarked-on aspects of Operation Turquoise was its heavy firepower and offensive combat capabilities. There were over 100 armored vehicles, 600 other motorized vehicles, a battery of heavy mortars, two light Gazelle and eight heavy Super-Puma helicopters, and four each of Jaguar fighter-bombers, Mirage ground-attack planes, and Mirage reconnaissance jets. There was also a wealth of communications and intelligence equipment.[46] As Lafourcade put it, "we were in a position to inflict severe harm on anyone who would oppose our mission."[47] Indeed, with the Mirages and Jaguars they had the ability to neutralize the FAR and RPF armies within a few hours. The idea behind all this firepower and the early use of the special forces was to create a meaningful deterrent threat that would avoid the need to actually use force by preventing attacks against the French and civilians in their areas of operation.[48]

Operation Turquoise was headquartered in Goma, Zaire, just across the border from northwest Rwanda. The original plan specified that it would be based entirely in Zaire, which is how it operated at first. Each day the troops would penetrate deeper into Rwanda and then try to return to Zaire at night. After the first few days these incursions were limited to the southwest of the country.[49] In the first week of July, however, the French decided to establish a Safe Humanitarian Zone (SHZ) in this area. The zone covered some 4,500 square kilometers or about a fifth of the country, and permitted the French to establish a "permanent foothold" in Rwanda.[50] The RPF were excluded from this area, a controversial decision I discuss below. From this point, the French were confined to the SHZ, which they worked to secure and stabilize in order to facilitate the work of humanitarian agencies and prepare for UNAMIR II's arrival.[51]

Because a number of people have argued that Operation Turquoise was a partial or even complete success, it is worth discussing what it accomplished before turning to its weaknesses.[52] First, the French saved some 10,000–20,000 threatened Tutsi who were otherwise likely to have been killed. These included about 8,000–10,000 people at the Nyarushishi IDP camp in Cyangugu province, plus various smaller concentrations of people.[53]

In addition, Operation Turquoise helped address the needs of displaced Hutu in various ways and spared many Hutu lives, at least in the short term.[54] In particular, it substantially improved the security environment in the SHZ, where many took refuge, thus allowing aid groups to work in the area. Meanwhile, the French helped group the displaced into camps where they could receive protection and assistance, and during the refugee crisis in Zaire they helped maintain order, again facilitating the work of humanitarian groups.[55] In both places, French troops also aided in distributing supplies, providing medical care and vaccinations, and burying bodies.[56]

It is also quite likely that the relative security of the SHZ helped prevent an even larger outflow of people to Zaire, first in mid-July and then again in August.[57] In the latter case, the Hutu population in the SHZ began to panic as Turquoise's August 22 departure approached, fearing that UNAMIR would not protect them from the RPF. The French worried this would lead to a new exodus and an even larger humanitarian crisis than in July. To prevent this they liaised with the UN and RPF, imploring people to stay put. Various observers and French military officials have, to different degrees, credited Turquoise with limiting the population outflow at this time and thus saving unknown thousands of lives.[58]

Despite these accomplishments, Operation Turquoise was unable to save more people for three broad reasons. First was its late deployment:

while the genocide was still in progress by late June, most victims had already been killed. Second, the force was simply too small. Third, and my main focus here, Turquoise exhibited an ambitions-resources gap. The last two problems were doubly unfortunate because the force's arrival reinvigorated the *génocidaires*, who at first sped up the pace of killing.[59] These issues were also related: as we will see, the competing pressures that explain the ambitions-resources gap also informed Turquoise's timing and size.

The ambitions-resources gap that plagued Operation Turquoise occurred because its resources—including its firepower and highly capable troops—were not used as efficiently to protect civilians as they might have been. As noted in chapter 1, in this book a force's ambitions refer to its goals and the decisions about military strategy that determine how they are pursued. In this case, two common problems—Turquoise's objectives and ROE—were actually quite appropriate for the conditions of ongoing genocide. Instead, it was hindered by various military strategy decisions that together were incompatible with its announced goals.

Two fundamental problems each stemmed, at least in part, from France's commitment to neutrality between the warring parties. The first was a tension between this commitment and the equally high priority given to presenting a strong deterrent threat, which in turn led to shortages of the personnel and materiel required for effective rescue operations.

As discussed in chapter 1, during mass violence against civilians, interveners can either focus on defeating the perpetrators or rescuing the victims. The first strategy requires the kind of combat-oriented, offensive weaponry that Operation Turquoise possessed in abundance. In contrast, rescuing victims involves different tasks and thus requires different units and equipment to pursue them. To be sure, such a force must also be able to deter and defend against attacks on itself or those it aims to protect.[60] Yet its main roles are locating people in danger, offering safe passage when they require evacuation, and providing protection and assistance at central locales.

To achieve its protection goals, then, Operation Turquoise either needed to confront the FAR and militia or to bring the right personnel and materiel for a full-throated rescue operation. Yet in practice it did neither. Confronting the *génocidaires* was never France's intention. Instead, Turquoise's extensive firepower was intended to deter conflict with both the RPF and FAR, and its focus on neutrality was supposed to show that it did not plan either to fight the RPF or assist the FAR. Yet neutrality also meant that the French would not systematically target the perpetrators or disrupt their ability to continue their attacks. Thus, as Olivier Lanotte has pointed out, the humanitarian benefits of the mission "could have been more evident if France had consented to conduct a more offensive operation with respect to the authors of the genocide."[61]

By ruling out a more aggressive stance, the French seemed to imply that they would pursue a rescue strategy. Yet, ironically, the top priority they placed on creating a strong deterrent meant that firepower ate up most of the budget. This combat orientation in turn served to crowd out equipment and personnel that would have been better suited to rescue-related tasks. According to one French officer familiar with the issue, "rather than special forces, we should have sent trains with trucks, more doctors, that is to say, to offer concrete aid to this defeated population."[62] As this comment suggests, there were too many armored vehicles and not enough of the trucks and transportation needed to evacuate threatened people to safer areas.[63]

Taylor Seybolt points out that there were also too few people to patrol and "handle small-scale, but no less deadly, attacks on civilians and aid organizations" throughout the safe zone.[64] While this was partly because of Turquoise's overall limited size, even that is not independent of the choice to bring so much expensive equipment, since spending less on firepower could have freed the money for more ground troops. This problem also reflects the extensive logistical support the combat forces required, which in effect meant that nearly one third of the French troops were there to perform jobs the French authorities hoped would prove unnecessary. Logistics teams located in Goma, Zaire, accounted for some 700 personnel and all logistics units save one—a military hospital—were related to combat support.[65] While these issues would not have been so serious if the French had not insisted on neutrality vis-à-vis the FAR and militia, as it was they created real limitations. Still, it is important to note that they did not reflect a lack of resources per se, but rather a set of decisions about France's strategy for how to pursue its announced goals.

Because they simultaneously insisted on neutrality toward the FAR and militia and overlooked the means for a robust rescue effort, the French were often unprepared to save endangered Tutsi. This was especially true for those who found themselves alone or in small groups in places where the killing was still proceeding rapidly, such as outside major population centers. Thus the French troops "often had to stand by in medium-sized towns while the killing went on unabated in the hills a few kilometers away."[66] In addition, on numerous occasions French soldiers came upon groups of Tutsi hiding in the bush but lacked both the vehicles to evacuate them and the numbers to stay and protect them. Although the troops would promise to return with appropriate transport, when they came back the Tutsi had often been killed. In one especially gruesome example in the Bisesero hills in Kibuye province, approximately one thousand Tutsi who had been in hiding since April emerged on learning of the French arrival. The French did not come back to evacuate them for three days, by which time most were dead.[67]

The second problem with France's commitment to neutrality was that it led to a limited focus on disarming and arresting the militia, FAR, and genocide ringleaders. In brief, the French did not initially plan to engage in these tasks. At the request of the UN and the RPF, however, they did subsequently work to disarm the militia and FAR within the SHZ. As Lafourcade put it, "Every time we met the militia, we disarmed them."[68] Yet these efforts were haphazard rather than methodical, and many FAR soldiers and militia who took refuge in the SHZ managed to keep their weapons. This was inconsistent with the creation of safe zones in other conflicts.[69]

To at least some extent, moreover, France's ad hoc disarmament efforts were intentional. As a July 10 telegram noted, "Except to provoke a systemic reaction against Operation Turquoise, disarmament of the militia cannot be systematic. It is currently practiced promptly in cases where militiamen threaten population groups."[70] Thus, France's reluctance on this issue reflected a desire not to threaten its perceived neutrality through a too-thorough disarmament effort that could risk serious militia and FAR backlash. Indirectly, moreover, by encouraging the priority on firepower over other kinds of units and materiel this same concern to limit the risk of confrontation also helped limit the available manpower for the tasks of arrest and disarmament.[71]

Because the French did not arrest the *génocidaires* who took refuge in the safe zone, Operation Turquoise was heavily criticized for allowing them to escape justice. While this is indeed important, it is tangential to the issue of civilian protection. More to the point here, France's limited efforts at disarmament and arrest also allowed these people to continue killing Tutsi, looting and destroying property, and coercing Hutu civilians to flee the country. As Lanotte describes, "In some places, as soon as the French paratroopers would leave, barricades were rebuilt, the weapons came out of hiding and the militia resumed 'working.'"[72]

Finally, a third problem—not related to the commitment to neutrality—was the initial decision to operate entirely from Zaire, which at first added to French difficulties in reaching threatened Tutsi in Rwanda. As Lafourcade put it, the daily need for the troops to return to Zaire was "untenable given that people were likely to be massacred as soon as we turned our back."[73] Similarly, Lanotte notes that the ban on occupying an area inside Rwanda made "hardly any sense."[74] Confronted with this reality and also with the Hutu influx into western Rwanda in early July, the French shifted strategy and set up the safe zone. Still, even after this only about half the force was deployed in Rwanda at any given time.[75] Added to the other limitations discussed above, this helps explain how the French evacuated only around 1,300 Rwandans aside from those at the Nyarushishi camp during the first three weeks of Operation Turquoise.[76]

Accounting for Turquoise

Why did France intervene in Rwanda when and as it did? What accounts for Operation Turquoise's ambitions-resources gap? In this section I describe the growth and impact of the normative pressures French leaders faced, mainly from society, to respond to the genocide. Next, I explain how the operational environment in Rwanda and France's history there inspired a laser-like focus by key officials—especially Balladur, Léotard and military leaders—on the potential physical and political perils of intervention. Further, France's upcoming presidential election magnified each of these concerns. Finally I show how these competing pressures worked together—though differently on different actors—to inspire the compromise of a French-led intervention that was designed more to minimize risks than to maximize lives saved. Still, this compromise worked as intended to help French leaders manage a delicate political situation.

NORMATIVE PRESSURES

Over the course of the genocide, France's leaders came to perceive intense societal pressure to help end the killing. On one hand, critics were vociferous in pointing out the inadequacy of the government's—and the UN's—initial responses. On top of this, they highlighted France's involvement in Rwanda's civil war and suggested that because of this, it had an important degree of responsibility for the current violence. While these charges were muted in April they grew rapidly in May and early June, building into a firestorm of political controversy. Unlike the situations in Darfur and East Timor that I discuss in Chapters 5–6, this pressure did not involve mass activism or ordinary people marching in the streets. Rather, it derived from a combination of advocacy by established NGOs—especially *Médecins Sans Frontières* (MSF), the renowned humanitarian medical group—and active media engagement that threatened to tarnish top politicians' reputations the year before a presidential election.

There are several reasons why NGOs and the media were at first subdued in their public reactions to the genocide. Initially, most humanitarian organizations already working in Rwanda—including major French groups MSF, *Médecins du Monde* (MDM), and *Action internationale contre la faim* (AICF)—withdrew most or all of their foreign staff. Only the International Committee of the Red Cross (ICRC) remained in Kigali, supported by a small MSF surgical team from France. Thus, aid groups were largely absent during the genocide's first weeks. For its part, MSF's French branch (MSF-France) was reticent compared with some other national chapters. Notably, after MSF-Belgium withdrew its last people on April 24, it began urging the UN to intervene and referring to "genocide." In contrast, MSF-France was quieter because it still had people working with the ICRC and did not want to use the word "genocide" prematurely. Still, it did criticize the UN's April 22 reduction of UNAMIR as an abandonment of Rwanda.[77] As for the press, early coverage of Rwanda reflected both the media outlets' business interests and journalistic confusion. During the first week, French newspapers and TV stations sent reporters to cover the evacuation mission, Operation Amaryllis, which was their main focus at this time. Indeed, at least one TV reporter was told to focus only on the evacuation of French citizens. Once the evacuation was complete, most journalists departed and attention to Rwanda temporarily fell. Throughout April, moreover, when the press did report on the violence its true nature was often obscured. Like many foreign governments, journalists tended to interpret the massacres as simply part and parcel of a return to civil war. Both in the written press and on TV, they portrayed the killings as chaotic and spontaneous rather than organized and premeditated, often overlooking that the perpetrators were overwhelmingly the Hutu extremists. Together, these and other misinterpretations tended to paint a picture of Rwanda as a general humanitarian morass and to obscure the kind of international responses that were needed. This was consistent with the dominant discourse promoted by French political and military leaders at the time.[78]

In contrast, starting in late April but especially in May and June, both NGOs—led by MSF-France—and the press began to communicate more clearly about the violence in Rwanda and to sharply criticize the French government and UN. On the NGO side, MSF was becoming increasingly uncomfortable with its self-censorship and felt a particular responsibility to speak out because of France's role in arming the killers. Thus, it launched a major media campaign to educate the French press and public, starting with two key initiatives in mid-May. The first was a series of media interviews by Rwanda Program Manager Dr. Jean-Hervé Bradol, beginning on Sunday May 16 during the 7 pm RTL radio show. The same day, a TV interview also opened the 8 pm bulletin on TF1, France's top evening news program, and aired again the next morning. In it, Bradol left no doubt that MSF saw the violence in Rwanda as genocide motivated by a fight for political power, not random tribal slaughter.[79] As for the French government, he added:

France has a particularly serious role and responsibility in Rwanda. Those now carrying out the slaughter, those who are implementing this policy of planned, systematic extermination have been funded, trained and armed by France. And that is something that hasn't been exposed properly yet. No French authority has explicitly condemned those responsible for the slaughter. And yet the French State knows these people only too well, since it has provided them with equipment.[80]

This interview was followed up with another published in *Libération* on May 18, which sounded the same themes of French responsibility and inadequate responses by France and the UN.[81]

MSF's other tactic was an open letter to President Mitterrand, announced by Bradol in the TF1 interview and published May 18 in *Le Monde*. In it, MSF accuses France of "serious responsibility" for the genocide and suggests that Mitterrand was disingenuous to claim that France lacked the influence to stop it. It concludes: "Mr. President, the international community, and France in particular, must accept its political responsibilities and put a stop to the massacres; it must ensure civilians are protected, and those guilty of war crimes are prosecuted."[82]

Several weeks later, on June 7, MSF-France decided to up the ante by publicly calling for military intervention to stop the genocide.[83] This was an unprecedented step for the group, and other MSF chapters initially expressed reservations. MSF-France was motivated, however, by a sense of deep unease that politicians were using its humanitarian work to avoid taking political actions to stop the killing. Drawing on this sentiment, the theme of its new appeal was, "You can't stop genocide with doctors," a phrase its officials repeated on multiple occasions.

MSF again published an open letter in *Le Monde*, this time addressed to Mitterrand, Balladur, and the representatives of the National Assembly. The letter did not come out until June 17, but in the meantime MSF leaders conveyed their intentions in meetings with Juppé on June 12 and then with Mitterrand and with Balladur's diplomatic adviser Bernard de Montferrand.[84] On June 15 MSF issued a press release calling for "immediate UN intervention" and wrote to the president of the National Assembly requesting his endorsement of its appeal. Two days later it held a press conference to coincide with its open letter. Both focused on the fact that the UN had acknowledged the genocide but failed so far to deploy UNAMIR II. According to the letter,

> As a matter of urgency, everything must be done to stop these massacres, by supporting the immediate intervention of the United Nations to genuinely oppose the murderers and protect the survivors. Since 16 May, the Mission of the United Nations in Rwanda has been authorized to use weapons to protect those in danger, yet it has not done so as it does not have the means at its disposal. We call on the Member States of the Security Council of the United Nations to guarantee protection for the survivors and to arrange for prosecution of those responsible for the genocide.

And for good measure, MSF added: "Mr. President of the Republic, Prime Minister, Honorable Ladies and Gentlemen, you have the power: stop the genocide!"[85] Meanwhile, a printed copy of the letter went out to all the group's donors requesting that they sign a petition in support. The appeal also "brought in significant donations from the public."[86]

Other NGOs also spoke to the media, met with French leaders, and criticized the international and French responses.[87] Yet an important distinction emerged in MSF's call for armed intervention. While MSF saw humanitarian aid as inadequate, others focused on it rather than military action. In *Libération* on June 15 a group of mostly humanitarian NGOs urged the public to "fight against the indifference of the states" and "arouse in France a great solidarity movement that will permit Rwanda to survive and prepare for the future."[88] Though the message differed from MSF's, it was a clear indictment of the world's governments, including in France.

After a few weeks, French media coverage also shifted noticeably. This was important because, when it comes to foreign policy, French officials tend to view the press as the most important indicator of public opinion. Compared to other major democracies, polling data and legislative opinion are not taken as seriously. Thus, when it comes to foreign crises like Rwanda, the amount and tenor of media coverage—especially by the major newspapers and TV outlets—can have considerable influence on leaders' perceptions of the pressures they face.[89]

In this case, the change was not so much a matter of volume as one of tone and content. Figure 4.1 shows a weekly count of articles that mention

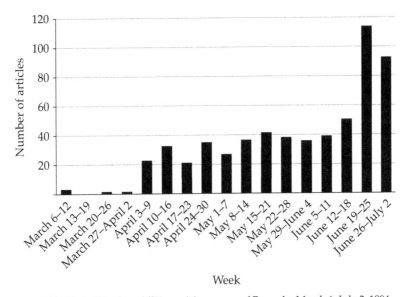

Figure 4.1. Weekly *Le Monde* and *l'Humanité* coverage of Rwanda, March 6–July 2, 1994

Note: Article counts are for full-text searches using "Rwanda" as the search term and conducted in the papers' archives at http://www.lemonde.fr/recherche and http://www.humanite.fr/search.

"Rwanda" in two national daily papers, *Le Monde* (France's "paper of record") and *l'Humanité*, between March 6 and July 2.[90] There is a notable jump in April from almost no prior mentions of Rwanda, followed by another modest increase from about mid-May to mid-June, and a large jump in late June as Turquoise began.

Yet while the total amount of coverage did not grow dramatically, beginning in late April and especially in May and June the emphasis changed in two key ways. First, the press started to explicitly acknowledge the genocide and to report more thoroughly on the nature of the violence and the identity of the victims and perpetrators. In this respect they often took their cues from NGOs. For instance, the wire service Agence France-Presse first used the term "genocide" on April 20 while quoting Human Rights Watch. Similarly, the first appearance of the term in *Le Monde* was on April 27, as used by an AICF administrator.[91] Among the major dailies, *Libération* and *l'Humanité* were most successful in presenting an abundance of timely and accurate information.[92] In general, moreover, the written press was ahead of the TV channels.[93]

This shift was significant because—like MSF's claim that "you can't stop genocide with doctors"—it focused attention on the limitations of the French and international responses. For instance, the Balladur Government was heavily critiqued for not condemning the massacres by the Hutu militia clearly and often enough.[94] In *Le Figaro* on May 19, Renaud Girard slammed Paris for launching a humanitarian approach "after six weeks of genocide against the Tutsi."[95] And in late May and June, reporters regularly invoked the UN's struggles to expand UNAMIR.

Second, many French papers began to write of their government's ties to the Hutu regime and thus of its "responsibility" or "culpability" in Rwanda's horror. While a few such references could be found in April this trend really took off in late May, drawing directly on MSF's advocacy efforts and in particular Bradol's May 16 TF1 interview.[96] According to MSF-France's communications director Jean-François Alesandrini, "In France it was Jean-Hervé's report that mobilized the rest of the media and perhaps public opinion too."[97] This was not just because of MSF's status in France but also because its argument was unique: "Instead of the usual response from a humanitarian organization, 'we go in with supplies, with doctors,' we showed that there was a different problem, a political problem, and faced with that, all the humanitarian organizations could do was put a sticking plaster on a wooden leg."[98]

Notably, in late May at least eight French print media outlets published critiques of this nature. For instance, on May 18 *Libération* charged the French government with organizing the escape of Agathe Habyarimana and her associates in April and then sustaining them in luxury in Paris while leaving the Tutsi employees of France's diplomatic mission to be massacred.[99] In *Le Monde* on May 20, Pierre Lainé scathingly denounced the UN's inefficacy and Mitterrand's military adventures in Rwanda, describing how French troops had helped keep the Habyarimana regime in power. Yet while such actions created "certain responsibilities . . . that [France] cannot escape without being accused of contempt and cowardice," he continued, the government had shamefully refused to rescue threatened civilians when it could have.[100] In *Ouest France* on May 24, Joseph Limagne charged that French leaders needed to tell the public "what logic, what friendships, what interests have at best blinded [France], and at worst made [it] complicit in what one can well call a crime against humanity."[101] Similar charges appeared in *Le Figaro* on May 19, *l'Humanité* on May 20, *La Croix* on May 21–23, the May 19 and May 27 editions of the weekly newsmagazine *Le Nouvel Observateur*, and the May 26–June 1 edition of the weekly *l'Humanité Dimanche*.[102] A flurry of comparable articles followed in early June.[103] Likewise, the TV channels—who "could not ignore what the print media revealed at column length"—also began to participate in these criticisms and to direct difficult questions at government officials.[104]

By mid-June, then, French leaders had faced a month of constant haranguing: they were not doing enough about a genocide that France itself had helped make possible. What is more, there was no sign of an impending reprieve: MSF was calling for immediate UN intervention, but it was abundantly clear to French officials that UNAMIR II would not be able to deploy any time soon. Meanwhile, the French public was losing patience with the constant reports of massacres. On June 10, the media reported a massacre of 170 Tutsi—mostly children—that a French priest, Father Blanchard, was protecting in Kigali. The next day, the evening TV programs returned to the killings. Father Blanchard, who called from Kigali, overwhelmed viewers and attracted strong TV ratings. Then, on June 14, Blanchard held a dramatic press conference in Paris that was covered by all the media. Recounting how the militia had killed forty children at his orphanage he concluded, "I prefer to believe in God than in men."[105] Under these societal pressures it is not hard to see how French-led intervention could seem like a reasonable response.

The pressure affected France's top politicians differently, but its timing a year before France's April 1995 presidential election was significant for everyone. As Léotard noted, the election "totally dominated national politics" at the time, with everyone having "eyes on the polls."[106] In general the French public was quite sensitive to humanitarian issues—as indicated, for instance, by the presence of a Minister for Humanitarian Action in the government.[107] Thus, on Rwanda the leading politicians felt compelled to demonstrate their "humanitarian credentials," which encouraged "an emerging competition to claim the moral high ground."[108]

Mitterrand and Juppé seemed to feel the pressure most acutely. For Mitterrand, the main issue was his legacy. Ill with cancer, he would not run for reelection and wanted to leave office on "a high moral note."[109] As a result, he was "very sensitive" to the NGO advocacy and media barrage, especially the charges about his responsibility for and indifference to the genocide.[110] Indeed, in late May MSF's Bradol and MSF-France president Philippe Biberson were invited to meet with Mitterrand's Africa advisers Bruno Delaye and Dominique Pin. As Bradol recalled, the advisers "tried very hard to convince [Bradol and Biberson] that they were in the right. . . . Delaye said, 'You must know that the president took your TV interview rather badly. It wasn't very bright of you. When you have problems like this it is better to see the president himself, to speak to him about it first.'"[111]

Later, both Mitterrand and his advisers would signal the issue's importance. For instance, when the former *Elysée* spokesman Jean Musitelli was asked what prompted the decision to intervene, he responded that it was "the emotion provoked in the population by the shock of the images" and "the rise of public opinion pressure as it took the full measure of the massacres that were going on in the country."[112] In August 1994 Mitterrand declared: "We could not see what was taking place in Rwanda, whose images were seen in every living room in Europe, and let it happen."[113]

Juppé also had reputational concerns to consider. On top of the conservatives' general incentives to show compassion in foreign policy, his own public image was under assault by a group of intellectuals known as the "List Sarajevo," who attacked him over France's "heartless" policy in the former Yugoslavia.[114] Significantly, it was May 16, the same day as Bradol's interview with TF1, that Juppé first used the word "genocide" in public. According to Lanotte, he was likely informed around this time that MSF was inquiring about evidence of ongoing French military cooperation with the FAR and of its imminent media campaign. It is thus quite likely that he used his declaration of genocide to demarcate French policy in Rwanda going forward from the policies of the past.[115] Then, in June, MSF's call for intervention and Father Blanchard's interviews had "the effect of an electronic shock" on Juppé.[116] In stark contrast to his statement of June 10, three days later he charged: "We cannot continue to permit such an abominable genocide."[117]

Still, there was more to Juppé's attitude than this. It was mainly in the foreign ministry that the moral concerns expressed by the media and NGOs drove pro-intervention attitudes among government officials who shared them. Juppé genuinely believed morality had a role to play in foreign policy and, like many in the diplomatic community, was troubled by the UN's delays.[118] As Lanotte notes, moreover, Juppé and his chief of staff Dominique de Villepin were broadly sympathetic to the charges of French culpability. For them, "The situation was all the more intolerable, and non-intervention even more untenable" because they "knew very well how much France . . . bore a part of the responsibility in the radicalization process that led to the genocide."[119]

Finally, despite their reluctance to intervene, even Balladur and Léotard felt the media and NGO pressure. For them, the result was a sense that they could not say no to military action once Mitterrand and Juppé proposed it. As one well-informed source noted, "The Prime Minister, confronted with a fait accompli, could not refuse a humanitarian intervention."[120] Moreover, like Mitterrand, Balladur publicly explained Turquoise in terms of societal concern, noting on June 29 that "the entire world and all of France were overwhelmed by the images that [they] saw, and it was apparent that the French government could not remain indifferent or immobile."[121]

THE OPERATIONAL ENVIRONMENT AND OTHER MATERIAL PRESSURES

For the French government there was also considerable material pressure rooted in very strong concern about the potential physical and political costs and risks of intervention. Not only was the operational environment difficult and unpredictable, but the risks it posed were amplified by political sensitivities related to the upcoming presidential election and recent French history in both Bosnia and Rwanda. Significantly, the officials most worried by these issues—the prime minister, defense minister, and military leaders—included those charged to design the force.

The operational environment for intervention in Rwanda—for France in particular—was challenging, but not overwhelmingly so. Certain aspects were fairly favorable, such as the nation's small size, in the bottom sixth of post-Cold War complex emergencies; total population of around 7 million, near the middle; and population density, among the world's highest.[122] On the other hand, geography posed notable challenges. Rwanda's land-locked location some 5,000 miles from France made it relatively inaccessible and meant that everything for the mission had to be brought in by air.[123] In addition, Rwanda ranks among the top complex emergencies in terms of the area covered by mountains. The result, as force commander Lafourcade relates, was windy roads and limited visibility that slowed the movement of the troops. To reach a hill 20 kilometers (12.5 miles) away could take two hours. This terrain also complicated the task of judging distances, and increased the risk of unexpectedly encountering hostile armed groups.[124]

Still, certainly the most concerning aspects of the operational environment were the various armed groups the French feared might try to oppose them. Most significant, the RPF was a disciplined fighting force that had

shown its strength against the FAR in 1993 and again throughout the genocide and was proficient at nighttime operations. The French estimated that
it had about 25,000 men in infantry battalions and 2 or 3 support battalions.[125] While this was by no means a large army and although it had no air
force, it represented a real threat because of its ground capabilities and stri-
dent opposition to French intervention. The RPF feared that France's true
intentions were to oppose them and to prop up the genocidal regime. When
Operation Turquoise was announced, the RPF president Alexis Kanyarengwe warned that "the French troops in Rwanda will be considered as an
enemy force and treated as such."[126]

Meanwhile, the French also worried about clashing with the FAR and the
Hutu militia, who they anticipated might use force to try to prevent Turquoise from accessing threatened Tutsi or even attack people already under
French protection.[127] The French estimated that the FAR had about 20,000
men in infantry, an armored battalion, an artillery battalion, a helicopter
squadron, and some 7,000 national police.[128] Altogether, the government
forces numbered about 40,000 between the FAR, the national police, and
the presidential guard. Except for the last of these, however, they had
largely been recruited during the civil war and were not very well trained
or effective. Similarly, the Interahamwe had an additional 15,000–30,000
men, most with no formal military training. Thus, there were some 55,000–
70,000 men on the extremist side.[129]

French concerns about the FAR and Interahamwe proved justified. As
has been widely reported, the extremists initially believed Turquoise was
there to help them and welcomed the French with open arms.[130] Yet relations between Turquoise and the FAR became tense within days as the latter realized their mistake.[131] Thereafter, the FAR and the militia could be
quite hostile and there were many small confrontations as the French
sought to secure the safe zone.[132]

Physically, then, the operational environment for French intervention
was of real concern to the opponents and planners of Operation Turquoise. According to the chief of the armed forces, Admiral Jacques
Lanxade, "Léotard and I were not favorable to an intervention, because
we felt that it would be very difficult to conduct and, also, very expensive.
Balladur was not hot either."[133] For his part, Balladur worried about
becoming "trapped much further than [he would] want and with incalcu-
lable risks, in a conflict that is likely to have repercussions throughout the
region." He continued: "At no price must we become bogged down alone
8,000 km from France, in an operation that would lead us to be targeted in
a civil war."[134]

Still, the operational environment could have been worse. Thus, it is
significant that three issues magnified these officials' disquiet and further
encouraged worries about limiting French casualties, minimizing clashes
with the RPF, and avoiding political embarrassment.[135] The first one again

related to the upcoming presidential election. As of June 1994, Balladur and Jacques Chirac were vying to become the conservative candidate. As Mitterrand adviser Bruno Delaye recalled, "we all understood that Balladur was in the presidential orbit and that he did not want to incur the least risk in taking responsibility for what he called an 'African adventure.'"[136] Indeed, Balladur saw little upside to intervening in Rwanda. In part, he disapproved of France's traditional close relations with Africa and with Mitterrand's conduct of Africa policy. But also, as Gérard Prunier put it, Balladur "felt that the whole Rwanda operation was directed against him. . . . To him and his men in the cabinet [it] was both dangerous (if it failed, he was bound to be blamed) and of very little profit (if it worked, the initiators, i.e. Mitterrand and Juppé who is a Chirac man, would get the credit)."[137] Meanwhile, Léotard was a Balladur supporter and so the Defense Ministry "felt that it was advancing through a political minefield and should be very prudent."[138]

The second issue was the specter of Bosnia, where French peacekeepers deployed with UNPROFOR had struggled to defend themselves against Bosnian Serb militias and snipers. This was of concern to both politicians and military leaders. The Rwandan genocide occurred at a time when French officials perceived the public as especially sensitive to casualties and attacks on their soldiers. As Lanotte notes, they had to account for "a public opinion that . . . would not have accepted a new 'Bosnian humiliation.'"[139] Further, the French general staff were "very marked by the traumatic experience of Sarajevo," where they had lacked the political and military means to respond to attacks, and were determined to avoid repeating that experience.[140]

The final concern was the prospect of political backlash if Operation Turquoise was not seen as a strictly humanitarian mission, a problem that directly reflected France's history in Rwanda. During the key week of June 16–22 while the Defense Ministry and military staff were planning the operation, there were new revelations about the delivery of French arms to the FAR during the genocide. Also, many NGOs and some in the press, especially the more liberal outlets, reacted negatively to the announcement of Turquoise. Echoing the RPF, they claimed that France should not lead a humanitarian intervention because it could not be trusted not to help the FAR. This critique was adopted by most of the NGOs that had so recently complained of France's abandonment of Rwanda, including MDM and AICF, and received broad coverage in the written press and on TV.[141] Indeed, among major NGOs only MSF-France supported the intervention, and even this was not clear until it announced on June 23 that while UN action would have been preferable, France could prove its good intentions through proper conduct.[142]

Ironically, then, societal concern about France's responsibility in the genocide put pressure on its leaders to act, but also led to loud criticism from many of the same actors when the government announced its plan to intervene. These critics seemed not to recognize the contradiction in lambasting the government for inaction and then objecting when it agreed to step in where the UN was clearly incapable. Yet they put French leaders in an impossible position and sharpened their concerns about how the force would be perceived. In particular, Balladur became fixated on avoiding any impression of behaving as a neocolonial power or supporting the Hutu government.[143] Nor were such concerns just limited to the politicians: top military officials also worried for the army's reputation. As Lafourcade explained to his second-in-command on arriving in Zaire, "our detractors were only waiting for one thing: to see us shoot at the predominantly Tutsi RPF and thus demonstrate our complacency vis-à-vis the perpetrators."[144]

PUTTING NORMATIVE AND MATERIAL PRESSURES TOGETHER

France's intervention in Rwanda reflected the conditions I would expect to promote ambitions-resources gaps and helped its leaders balance a delicate set of normative and material pressures. Consistent with my argument, the French public broadly supported Operation Turquoise despite—and without understanding—its flaws, and even its early critics soon largely quieted down. Meanwhile, French leaders used the rhetoric of organized hypocrisy to promote this outcome. The type of ambitions-resources gap Turquoise represented—the resources France deployed did not live up to their protection potential because of restrictions that effectively limited the force's ambitions—was also the only one realistically available by the middle of June.

For the first month or more of the genocide, the French government faced little if any political dilemma about how to respond thanks to the delay in serious media and NGO activism. In these circumstances I would not predict an intervention or ambitions-resources gap. By late May and into June, however, French leaders confronted a real quandary: how to respond to the growing societal concern over Rwanda without getting too many soldiers killed or conveying the wrong message about France's intentions. On one hand, the NGO and media pressures led Mitterrand and Juppé to worry about how the broader public would judge their past and current policies. On the other, Léotard, Balladur, and military leaders were anxious about costs and risks. These circumstances were ripe for an ambitions-resources gap. As we have seen, the French government's first preference was for UN intervention under UNAMIR II. Yet as the passing weeks made abundantly clear, France could not ensure a timely UN deployment. Thus, the intensity of both the killing in Rwanda and the public criticism at home left French intervention as the only viable military option. The solution, Operation

Turquoise, became, as African Rights put it, "a prime example of gesture politics."[145] By imposing the limits they did, French leaders reached a classic compromise between the pressures to act and to control the consequences of doing so.

First, by imposing numerous conditions on Operation Turquoise, its reluctant designers were able to reduce the political and military risks they were most concerned about. Indeed, not a single French soldier was killed in confrontation with the RPF, FAR, or militia.[146] To achieve this, after the June 15 decision to intervene, Balladur, Léotard, and their supporters spent the next week working "to minimize the scope and framework of Operation Turquoise" in order to limit conflict with the RPF and the appearance of anything other than purely humanitarian motives.[147] As Prunier notes, "Edouard Balladur had been pushed into doing something he did not particularly want to do, and he was going to do it as quickly and cheaply as possible."[148]

In the end, virtually every aspect of Operation Turquoise reflected these efforts, including many that were unrelated to the ambitions-resources gap. For instance, Balladur insisted on UN authorization, participation by other states, and a short few weeks' timeframe for the mission.[149] To promote transparency, Léotard—supported by Lafourcade—insisted that the media could accompany the troops, who would assist them with transportation and logistics. Léotard also reached out to Prunier, an expert on Uganda and the RPF. On Prunier's advice he scrapped the army's plans to enter Rwanda in the northwest, the Hutu hardliners' base where risks of confrontation with the RPF and of embarrassing threats to the mission's image seemed especially high. Also on Prunier's advice, the French sought to reduce RPF hostility by inviting its representatives for consultations in Paris and then negotiating the parameters of the SHZ with them in early July.[150]

Yet the key decisions that led to the ambitions-resources gap were also about risk-management. First, Balladur's insistence on avoiding durable occupation or penetration of Rwanda drove the initial decision to base the force in Zaire. As Mitterrand's chief military adviser Christian Quesnot recalled, "Balladur, Léotard and Lanxade did not want to go into Rwanda. This is why we played the game of an operation conducted from Zaire but prolonged by progressive incursions into Rwanda, loudly proclaiming that it concerned a strictly humanitarian operation."[151] Second, Balladur required that the force would remain neutral (not interpose itself) between the warring parties. This, as we have seen, discouraged efforts to target, disarm, and arrest the *génocidaires*.[152] On the last issue, Juppé later noted, "The government planned to confine itself to a limited operation. The arrest of the assassins would have involved many risks of confrontation with the FAR and militias. Such an operation would have required military means to deal with these risks. This the government did not want."[153] As Lanotte concludes, the French seemed intent on avoiding the problems the United States had faced in Somalia, "where the operations to search for arms caches and efforts to arrest General Aidid—whose head had a price on it—had ended in October 1993 with the death of 18 Marines."[154]

Last but not least, for France's military staff—including the top planner for Operation Turquoise, General Mercier—the decision to prioritize firepower that was at odds with the force's commitment to neutrality reflected the same concerns. Drawing on the lessons of Bosnia, the goal was to reduce the risk of clashes by ensuring the capacity to respond to any attacks, even while this was only seen as contingency planning.[155] And indeed, in the end there were only a few confrontations with the RPF, which Turquoise's offensive capabilities helped prevent from escalating. For instance, in mid-July when the RPF launched shells near the French headquarters in Goma, General Lafourcade received permission to conduct a low-altitude aerial survey of the RPF positions. After this, the bombardments stopped immediately.[156]

Still, despite its limitations, Operation Turquoise also worked as a response to the normative pressures on the French government. For Juppé and the diplomatic community, satisfying their own moral imperative to act was a real consideration.[157] In this sense the mission had important symbolic value. Mainly, though, intervening in Rwanda offered a chance for the politicians to manage their political images. Mitterrand hoped it would allow him to leave office on a high note and complete his term as president with a "gesture of political spectacle" that would overshadow "the dramatic errors of his Rwanda policy."[158] Meanwhile, Juppé wanted to silence the critics who had accused him of heartlessness over Yugoslavia and to deny the Socialists the advantage of claiming a "monopoly of the heart" before the upcoming election.[159]

Fortunately for them, once Turquoise was underway, the early NGO and press criticism quickly died down. Media coverage was generally good, as the force seemed to operate smoothly and the government worked hard to ensure transparency. Yet this also reflected a new attitude by humanitarian groups, who depended on donations to fund their operations and found themselves in a difficult position when it became clear that the French public did not understand their suspicion of Operation Turquoise. In this sense, they found that they had meaningful material incentives to acquiesce in the operation, and most soon moderated their tone or began working in the SHZ.[160] In terms of the ambitions-resources gap, MSF-France did criticize Turquoise for not going after the killers more aggressively, but this was accompanied by strong overall support for the mission.[161] Finally, there was also confusion created by the July refugee crisis in Zaire. While the media presence in Rwanda was limited before Turquoise, journalists and TV stations now flocked to Goma. The refugees' plight thus received extensive coverage and the public image of the genocide became confused with that of the camps and the cholera epidemic. While talk of French responsibility declined, the French troops in Zaire were now "on every television screen, shown as trying to alleviate the terrible suffering in Goma."[162] As Pierre Favier and Michel Martin-Roland point out, "No one criticized the French intervention anymore. Public opinion and the international media now worried about the consequences of a potential premature withdrawal of the French soldiers, whose devotion was unanimously welcomed."[163] Indeed, as Turquoise's departure approached, the UN and United States began calling for the French to stay.[164]

On top of all this, as I would expect, French officials used the language of organized hypocrisy to promote Operation Turquoise, describing it as a humanitarian triumph while overlooking what it did not accomplish due to its late arrival and ambitions-resources gap. For instance, on July 14 Mitterrand claimed not only that France had saved tens of thousands of lives, but also that with respect to the goal of saving the maximum number of Tutsi Turquoise had done very well.[165] Moreover, once the mission was underway Balladur and Léotard joined the chorus promoting it and claiming political credit. Indeed, perhaps recognizing that their earlier hesitation was "not ideal" for Balladur's presidential aspirations, their claims were among the most grandiose of all.[166] Thus, on July 11, after asserting that France had intervened "without delay," Balladur declared that Turquoise's "humanitarian goal has been largely attained: almost a million refugees find themselves at present assembled under the protection of the French and Senegalese forces in a zone where, in essence, the massacres have been stopped and the refugees are safe."[167] On July 22 in *Libération*, Léotard wrote: "We have stopped the violence, cared for the victims and prepared the way for those who deserve the beautiful name of humanitarians."[168]

In the end, Turquoise was a public relations coup.[169] The primary audience—the French public who Mitterrand and Juppé feared would judge them harshly if media and NGO criticism continued—largely accepted their claims of success and forgot about France's problematic earlier policies. As Prunier put it, in the face of the media images of Goma and the politicians' promotional efforts "the mechanics of Turquoise on the ground were overlooked."[170] Similarly, according to *Libération*'s Africa editor Stephen Smith, "The broad public opinion is that France was the only nation to care about human suffering. They did something and then got out, but by that time everyone wanted them to stay. Most people would say it was a success."[171] Consistent with these assessments, both Mitterrand and Juppé saw their approval numbers go up, but ironically Balladur's climbed most of all, from 52% in July to 60% in the September edition of the *Baromètre TNS Sofres* poll.[172]

ALTERNATIVE EXPLANATIONS

Despite the mostly positive reception it earned at the time, Operation Turquoise has been the subject of more suspicion and conspiracy theories than any other peace operation I am aware of. The most common claim, as noted earlier, is that its true purpose was to save France's former Hutu allies from defeat and prevent the RPF from taking power. Some journalists and the post-genocide Rwandan government have even suggested that France and its soldiers were complicit in the genocide.[173] If true, such charges—and several similar ones—would support the idea that ambitions-resources gaps occur because leaders use humanitarian language to cover their true, strategic motives for intervention. On close inspection, however, there is little evidence to support this claim. Critically, while Mitterrand and, even more so, some of his advisers and military personnel were partly inspired by considerations of France's position in Africa, these issues were not significant for Balladur, Juppé, or Léotard and had virtually no influence on how Turquoise was designed. Finally, this case also does not appear to support the notion that great power democracies create ambitions-resources gaps unknowingly.

It would be impossible to address here all the arguments critics have employed to suggest that Operation Turquoise was intended to help the *génocidaires*. Indeed, it is fair to say that nearly every angle of French policy on Rwanda both before and during the mission—and even before the genocide—has been used to question France's motives. Thus, I will focus on only a limited number of the most relevant issues that arose during Turquoise itself.[174] Before this, any French actions to support the Habyarimana regime do not preclude a change in attitude by June 1994. What is more, the decision-makers in charge of Turquoise were not always those responsible for earlier policies that have aroused suspicion.[175]

We have already seen considerable evidence against the hypothesis that Operation Turquoise was intended to support the FAR and undermine the RPF. Indeed, this would essentially contradict my claim that the French sought to minimize political and military risks, especially of confrontation with the RPF. Operating at first entirely from Zaire and then leaving half the force there, declaring neutrality between the RPF and FAR, committing to a short time-frame, inviting the media to accompany the troops, seeking other countries' participation, and successfully avoiding more than a few clashes with the RPF: all these aspects of the mission tend to refute the notion that the French sought to alter the course of the war. What is more, several careful scholarly assessments have reached the same conclusion. In their major study of the Mitterrand presidency, Favier and Martin-Roland could not be clearer:

> There is no trace in support of this view in the papers on Rwanda from the Presidency of the Republic. The authors were able to view all the reports

classified as "Confidential Defense" from the Cabinet meetings at the Ely-sée, the notes of the Chief of the Armed Forces [Lanxade], and those of the Africa adviser and the chief of the president's military staff [Quesnot] informing François Mitterrand on the day to day of the preparation of Oper-ation Turquoise and its development. There is nothing, even in the form of allusions, to establish that Turquoise had from the beginning a political-military objective related to France's past support of the Hutu camp embod-ied by the late President Habyarimana. At no moment, in the innumerable exchanges of view between the responsible French officials revealed in these secret documents, appears the least doubt about the inevitability of the RPF military victory or the idea that France could oppose it. Concerning the fate of the former Hutu leaders, it is never mentioned.[176]

Similarly, according to Lanotte, "it is undeniable that the many imputed motives regarding the French troops' lack of impartiality or will to steal the victory of the RPF are not verified by the facts."[177] Still, given the persis-tence of the accusations, it is worth addressing several directly.

One major source of suspicion involves the equipment and troops selected for Turquoise. In particular, the volume of firepower and the use of special forces inspired speculation that such combat-oriented resources must be intended for offensive action against the RPF. Yet as we have seen, these decisions reflected the French authorities' emphasis on deter-rence and desire to deploy as quickly as possible after Resolution 929. Similarly, critics have charged that by bringing troops who had been to Rwanda before and would likely see the FAR as friends, the French were aiming to assist the Hutu extremists. Yet according to Lafourcade, these units were selected "to take advantage of their knowledge of local atti-tudes and mentalities" and while it was understood that some might be tempted to assist their former comrades, he made it very clear that this was not their role.[178] In addition, in deciding who would go to Rwanda General Mercier explicitly sought to weed out hawkish officers who might wish to help their old allies or fight the RPF.[179] Then, after a July 3 clash revealed that some soldiers still seemed to be "spoiling for a fight with the RPF," some 400 troops were removed from the force to avoid a threat to the mission.[180]

Critics have also latched onto the surprise of some French troops when they arrived in Rwanda to discover that the genocide's victims were mainly Tutsi rather than Hutu, and that they would not be going to Kigali to fight the RPF. In the skeptics' view, this surprise suggests that the soldiers were given false information by superiors who wanted to support the interim government and FAR.[181] While this is possible, it is also possible that the troops who had been to Rwanda before arrived with preconceived expecta-tions based on their past experiences. Yet even if some troops *were* fed false information, this does not necessarily reflect the motives of those who initiated and designed Operation Turquoise. To be sure, there were those in the French defense establishment who did want to forestall an RPF victory and who may have conveyed this to the troops. Notably, Mitterrand and his chief military adviser, General Quesnot, originally favored a more offensive operation throughout western Rwanda and a French presence in Kigali. It appears Quesnot believed there were moderates in the FAR and interim government who could still be supported against the RPF, a view Mitterrand may have shared.[182]

Yet as we have seen, decision-making was not solely up to Mitterrand or his personal military staff. Under the Balladur government's influence, as a former member of the Defense Ministry's crisis cell explains, "The scenario chosen was that of letting go: dropping the interim government and the Rwandan army, too compromised in the genocide; evacuating our people still present on the government side; and contenting ourselves with leading a humanitarian operation."[183] Ultimately, those with other ideas lost the debate about what the force would do and where it would go, as even one of its most vociferous critics admits.[184] Thus, even if Mitterrand did want to assist the FAR and interim government—which seems unlikely since in June he called the latter a "bunch of assassins"—this did not inform the design of Turquoise.[185]

A final major charge against Turquoise contends that the French established the safe zone to shield the interim government and FAR from the RPF by helping them escape the country. By this logic, Turquoise did not aim to deny the RPF its victory outright, but hoped to help the FAR and Hutu power structure live to fight another day. Its proponents focus on the fact that the RPF was excluded from the SHZ, that the French encouraged the RPF to declare a ceasefire before achieving complete military victory, that they did not thoroughly disarm the FAR and militia in the zone or arrest known *génocidaires*, and that at least some of these people transited through the safe zone as they left the country.

In reality, two primary goals explain these French decisions on the safe zone. The first was the desire to avoid confrontation with the RPF, FAR, and militia. As we have already seen, Turquoise's limited efforts at disarmament and arrest mainly reflected the French desire not to provoke excessive hostility from the *génocidaires*.[186] Likewise, the decision to create a safe area that excluded the RPF arose in part out of similar worries. The first days of July saw several clashes between the RPF and Turquoise troops, and the French authorities worried that if they did not take preventive action such incidents would become more frequent as the RPF kept advancing into the southwest where the French troops were operating.[187]

The second motive was to minimize further civilian suffering by creating a space where the uprooted population could receive humanitarian assistance in an environment free of ongoing combat. In this respect the

French authorities worried not only about the RPF but also that the safe zone could become a sanctuary and rear base for the FAR and interim government. Thus, on July 7 they issued orders to end all contact with the interim government and ban its representatives from the SHZ. While some did still enter the area, once informed they were unwelcome they headed south to Bukavu in Zaire. In the most publicized incident, there was a delay of one day in order for the Zairean authorities to prepare to receive the Rwandan parties, which led to charges that the French were "exfiltrating" the *génocidaires*.[188] Yet not only is there no solid evidence to support this as the French government's intent, it is also unlikely that the safe zone materially facilitated the escape of the genocidal authorities. As Lanotte points out,

> While it is true that the arrival of more than a million Rwandan refugees destabilized eastern Zaire, it is totally illusory to think that without the French intervention there would have been no withdrawal of the genocidal forces to Zaire. Neither the militia nor the Rwandan army nor even the members of the interim government needed Operation Turquoise to take refuge in Zaire. They withdrew in a more or less orderly way everywhere, even where the French were not present.[189]

Indeed, as we have seen, in April several hundred thousand Hutu had already fled to Tanzania without assistance, and in July the major exodus to Goma, Zaire, went through northwest Rwanda where the French were not present. Most of the FAR never even passed through the SHZ.[190]

Still, the French were worried about the RPF, for two reasons. First, they feared that under their noses it would target the Hutu population.[191] Although critics have accused them of insincerity on this, their worries were not necessarily far-fetched. The RPF had already killed thousands of Hutu between April and June, and subsequently committed numerous serious abuses, including contributing to the deaths of several thousand Hutu at the Kibeho IDP camp in April 1995.[192] Second, the French feared that the RPF's advance into western Rwanda would prompt a mass Hutu exodus and hoped that by providing a space where uprooted Hutu could congregate without fear of the RPF, they could prevent this. These concerns thus further motivated excluding the RPF from the safe zone, and also explain why the French encouraged it to agree to a ceasefire. While an earlier ceasefire would have prevented the RPF from stopping the genocide, by July this was no longer a top concern. Indeed, the UN agreed and joined France in urging the RPF to accept a ceasefire rather than push on to take the entire country.[193]

Still, preventing RPF victory is not the only strategic motive attributed to Operation Turquoise. Another is that it aimed to help maintain French influence in Africa. Some in the Elysée wanted to reassure friendly and allied states that France could still act effectively on the continent, and would uphold its security commitments. Worried about destabilization and the precedent of letting the RPF take power in Rwanda, several regional leaders wanted France to once again halt its advance.[194] Mitterrand also likely hoped either to preempt an intervention by "Anglo-Saxon" South Africa or to curry favor with its new president, Nelson Mandela.[195]

Yet in judging the significance of these objectives it is again vital to consider the role of Balladur, Juppé, and Léotard. Not one of these conservative politicians shared the president's commitment to a special role for France in Africa, and they had come to power intent on reducing the president's control over Africa policy. As Prunier has noted, Balladur "dreamed of 'multilateralising' France's relations with Africa, which in normal language means weakening them and making them less of a family melodrama."[196] For none of these men was France's place in Africa a reason to intervene in Rwanda. Indeed, rather than showing France's will to intervene against threats to its partner countries, if anything the many limits they imposed on Turquoise showed the opposite. Thus, while these concerns may have mattered to Mitterrand and some of his associates, at best they played a marginal role in the decision to launch Operation Turquoise and none at all in the design decisions that led to its ambitions-resources gap.

Finally, what of the chance that French authorities created Operation Turquoise with an ambitions-resources gap unintentionally and unknowingly? It is abundantly clear in General Lafourcade's operational orders that whatever some troops may have initially thought, the officials in charge of the mission understood the nature of the violence and the primary need to halt the killings of the Tutsi population. For instance, the first paragraph notes that the civil war in Rwanda had led to "a genocide perpetrated by certain Rwandan military units and by Hutu militias against the Tutsi minority." Meanwhile, the force's mission is described as "to end the massacres wherever possible."[197]

Perhaps, then, French political and military leaders did not realize that the limits they imposed on Turquoise would restrict the civilian protection it could provide. Yet we have already seen clear evidence to contradict this as well. Generals Lafourcade and Quesnot were very clear that the initial decision to operate from Zaire made it harder to access and protect civilians in need of rescue. Likewise, the French authorities understood that a haphazard approach to arrest and disarmament would limit military risks, and defended it on these grounds; at no time did they claim this would save Rwandan lives.

This is not to suggest that these leaders foresaw every possible way the limitations they placed on the force could play out. Notably, I have seen no hard evidence on whether they understood the implications of combining neutrality with an emphasis on firepower rather than the materiel for a rescue-oriented mission. Given Balladur and Léotard's obsession with risk management, it seems unlikely that they would have acted differently even if they clearly understood this tradeoff. If this is correct, then even an incomplete understanding of the effects of the constraints they imposed still would not account for the ambitions-resources gap. More broadly, though, the idea that politicians must predict every potential consequence of an ambitions-resources gap is not the proper standard for judging whether support for such a gap is intentional. Certainly, no one in the French political or military hierarchy decided to bring an insufficient number of trucks with the intention of leaving stranded Tutsi to die. But on the key question of whether they understood that they were imposing constraints on the force that could limit its humanitarian potential, there is no doubt.

The politics of Operation Turquoise support all four of my hypotheses about ambitions-resources gaps. First, by examining how French leaders saw the pressures they faced to address the violence in Rwanda and to control associated physical and political risks this case confirms the findings from chapter 3 about the circumstances that encourage these gaps (hypothesis 1). Extensive, critical media coverage and NGO activism combined with a challenging operational environment, France's fraught histories in Rwanda and Bosnia, and a presidential election to ensure that perceived normative and material pressures were both intense. The compromise that Operation Turquoise represented was not only a bargain between the positions of different players in the executive, but also a way to balance society's clear sympathy with the victims of the genocide against its likely anger at a too-costly intervention.

This chapter has also provided vital evidence to support the causal mechanisms that explain how leaders benefit politically from ambitions-resources gaps. Indeed, all four of the reasons laid out in hypothesis 2 to explain why concerned citizens, activists, and officials might accept such policies played a role in this case. The French public, the key audience for Turquoise, was broadly unaware of the major limits on its effectiveness. MSF, which *was* aware, nonetheless supported the force as the best of the apparent alternatives. Other humanitarian NGOs, meanwhile, faced material incentives to acquiesce once it became clear that the French public did not understand their reservations about Turquoise. And finally, the intervention had symbolic and expressive value for diplomatic officials—notably Juppé—who felt morally compelled to respond to the suffering in Rwanda. Key French officials' use of the rhetoric of organized hypocrisy (hypothesis 3) also suggests that they understood these dynamics and actively sought to use them to their advantage.

Finally, as we will see in the next chapter, in all these respects the politics of Operation Turquoise resemble those behind U.S. support for AMIS and UNAMID in Darfur. Yet in one key respect these cases are different.

Consistent with hypothesis 6, the French decision to intervene directly in Rwanda but to limit the ambitions of their mission reflected the slow pace of action at the UN and the lack of any other option for a speedy military response. In contrast, American policymakers were able to avoid a choice between leaving Darfur with no protection force at all and committing U.S. troops by actively cultivating the chance to support first the African Union and then a UN mission.

The United States in Darfur

> The Security Council and the international community were very happy
> to say African peacekeepers could go in, when everybody knew they
> did not have the capacity or resources.
>> —Kofi Annan, UN Secretary General, *Fighting for Darfur*

Civil war and mass killing in Darfur, Sudan, attracted perhaps more global
attention than any conflict of the 2000s aside from Iraq and Afghanistan.
Nowhere was this attention greater than in the United States, where Darfur
became an issue in two presidential elections and a recurring topic in Congress. This chapter analyzes the George W. Bush administration's Darfur
policy between 2003 and the end of 2007. Though serious violence continues and peacekeepers remain as of 2017, these five years cover the major
peacekeeping and civilian protection debates.

In terms of U.S. policy I divide this period into three phases. For roughly
the first year, from February 2003 through March 2004, the American
response was limited to providing humanitarian aid while trying not to
draw attention to the Sudanese government's targeting of Darfuri civilians.
Later, from spring 2004 through the end of 2005, the administration focused
on pushing for and supporting the African Union Mission in Sudan (AMIS).
But despite aid from the United States and other wealthy nations, AMIS
simply could not deliver the level of civilian protection it was asked to provide. Finally, a third phase began in early 2006 with an extended diplomatic
push to replace AMIS with a UN mission. Yet the hybrid UN-AU force
known as UNAMID that took over on December 31, 2007, faced nearly the
same limitations as AMIS and did little if any better at protecting civilians
from an increasingly anarchic security environment.

This is a compelling case in which to assess this book's central claims about
ambitions-resources gaps. Initially the Bush administration treated Darfur as
a purely humanitarian problem and then later facilitated these gaps in two
separate and consecutive peace operations. This policy evolution offers a

chance to examine how my argument performs in a single, extended complex emergency and to show that it can help explain not just variation in discrete events, but also how leaders respond to temporal changes in the political demands they face. What is more, while the other great power democracies pursued similar policies toward peace operations in Darfur during these years—both the United Kingdom and France also supported AMIS and then UNAMID without sending their own troops—U.S. diplomacy, and, later, civil society activism, were especially critical to bringing these missions about.[1]

The evidence adheres closely to my expectations about both when leaders will help create ambitions-resources gaps and how they can gain from doing so. Conditions ripe for these policies began to develop in the spring of 2004 as key elements of the Bush administration came to see existing policy as inadequate and as emerging civil society interest in Darfur blossomed into a powerful advocacy movement. These developments led to stark tension between normative and material pressures on the administration: not only was the operational environment for intervention quite unfavorable, but concerns about the costs and risks of U.S. military action were magnified by the wars in Iraq and Afghanistan. Meanwhile, several other policy priorities reinforced opposition to confronting the Sudanese national government in Khartoum from within the administration. This basic situation persisted through 2007, inspiring support first for AMIS and then—starting in early 2006—the drive to deploy a UN force. As I would anticipate, these policies allowed the Bush administration to avoid the costs of more robust action while still responding to pressure from concerned citizens and officials, whose backing for them strongly supports the logic laid out in chapter 2. Within civil society and government, those most concerned about Darfur often failed to grasp the AU's key weaknesses or UN peacekeeping realities, saw more robust military action as impracticable, had organizational interests in accepting what action they could get, or were focused on the act of expressing their outrage. Meanwhile, Bush administration officials used the language of organized hypocrisy to promote their successive policy approaches.

This chapter marshals evidence from a wide variety of sources. In addition to the excellent secondary literature, I rely on various official documents and statements from the U.S. government and African Union, media reports, memoirs, and advocacy materials. For an additional perspective I also conducted select interviews with well-placed Darfur activists. The first section reviews the complex emergency and civilians' core protection needs, discussing major changes as the war progressed. Next I lay out the three phases of U.S. policy. Third, I examine how these policies fit with the evidence on societal and bureaucratic pressure for civilian protection, the operational environment, and other sources of official opposition to direct U.S. military action. Finally I assess the possibilities that U.S. officials did not understand the limitations of supporting AMIS and UNAMID or that doing so was a fig leaf to cover for other U.S. interests.

The Complex Emergency

The origins of the war in Darfur have been laid out in detail elsewhere.[2] Briefly, repeated droughts beginning in the 1970s contributed to the gradual breakdown of traditional land-sharing mechanisms between the region's pastoralist groups—variously referred to as blacks, Africans, or non-Arabs—and its nomadic, livestock-herding groups, typically identified as Arabs. Violence erupted in the 1990s as the nomads began to attack the farming communities in pursuit of greater access to water and grazing land for their animals. Darfur's African communities, who had long been denied a fair share of political power and national resources, lacked government support in dealing with these new threats. Frustrated, but also encouraged that Sudan's leadership appeared poised to accept a power-sharing deal to end its long-running civil war with the similarly marginalized South Sudanese, they launched an insurgency in early 2003.

Initially there were two rebel groups, the Sudan Liberation Movement/ Army (or SLM/A) and the Justice and Equality Movement (or JEM). While the former garnered support among all the country's major ethnic groups, the latter had links with its political Islamist movement. In part, these groups hoped to have their own grievances addressed as part of the north-south peace negotiations that had been taking place in Naivasha, Kenya, since 2002. In addition, JEM was most likely influenced by Hassan al-Turabi, a hard-line Islamist and former head of the ruling National Congress Party with dreams of unseating the national government.[3] Thus, President Omar al-Bashir saw the Darfur rebels as a threat to both the ongoing peace process and his own hold on power, and resolved to end the revolt as soon as possible.

The first stage of the war that followed was dominated by a government-led counterinsurgency campaign involving large-scale attacks against civilians in their villages and homes. While clashes between the Darfur rebels and government forces began in earnest in February of 2003, counterinsurgency operations escalated that summer and reached their height between July of 2003 and the spring of 2004. In the words of former UN peacekeeping chief Jean-Marie Guéhenno, this was "the worst time for Darfur."[4]

To conduct its counterinsurgency campaign, the national government in Khartoum exploited the existing ethnic tensions and the nomadic communities' desire for land by employing Arab militias—known as Janjaweed—to carry out most of the attacks, typically in coordination with the government's air forces. The tactics they employed are well known. Entire villages were destroyed with the intent of preventing the inhabitants from ever returning, both through the physical destruction of the means of survival—such as the poisoning of wells and destruction of homes and belongings—and through traumatizing violence, including the killing of men and boys and the widespread rape of women and girls. During this time Bashir's government also largely refused aid organizations access to the people displaced by these attacks. Although it did begin to authorize some visas for relief workers in 2004, restrictions often prevented them from entering Darfur and strict limits on what could be imported seriously hindered their work.[5]

The disruption to civilian life was extensive. Already by mid-September of 2003, government and Janjaweed counterinsurgency operations had displaced nearly 500,000 people.[6] Over the next year, as fewer and fewer villages were left intact, more and more people became internally displaced within Darfur or fled to neighboring Chad. By August 2004, the UN estimated that some 1.8 million war-affected people were in need of international assistance.[7]

Most mortality estimates that cover this intense counterinsurgency period extend into 2005. Deaths due to war-related violence and disease through early 2005 may have been as low as 63,000 or as high as 380,000.[8] Analyzing some of these estimates, Gérard Prunier concludes that about 280,000–310,000 civilian casualties for the first two years is probably most accurate.[9] A survey-based mortality analysis published in 2010 offers some more fine-grained insight, estimating that there were 43,289–45,137 conflict-attributable civilian deaths from September 2003 to March 2004 and another 70,451–76,539 from April to December 2004.[10]

Khartoum's mass targeting of civilians obviously created severe security needs for the civilian population. These revolved primarily around an end to the attacks against villages, and, secondarily, access to humanitarian relief. Critically, halting the counterinsurgency campaign before the spring of 2004—whether through diplomacy directed at Khartoum or through military intervention—would have prevented much of the eventual death and displacement and obviated the even more difficult job of trying to reverse the mass displacement later on.

Instead, with much of what Khartoum sought to achieve already accomplished by the late spring of 2004, the conflict began to change in two key ways. First, government-sponsored attacks on villages gradually gave way to new forms of violence. There were more direct clashes between the Sudanese army, the Arab militias, and rebel groups; there was an increase in intra-group conflict; and there was growing banditry.[11] Thus, the situation on the ground became more complex, if somewhat less severe. Although insecurity was rampant, the reduction in attacks on villages led to many fewer violent deaths.[12] By 2005, moreover, these were mostly caused by intra-group fighting among rebels and Arab militias.[13]

The second trend was the growth in the conflict-affected population and their increasing concentration in dangerous and unhealthy IDP camps. By the second half of 2004 Khartoum was more accommodating of international relief organizations. This improved access to remote areas and allowed the international humanitarian community to collect new information about the war-affected population. They quickly found far more internally displaced and conflict-affected people than had previously been recorded.[14] Largely as a result, estimates of the war-affected population doubled between April and December.[15] By February of 2005, the UN estimated that there were 2.5 million in need of international assistance.[16]

The IDP camps in which many of these people took refuge were profoundly hazardous places. The camps became frequent targets of attack for Janjaweed militia, with civilians who ventured outside at high risk of being raped or killed. In addition, conditions were often overcrowded and squalid, and residents became totally dependent on humanitarian assistance for survival. By 2005, hunger and disease associated with disruptions in international relief and unsanitary conditions in IDP camps had become the primary causes of death.[17]

These changes in the war created a catch-22 for the growing displaced population: it was neither safe to stay in the IDP camps, nor was it safe to leave. To overcome these combined problems, it was too late to focus just on Khartoum's large-scale attacks on villages. An end to the war that would allow people to leave the camps and begin rebuilding their lives would ultimately require a political settlement acceptable to all the major parties—Khartoum, the rebels, and Darfur's Arab community. This would also improve the odds of survival for those who had been displaced but remained outside the camps. Yet given the complex political tensions and long-standing grievances behind the war, such a settlement would take time to negotiate. In the meantime, civilians and relief workers remained extremely vulnerable. A peace operation with the capacity to protect IDPs and aid workers could make survival in the IDP camps more likely, and life more bearable, until a peace deal could be struck.

As discussed below, the Darfur Peace Agreement (DPA) was signed on May 6, 2006. The six months beforehand saw intensified fighting as all sides jockeyed for political advantage in the ongoing peace negotiations. Rival SLA factions fought each other in pursuit of international recognition. Khartoum invited Chadian rebels into Sudan, supporting their efforts to oust the Chadian government in hopes of ending its support for the Darfur rebels.[18] Attacks against aid operations and AMIS by rebels, Arab militias, and government agents increased.

Unfortunately, circumstances failed to improve with the deal in place. The DPA lacked both the support of key rebel leaders and the involvement of the Arab community, and in its wake the war became increasingly complex and violent. The rebel movement fragmented further, with new groups vying for resources and attacking relief operations to obtain loot and, to a lesser extent, to intimidate distrusted foreigners. Meanwhile, Khartoum progressively lost control of the Arab militias that had helped it prosecute its counterinsurgency campaign.[19]

Predictably, these trends led to reduced services and relief for Darfur's displaced. Some areas were completely cut off, while aid agencies curtailed operations in others. By August 2006, humanitarian access was at its lowest point since 2004.[20] Meanwhile, the displaced population grew rapidly—by 40% from July 2006 to September 2007—and this period saw the most conflict-related (but not violent) deaths of the entire war, with up to 98,187 civilian fatalities.[21]

The U.S. Response

FEBRUARY 2003–MARCH 2004

For some 14 months, the Bush administration treated Darfur as a humanitarian problem rather than a security issue. To their credit, in the summer of 2003 Andrew Natsios and Roger Winter, senior officials in the U.S. Agency for International Development (USAID), began a campaign to improve aid groups' access to the conflict-affected population, and committed $40 million of food aid that fall. They helped convince Khartoum to lift restrictions on aid workers and bring relief to the region, including $300 million worth of aid from the United States by the summer of 2004 and nearly $1 billion by 2006. Their efforts most likely saved tens of thousands of lives.[22]

Still, humanitarian relief did nothing to stop the attacks against civilians or the growth of the affected population. When it came to the violence itself, the U.S. government's response during this period can best be described as willful evasion of the issue. Indeed, the Bush administration took a series of actions that aimed to avoid bringing attention to the attacks against civilians in Darfur or pushing Khartoum to end them. On his arrival in Sudan in the fall of 2003, for example, the State Department's new chargé d'affaires Gerard Galluci received instructions to focus exclusively on two goals: improving counterterrorism cooperation with the Sudanese government and completing the ongoing peace negotiations to end the civil war between northern and southern Sudan, which the Bush administration had been facilitating since 2002.[23] Meanwhile, U.S. officials even went so far as to pressure aid workers arriving in Darfur not to talk about what they saw.[24] Finally, from December 2003 to March 2004, the United States (along with the United Kingdom) repeatedly resisted entries by Jan Egeland, head of the UN's Office for the Coordination of Humanitarian Affairs, to have Darfur placed on the Security Council agenda.[25]

The spring of 2004 saw the beginning of a significant transformation in U.S. policy on Darfur. In March, senior State Department officials admitted for the first time that humanitarian assistance alone would not suffice as a response and authorized their subordinates to report accurately about the violence.[26] Thereafter, the United States took various actions to save lives, end the war, and pursue justice against the perpetrators of atrocities. Over the spring and summer verbal pressure on Khartoum from Congress and top administration officials escalated dramatically, culminating in September in statements from Secretary of State Colin Powell and President Bush that its actions in Darfur constituted genocide.[27] In the summer the United States also began providing diplomatic support for negotiations in Abuja, Nigeria, for a permanent peace in the region. These talks saw little progress through 2005, however, and the administration has been criticized for not devoting the energy or resources needed for a real chance at brokering a sustainable agreement.[28] In addition, notable initiatives pursued through the UN in 2004–5 included pushing for an International Commission of Inquiry to investigate abuses, helping impose a travel ban and asset freeze on those found guilty of provoking violence in Darfur, and agreeing to refer alleged crimes against humanity to the International Criminal Court.[29]

Still, throughout this period the centerpiece of the administration's Darfur policy was its support for AMIS. The prelude to this support was State Department pressure for the resumption of talks between Khartoum and the Darfur rebels that had broken down in September 2003. The United States paid to fly the rebel leaders to Chad for discussions mediated by the Chadian government and the AU and pressured both Khartoum and the rebels to take them seriously. Several U.S. envoys attended the meetings, which began on March 31, 2004, and led to an April 8 agreement for a forty-five-day "humanitarian ceasefire" as well as a Ceasefire Commission to monitor the deal.[30]

Unfortunately, the agreement had serious problems. With no maps and two different, contested versions of the text, military officers on both sides warned that it would be impossible to monitor.[31] Still, while the ceasefire was quickly broken and had little if any effect on the violence in Darfur, it did help lay the groundwork for AMIS. At U.S. urging, the AU agreed to lead the force that would monitor the deal and Khartoum cooperated with the planning process.[32] The mission became operational in June with the arrival of the first military observers, and in August the AU sent a contingent of troops to protect them. By October AMIS included 135 observers plus 310 troops.[33] During these initial months, however, it was not envisaged as a force to protect civilians or aid workers. Rather, its mandate focused on tasks associated with monitoring and helping implement the humanitarian ceasefire.[34]

Over the summer, as all sides breached the ceasefire agreement, it quickly became clear that AMIS was much too small and also that the security situation continued to pose a grave threat to civilians. Thus, discussion soon began of increasing AMIS's size and giving it a stronger mandate, potentially including the direct protection of civilians. The United States actively pressed for this expansion, favoring both more troops and a more ambitious mandate.[35] Indeed, when Khartoum resisted the Bush administration pushed until it gave in. Then, on September 18, the United States cosponsored a UN Security Council resolution that threatened Sudan with sanctions if, among other actions, it failed to abide by its commitment to accept the strengthened AU force.[36]

On October 20, the AU authorized an increase in AMIS's size to 3,320 civilian and military personnel and allowed it to begin providing at least some limited civilian protection. The new mandate asked the force to "contribute to a secure environment for the delivery of humanitarian relief" and to patrol and establish outposts for the purpose of deterring attacks against civilians. Troops could also protect both aid operations and civilians encountered "under imminent threat and in the immediate vicinity."[37] On the other hand, they were not supposed to pursue perpetrators of violence against civilians or compel them to halt their attacks. After this, the United States continued to push the AU to fully implement the new expanded mandate.[38]

The deployment of the additional troops took nearly six months, and even once they had arrived AMIS was still stretched too thin to perform its mandate.[39] Along with various international partners, the United States again urged the AU to expand the mission.[40] At the end of April 2005 it did so, authorizing a force increase of up to 6,171 troops and 1,560 civilian police. Although the AU did not otherwise alter AMIS's mandate, it did approve a greater focus on creating a secure environment in and around IDP camps and for the delivery of humanitarian aid.[41] Deploying so many more personnel posed a major logistical challenge, and at U.S. urging NATO agreed to provide additional logistical support, primarily in moving in the new troops.[42]

In addition to its diplomatic initiatives the Bush administration also provided vital material support for AMIS's initial deployment and subsequent expansions. Indeed, the AU relied on the United States and various other donors to fund every aspect of the force. Beginning in June 2004, the United States provided logistical assistance and paid a contractor to set up the headquarters and to build, support, and maintain camps for AMIS troops. In addition, a small number of U.S. military observers were sent to participate in the monitoring aspects of the mission and to advise and coordinate with the AU. In March of 2005 the Bush administration used its position on the Security Council to help direct the new UN Mission in Sudan (UNMIS) to provide AMIS with technical assistance and training. Finally, as part of NATO's assistance with the 2005 force expansion, the United States established a logistics and transport base in Kigali, Rwanda, and provided training, equipment, and transport for AMIS battalions from Rwanda and Nigeria. By the summer of 2006 the United States had allocated some $280 million in assistance to AMIS.[43]

Despite the international support, however, AMIS faced extraordinary challenges in providing meaningful civilian protection and security. On one hand, it was constrained by the limited circumstances in which its mandate allowed it to protect civilians. Frustrated by these restrictions, the initial force commander sought to do more by pushing the boundaries of, or even exceeding, his instructions.[44] More important, however, the AU lacked many of the key resources and capabilities needed to fulfill (let alone exceed) its mandate. First, by any standard AMIS's authorized size was always much too small to handle Darfur's protection needs.[45] Yet despite the small size, it deployed at a glacial pace, even with extensive international help. After more than a year, the force had reached only 90% of the strength authorized in April 2005.[46] What is more, these difficulties were mirrored on the ground. Among other problems, limited intelligence collection and communication capabilities, inadequate ground and air transport, and the inability to fly or patrol at night often meant that AMIS arrived at the scene of an attack too late to protect endangered civilians.[47] The troops' poor night mobility, in particular, limited their responsiveness to attacks against villages, which often occurred in the predawn hours.[48]

AMIS's biggest problems, however, were in organization and operational planning. As Julie Flint and Alex de Waal put it, "The fundamental problem was neither numbers nor mandate, but organization—lack of it. . . . The AU was so weak in capacity that it did not have the ability even to recruit essential staff. It ran its Darfur operation with fewer personnel than the Sudan desk of a small NGO—and frequently diverted them to other tasks."[49] Citing the mission's apparent inability to request desperately needed telephones as an example, one Western military officer who liaised with AMIS for a number of years concluded that the mission "neither had the capacity to ask for what it needed nor the ability to manage what it had."[50]

The international assistance AMIS received could not overcome these problems. Thus, while it was successfully able to intervene to prevent violence against civilians in some cases, on the whole the force proved unable to implement even its relatively restrained civilian protection mandate. As a result, U.S. support for AMIS served to sustain the deployment of underprepared troops mandated to provide a level of civilian protection they had little hope of achieving. In this sense it is a classic example of a policy that promoted an ambitions-resources gap, especially because of the role the United States played in pushing for the stronger mandate and troop expansions. Critically, moreover, there was little reason to hope that more financial and logistical aid could have significantly changed this outcome. While more assistance might have alleviated certain difficulties, it could not solve the AU's basic lack of organizational capacity. As one State Department official remarked, "You can't run a peacekeeping operation on voluntary contributions and have your partners do all the logistics for you."[51] What most fundamentally constrained the U.S. contribution to civilian protection in Darfur during this period, therefore, was American willingness to "farm out" the bulk of the work to the African Union.[52]

2006 AND BEYOND: THE UN AS SAVIOR

The beginning of 2006 saw yet another significant shift in U.S. Darfur policy. While it continued to provide financial assistance for AMIS, the Bush administration simultaneously initiated a full-court diplomatic press to replace it with a UN force. This effort began by addressing the opposition of the AU itself, which was initially reluctant to surrender its authority to the UN. In January, however, AU leaders agreed in principle to a UN handover after the United States and other donors declined to provide further financial support for AMIS and it became clear that the force would otherwise run out of money by March.[53] Yet Khartoum immediately and repeatedly expressed intense opposition to this plan. In one notable incident in February, President Bashir threatened that Darfur would become a "graveyard" for UN troops.[54]

Despite this, the Bush administration pressed ahead. The next step was to secure a peace deal so that the UN, which is poorly equipped to conduct coercive missions that lack the local government's consent, would agree to deploy. Not wishing to be saddled with an operation they knew would be out of its depth, UN officials emphasized that they would act in Darfur only if the trappings of traditional peacekeeping—that is, a peace agreement and Khartoum's consent—were in place. As Hedi Annabi, the assistant secretary-general for peacekeeping, told the Security Council in April, a mission that lacked Sudanese government approval would be "better undertaken by means other than a UN operation."[55] Yet ongoing peace talks in Abuja, Nigeria, seemed to be getting nowhere. Thus, impatient with the lack of progress, the United States and other international players began trying to hurry things along. Finally in early May, after months of missed deadlines and intense international pressure to reach an agreement, the administration sent Deputy Secretary of State Robert Zoellick to Abuja to try to finalize a deal.[56]

The primary U.S. goal at the negotiations was to obtain a settlement that would allow the UN to deploy as soon as possible.[57] Although Zoellick was able to broker an agreement within a matter of days, the rushed timetable had a number of important consequences both for the war itself and for the proposed UN mission. First, as noted earlier, the DPA lacked the consent and participation of all the major parties to the conflict. Despite their pleas to be included in the negotiations, Darfur's Arab population—whose support would be needed for any lasting peace—was left out entirely. In addition, only one rebel leader signed on to the deal. By 2006, the SLA had broken into two factions, led by Minni Minawi and Abdel Wahid. Of the two, Wahid had greater support in Darfur and an agreement with him would have had greater value to Khartoum. Along with JEM, however, Wahid refused to sign Zoellick's proposed text without additional guarantees that would have taken longer to arrange. Unwilling to wait any longer, the Bush administration decided that an agreement with Minawi was good enough.[58]

The result, as both the AU's security advisers and Darfuri tribal leaders had warned, was that the DPA only served to worsen the security situation in Darfur.[59] For one thing, the rebel movement fragmented further, with the number of groups ballooning to at least 12 and the count sometimes changing on a daily basis. For the AU troops, this greatly increased the challenge of maintaining working relations with the various armed groups, a necessity for effectively carrying out their mandate. It also led to a major increase in looting and attacks on aid workers. Yet the DPA also further reduced AMIS's already limited ability to protect civilians and aid workers by undermining its respect in Darfur. As the United States pushed the AU to enforce the agreement by cracking down on the non-signatories, AMIS found itself aligned with Khartoum and Minawi and at odds with the other rebels and the Darfuri population. The AU not only lost the trust of the displaced people it was trying to protect, but also became the target of more frequent and deadly attacks.[60] While the Bush administration sought to secure approval for a new UN force, AMIS was neglected and dwindled in size as morale and effectiveness fell.[61]

The Bush administration's haste also led to a second key omission at Abuja. By failing to provide specifically for a UN peacekeeping operation in the text of the DPA, Zoellick may well have missed an opportunity to deploy UNAMID more quickly. Although Khartoum opposed a UN mission, Bashir might have consented if Zoellick had made this a clear prerequisite for an agreement—especially if that agreement had included Abdel Wahid. Instead, according to UN special representative for Sudan Jan Pronk, the United States and United Kingdom opposed his pleas to specify the transition to a UN force because this would have created an unwanted delay.[62]

What followed, therefore, was a long diplomatic struggle that resulted in major limitations on the design and composition of UNAMID. Once the DPA was signed, the Bush administration moved to get UN approval for a new peacekeeping mission. But when Khartoum objected, U.S.

diplomats were surprised to find that it was under no obligation to accept a new mission. In August, President Bush promised Bashir a personal meeting if he would consent to a UN force.[63] When he refused, the administration enlisted the Security Council to pressure him. Resolution 1706, approved on August 31, "invited Sudan's consent to a UN force—implying that if consent was not forthcoming, such a force might be dispatched without it."[64]

Bashir quickly declined this "invitation," however, and progress stalled. In November 2006, UN Secretary General Kofi Annan suggested replacing AMIS with a hybrid AU-UN force.[65] Over the next seven months Khartoum resisted American, European, and UN pressures to accept key features of this new plan, including the inclusion of non-African troops and UN command of the mission. Finally, on June 17—almost 10 months after Resolution 1706—Bashir appeared to relent on these issues, paving the way for unanimous adoption of Security Council Resolution 1769 of July 31, which authorized UNAMID to take over from AMIS on December 31. Pressure from China, a major purchaser of Sudanese oil and Khartoum's closest ally on the Security Council, was widely seen as crucial in eliciting this change. Mindful of its image before the 2008 Beijing Olympics, the Chinese government urged Bashir to accept the new plan.[66]

Still, Khartoum was able to dictate terms and strictly limit the new force's composition and freedom of action. Notably, it refused to approve the deployment of specialized units of non-African soldiers considered vital to the mission, and for which the UN had no viable alternatives. Partly for this reason, UNAMID was slow to reach capacity. Even though many personnel transferred directly from AMIS, barely 9,000 of the mandated 26,000 had deployed by early 2008, only 15,000 had deployed by the end of the year, and not quite 20,000 were in place by the end of 2009. Other roadblocks included failure to approve the land needed for UNAMID bases and refusing to allow UN planes to fly at night.[67]

As a result, the transition to UNAMID had little effect on civilian protection and the new mission suffered—like AMIS before it—from a clear ambitions-resources gap. UNAMID's mandate was very similar to AMIS's: soldiers were expected to help restore safe conditions for the delivery of humanitarian aid and to protect civilians within their capabilities and areas of deployment. To do so they were asked, among other tasks, to proactively patrol; deter violence; and prevent attacks against civilians.[68] Still, the mission's primary limiting factor remained its lack of capacity to deliver this protection. As Prunier describes, "the AMIS soldiers solemnly took off their green berets and put on blue ones. Apart from this 're-hatting' they were still as unmotivated, as inefficient and as under-equipped as they had been under their previous name."[69] Indeed, in the worsening security environment UNAMID was often unable to protect even itself.

Accounting for U.S. Policy

Why did the Bush administration begin by trying to draw attention away from the horrors of Darfur, later switch to pushing for and supporting AMIS, and then finally seek to replace it with a UN force that faced long odds of doing much better? In this section I first lay out the normative pressures the administration faced from society and from within. I then explain how the operational environment in Darfur, the wars in Iraq and Afghanistan, and other diplomatic priorities related to Sudan's north-south peace process and the U.S. war on terror combined to create substantial reluctance within government to push Khartoum too hard on Darfur, and especially to engage in military action. Finally I explain how putting these pressures together and accounting for changes over time—particularly in normative demands from society—can help us understand the administration's assistance to AMIS and UNAMID, and how its support for these missions helped it balance a tricky political dilemma.

NORMATIVE PRESSURES

The Growth of Societal Demands. In 2003 and early 2004, U.S. society was virtually silent on the war in Darfur. Few Americans had heard of the region, and the lack of interest was reflected in the dearth of media coverage. News reports on Sudan at this time were dominated by the Naivasha negotiations for peace between north and south, and Darfur was barely discussed. For instance, the *New York Times* mentioned the region only six times and the *Washington Post* nine times from 2003 to the end of March 2004.[70] What is more, although Darfur was the subject of a few reports by elite advocacy groups like the International Crisis Group (ICG) and Amnesty International, in general even NGOs with a history of working on Sudan paid little attention during 2003.[71]

In contrast, the spring of 2004 saw the beginning of a dramatic shift in Darfur's place in U.S. politics. After more than a year out of the American public eye, Darfur now became the object of a deluge of concern. The spark that ignited this change was the ten-year anniversary of the start of the Rwandan genocide on April 6. In the lead-up to and during the official commemorations of that event, explicit comparisons between Darfur and Rwanda by high-level UN officials resonated broadly.[72] On April 7, President Bush released his own first statement on the conflict, calling on Khartoum to stop the atrocities.[73] After this, Darfur saw an explosion of public and media attention. As shown in figure 5.1 below, mentions of "Darfur" in U.S. newspapers increased from 7 in March to 429 in September. Moreover, from this point, media coverage and advocacy worked in tandem, with the former both attracting concerned citizens to the emerging advocacy movement and reflecting activists' efforts to heighten public awareness.

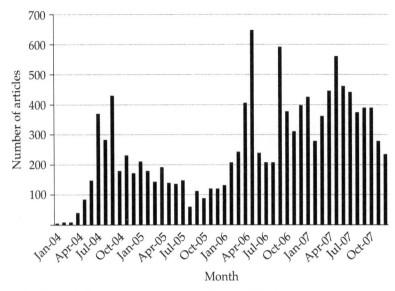

Figure 5.1. Monthly U.S. newspaper coverage of Darfur, 2004–7

Note: Article counts are for full-text searches conducted in LexisNexis using "Darfur" as the search term.

The founding of the Save Darfur Coalition in July 2004 at a meeting called by the U.S. Holocaust Museum and American Jewish World Service laid the foundation for the considerable political influence the advocacy movement would muster over the next several years. Save Darfur quickly found itself helping to coordinate the work of a wide range of groups, including the many Darfur-related organizations that formed on college campuses and through community and church groups starting that fall. As David Lanz describes, this strategy of coordination and coalition building among groups from across the political spectrum helped ensure that they reached a wide audience: "They created a movement, whose cause was sufficiently vague and non-menacing to allow it to become a catch-all for various civil society groups. They managed to tap into traditional Christian advocacy for Sudan, Jewish preoccupation with genocide, human rights groups' support for international criminal justice, the conflict resolution community's enthusiasm for R2P, student idealism, and the philanthropic impulse of celebrities."[74]

As their movement grew, over the next few years activists assiduously used the media to press their policy demands and to publicize their growing numbers and political clout. In 2005, for example, the Center for American Progress and a student group called the Genocide Intervention Network (GI-Net) created a petition to increase reporting on Darfur, while Save Darfur asked its followers to write letters-to-the-editor and op-eds in their local papers to boost awareness.[75] As a result, after the initial burst in mid-2004, media coverage of Darfur grew once again. As shown in figure 5.1, average monthly newspaper references grew from 150 in 2004–5 to 359 in 2006–7.

Significantly, from the very beginning a major (though not the only) focus of all this media and advocacy attention was the need for military action to directly protect civilians from violence. According to one study of opinion pieces in major U.S. newspapers between March and September of 2004, there was heavy emphasis on potential military solutions for Darfur.[76] Also at this time, and analogizing from the Clinton administration's refusal to refer to the violence in Rwanda as genocide to avoid a vigorous response, activists and journalists pushed Congress and the Bush administration to call the situation in Darfur "genocide" in the belief that this would legally commit the government to support military action.[77] And, according to Prunier, when Colin Powell declared in September that genocide had occurred in Darfur, he had "practically been ordered" to do so.[78] Still, most activists did not call for direct U.S. or NATO intervention without Khartoum's agreement.[79] Instead, they focused on two goals that aligned with the policies the administration actually pursued: first, bolstering AMIS, and later, replacing it with a UN force.

Efforts to strengthen AMIS formed the core of most of the movement's strategy for well over a year. Beginning in the summer of 2004, and in at least one case even before the AU had begun deploying its ceasefire monitors, influential individuals—including Pulitzer Prize winner and advocate Samantha Power, U.S. senator Jon Corzine, and former UN ambassador Richard Holbrooke—began calling on the U.S. government, both explicitly and implicitly, to assist and strengthen AMIS. They were joined by Human Rights Watch and by the editorial boards of various national and regional newspapers, and pushed for a stronger mandate, a larger force, and more logistical and financial aid.[80]

Soon, new Darfur-specific advocacy groups, including Save Darfur, took up these themes. For many of the advocates, there was a compelling link between AMIS's lack of resources and the earlier argument of Roméo Dallaire, commander of UNAMIR in Rwanda, that with more troops his force could have stopped the slaughter there. Driven by such thinking, a key focus for the rest of 2004 and throughout 2005 was on getting AMIS the funding and equipment that many activists presumed would allow it to act effectively.[81] To promote this idea, GI-Net took the novel approach of raising money for AMIS directly in the hope of embarrassing the government into providing more support itself. As one of the group's founders explained, supporters would visit their congressional representatives and say, "I've put $20 down to protect the people of Darfur. What are you doing?"[82]

Thanks to this advocacy activity, the Bush administration faced substantial and growing societal pressure, beginning in mid-2004, to help protect

Darfuri civilians. Although much of the advocacy movement's focus involved encouraging Congress to open the federal pocketbook on behalf of AMIS, it was clearly relevant to the administration as well. Executive leadership was required for U.S. diplomatic efforts to expand the force and strengthen its mandate, and for decisions about directing U.S. logistical support. Thus, for instance, when Darfur became a topic of conversation in the 2004 presidential election, U.S. support for AMIS allowed President Bush to highlight his cooperation with the AU and point to the aid the government was committing.[83]

Still, the enthusiasm for AMIS did not last forever. At the start of 2006 the advocacy movement turned the full force of its attention to promoting precisely the goal the Bush administration now pursued—a UN operation to replace the overwhelmed AU force.[84] In the first half of 2006, Save Darfur organized to send one million postcards to the president, urging him to use "the power of [his] office to support a stronger multinational force to protect the civilians of Darfur."[85] On April 30—the day before Deputy Secretary Zoellick traveled to Abuja to make the final push for the DPA—thousands gathered in 30 different locations around the country to press for UN troops. By this time the movement's size and influence had reached new heights, with Save Darfur boasting 165 member organizations.[86]

The long delay in achieving the deployment of a UN force, as described above, continued to spur the activists on through the rest of 2006 and 2007. On September 16, 2006, in yet another series of rallies, demonstrators wore blue berets to symbolize their demand for a UN force.[87] Save Darfur alternately praised the administration's efforts to secure the new mission while pushing to make sure the president and his aides did not drop the ball.[88] The international diplomatic challenges of convincing Khartoum to accept a new force also inspired new advocacy tactics. Notably, activists worked loudly to link China's role as host of the 2008 Olympics with Darfur through Beijing's diplomatic support of Khartoum. Their efforts were critical in getting China to encourage Khartoum to accept the concept of a hybrid AU-UN force in 2007.[89]

The Bureaucracy. During the first stage of U.S. policy, through March 2004, there was somewhat more concern about Darfur from within the bureaucracy than there was from American society. In particular, those paying closest attention to Darfur in the State Department and USAID clearly understood the futility of relying on humanitarian relief to address the conflict and advocated for a different approach. Beginning in the fall of 2003, Roger Winter and Andrew Natsios of USAID convinced the U.S. embassy in Khartoum to begin referring to the violence in Darfur as "ethnic cleansing" in internal cables; in February of 2004 Winter was the first official to use this language in public. Meanwhile, from Khartoum, the State Department's envoy Gerard Galluci begged his superiors to move beyond simply providing emergency assistance. Still, at this point these voices were a clear minority, as most State Department officials had not yet come to see Darfur as a human rights crisis, and not merely a humanitarian one.[90]

As noted above, however, March of 2004 was a turning point when top officials within the State Department became convinced of the need to address Darfur's political problems as well as its humanitarian ones. From this point forward, in various offices and agencies throughout the administration, from the State Department and USAID to the White House and the National Security Council, there were numerous high-level people (including the president himself) who cared about Darfur and wanted to help end the violence and the attacks against civilians.

Yet for the most part this concern did not translate into pressure for the president to send U.S. troops and it was consistent with the policy compromises involved in supporting AMIS and UNAMID. There were several reasons for this. First, for at least some officials U.S. military action threatened to do more harm than good. For instance, Natsios—who also served as the president's special envoy to Sudan from 2006–7—worried about Khartoum's antagonism toward aid workers and opposition to the deployment of any Western troops. For him, the biggest problem with any potential U.S. military operation was that it would threaten the ongoing humanitarian operations that by 2004 were saving thousands of lives.[91] Second, as discussed below, the Bush administration had a complex set of diplomatic and political interests in Sudan that extended well beyond the war in Darfur and in important respects conflicted with addressing it. Even those who cared about Darfur, therefore, often hesitated in pushing to do too much to end the violence or in advocating a coercive military solution against Khartoum's wishes. Third, a number of bureaucrats were, unlike most activists, more focused on diplomatic rather than military initiatives as the most promising approach to ending the conflict and addressing civilians' needs. For them, too much emphasis on a military response—of any kind—threatened to distract the administration from the bigger picture.

For these various reasons, many of the most concerned officials either were themselves convinced of the need for compromise when it came to military action in Darfur or believed that there were equally if not more important initiatives to pursue. Still, as my argument anticipates, the growth of the advocacy movement also mattered for those in government who were most focused on Darfur. For some who were skeptical of the value of military action without Khartoum's wholehearted approval, the activists' influence was problematic, if not unwelcome. As Natsios complained in a 2007 memo to then–deputy secretary of state John Negroponte, for instance, the activists' intense oversight of U.S. diplomacy "is constraining what we may be able to do to resolve the crisis" by making it difficult to engage with Khartoum and offer incentives for good behavior.[92] For others, though, the civil society engagement was generally helpful. According to

Natsios's replacement as special envoy, Richard Williamson, civil society helped keep Darfur on the agenda and provided different sources of information than he received from traditional governmental channels.[93] And in the White House, presidential adviser Michael Gerson would use media articles and advocacy statements that criticized the administration's policies to "stoke the president's interest" on Darfur and push him to do more to protect civilians.[94]

THE OPERATIONAL ENVIRONMENT AND OTHER MATERIAL PRESSURES

The obstacles to protecting civilians in Darfur arose from various sources, including a formidable operational environment and associated opposition to U.S. military action from the defense establishment. In this case, moreover, the costs and challenges associated with this situation were amplified by the ongoing wars in Iraq and Afghanistan. Meanwhile, two other calculations further added to domestic political and bureaucratic pressures against intervention.

The operational environment for any peace operation in Darfur was always going to be inhospitable. The territory is very large, roughly the size of France. This places Darfur in the top third of post-Cold War complex emergencies in geographic size. Its prewar population of roughly six million, though hardly enormous, places Darfur in the middle among complex emergencies, and is several times larger than places like East Timor or Kosovo that received large intervention forces.[95] In addition, Darfur's population was widely dispersed (though less so once so many people became concentrated in IDP camps). Poor infrastructure made land travel challenging and many villages difficult to access. What is more, the presence of multiple rebel groups and, with the militias, multiple groups on the government side complicated the tricky task of negotiating relations with the belligerents. Indeed, this problem worsened over time as the rebel movement splintered and Khartoum lost control of the militias.

One especially important factor was also particularly relevant for any prospective Western troop deployment. Khartoum clearly and repeatedly indicated that it would not consent to the presence of any Western forces, beginning with warnings to the United States and United Kingdom against interfering in Sudan's internal affairs when they briefly raised the possibility in 2004.[96] Thus, any U.S. forces would face the prospect of fighting the Sudanese Army (which, at 100,000 men, was in the top third among complex emergencies without even counting the Janjaweed).[97] As a result, while the operational environment for intervention in Darfur would have been challenging for any outside force, it would have been especially so for U.S. or other Western troops.

The formidable operational environment was accompanied by strong opposition within the bureaucracy to the use of U.S. forces in Darfur. As the *Washington Post* reported, "skepticism about using U.S. soldiers, even in a limited way, cut across agencies and bodies that often disagree, from the State Department to the Pentagon to Vice President Cheney's office, according to many current and former officials."[98] In this case, the ongoing U.S. commitments in Iraq and Afghanistan provided an easy justification for this opposition: with the military already stretched by these operations, it lacked the capacity for a third mission as challenging as Darfur. Still, in other respects intragovernmental debate closely resembled discussions that had taken place during earlier complex emergencies. To some officials, such as Assistant Secretary for African Affairs Jendayi Frazer, Defense Department estimates of the troops needed for a U.S. deployment appeared inflated to discourage doing anything at all. Meanwhile, Defense Secretary Donald Rumsfeld argued that even a small U.S. deployment could require sending more troops later to bail them out in case of trouble, and the military worried that a Darfur deployment would turn into a quagmire with no clear exit plan.[99]

Yet extenuating circumstances related to the war on terror and the conflicts in Iraq and Afghanistan did not only matter for U.S. capabilities. They also bolstered opposition to U.S. action within the government in two further ways that magnified the dangers of the operational environment. First, regional allies warned that U.S. troops would draw foreign al-Qaeda fighters to the region to fight the Americans. This altered officials' expectations about the operating environment in Darfur in a way that raised anticipated costs of a U.S. deployment and lowered expectations of its efficacy. Senior officials such as Deputy Secretary of State Zoellick expressed fears that U.S. troops could be vulnerable to attacks by "bloodthirsty, cold-hearted" terrorists who might flock to Darfur from Somalia or other regional trouble spots in search of soldiers to kill.[100] Second, Iraq and Afghanistan increased U.S. officials' sensitivity to the costs of another difficult deployment. Indeed, for some this was more relevant than the limits on U.S. capabilities. According to UN ambassador John Bolton, for instance, "We had the capacity. The issue was that we had a war in two Islamic countries and how many dead Americans can you have at any given time?" Similarly, in the words of one senior Defense Department official, not being asked to deploy to Darfur was "a weight off the nation in terms of sweat and blood."[101]

The operational environment combined with the related complications of Iraq and Afghanistan, then, accounted for substantial opposition to any U.S. deployment to Darfur from within the Bush administration. Yet another impediment had to do with the north-south peace process. As noted above, the Bush administration was a key player in the ongoing Naivasha negotiations for an agreement to resolve the Sudanese civil war. Its primary motive was to repay a core domestic constituency of Christian evangelicals with a long-standing concern about the suffering of south Sudan (a mainly Christian region) for their support in the 2000 U.S. presidential election. When war in Darfur flared in 2003, the negotiations appeared to be making real progress and the administration hoped to conclude them before the 2004 presidential election. Not only would this help bolster President Bush with his key supporters, but for the diplomatic community the prospect of a triumph in the Arab world during the furor over Iraq was enticing. Yet there was significant concern within the administration that too much public criticism of Khartoum over the situation in Darfur, let alone more forceful action, could undermine the Naivasha process. This not only had potential electoral implications for the president, but there was also a powerful pull from the State Department to see the process through since it had invested a great deal of energy in the initiative.[102] Indeed, according to one senior official, fear of destroying the Comprehensive Peace Agreement (CPA) that was ultimately signed in January 2005 remained the main factor in restraining U.S. pressure on Sudan over Darfur, even after the election.[103]

Finally, as hinted at earlier, after 9/11 the Bush administration was very desirous to maintain good relations with the Sudanese government in order to benefit from its extensive intelligence on Al Qaeda (Osama bin Laden had lived in the country from 1991 to 1996). The CIA in particular established a close working relationship with Khartoum, and the administration offered diplomatic carrots to help ensure effective cooperation. Specifically, through the combination of intelligence sharing and the Naivasha negotiations, Khartoum hoped to achieve normalization of diplomatic relations and, as a result, Sudan's removal from the U.S. State Sponsors of Terror list and an end to economic sanctions imposed by the Clinton administration. The United States repeatedly offered assurances on these issues and, as with the peace negotiations, the prospect of losing Khartoum's counterterrorism cooperation helped deter criticism of its actions in Darfur.[104] Despite opposition from some in the State and Justice Departments, moreover, there was also strong support for this approach from others at the State Department as well as from the CIA and the Defense Intelligence Agency (DIA).[105]

PUTTING NORMATIVE AND MATERIAL PRESSURES TOGETHER

Across all three periods, the Bush administration's actions on Darfur were consistent with my expectations about the conditions that encourage ambitions-resources gaps and about how leaders use these policies to balance conflicting normative and material pressures. Notably, from mid-2004 onward there is evidence that concerned citizens and bureaucrats supported the administration's focus on aiding AMIS and then UNAMID for all of the reasons I would expect, and that these policies were accompanied by the rhetoric of organized hypocrisy.

February 2003–March 2004. The administration's reluctance to acknowledge Darfur as a security problem in 2003 and early 2004 reflected, first, the near total absence of societal interest or even awareness of the conflict and the limited pressure within the bureaucracy to deal with the attacks against civilians. In particular, these circumstances allowed plenty of political space for the administration to pursue other priorities in its relations with Khartoum. Indeed, barring some other reason for action, the potential operational environment for a peace operation was effectively irrelevant. Yet in this case the administration's other concerns—to avoid offending Khartoum or taking actions that could delay the north-south peace process—pointed clearly away from any actions on Darfur that did not have Khartoum's full endorsement.

It is these other priorities, then, that explain why the administration went so far as to actively deflect attention from Darfur during this period. Moreover, these motives were quite transparent to the Bush administration's African interlocutors. As journalist Richard Cockett wrote, paraphrasing a senior Sudanese official, the Americans downplayed Darfur because "they were as eager as the Sudanese, if not more so, to clinch the politically valuable CPA and to get more intelligence on al-Qaeda."[106] Similarly, in the words of chief Naivasha negotiator Lazaro Sumbeiywo, "The Americans knew about Darfur—I knew that. And they did sacrifice the people of Darfur for the CPA, for a success for Bush."[107]

Spring 2004–End 2005. Beginning in the spring of 2004, however, the societal and governmental pressures President Bush faced over Darfur intensified greatly, leading to a serious dilemma: how to demonstrate a commitment to protecting Darfuri civilians without bearing unacceptable costs to do so? On one side were the expectations of the growing advocacy movement and the late but crucial recognition by various senior officials of the need for a new approach to the conflict. On the other were Darfur's inhospitable operational environment, the ongoing wars in Iraq and Afghanistan, and the related opposition to U.S. military involvement in Darfur especially, but not only, from the defense establishment. The latter were reinforced by the State Department and intelligence community's continued emphases on counterterrorism and completing the Naivasha process. As Prunier put it, President Bush "found himself under pressure from an array of public opinion elements too wide to be ignored during an election year. But since the 'realists' in the intelligence community kept insisting that Khartoum was too important to be harshly treated, these contradictory pressures led the White House to compromise on all fronts."[108] In particular, by supporting AMIS diplomatically, financially, and logistically, the administration was able to limit the costs of its Darfur policy while finding a middle ground between the different positions in government and convincing concerned citizens it was making an effort on civilian protection.

First, promoting and assisting the AU operation had the benefit of keeping the physical, political, and strategic costs of U.S. involvement in Darfur firmly in check. Significantly, no Americans died in Darfur. As James Traub noted, promoting AMIS allowed the United States and other Western powers "to say that they were addressing the problem without having to commit anything save money."[109] What is more, even the financial costs were relatively limited. While the United States did spend several hundred million dollars on AMIS, this pales in comparison to what it would have spent to deploy substantial U.S. military assets and what it has spent on other peace operations.[110] Nor did the policy require much of intervention opponents in the Pentagon, since the Defense Department's direct contributions to AMIS were "limited to staff expertise, military observers, training and the provision of airlift to move troops in and out of Darfur."[111] Finally, unlike committing troops, supporting AMIS—which had Khartoum's grudging consent so long as it remained small and under AU leadership—was not so confrontational as to fundamentally challenge the administration's priorities on counterterrorism and the Naivasha negotiations.

At the same time, the policy was acceptable to bureaucrats who wanted to see the administration do more for Darfur than provide humanitarian aid. The administration's initial moves to bring about the April 2004 humanitarian ceasefire and the AU's monitoring of it occurred on the State Department's initiative and before the birth of the advocacy movement. Later on, its efforts to expand AMIS's size and mandate—the moves that led to promoting an ambitions-resources gap—occurred in the shadow of growing pressure from the advocacy movement. Yet the officials who favored these moves and wanted to see AMIS become more effective were often among the same people who worried about Naivasha, counterterrorism, and the risks of a U.S. deployment. Although they were morally outraged at the suffering in Darfur they also weighed the consequences of different means to combat it against other values and interests and had a variety of reasons for not wanting to send U.S. troops. For some, supporting AMIS seemed the next best option given the threat that more robust action would pose to relations with Khartoum. They hoped the AU force would be able to do some good. For others, the only military option they could ever potentially condone was one Khartoum would willingly accept. Supporting AMIS, despite its limitations, was the most these officials found prudent.

As discussed earlier, supporting and pushing to expand AMIS largely met with the Darfur advocacy movement's approval as well, at least through 2005. Indeed, not only did activists accept this approach, but it was the one that most were pushing for. Their optimism reflected the full range of reasons I would expect for why concerned citizens may accept ambitions-resources gaps, including factors that were similar to and different from those underlying concerned bureaucrats' positions. Notably, Darfur advocates and their followers tended to be much less interested in the value of Sudan's counterterrorism cooperation. This was highlighted in the spring of 2005 when a secret visit to Washington by Sudan's intelligence chief, Salah Gosh, became public and prompted activist outrage. Director of Africa Action Salih Booker, for instance, accused the Bush administration of creating a hierarchy of U.S. interests in which "African lives are at the bottom while collecting intelligence, even dubious intelligence . . . is clearly at the top."[112]

On the other hand, certain activists' views were influenced by the north-south peace process. In particular, some who had also worked on South Sudan were reluctant at this time to push the Bush administration too hard on Darfur because they were satisfied with its role in the Naivasha negotiations and were reluctant to risk upsetting them.[113] Further, thanks to the wars in Iraq and Afghanistan, many advocates also accepted that the United States lacked the capacity to intervene itself or that, if it could, it might inflame rather than calm the violence in Darfur. As GI-Net activist Chad Hazlett put it, a coercive U.S.- or NATO-led mission was viewed by many "as a political impossibility at best and a bad idea at worst." Seen from these perspectives, the force that was already on the ground provided an obvious focal point for citizens' attention and—as for many officials— appeared to be the next best option, even if an imperfect one.[114]

Yet many activists also held overly sanguine attitudes about what the AU could hope to accomplish and about the benefits of a U.S. strategy of supporting it. Although there were key exceptions among experienced Sudan watchers such as Smith College professor Eric Reeves and a few elite NGOs like ICG and Africa Action, the belief that the AU could do the job in Darfur if it just had the right mandate and resources was widespread.[115] As Reeves complained in July 2005, "Human rights groups have, in the main, refused to articulate" the AU's core weaknesses, thus allowing AMIS to remain "the unchallenged policy of the international community."[116]

In part, this situation reflected certain challenges to recognizing some of AMIS's most intractable flaws. Not only were the force's greatest downsides—its operational planning and organizational capabilities—quite difficult to observe from the outside as a non-military expert, but the AU had little prior experience in peacekeeping that could be used to judge its strengths and weaknesses. Thus, as late as December 2005, even so veteran an organization as Human Rights Watch was still focused on increasing AMIS's size and clarifying its ROE, and on urging the United States and other Western donors above all to "provide increased financial and technical resources to AMIS to strengthen its capacity to protect civilians."[117] Further, a second important factor was that most members and followers of the advocacy movement were new to Darfur or to advocacy generally. As Colin Thomas-Jensen and Julia Spiegel put it, "most within the movement have never been to Darfur—most have never even met a person from Darfur."[118]

For these inexperienced activists, the AU's dearth of operational planning and organizational capacity—and the possibility that more troops, more money, and a stronger mandate would not transform it into a capable and effective protection force—could be especially hard to grasp.

One late 2005 incident, when a GI-Net activist visited AMIS headquarters to discuss how to disperse the funds the group had collected, starkly illustrates this point. The trip proved an eye-opening experience. After a year of focusing on fundraising, he realized that "they had 12 guys trying to coordinate a 7,000-person mission. They were maxed out. We had $300K to offer, and it was a billion dollar project."[119] GI-Net soon gave up working with the AU directly.

There is even evidence that these oversights by advocates influenced the particular forms of U.S. assistance to AMIS. According to one mid-level State Department official the types of support the United States offered were selected for maximum political visibility, even at the expense of efforts that might have done more for AMIS's capacity. As Rebecca Hamilton describes,

> For those under political pressure, airlifting in an additional 400 AMIS troops, with pictures to show for it, was a better way to manage advocacy demands than coming out with a statement that they were working to improve AMIS management techniques. "Those of us working closest to the AU realized that you could expand ten times over and they still wouldn't have the capacity," the same official recalls. . . . "We knew we couldn't solve it with more money or more personnel. But the politicos all pushed for an expansion of AMIS throughout 2005."[120]

In line with the activists' focus on AMIS's most easily observable problems, then, the emphasis in Washington tended to overlook the force's most fundamental weaknesses.

Further, pushing to support and expand AMIS was also consistent with other motives within the advocacy movement. On one hand, these included the professional incentives of organized groups. In the face of clear opposition to a U.S. deployment from the Pentagon and other high-level officials, focusing on getting the government to bolster AMIS was a much easier way for advocacy groups to show their followers and donors that they were having an effect on policy than promoting more direct U.S. military involvement.

On top of this, the expressive benefits that accrued from participating in the movement were clearly an important element for many. For religious groups, becoming involved was at least partly about upholding an obligation to behave in ways consistent with their own self-identities. As explained by David Saperstein, head of Reform Judaism's Religious Action Center in Washington, Darfur advocacy reflected the "well-established pattern of the faith community believing they have a prophetic witness, an obligation to be a goad to the conscience of the country." Similarly, according to Rachel Cornwell, a pastor in Bethesda, Maryland, "By being silent we're being complicit."[121] Such statements suggest that for members of these communities, expressing outrage about violence in Darfur had its own value in affirming members' sense of their own morality. A similar dynamic played out among followers of Darfur-related advocacy groups. As one University of Pennsylvania student declared, "Once you know about it [Darfur], you have to do something."[122] And indeed, these groups organized numerous opportunities for citizens to express their concern and outrage without having to invest in deep knowledge about the AU or the practical challenges of civilian protection. These included participating in "die-ins"; giving up a minor luxury, like a coffee, and donating the proceeds; and wearing green bracelets branded with the Save Darfur slogan "Not on Our Watch." Insofar as such actions point to people's need to "do something" as a dominant impulse, they can also help explain some of the enthusiasm for AMIS that persisted through 2005.

Finally, the Bush administration regularly employed the rhetoric of organized hypocrisy, though perhaps not so flamboyantly as French leaders did in 1994. Despite AMIS's difficulties on the ground and in deploying the mandated troop numbers, U.S. officials asserted their confidence in the AU and touted its accomplishments throughout 2004 and 2005. For instance, anticipating AMIS's initial expansion the next month, in September 2004 Colin Powell testified: "I am pleased that the African Union is stepping up to the task. It is playing a leadership role and countries within the African Union have demonstrated a willingness to provide a significant number of troops. And this is the fastest way to help bring security to the countryside through this expanded monitoring presence."[123] A year later, in October 2005—as UNHCR chief António Guterres declared that AMIS "cannot effectively protect the people of Darfur"—the State Department was still expressing its "unequivocal support" for the AU mission.[124] Similarly, the following month, Assistant Secretary of State for African Affairs Jendayi Frazer asserted, "It is vital that the AU effort succeed, and we are helping to ensure that it does. Our logistics support for [AMIS] is key to its success." Frazer further credited AMIS with achieving "impressive" results and "playing a crucial role to help bring about an end to violence."[125] While it is difficult to know for sure, such statements may well have helped the Bush administration in keeping activists focused on the goal of improving AMIS during this period.

2006 and Beyond. The political pressures working on the Bush administration when it began seriously pushing for a UN force in 2006 were very similar to those it had faced for the past 18 months. A U.S. deployment continued to remain unattractive for various reasons. By this point, bureaucratic concerns revolved somewhat less around the CPA (which had been signed a year earlier) or the value of maintaining good relations with Khartoum (this relationship had already begun to deteriorate). Yet the issues of limited capacity due to Iraq and Afghanistan; fears of the specter of dead American soldiers; and worries about worsening the conflict remained as strong as ever.

On the other hand, within government there was also growing frustration with AMIS's ineffectiveness. This sentiment went all the way up to the president himself, who made it abundantly clear he wanted to find a stronger military option. As reported by the *Washington Post*, in late 2005 Bush asked his senior advisers "whether the U.S. military could send in helicopter gunships to attack the militias" if they attacked displaced Darfuris, or if the United States could "shoot down Sudanese military aircraft." According to a senior official who was familiar with the episode, Bush "wanted militant action, and people had to restrain him. . . . He wanted to go in and kill the Janjaweed."[126] Indeed, before focusing fully on the UN, in February 2006 the president tried to secure a lead role for NATO in Darfur, but found the alliance resistant. On top of this, by late 2005 the administration and other AMIS donors had grown tired of paying for the mission, given how little it seemed to be achieving. Financially, a UN deployment would be attractive because it would commit all UN members to help fund peacekeeping in Darfur.[127]

At the same time, by this point the broad majority of the advocacy movement had determined that AMIS was unlikely to ever provide adequate civilian protection. Together, the movement's political clout combined with its new focus on replacing AMIS to create a powerful incentive to heed its demands. Indeed, in addition to his own personal horror at the violence in Darfur, Bush's search for alternative military options seems to have been driven at least partly by this instrumental motive. According to adviser Michael Gerson, it was a desire to respond to media accusations that he was not truly committed to improving conditions in Darfur that inspired the president's February 2006 outreach to NATO.[128] Thereafter, with a major role for NATO off the table, it was advantageous to be seen making progress toward a UN force.

The switch to pushing for a UN force again played the politically useful role of balancing these conflicting pressures. In terms of restraining costs a UN mission would have all the advantages of AMIS, including allowing the military to limit its direct involvement in Darfur to logistical assistance. In addition, the financing would be spread more widely, among all UN member states. For those in the administration who wanted to see more effective protection of civilians, on the other hand, bringing in the UN at least offered the hope of some improvement on the AU force. Thus, as UN ambassador Bolton noted, the administration's approach to replacing AMIS "showed the competing pressures on Bush, on the one hand from people like . . . Gerson, who wanted to do something muscular in Sudan because it was the 'moral' thing to do, and on the other from people like Rumsfeld, who wondered how 'moral' it was to risk even more Americans' dying far from home in a conflict in which our national interests were remote."[129] As my argument would expect, promoting UNAMID was a compromise that reflected, in part, the intragovernmental bargaining process.

Importantly, the new strategy also had the backing of the advocacy movement. Indeed, as Flint and de Waal put it, UNAMID "was designed to satisfy western public demand for military intervention."[130] Yet given that U.S. support for UNAMID ended up promoting another ambitions-resources gap right on the heels of the first one, it is especially significant and revealing that it had such support from diverse elements of civil society. This situation again highlights the various reasons I expect concerned citizens may be willing to accept such policies.

First, it is clear that especially for some of the best-informed and experienced members of the advocacy movement, supporting a UN or hybrid force represented a clear-eyed concession to the political obstacles that stood in the way of their preferred policies. For instance, in March 2006 the International Crisis Group urged the AU and UN Security Council to move forward with a transition to a 15,000-person UN force within six months, preferably spearheaded by a 5,000-person stabilization element that would deploy immediately to assist AMIS in the meantime. Yet ICG was a rare organization that had been arguing since mid-2005 for a NATO deployment to bridge the gaps between AMIS's capabilities and Darfur's security needs. Thus, even in pushing for a UN force, they clearly laid out their continued reservations:

> This is not ideal. Crisis Group has long contended that because AMIS has reached the outer limits of its competence . . . a distinct and separate multinational force should be sent to Darfur to bridge that gap and help stabilise the immediate situation. We have argued, and continue to believe, that NATO would be best from a practical military point of view. Unfortunately, political opposition . . . means it is not achievable at this time. What we now propose, therefore, is a compromise driven by the urgent need for a more robust force in Darfur.[131]

Similarly, some advocates recognized that getting a UN mission deployed would be just a first step, and tempered their demands in the hope of improving its effectiveness later on. As the activist Omer Ismail described, "Experience had told us that if we ask for everything we are not going to get it, so we became a little bit more pragmatic. . . . We cannot say we want all the bells and whistles at once, so we got the better operation in terms of command and control, in terms of the link to the United Nations, in terms of the backing by Security Council resolutions." As for the other elements needed to make the force more robust, "you have to fight for these in due time."[132]

Second, as with their initial faith in AMIS's potential as a protection force, many activists were overly optimistic about both what a UN force could accomplish and when it might deploy. This was in part due to unfamiliarity with the UN's relative strength in traditional peacekeeping and poor record in peace enforcement. As Flint and de Waal relate, "The high expectations for what UN peacekeepers would do was frankly astonishing to those in the UN's Department of Peacekeeping Operations and others who had witnessed UN peacekeeping operations from Sierra Leone to Congo."[133] Many activists also did not fully understand the need for Khartoum's consent in deploying a UN force. Despite Bashir's clear opposition to a transition from AMIS, the possibility that he could prevent it did not occur to them until after he rejected Resolution 1706 in August 2006. As one activist remembered, the assumption had been that "if the Security Council authorizes it, then we've overcome the big barrier. What are they going to do? Not accept the peacekeepers?!"[134] Under the circumstances, Khartoum's power to dictate decisions concerning operational design and force composition—and the possibility that a new UN force might thus be unable to improve much on AMIS—came as a similar surprise to many activists.

Third, the proliferation of mass rallies and other public events in 2006–7 again demonstrates the relevance of expressive benefits. For various supporters of the advocacy movement, the experience of speaking out and demonstrating their concern for Darfur appeared to matter at least as much as identifying the most promising ways to leverage their influence. For instance, as a spokesman for the American Jewish World Service described, the group's leadership was initially reluctant to invest in the April 30, 2006 Save Darfur rally in Washington, D.C., "because it meant a lot of resources and energy." Ultimately, though, a grant was secured to fund and organize the event because "this is what people want; there's an itching to march and demonstrate."[135] Similarly, when activists were working to find a way to tie the upcoming Olympics to Beijing's diplomatic support of Khartoum in 2007, a group called Dream for Darfur organized a series of torch relays to call attention to the issue. Yet while others within the Save Darfur Coalition were skeptical that this would affect the Chinese government, they supported the events because of their followers' evident desire to participate. As one GI-Net leader put it, "Our Vermont people really wanna do a torch relay, dammit!"[136]

More broadly, for advocacy groups seeking to sustain a mass following, such activities proved vital to maintaining the engagement of ordinary citizens over time. As Mark Hanis of GI-Net stressed, it was important to keep advocacy fun and easy. "If you can't get someone to do something in five minutes, you've failed in a key way of organizing," he noted.[137] Notably, not everyone could connect all the dots between what was happening on the ground in Darfur and the intricate international diplomacy required to deploy UN troops there. Thus, for some advocacy leaders this was not the movement's purpose. For instance, both David Rubenstein of Save Darfur and actress Mia Farrow emphasized that the activists' main job was to get

Darfur on the agenda and keep it there. Farrow once advised concerned citizens to "leave it to the government to decide how to best help the people of Darfur, but let them know you want to help."[138] Meanwhile, for Rubenstein, "the closer we could get to a bumper sticker, the better we'd do as an organization."[139] While these views were by no means universal, they do help explain how demonstrating their concern could be more attractive for some citizens than working to understand the various merits and disadvantages of different policy options.[140] Notably, this advocacy approach also makes it easier for organizations to claim success at influencing policy, since it does not depend on the government adopting any single strategy.

Finally, the Bush administration's rhetoric during this period was, again, often decoupled from the reality of its efforts to secure a UN force for Darfur. For instance, administration statements repeatedly expressed horror at the continuing violence in Darfur, referred to it as ongoing genocide, and indicated that time was of the essence in ending it.[141] Such declarations conveyed a sense of urgency that was undermined by the diplomatic constraints involved in deciding to work through the UN to replace AMIS, and led Eric Reeves to conclude that the administration was full of "bold talk, [but] no action."[142] Further, although the administration clearly acknowledged Khartoum's obstructionism, a number of statements also seemed to obscure the lack of tangible progress and to oversell the changes that could be expected from a UN transition. For instance, in December 2006, after nearly a year of effort, President Bush announced: "We continue to work on establishing a credible and effective peacekeeping force to stop the violence in Darfur. To this end, we are aggressively engaging all stake-holders to implement UN resolution 1706 to transition the African Union Mission in Sudan to a strong international peacekeeping operation."[143] Similarly, in April 2007 the White House asserted the United States' leadership role on Darfur by pointing to two still entirely unimplemented initiatives: Resolution 1706, and the November 2006 UN-AU agreement that established the idea of a hybrid force.[144] That September, as Khartoum was rejecting the presence of non-African forces with capabilities that UN planners considered vital, Deputy Secretary of State Negroponte referred to UNAMID as "an absolutely crucial element of establishing the kind of stability that is going to permit the implementation of the other aspects of the Darfur peace agreement."[145]

ALTERNATIVE EXPLANATIONS

Neither of the two main alternative explanations for policies that promote ambitions-resources gaps goes very far toward explaining the Bush administration's support for AMIS and UNAMID. First, it is evident that these policies were not a fig leaf for pursuing other U.S. interests. As thoroughly discussed above, various elements within the U.S. government had different interests in Sudan during the period covered by these policies, but each of them pointed clearly toward maintaining good working relations with the Sudanese government. Yet beginning in the summer of 2004, each time the administration pressured Khartoum to accept a larger AU force or a more ambitious mandate, and each time it pushed for a UN replacement for AMIS, it risked antagonizing President Bashir. In taking these actions the administration sought, especially at first, not to go too far. It thus seems very unlikely that the administration would have changed direction from the very different approach that it pursued before March 2004 without the growing normative pressure from both its own ranks and civil society.

The second possibility—that decision-makers promote ambitions-resources gaps unknowingly and unintentionally—is more plausible. Perhaps the Bush administration was—like many activists—just too optimistic about AMIS and UNAMID's potential. Yet here, too, while officials did not always grasp the obstacles to aspects of the U.S. policy strategy, when it came to the fundamental relationship between the protection they wanted to see in Darfur and the resources the AU and UN had to provide it, the administration was not in the dark.

It is true, as noted above, that in public senior officials professed considerable faith in AMIS throughout 2004 and 2005. Overall, however, various types of evidence tend to suggest that they understood it was not up to the job in Darfur but made supporting it the centerpiece of U.S. policy anyway. Certainly, this was the opinion of the State Department official who deplored the administration's focus on expanding the number of AU troops through 2005. In addition, in 2004 the Defense Department informed the State Department that it would take at least 35,000 U.S. troops to protect the IDP camps in Darfur, assuming a consensual deployment that had Khartoum's cooperation.[146] Since it was always clear that the AU could not possibly deploy nearly so large of a force, this was one early indication of the limited use in helping AMIS to expand by a few thousand personnel.

Later, in December 2004, high-level UN officials began actively discussing possible solutions to what they saw as the AU's obvious inability to handle the security situation in Darfur. Unlike many U.S. activists, they understood that AMIS not only was too small, but that "the AU didn't seem to know how to use" the money it had.[147] U.S. diplomats may have been exposed to these conversations, but at the very latest UN Secretary General Kofi Annan pointed out to the Security Council in March of 2005 that further strengthening the AU would almost certainly fail to improve conditions in Darfur. A multinational force similar to INTERFET in East Timor was, in Annan's view, the only military option with a real chance of accomplishing what was needed.[148] The next month, Deputy Secretary of State Zoellick made his first visit to Darfur after joining the Bush administration in February. He observed the effects of the AU's limited organizational capacity firsthand and "immediately saw that AMIS was out of its depth."[149] Such experiences appear to support Kofi Annan's later claim that, from an early date, "The Security Council and the international community were very happy to say African peacekeepers could go in, when everybody knew they did not have the capacity or resources."[150]

When the administration began pushing to replace AMIS in 2006, its efforts to secure a UN force were delayed by the need for a peace agreement and Khartoum's refusal to give its consent. Here, there is evidence that at least some officials were surprised by these obstacles and—like the advocacy movement—underestimated how long it would take to deploy the new force. For example, in a series of State Department interviews, Hamilton found that the need for Khartoum's consent for a UN mission "was a fundamental point that many U.S. officials were either unwilling or unable to absorb. . . . The possibility that their demands would be met by the word 'no' was never seriously factored into the calculations of many U.S. bureaucrats."[151]

However, on the key issue of whether those in charge grasped that a UN mission—or, subsequently, the joint AU-UN force that was deployed— would face many of the same structural obstacles as AMIS in trying to protect civilians, there can be little doubt. First, President Bush's evident interest in U.S. military options and effort to secure significant NATO involvement before turning to the UN suggests that he understood this. In addition, the delays in deploying UNAMID and the limitations of its troop composition were clearly predicted. From the earliest discussions of a UN force, UN officials stressed the importance of including Western troops with sophisticated equipment and military capabilities.[152] Likewise, in April 2006 Ron Capps, a Foreign Service officer then serving in Khartoum who was an expert on the war in Darfur and who had previously worked in military intelligence, wrote a widely distributed State Department cable with a similar message. In it, Capps argued that "stopping the violence in Darfur will require a military force with first-world leadership, first-world assets, and first-world experience."[153] Still, in deference to Khartoum and the AU, the United States accepted the idea of a primarily African force with African leadership even while senior administration officials privately recognized that Khartoum had no intention of permitting the deployment of an effective force. As Natsios tellingly noted in April 2007, nearly nine months before the handover to UNAMID, "No matter what they agree to I doubt the [Government of Sudan] will actually allow us to put competent peacekeeping troops under UN command and control in Darfur. They may agree to it, but they will find ways to stonewall and delay them."[154]

The evidence about U.S. Darfur policy introduced in this chapter provides support for five of this book's six hypotheses. First, like the French government on Rwanda and in line with hypothesis 1, when the Bush administration faced strong moral pressures to protect civilians combined with an inhospitable operational environment and multiple other concerns within its ranks about the costs and risks of military action, it facilitated two consecutive ambitions-resources gaps through its support for AMIS and UNAMID. In contrast, in the absence of significant internal or civil society pressure to address the violence in Darfur before the spring of 2004, the first phase of U.S. policy was consistent with hypothesis 5: other priorities in U.S.–Sudan relations took precedence in guiding policy, and a peace operation was not on the table.

The evidence also supports my expectations about how leaders can benefit from ambitions-resources gaps. U.S. support for AMIS and UNAMID was not just the result of intragovernmental bargaining; it was also a way to placate activists without taking risks that could threaten serious public backlash. As in chapter 4, the assorted reasons highlighted in hypothesis 2 for concerned citizens and officials to accede to these policies were on full display. Notably, forces ranging from naiveté to sophisticated calculations of political feasibility pushed different elements of the diverse advocacy movement to accept these missions, while competing priorities and efficacy concerns often led the officials most committed to Darfur to see them as acceptable compromises that could hopefully do some good. Further, as highlighted in hypothesis 3, U.S. officials repeatedly portrayed their policies of support for the AU and then the UN-AU hybrid as more impressive in addressing civilians' security needs than they really were.

Finally, U.S. Darfur policy also supports hypothesis 6, my tentative expectation that if they have the chance to do so, leaders will sooner support foreign troops who may be unable to provide the protection they are asked to deliver than deploy and constrain their own capable forces. For the Bush administration the opportunity to support AMIS and UNAMID was a convenience made possible by the availability of the AU and UN as alternatives to U.S. intervention. Yet the administration also worked hard to make these viable options, first urging AMIS's initial deployment and expansion and then pushing the UN peacekeeping bureaucracy into a mission it wanted no part of. By using its political clout in these ways it was able to create the conditions that allowed it to support these missions without having to commit its own troops.

This was a stark contrast to the French experience in Rwanda, where French leaders were prevented from using the UN in similar fashion despite a clear preference for doing so. In that case, this was partly due to resistance from other Security Council members, but it also reflected the faster pace of killing in Rwanda and the much quicker emergence of civil society pressure for action. By the time UNAMIR II was approved the French press and NGOs were already focused on the genocide, and had no patience for delays in deployment. In contrast, the framework for AMIS was in place by the time the Bush administration came under significant pressure for stronger action on Darfur, in part due to the administration's own diplomatic legwork. As we have seen, this helped the administration manage advocacy demands, since so many concerned citizens were open to the approach of expanding the existing force.

Australia in the Southwest Pacific

The Australian public were screaming out . . . to do something to stop
it. People were ringing up, crying over the phone, we had more calls
on that issue than I've ever had in my life on anything.
　　—Alexander Downer, foreign minister of Australia, *Deliverance*

The late 1990s was both a difficult and exciting time for Indonesia. The
Asian Financial Crisis that began in 1997 badly damaged the nation's economy and led to the resignation of the long-time dictator, President Suharto,
in May of 1998. Suharto's departure paved the way for the emergence of
democracy but was accompanied by instability and violence across the
archipelago. Indeed, three separate complex emergencies began in 1999—
one-sided militia violence against civilians in East Timor, civil war in the
province of Aceh, and communal conflict between Christians and Muslims
in the Moluccas.

This chapter investigates and compares the Australian government's
responses to two of these conflicts, in East Timor and Aceh. These responses
could hardly be more different, though they involved the same Australian
leadership—under Prime Minister John Howard—and both conflicts
revolved around separatist demands for independence from Indonesia. In
East Timor, Australia led a large and robust civilian protection operation,
the International Force for East Timor (INTERFET). This case is a clear
example of how the combination of extraordinary normative pressure—
mainly in the form of demands from society but also acting directly on top
leaders themselves—can combine with a fairly favorable operational environment to inspire robust civilian protection efforts, rather than ambitions-
resources gaps. Together, these factors provided the Howard government
with both the motive and the political space it needed to launch an ambitious protection force. Notably, moreover, Australia's leadership of INTER-
FET is not explained by traditional "national interest"–type arguments,
either strategic or economic.

In response to the civil war in Aceh from 1999 to 2004, in contrast, Australia took no part in any peace operation and made no other significant effort—diplomatic or otherwise—to address security threats to civilians. Here, too, the configuration of domestic pressures differed dramatically from the cases of ambitions-resources gaps discussed in chapters 4–5, but in an entirely different way from East Timor. With Aceh, Australian leaders instead faced very little domestic pressure from society or the bureaucracy. This lack of concern, in turn, rendered the operational environment virtually irrelevant and allowed the government to pursue a key strategic interest it had abandoned over East Timor—a strong relationship with Indonesia—without facing any real political dilemma about how to respond to the war in Aceh.

These cases complement the other empirical chapters in various ways. Together they further support my expectations about when leaders turn to ambitions-resources gaps. Both are examples of circumstances where, for very different reasons, we would not expect to see these policies and indeed do not. Yet Australia's leadership of INTERFET is also significant for several other reasons. Though not an instance of an ambitions-resources gap, it does confirm some of my expectations about why concerned citizens support these policies, since many Australians were unaware of the most basic challenges of intervening in East Timor. In addition, it builds on the statistical support for hypothesis 4 by showing how strong moral pressure may inspire robust protection even without strategic or economic grounds for intervention, if leaders also expect that costs can be held to an acceptable level. Further, INTERFET highlights an issue with implications for the distinction between ambitions-resources gaps and robust protection efforts by showing that some aspects of the operational environment, notably local consent for intervention, may at times be malleable. I return to this issue at the end of the chapter.

Finally, these two cases provide a unique opportunity to examine the validity of my arguments outside the context of the American, French, and British policies that provide the basis for so many studies of humanitarian military action (and non-responses to atrocities). Australia is the only Western democracy besides the United States, United Kingdom, and France that consistently possesses the military capacity and political influence needed to lead ambitious civilian protection missions. Indeed, Australia has initiated or provided crucial support for several highly regarded peace operations and has oriented post–Cold War defense planning around the ability to serve as the lead state in peace enforcement, peace-keeping, and civilian evacuation missions in its own neighborhood. To do so, a 2000 defense review asserted, the Australian Defence Force (ADF) might need "to contribute to regional peacekeeping and humanitarian relief operations and help evacuate Australians and others from regional trouble-spots." The review continued: "We should be prepared to be the largest force contributor to such operations. Our planning needs to acknowledge that we could be called upon to undertake several operations simultaneously."[1] The government later adopted the review's plans to emphasize the development of logistics and deployment capabilities for land forces and to increase the number of full-time ADF personnel.[2] Thus there is every reason to think that this book's arguments apply to Australian decision-making within its own region.

Australian policy on East Timor—and, especially, Aceh—has received less attention in the secondary literature than was true for the previous case studies. For this chapter I thus conducted an extensive, in-depth analysis of elite Australian media coverage of the two conflicts as well as a series of interviews in Australia with former politicians, policy advisers, academic experts, and activists. For the media analysis, as in the statistical work, I relied on coverage in the *Sydney Morning Herald* (*SMH*).[3] While the hundreds of articles I looked at provided important information about the conflicts and Australian policy, I also used the volume and content of reporting to help assess the extent of concern and activism about each complex emergency. To my knowledge this is the first in-depth scholarly investigation of Australian media coverage of either of these conflicts. Finally, in addition to various secondary sources, I also sought out key players' and activists' media interviews and firsthand accounts; every publicly available opinion survey about East Timor (there were none for Aceh); and every related petition submitted to the Australian Parliament in the years preceding and during the complex emergencies.

The chapter begins with a brief introduction to the Australian political system and foreign policy process. I then lay out my argument as it relates to East Timor, followed by Aceh. As in the previous chapters, for each case I discuss the complex emergency and Australian policy toward it, and then relate this to the relationship between pressures to protect civilians and control costs. For East Timor I also address the top alternative explanations for INTERFET.

Foreign Policy Making in Australia

Australia has a Westminster political system with two primary political blocs, the Australian Labor Party (ALP, or Labor), and the Liberal-National Coalition (the Liberals, or the Coalition).[4] Parties are highly disciplined, and parliamentarians rarely cross the aisle, giving the majority party strong control over both domestic and foreign policy.

Although major policy decisions are subject to the approval of Cabinet, Australian prime ministers have a great deal of authority. The prime minister takes advice from Cabinet but makes the final decision on the deployment of military force. What is more, the Australian constitution places virtually no constraints on the government's ability to use armed force abroad. As one former senior Defence Department official described it, "The prime minister must have the confidence of Cabinet, Cabinet must have the confidence of the party room, the party must have a majority in the House of Representatives, and if they do they can do whatever they want."[5] As in the United States and France, then, it is the preferences and decisions of the national executive—in particular, the prime minister and foreign minister—that require explanation.

Given this system, there are two primary political components of foreign policy-making in Australia. The first is party room politics: the government must convince the party to support what it wants to do. The second is public politics. Although the government need not garner support from outside its caucus in the short term, it must concern itself with how its decisions may affect the next election, and thus with public opinion. As in all democracies, the opposition may seek to score political points or affect policy through its influence in public debate.

East Timor: The Complex Emergency

A former Portuguese colony, East Timor comprises the eastern half of the island of Timor, some 240 nautical miles across the Timor Sea from northern Australia. After Portugal withdrew from the territory in 1974, Indonesia invaded and annexed it in December 1975. A bloody 23-year occupation and war between Indonesia and Timorese resistance forces followed. This war involved extraordinary brutality by the Indonesians against the civilian population, especially in its early years. By the early 1980s, up to 200,000 East Timorese had died from violence, disease, or starvation associated with the occupation, out of a population of no more than 800,000.[6] Over the next two decades the East Timorese and their allies abroad advocated for independence from what most saw as a cruel and illegitimate occupying power.

The first major signs that this quest might someday succeed came with the dramatic political changes of the late 1990s in Indonesia. After the fall of Suharto, the new Indonesian president, B. J. Habibie, was eager to put an end to constant international pressure about East Timor, whose incorporation into Indonesia most countries had never recognized. Although Habibie did not want to see the territory go, he announced in January 1999 that the East Timorese would be allowed to vote on whether they wished to remain in Indonesia or become independent. A UN-supervised referendum was scheduled for the following August.

Habibie's decision was deeply unpopular with the Indonesian military—TNI (Tentara Nasional Indonesia)—and with a portion of the local population who benefited from association with Indonesia. Throughout 1999, as planning and preparation for the referendum progressed, local militia supported by elements of TNI instigated violence in a bid to delay or cancel the vote, or at least to frighten the East Timorese into casting their ballots against independence. Tens of thousands of East Timorese were uprooted, and several hundred died.[7] The militia held civilians hostage, cut them off from access to humanitarian aid in an effort to influence their votes, and threatened the UN personnel who were preparing for the ballot.[8] TNI—which was responsible for security—took no effective action to prevent this escalating violence.

After a delay due to the violence, the referendum was held on August 30, 1999, and the nearly 99% turnout was widely interpreted as a sign that the result favored independence. Immediately, the militias escalated their attacks against civilians, further accelerating their efforts after the result—78.5% for independence—was announced on September 4.[9]

The scale of the violence in East Timor over the following weeks was extraordinary. According to one estimate, "In less than three weeks 72 percent of all buildings and houses were destroyed or damaged, and hundreds of East Timorese were killed. . . . More than 250,000 people were deported to West Timor [the neighboring Indonesian province]. The casualty rate would have been much higher had not hundreds of thousands of Timorese fled to the mountains where they faced severe food shortages."[10] Indeed, some 600,000 people—around three-quarters of the total population—were displaced during this period.[11] The number of Timorese that died in the violence in September 1999 is uncertain, but was probably between 1,000 and 2,000 people.[12] Some of those who went to West Timor were supporters of Indonesia who feared the prospect of remaining in an independent East Timor. Most, however, were forced across the border against their will by militia who hoped to convince outside observers that the vote had been rigged.

Given the nature of the violence in East Timor, an international peace-enforcement mission offered the only realistic hope of providing for civilians' security and protection needs.[13] First, there was no political settlement that could be mediated to end the violence. The militia forces had no official authority, and in any case were conducting exclusively one-sided attacks against civilians. What is more, the Indonesian government—though ostensibly in charge—was not entirely in control of TNI, and TNI was clearly not in control of the militia. Thus, coercive diplomatic or economic pressure on Jakarta alone offered little hope of restoring security.

Australia's Response

Australian involvement in these events took place in two phases: first, before the referendum, from December 1998 through August 1999; and second, during the rapid post-ballot escalation of violence in September. The contrast between these periods, moreover, is stark: while the Australian government initially hoped to avoid both independence for East Timor and a major peacekeeping role there, by the end of September it found itself leading a major international coalition to protect civilians and, ultimately, uphold the results of the referendum.

PREPARING FOR THE REFERENDUM

In December 1998, the Australian prime minister, John Howard, sent President Habibie a letter urging him to think about ways that Indonesia might develop more progressive policies toward East Timor. Howard knew that Habibie was already contemplating various liberalizing reforms and hoped to encourage this process. He did not, however, wish to see East Timor become independent in the near future, and his letter focused on suggestions about how Indonesia might best prevail on the people of East Timor to accept an agreement for political autonomy within the Indonesian state.[14] Habibie's subsequent announcement that East Timor would be permitted to vote on its future within the year therefore came as a considerable and unwelcome surprise to the Australian government, which nevertheless felt that it had no choice but to support the process. It did so, however, with considerable trepidation regarding the prospects for violence and the viability of a potentially independent East Timor.[15]

During February and March of 1999 the Howard government developed four key policy objectives with respect to East Timor. First, they wanted the territory to remain in Indonesia. Second, Australia's relationship with Indonesia would take priority over the future of East Timor, and therefore they would seek to avoid policies that might damage that relationship. Third, because they expected TNI to continue to play a prominent role in Indonesian politics, it was of special importance to maintain a positive relationship with it. Finally, Australia would—if at all possible—prefer to avoid deploying a large military force to East Timor. The Howard government recognized, however, that there was a good chance that a UN peacekeeping force would be needed in the event of a sudden Indonesian withdrawal from East Timor following a vote for independence, and that Australia would need to be prepared to play a major role in such an operation. In March, therefore, they began the process of bringing a second ADF brigade up to 30 days' notice to move (only one was normally maintained at this state of readiness), and shortly thereafter began consultations with the UN on what such a peacekeeping force might look like.[16] At the same time, they hoped that it would not prove necessary.

Given subsequent events, it is significant that at this time the Australian government anticipated that at least three things would need to happen before any peacekeeping operation could occur. First, the Timorese would have to vote for independence. Second, the Indonesian parliament would have to ratify this result. And third, TNI and other Indonesian personnel would have to leave East Timor. Any Australian deployment would thus occur no earlier than November 1999, and only as part of a UN effort to prepare the new nation for independence.

In the meantime, maintaining security in East Timor during the months before the vote posed a major challenge. In March and April, Indonesia, Portugal, and the UN negotiated a tripartite agreement that laid out the provisions for implementing the referendum. A UN civilian operation, the United Nations Mission in East Timor (UNAMET), would oversee the preparations for and conduct of the election, while Indonesia insisted that TNI—which strongly opposed independence—would take responsibility for maintaining security.

By late March, while the tripartite agreement was being negotiated in New York—and certainly by the time its terms were announced in late April—it was clear to Australian officials that TNI could not be trusted to maintain a secure environment for the vote. Australian intelligence indicated that TNI's relationship with President Habibie was shaky and that TNI was actively supporting the militia's violent efforts to influence (or ideally cancel) the vote.[17] Given their wish to preserve positive relations with TNI, however, Australian officials were not always forthcoming about this information in public. Still, as time passed, Prime Minister Howard, Foreign Minister Alexander Downer, and others increasingly criticized TNI involvement in the pre-ballot violence, and the government reached out repeatedly behind closed doors to encourage senior Indonesian civilian and military officials to bring security under control.[18]

Australian ambivalence about participating in a major peacekeeping operation also appears to have influenced the Howard government's handling of the intelligence at its disposal. In late March, the Australians proposed to a visiting UN official that UNAMET should include peacekeepers in order to keep a watchful eye on TNI during preparations for the referendum and to ensure the safety of the East Timorese and UN civilian staff. Australia, they suggested, would be willing to participate in such an operation. Subsequently, however, the government did nothing more to ensure that the tripartite agreement would include provisions for peacekeepers within UNAMET, instead assuming that the UN would do so.[19]

When the provisions of the tripartite agreement were announced in late April after weeks of escalating violence, the Australians were surprised to learn that there were to be no peacekeepers in UNAMET. Howard flew to Bali to encourage President Habibie to do more to provide security and to seek his consent to revise the tripartite agreement to include peacekeepers.

Habibie refused, and Howard later admitted that this was the last time he raised the issue with the Indonesians until the day before the vote, when it was too late.[20]

THE DEPLOYMENT AND DESIGN OF INTERFET

Despite the dramatic escalation in violence at the beginning of September and TNI's inability and unwillingness to control the militia that were responsible, the Indonesian government adamantly opposed the idea of an international force to protect civilians and restore order. For a critical period of just over a week after the September 4 announcement of the ballot result, the Howard government devoted itself to changing President Habibie's mind, both directly and by engaging the efforts of the United States, the UN, the International Monetary Fund (IMF), and numerous other governments. On September 7 Australia announced that it would be willing to lead such an operation if Indonesia could be prevailed on to consent.[21] It initially offered 2,000 troops and increased this to 4,500 two days later. After the United States suspended military ties with Indonesia on September 9, Australia followed suit.[22]

During this period, the Howard government and its international partners used every diplomatic measure they could conceive of to pressure the Indonesian government. The crippling of its economy in the Asian Financial Crisis had left Indonesia particularly vulnerable to the potential loss of international loans from the IMF if Habibie refused to accept a peace enforcement mission. Late in the evening of September 12, therefore, Habibie conceded and announced that an international force could deploy as soon as possible. Although his preference was for a UN mission consisting mainly of Asian troops, only Australia had both the will and the capacity to lead on short notice.[23] Unlike the Sudanese government in Darfur, Habibie did not absolutely rule out an Australian-led force. Thus, although the Australian government had not previously considered the possibility of leading this kind of enforcement mission, by September 20—only three weeks after the vote and a week after Habibie gave his consent—the ADF was on its way to East Timor. This quick deployment was possible partly due to the preparations the Howard government had already made for contributing to the anticipated UN operation.[24]

Australia's leadership of INTERFET qualifies as among the most robust of all post–Cold War civilian protection efforts. The operation's goals were, first, to re-establish peace and security, and second, to facilitate humanitarian aid and reconstruction. In this context, the former involved both directly protecting civilians under threat of violence and, more broadly, neutralizing the threat represented by the militia.

The mission's military strategies were equally ambitious. It was approved under Chapter VII of the UN Charter—assured through Australian diplomatic efforts at the UN—with a mandate to "take all necessary measures" to fulfill its goals.[25] Permissive rules of engagement allowed soldiers to pursue and disarm militia engaged in violence against civilians. As force commander Peter Cosgrove later described, these rules "would actually have excused any soldier who, in fearing for his or her life, had fired their rifle" while participating in these activities.[26] In addition, they "would have allowed him to open fire on the militia because they were threatening our troops directly by pointing their weapons at them."[27]

What is more, INTERFET's core protection tasks were carried out by ground forces supported from the air and sea. This allowed soldiers to interpose themselves between militia and civilians, create a credible threat, and thus serve as a deterrent to the militia.[28] As Cosgrove put it, "Our troops were able to starkly demonstrate to all interested parties the penalties and sanctions that would accompany any attempt to deliver on the wealth of violent rhetoric."[29]

In addition to appropriate operational goals and military strategies, Australia provided an impressive array of resources. In the end, it contributed some 5,500 personnel, and was supported by contributions from the United States—which played a critical role in logistics, communication, and intelligence—and some twenty-two other countries.[30] The Australian soldiers, the bulk of the force on the ground, were highly trained and exceptionally well equipped.[31] As John Birmingham describes, "Using the aggressive mobility provided by Blackhawk choppers and Light Armoured Vehicles to act on intelligence gathered by INTERFET's vastly superior surveillance net, the Australian-led forces were able to create the impression of overwhelming presence from the moment of their arrival."[32] Thanks to these high-end mobility and surveillance capabilities, Cosgrove later noted, the Australians "were able to seem ubiquitous."[33]

INTERFET quickly succeeded in bringing the violence in East Timor under control. By protecting civilians and confronting the militia, it helped create the conditions for hundreds of thousands of people to emerge from hiding and begin resuming their lives. In addition, aid organizations, which had been evacuated when the violence began, were able to return and provide desperately needed help to the terrorized and uprooted population. On October 20, the Indonesian parliament officially recognized the result of East Timor's referendum, and the last of the TNI troops departed on November 1.[34] In February of 2000, responsibility for the territory transferred to the UN Transitional Administration in East Timor (UNTAET), which included peacekeepers and a large civilian component to help with the transition to independent statehood. Australia provided about 1,650 troops (plus civilian police) to UNTAET, whose military component continued to focus on maintaining law and order.[35]

Accounting for INTERFET

Why did the Howard government lead such a robust civilian protection mission in East Timor, especially given its initial desire to avoid a major peacekeeping operation? First, by foreign policy standards the events in East Timor in 1999 generated enormous concern in Australia, and tremendous anger against Indonesia. This response was manifest in extensive and well-organized activism by various civil society groups both before and after the referendum, and in spontaneous outpourings of emotion by Australians from across the political spectrum. In early September, this led to intense pressure on Howard to send the ADF to protect the people of East Timor. On top of this, Australia's top political leaders have expressed a sense of moral responsibility that intervening in East Timor was "the right thing to do." At least on the margins, this added strength to the normative pressure from society. Second, material pressures were, though real, relatively muted. In particular, with Habibie's reluctant consent for an Australian-led mission and several other favorable circumstances, it was possible to envision keeping the risks and dangers at a tolerable level. This was important not just for the prospect of maintaining public and international backing, but also for ensuring support from within the Defence Department and the ADF. Overall, then, the weight of domestic moral pressures for action exceeded that of material concerns about expected costs, supporting the idea that this may at times be enough to prompt robust civilian protection efforts. In contrast, two alternative explanations for INTERFET that relate to Australia's strategic and economic interests directly contradict the available evidence.

NORMATIVE PRESSURES

East Timor in Australian Politics: Societal Pressure before and after the Ballot. Even before the August 30 vote, the Howard government faced domestic pressure over its policies on East Timor. This came primarily from organized groups with a long history of advocacy on Timorese self-determination and human rights, whose very existence reflected the special place that East Timor holds in Australian politics.

During World War II, Australian soldiers were stationed in East Timor, where the local population aided them (and a large number gave their lives) in the fight against Japan.[36] Thus, Australia boasted a large community of veterans with personal experience of the island and its people. A number of these men had also returned after the war as vacationers with their families, reinforcing their ties and increasing the number of Australians with a personal connection to Timorese society.[37] Many former soldiers also felt intense gratitude toward the Timorese for their help during the war, and had already taken an active interest in East Timor after the Indonesian annexation. They thus shared an established emotional commitment, a base of knowledge about the political situation, and a network of East Timor connections.[38] As violence mounted in 1999, they used their considerable political clout—organized through the Returned Services League, Australia's foremost veterans' association—to express their outrage.[39] Significantly, this group tended to be more politically conservative—and thus more likely to be supporters of the Howard government—than many other Australians who expressed similar concerns. This helped to ensure that in 1999 Howard faced political pressure from across the political spectrum, including a core constituency of Liberal Party voters.

The Indonesian occupation also helped lay the groundwork for the outpouring of support for East Timor in 1999, in three ways. First, it spawned a sizeable diaspora. According to East Timor's Commission for Reception, Truth and Reconciliation (CAVR), "Australia was the destination for the first East Timorese refugees from the civil war, a development which in time greatly strengthened the campaign for Timor-Leste in Australia and the region."[40]

Second, and relatedly, the annexation spawned a large international activist movement that advocated on behalf of Timorese independence and human rights for the next 25 years. Australia was one of the primary centers of this movement, partially due to the diaspora and its proximity to East Timor. In the 1970s, the movement attracted the attention of "academics, human rights activists, journalists, politicians, aid agencies, churches, returned soldiers, students and trade unionists, a good number of whom had already visited the territory," as well as a few parliamentarians.[41] Major organizations included the Campaign for an Independent East Timor and the Australia East Timor Association.

In addition to these solidarity groups campaigning for Timorese independence, a range of development, church, and human rights NGOs adopted a less party-political and more human rights–oriented approach, which was more appealing to a wider public.[42] Aid agencies such as the Australian Council for Overseas Aid (ACFOA) delivered humanitarian assistance after the Indonesian annexation, leading to long-term advocacy.[43]

After a number of setbacks the activism of the 1970s gave way to a more subdued level of activity in the 1980s. The 1990s, however, saw renewed attention and advocacy, both in Australia and elsewhere. Indonesia's 1989 decision to admit foreigners into East Timor for the first time since 1975 led to thousands of visits by individuals and civil society representatives. In addition, on November 12, 1991, Indonesian security forces were caught on film murdering several hundred funeral mourners in what became known as the Santa Cruz Massacre. According to CAVR, this event "was a turning point in world opinion on the territory . . . due to the presence of international observers . . . and their projection of the tragedy through print, radio and television to the world."[44] Moreover, in 1996, two Timorese—Bishop Carlos Filipe Ximenes Belo and José Ramos-Horta, the face of the Timorese resistance campaign's international diplomatic efforts since 1975—received the Nobel Peace Prize. This proved a boon to the activist community: as CAVR noted, "The global media coverage it attracted . . . generated new public interest and support for the civil society campaign in many countries."[45]

Nowhere was the effect greater than in Australia, where new organizations continued to form. According to CAVR, "These included Australians for a Free East Timor, . . . a Sydney branch of the Australia East Timor Association in 1992, Perth-based Friends of East Timor, the Mary McKillop Institute of East Timorese Studies established in Sydney in 1993, . . . the East Timor International Support Centre in Darwin, . . . in Melbourne the University Students for East Timor and the East Timor Human Rights Centre, . . . [and] Action in Solidarity with Indonesia and East Timor."[46] Australians also submitted no fewer than ninety-three East Timor-related petitions to Parliament between 1991 and 1997. These called for such actions as supporting UN resolutions on East Timor, supporting Timorese self-determination, working for the release of Timorese political prisoners, and ending military cooperation with Indonesia.[47]

The third effect of the Indonesian invasion and annexation was that Australia's response to these events had, by the 1990s, generated widespread feelings of remorse and guilt among the public—and some politicians—for their failure to have done more to prevent or halt Indonesia's actions. In 1975, Australia—preoccupied with a dramatic political crisis at home—had acquiesced in the Indonesian annexation. Three years later, in 1978, it became the first and only Western government ever to officially recognize Indonesian sovereignty over East Timor, a policy that continued unbroken into the 1990s. A belated understanding of the scale of violence wreaked on East Timor in the 1970s and 1980s now fueled the conviction among many Australians that their government must not repeat the mistakes of the past.

Thus, building on their advocacy of the previous decades, Australian solidarity groups and development-oriented NGOs spent the first eight months of 1999 preparing for the referendum and the prospect of an independent East Timor. Their long history of advocacy made it easy for these groups to mobilize quickly in support of the ballot process and coordinate with one another and with other relevant groups, such as the East Timorese diaspora.[48] Indeed, Habibie's decision to permit the referendum, combined with unprecedented media coverage of East Timor, "invigorated civil society like never before."[49]

Members of the media and the Labor Party joined these groups in urging the Howard government to do all it could to ensure that the ballot process would be fair and secure. This included advocating for strong pressure on Indonesia to admit a peacekeeping force after Howard's failed visit to Bali in April.[50] The Labor Party's foreign affairs spokesman, Laurie Brereton, pushed hard on this issue, noting in August that it was "a disgrace that there was no Australian commitment to peacekeepers, nor any Australian campaign to press Jakarta to accept them, during the most dangerous stage of the process."[51] Although these efforts to encourage stronger pre-ballot pressure for peacekeepers were unsuccessful, the sustained mobilization of civil society groups in the months leading up to the vote played an important role in helping galvanize broader public concern very quickly once the violence escalated in September.

After the referendum, Australian society exploded with indignation about the violence in East Timor. Suddenly, the Howard government came under pressure not just from the established activist community but also from a larger, more diverse set of concerned citizens.[52] This pressure, moreover, now focused on convincing Howard to send the ADF to restore order.

The growth in concern can be seen, for example, in changes in news coverage in the *Sydney Morning Herald*. Figure 6.1 shows the monthly count of

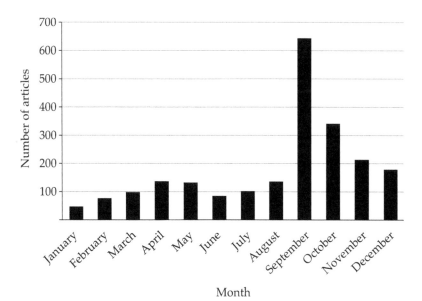

Month

Figure 6.1. Monthly *SMH* coverage of East Timor, 1999

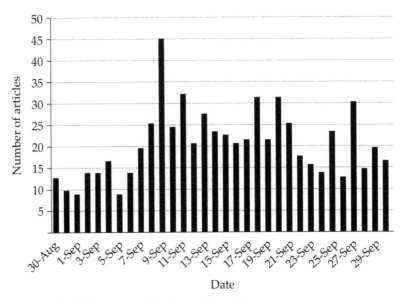

Figure 6.2. Daily *SMH* coverage of East Timor, September 1999

Note: Article counts for figures 6.1 and 6.2 are for full-text searches conducted in LexisNexis using "Timor" as the search term.

articles in 1999 that mention "Timor," with a striking increase in September. A closer look, moreover, reveals that coverage not only increased dramatically in September but also did so before the decision to deploy INTERFET. The critical period was between the vote—especially the announcement of the result on September 4—and President Habibie's consent on September 12. During this time violence was rampant, but it was not yet clear if an international force would be deployed to stop it. Figure 6.2 shows the daily volume of reporting starting August 30. Coverage shot up dramatically over the next two weeks and actually peaked at a higher level than for most of the days after INTERFET was announced and deployment began. This suggests that the increase was a response to the violence in East Timor, and not just the decision to deploy INTERFET.

An examination of concerned citizens' and civil society groups' actions and demands, however, offers clearer evidence of the pressure on the Howard government. During the critical week of September 4–12, calls for military action came from all directions. Prominent citizens with ties to East Timor, such as James Dunn, former Australian consul, urged intervention.[53] So did the Australian Green Party, many members of the media, and East Timor solidarity groups. Many of these calls for action pushed for military force even without Indonesian permission.[54] Even groups not normally associated with militaristic attitudes, including development NGOs such as

ACFOA and Oxfam, were in favor.[55] This attitude also extended to leaders in the Catholic community, which maintained close ties with overwhelmingly Catholic East Timor. On September 6, the Archbishop of Sydney warned that a failure to send troops "would leave a scar on Australia's reputation."[56] A Sydney nun stated, "This is a humanitarian crisis of enormous proportion, and if the world and Australia doesn't do something now we will never, never be forgiven."[57] Australian unions organized protests and boycotts—notably against the Indonesian airline, Garuda—in Sydney, Melbourne, Brisbane, Darwin and elsewhere.[58]

Crucially, moreover, during this time an unusually large number of ordinary Australians who had not previously sought to influence government policy added their voices to the call for military action. Partly, they expressed their views through spontaneous outpourings of emotion in letters to newspapers and calls to radio stations and to their parliamentary representatives. Partly, however, they participated in demonstrations and events organized by the many civil society groups who had been following events in East Timor for months. In this sense, these groups' high level of activity over the previous months was critical to the speed at which the Howard government came under pressure to act. Prepared for probable violence and mobilized for action, East Timor solidarity groups and other civil society organizations were able to provide concerned citizens with public avenues for expressing their views on almost no notice.[59]

The media devoted considerable coverage to this phenomenon of public indignation. As one article noted, "the vast majority of Australians are outraged and are demanding action. Indeed, we are more united in our anger and concern than at any other time since World War II."[60] Another marveled that "East Timor dominated Letters last week. . . . There were many, many calls for a UN peacekeeping force to be sent to end the violence and bloodshed and deaths, and calls for Australia to adopt a harder line with the Indonesian Government. It is a topic that attracts very few opposing positions, unlike most other controversial subjects."[61] One telling article outlined reports from members of Parliament about the activities of their constituents:

> Federal MPs across Australia . . . reported a flood of phone calls and e-mails from constituents, with the Liberal member for the Sydney seat of Cook, Mr. Bruce Baird, saying "my phones have gone crazy." In Bathurst, 200 people attended a candle-light vigil, called at less than a day's notice, and passed a resolution calling on the Government to send in troops. . . . Mr. Baird said his largely Anglo-Celtic, Australian-born electorate had deluged him with calls on East Timor, more than on any other issue. "To a man and a woman, they are saying, 'go for it,' that we've let the East Timorese people down before and we just can't do it again."[62]

The same article reported that calls to political radio programs, popularly known as talkback, had exploded: "This week . . . there's been more than 1,000 calls, and many say we have to return the favour after what the East Timorese did for us in World War II. The last 72 hours has completely galvanised public opinion."[63]

Such calls for military intervention even in the face of Indonesian opposition reflected a widespread misunderstanding of Australia's own military capabilities and of the import of taking such aggressive action. Leading a peace operation was one thing, but a unilateral invasion without Indonesian consent would certainly prompt fierce resistance from TNI, which could field a much larger force than the Australians. Many concerned citizens, then, were effectively calling for a war that their country could not hope to win. As a result, their pleas also prompted a reaction. One *SMH* contributor wrote, "The most unexpected fact of the week: that so many Australians seriously believe we should land troops in East Timor without Indonesian permission. . . . There seems a real lack of caution among those who tell our Government to 'just get in there.' . . . The mood seems to be to shame all those Australians who have tried to establish a dialogue and cordiality with our most important neighbour."[64] According to another, "Only after a few days did it apparently dawn on the callers to talkback radio that our military capacity was not even remotely up to unilaterally mounting some sort of presence in East Timor."[65]

Finally, available survey evidence confirms the impression that many Australians wanted to see strong action from their government, and also suggests that the broader public favored the possibility of military action. A poll conducted September 10–12, before Habibie's decision to let INTERFET deploy, asked two relevant questions. First, "Do you personally think the Australian government is currently doing too much, doing enough or should they do more to help the situation in East Timor? If do more—do you think the Australian government should do a lot more or only a little more?" Fully 31% of respondents felt that the Australian government should do "a lot more" for East Timor, while an additional 10% felt it should do "a little more." The Australian government was "doing enough" according to 45%, and only 6% thought it was "doing too much." Second, the poll asked: "Are you personally in favour or against Australia sending troops to East Timor as part of an international peace-keeping force? If in favour—is that strongly in favour or partly in favour? If against—is that strongly against or partly against?" Fully 54% of respondents answered "strongly in favour," and an additional 23% answered "partly in favour," for a total of 77% in favor. Only 15% answered either "partly against" or "strongly against."[66] Given that it was unclear at the time whether Indonesia would consent to such a force, this high level of support is especially impressive.[67] More subtly, a pollster for the Howard government, who had access to far more polls than are publicly available, later recalled of this period that "the imperative there politically was to do something."[68]

In sum, the message to the Australian government was loud and clear: not only were a great many citizens extremely concerned about the Timorese and willing to firmly support military action, but a significant portion—from activists to the average citizen—wanted to send the ADF even without Indonesian consent. As evident in the surveys, moreover, even members of the broader public who were not expressing these views aloud mostly supported them.

Howard and other senior officials have since acknowledged the intensity of this pressure. Some years later Howard recalled that "the reaction in Australia got increasingly alarmed as the result of the ballot was known and the violence and the apprehended violence increased, people got more and more concerned and more and more demanding that we do something."[69] Joe Hockey, Minister for Financial Services, remembered: "It was an extraordinary period. The reaction right across the electorate was you've got to do something. And even when you said 'Look, do you really want to invade our nearest neighbour?' they'd say 'Yes, do it.'"[70] According to Foreign Minister Downer, "The Australian public were screaming out, everybody was—I mean it wasn't a party thing, a Left-Right thing—screaming out to do something to stop it. People were ringing up, crying over the phone, we had more calls on that issue than I've ever had in my life on anything."[71]

Moral Responsibility Within Government: "The Right Thing to Do". A further source of normative pressure to protect civilians appears to have been a sense of moral responsibility for the welfare of the Timorese population among Australian officials, including notably Howard and Downer themselves. As they repeatedly asserted in INTERFET's aftermath, protecting the East Timorese and helping them realize their independence was "the right thing to do."[72] This sense of responsibility mirrored the sentiments of many everyday Australians but also seems to have reflected the government's unintended role in the events that led to the violence. Although Howard's December 1998 letter to Habibie did not push for independence, it is thought to have had considerable influence over his decision to call the referendum.[73] What is more, after the referendum the evidence is consistent with this story since Australia's leaders did expend considerable effort and expense on behalf of the Timorese.

Still, Australian policies before August 30 are not especially consistent with a major role for such sentiments. Since the government was well aware of the prospect of severe violence, it might have devoted greater effort to convincing the Indonesians to accept peacekeepers before the ballot if avoiding this outcome were a top priority. And as Hugh White has noted, subsequent claims that official support for East Timorese independence had developed by late 1998 or early 1999 are "simply inconsistent with all of the Government's words, and most of its deeds, until at least the middle of 1999."[74] Thus, the government's priorities as expressed through the policies of the preceding months seem to suggest that INTERFET was not simply the right thing to do. Rather, this view probably acted to reinforce the pressure for action from across Australian society as this pressure climbed to a fever pitch.

THE OPERATIONAL ENVIRONMENT

Society's calls for military action created a real quandary for the Howard government during the two weeks after the referendum. The biggest problem was Habibie's opposition to an international force, which threatened to create an untenably dangerous operational environment for intervention. Without Indonesian consent, Australian troops would certainly face fierce resistance from TNI and a real possibility of full-scale war between the two countries. This was undesirable for a host of reasons. Obviously it would involve much higher financial and human costs, and despite the initial unconcern of some Australians about Indonesian consent, maintaining public support over time would have been an entirely different proposition. As Don Greenlees and Robert Garran note, "Aside from the political unacceptability, the number of casualties would be intolerable."[75] Relatedly, the main concern of both top ADF officials and Defence Department bureaucrats was to avoid fighting TNI, and so they viewed Indonesian consent as a prerequisite for any deployment. Not only did they not want to see their people killed, but they did not want to permanently destroy the strong working relationship the ADF had carefully built with the Indonesian military or expose Australia to a long future of antagonistic relations with its most important neighbor.[76] As backup, the Defence Department also wanted a clear signal from the U.S. government to the Indonesian government that a fight with Australia would also mean a fight with the United States.[77]

Thus, Howard and Downer made it clear that Australia would not intervene without an invitation from Indonesia, while at the same time doing everything they could to bring this about. In the meantime, they faced the difficult task of convincing an agitated public of the folly of a course of action that many citizens preferred. As Howard's chief of staff Arthur Sinodinos put it, the problem was "to manage the wild horses of public opinion to make sure that we [didn't] end up by accident in a shooting war with Indonesia."[78] To this end, Howard and Downer repeatedly emphasized that there were 26,000 Indonesian troops in East Timor, that sending forces without Indonesian permission would be tantamount to declaring war with Indonesia, and that Australia could not unilaterally save the Timorese.

When Habibie finally consented to INTERFET's deployment on September 12, he dramatically changed the anticipated operational environment. Rather than risking a war that the public would soon tire of, Australia could now intervene under relatively favorable circumstances, at least by the standards of complex emergencies. What is more, in addition to its other contributions the Clinton administration came through with both a verbal warning to Jakarta and a Marine expeditionary unit that parked offshore—just in case—for part of the operation. Thus, Australian officials could now at least anticipate that TNI would mostly cooperate, and several other aspects of the operational environment were quite auspicious. The total civilian population requiring protection was very small at well under a million people, as was the size of the territory. At less than 15,000 square kilometers, East Timor is the third smallest in land area among all the post–Cold War complex emergencies analyzed in chapter 3.

Also of significance, with this key issue resolved the ADF was enthusiastic about the mission. It was to be Australia's largest overseas deployment since the Vietnam War, and it was meaningful for service-members—from chief of the Defence Force Chris Barrie all the way down through the ranks—that the public were expressing their strong support.[79]

To be sure, there remained legitimate reason for concern. Australian leaders fully expected the militia, who were well armed but not particularly well trained, and who had excellent knowledge of the mountainous terrain, to resist INTERFET's efforts to halt their attacks against civilians. What is more, some officials continued to worry that INTERFET might be drawn into fighting with Indonesian forces.[80] Although TNI was supposed to withdraw from the territory, there would be some time during which both Australian and Indonesian soldiers would be on the ground and in which tension or misunderstandings could lead to violence. Likewise, there remained some uncertainty about Habibie's control over TNI.[81] Still, despite all of this, the situation compared favorably with places like Darfur, Kosovo, and even Rwanda.

Alternative Explanations

There are two alternative explanations for the deployment and design of INTERFET that coincide with standard realist or national-interest accounts of humanitarian intervention: the mission may have reflected either traditional Australian strategic interests or a quest for natural resource wealth. To assess these possibilities it is helpful to consider them in the context of Australian policy throughout 1999, not just beginning in September. On close examination, both are contradicted by substantial evidence.

First, although strategic imperatives can sometimes explain the robust use of force to protect civilians, this is clearly not the case here. Indeed,

INTERFET defied the most sacred tenets of decades' worth of Australian strategic doctrine.

Indonesia is Australia's largest and most powerful neighbor. Thus, as hinted above and as the policy objectives developed in the spring of 1999 suggest, Australia has very strong strategic interests in maintaining good relations with Indonesia and TNI. Successive Australian governments have, moreover, pursued these interests enthusiastically since Indonesian independence from the Netherlands in 1949. When Australia failed to protest Indonesia's original annexation of East Timor in 1975 and then officially recognized its incorporation in 1978, maintaining a firm relationship with Suharto was a key part of the motivation for its silence. Likewise, Australian strategic planning has consistently emphasized the importance of these relations to Australian security. Efforts to promote close defense ties with Indonesia included several decades of extensive military cooperation programs, including regular meetings between defense ministers, combined military exercises, and considerable Australian training assistance to the Indonesian military.[82] What is more, these policies have never been popular with the Australian public. Notably, Paul Keating's Labor government negotiated a 1995 defense cooperation agreement with Indonesia in secret because the expected public opposition in Australia was so strong that this appeared the only means to ensure its passage.[83]

Australian policies through August 1999 largely followed in this tradition, although they were also partly consistent with the preferences of the activist community. On one hand, decisions to raise the issue of peacekeepers with Habibie in April, to call attention to Indonesia's failure to maintain adequate security, and to call for the deployment of more civilian police were generally consistent with both the government's desire not to be forced into a large and dangerous military deployment and the demands of concerned Australians. On the other, Howard's decision not to push the Indonesians harder to accept peacekeepers before the vote is consistent with seeking good relations with Indonesia and TNI. Given the strength of pro-Timorese and anti-Indonesian sentiment in Australia, moreover, it may have increased the probability of an outcome—heightened post-ballot violence—that officials knew would generate widespread anger at home.

Indeed, the extent to which the Australian government did or did not try—and should or should not have tried—harder to gain Habibie's acquiescence for peacekeepers before the referendum is the subject of some controversy. Downer defended the government's actions, arguing that Habibie was firmly resolved not to allow peacekeepers at that time.[84] That Australian officials repeatedly urged Indonesia—both publicly and in private—to do a better job in providing security does provide some support for Downer's position that the government's focus was on the Timorese people. Still, as then-deputy secretary for strategy in the Department of Defence Hugh White concludes,

> It was clear . . . that there would have been huge resistance in Indonesia to the deployment of a major PKF [peacekeeping force] to East Timor before the ballot. But it was also clear that no sustained and focused effort was made either by Australia or, it seems, by the UN to overcome that resistance. We can never now know whether, if pushed harder, Indonesia would have acquiesced. But it may well be that by not pushing harder at this time . . . we missed the last best chance to avoid the disasters of September.[85]

Although this debate cannot be resolved here, at the very least the evidence does seem to indicate that Australia's relationship with Indonesia played a critical if not a predominant role in the development of policy toward East Timor during the period before the referendum.

Importantly, this history of efforts to maintain good relations with Indonesia right up through 1999 illustrates the extent to which INTERFET represented both a break with long-standing Australian strategic priorities and a total failure to achieve the strategic goals the Australian government had laid out in the spring.[86] What is more, the goal of minimizing the unavoidable rift with Indonesia over INTERFET persisted throughout the planning and conduct of the mission. As Sinodinos put it, Howard knew that the Indonesians would be upset and "probably would not talk to us for a while," but aimed to "act in a way that [would] give them the least cause for offense."[87] In the end, the operation led to years of tense relations with both the Indonesian government and TNI.

The second alternative explanation for INTERFET, put forward by some on the left, is that the Howard government was driven by the opportunity to increase Australian revenues from the Timor Gap oil and gas fields—located between East Timor and Australia—if East Timor were to become independent. This, too, is inconsistent with the available evidence. As noted above, the government's preference as of early 1999 was for East Timor to remain in Indonesia. It held this preference, moreover, despite having sponsored a 1998 study of East Timorese public opinion that clearly showed that any imminent vote on the territory's status would likely favor independence.[88] Its preference for East Timor to stay in Indonesia, therefore, suggests that it made no effort through the spring or summer of 1999 to capitalize on any potential that an independent East Timor would represent.

Even if East Timor were to become independent, however, it was hardly clear at the time how this would affect Australian revenues from the Timor Gap fields. In 1989 Australia and Indonesia had negotiated a treaty over drilling rights that was already highly favorable to Australia as a reward for its status as the sole Western power to recognize Indonesian sovereignty over East Timor. Indeed, the Timor Gap fields had served as a partial incentive for Australian recognition of Indonesian sovereignty in 1978.[89] While Australia could reasonably expect—and indeed would later gain—considerable leverage with a newly independent East Timor on the negotiation of a new treaty, the Howard government could hardly have predicted in 1999 how such negotiations would progress. According to international law, an independent East Timor would have a strong territorial claim to areas Australia controlled under the existing treaty. Had East Timor pressed this claim in the International Court of Justice, Australia could well have ended up with a worse deal than it already had. INTERFET, moreover, was a very expensive mission: the Government actually planned a special tax to pay for the budget deficit it was expected to cause. Given this, and given the threat to the relationship with Indonesia, it stretches the imagination to believe that Australian leaders would have initiated INTERFET for the uncertain benefits of a new and more favorable treaty governing the Timor Gap fields.

Aceh: The Complex Emergency

In 1999 a long-running conflict between the Free Aceh Movement (Gerakan Aceh Merdeka, or GAM) and the Indonesian government erupted into full-scale civil war. Although low-level fighting had plagued the province since the 1970s, the worst of the violence was between 1999 and 2004. The roots of the conflict lay in resentment by the local population at perceived exploitation by the Indonesian government and the arrival in Aceh of some 160,000 Javanese settlers during the previous decades as part of the government's so-called "transmigration policy."[90] The renewed outbreak of violence in 1999 was associated with the broader upheaval in Indonesia after the fall of Suharto, which included the violence in East Timor. Indeed, GAM's aspirations were influenced by events in East Timor. Before 1999, unrest in Aceh had never generated calls for a vote on the province's future, but such calls emerged in the wake of the decision on the Timorese referendum.

Both sides perpetrated human rights abuses—including extrajudicial killings, forced disappearances and torture—although the Indonesian security forces were the bigger culprits. The war is thought to have directly affected a majority of the province's population, forcibly displacing from one-third to two-thirds of residents at some point in time—up to 600,000 people between 1999 and 2004.[91] Both sides used forced displacement strategically: the rebels to draw attention to the conflict, and the government during counterinsurgency operations. By the end of 2002, the U.S. Committee for Refugees estimated that over 10,000 people, mostly civilians, had died since the beginning of the conflict.[92] Then, during a single year of martial law and Indonesian military offensives between May 2003 and May 2004, TNI claimed to have killed nearly 2,000 GAM members, although human rights groups argued that most of these were civilians.[93] Ironically, the December 2004 tsunami that devastated Aceh and other parts of Southeast Asia helped pave the way for peace. A memorandum of understanding providing for demobilization and disarmament of GAM and the removal of Indonesian forces was signed in August 2005, and peaceful elections were held in December 2006.

The Australian Response

The Australian government, still under Prime Minister John Howard, showed no interest in any significant involvement, military or otherwise, in the conflict in Aceh. Instead, Foreign Minister Downer consistently asserted that Aceh's claim for independence was distinctly different—and less valid than—East Timor's, because Aceh had been part of Indonesia since independence in 1949.[94] Although he urged both Indonesia and GAM to respect human rights and noted that a diplomatic solution to the conflict would be preferable, Downer left no doubt about Australian support for Indonesia's "right to deal with organisations that mount militant acts against their own people," calling attention to the atrocities also committed by GAM and noting that they "should not be seen as some sort of honest and honourable victims."[95]

But GAM's pursuit of independence was not the only relevant issue. More pertinent from a humanitarian perspective were the violence and human rights abuses that accompanied the Indonesian counterinsurgency campaign. Beginning in 2000, a small Swiss NGO called the Henry Dunant Centre for Humanitarian Dialogue took charge of coordinating a three-year-long peace process. Initial negotiations led to a ceasefire, known as the "humanitarian pause," which ended with the launch of major military operations in April 2001. On December 9, 2002, the parties signed a more wide-ranging cessation of hostilities agreement, but, following repeated ceasefire violations over the next few months, in May 2003 the Indonesian government launched the most extensive offensives yet in the province.

Over time, as Konrad Huber notes, the Henry Dunant Centre "increasingly reached out to key states, including Norway, the U.S., and others, to secure financial support and political backing for its dialogue efforts."[96] The Australian government did provide some funding to this process, but it was less than that provided by the United States, Europe, or Japan, and Australian diplomats were less involved than those of other donors.[97] Moreover, by 2002, the Henry Dunant Centre had recognized its limited capacity, as a small NGO, to bring about a sustainable peace and sought to encourage donor states to take a more active role in the peace process. According to Huber, however, it found that, after East Timor, "Jakarta opposed any formal role for an international organization, and donor countries side-stepped direct responsibility for implementing the peace process."[98]

Accounting for Australia's Inaction

MATERIAL, BUT NO MORAL PRESSURE

Australia's lack of engagement with the war in Aceh is consistent with the overall argument of this book. There was virtually no moral pressure from society or in government to address civilian suffering and human rights abuses diplomatically let alone militarily, and so countervailing concerns about the potential operational environment for a peace operation never arose. Thus, this was not a situation in which I would expect to see Australia promoting or creating an ambitions-resources gap. Still, if perceived strategic or other interests suggested it, a limited contribution to a peace operation might have been a possibility.[99] In practice, however, the Howard government's strategic priority of repairing relations with Indonesia after East Timor dictated against any such action and guided the nation's approach to the war.

By all accounts, concern about events in Aceh was exceedingly low in Australia. In stark contrast with East Timor, Australians lacked strong personal connections with the people of Aceh. Aceh is not only located farther from Australia than East Timor, but the Acehnese population in Australia is tiny, and most arrived since 1999. In addition to their shortage of long-term ties to Australia, most had little education and lacked the language skills needed for effective communication and liaison with the Australian media and NGOs. Thus, they tended to be poorly organized and were—unlike the Timorese—unable to conduct effective advocacy efforts within Australia. Occasionally the Acehnese community held protests in Sydney, but these failed to attract many non-Acehnese participants, and always remained very small.[100]

The institutional connections that helped connect Timorese and Australians—such as veterans' organizations and churches—were also lacking. According to Hugh White, this played directly into the low level of concern about the conflict, and in turn, the government's lack of interest:

> The political oxygen that was available in Australia in relation to Indonesia's treatment of separatist movements was entirely absorbed by East Timor and to a lesser extent West Papua. There was none left over for Aceh. If you wanted to bitch and moan about what those bloody Indonesians were

doing you'd focus on East Timor. Aceh just seemed like a lesser case, from the public's point of view and from the government's point of view. Why, having put this huge investment in East Timor, would you then go and focus on something that nobody in Australia cares about?[101]

Other policymakers shared this impression of low public interest in Aceh. Foreign Minister Downer, for example, claimed never to have seen a demonstration in Australia on the human rights abuses in Aceh.[102] In stark contrast to East Timor, moreover, between 1999 and 2004 not a single petition was filed in the Australian Parliament concerning the conflict in Aceh.

In addition, during the war, most Australian development and human rights NGOs had very little engagement with events in Aceh.[103] Paradoxically, Australia's involvement in East Timor may actually have served to limit pressure on the Howard government from these groups. Many of the NGOs that might otherwise have urged a more active Australian role in promoting human rights in Aceh were extremely busy with Timor-related work during and after 1999. They were closely involved not only in the preparation of the ballot and its immediate aftermath in East Timor, but also in the two-and-a-half-year transition period of UN administration, which involved both development and reconstruction work as well as extensive political groundwork to lay the foundations for independence.[104] This left them less time than they might otherwise have had for Aceh-related activism. Religious affiliation may also have contributed to the limited NGO activity. The Catholic Church and Catholic charities had worked to draw attention to events in East Timor in part because it is strongly Catholic. Yet according to Downer, these groups "didn't care about human rights abuses in . . . Aceh because that was Muslim on Muslim."[105]

The lower level of public interest in—and access to information about—Aceh can be seen through the volume of related media coverage, both prior to and during the conflict. From 1991 to 1997 fewer than ten *SMH* articles mentioned Aceh annually, and there were 38 in 1998. In contrast, typically some 200 to 300 articles per year mentioned Timor during this period.

Figure 6.3 shows the number of *SMH* stories containing the word "Aceh" on a monthly basis between 1999 and 2004. During this time, the number of articles per year ranged from 58 in 2004 to 154 in 1999. The larger average volume of coverage in 1999 and 2000 reflects the fact that what public discussion there was of Aceh followed to some extent from interest in the situation in East Timor. A number of journalists who reported on the crisis in East Timor in 1999 subsequently turned their attention to the conflict in Aceh.[106] In addition, because it was another separatist conflict within Indonesia and therefore had a bearing on broader political developments there,

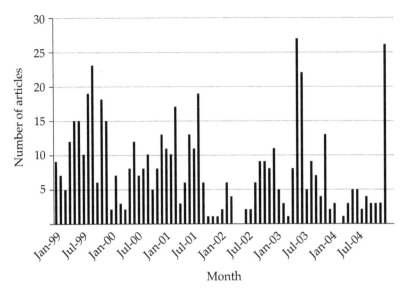

Figure 6.3. Monthly *SMH* coverage of Aceh, 1999–2004

Note: Article counts are from full-text searches conducted in LexisNexis using "Aceh" as the search term.

Aceh was often mentioned in passing in articles that mainly concerned developments in East Timor or the Indonesian political landscape more generally. Yet despite being mentioned in so many articles that did not primarily concern it, not once in the five year period shown here did the number of articles that mentioned Aceh reach the number of articles that mentioned East Timor in any month of 1999.

In terms of content, several aspects of this coverage are striking and contrast sharply with East Timor. First, efforts to influence government policy were noticeably absent among articles mentioning Aceh. This may have been because, whereas with East Timor there was a sense that Australia both could and should do something, this simply was not the case with Aceh.[107] Second, the coverage of Aceh attached blame to both sides in the conflict. Although most articles placed greater emphasis on rights abuses committed by the Indonesian military, they also reported on abuses committed by GAM, and on its role in sinking the peace process. Finally, reflecting the lower level of government interest in Aceh, the coverage was striking for the rarity of reports on Australian policy. Articles mentioning Aceh included few statements by government officials, and the occasional mentions of government policy were generally references to its lack of support for GAM's political objectives.

One reason for the limited coverage of Aceh that also limited the potential for significant growth in Australian concern about events there was that the Indonesian government periodically restricted foreign journalists' access to the conflict zone. For example, in June 2003, after the start of its renewed military offensives, the government introduced regulations that "effectively stopped all foreign aid workers and journalists from visiting most parts of the province."[108] Human Rights Watch claimed that such restrictions, in combination with threats against Indonesian reporters, prevented information about rights abuses committed during the offensives from being examined or publicized and "stopped most serious reporting of the conflict."[109] In November 2004 the Indonesian government officially barred all foreign journalists from Aceh for the first time in four years.[110] As shown in figure 6.3, however, the volume of coverage of the war in Australia was low even before these restrictions were put in place.

Thus, Australian civil society and media offered no incentive for a stronger response to the human rights crisis in Aceh. Neither, however, did Australia's perceived strategic interests, which after the breach over East Timor focused on repairing the severely strained diplomatic relationship with Jakarta and avoiding any actions that might encourage further fragmentation of the Indonesian state. Indeed, these goals provided clear grounds for staying out of the conflict.

Australian actions in East Timor had fostered the belief among many Indonesians that Australia secretly longed for the disintegration of their country. This generated considerable suspicion and ill will at a time of tremendous political upheaval in Indonesia, as Australian elites were well aware. As White noted, for example, among Indonesians the belief was widespread "that what happened in 1999 was that Australia set about to humiliate Indonesia and to take East Timor from Indonesia . . . and make East Timor an Australian military base."[111] Given these suspicions, repairing relations with Indonesia necessitated, more than ever, careful avoidance of any statements or activities—such as real or apparent political support for GAM—that could be construed as encouraging the break-up of the Indonesian state. Thus, "Australia had good diplomatic reasons not to make a fuss about Aceh."[112] And, indeed, at the height of Indonesia's 2003 offensives in Aceh Australia resumed joint military exercises with Kopassus, TNI's special forces, for the first time since September 1999, despite their reputation for rights abuses in Aceh, East Timor, and elsewhere.[113]

Finally, aside from the quality of diplomatic relations, the Howard government also believed Australia had a strong strategic interest in a stable and united Indonesia. The prospect that multiple small, weak, poor, and potentially non-viable states could splinter off from Indonesia seemed a real possibility in the late 1990s and early 2000s, and these were not the kinds of states that Australian policy-makers wanted to see in their immediate neighborhood. In a typical statement, in 2000 Downer remarked that the Howard government and the bureaucracy believed "without exception that the break-off of parts of Indonesia . . . would be a strategic disaster for Indonesia's neighbours, including Australia."[114] However, it was not clear that Australian diplomatic involvement in the conflict in Aceh could help prevent this outcome, given Australia's lack of credibility in Indonesia at the time, and might only have hurt matters. It made more sense, therefore, to entrust any peace negotiations to other actors who were willing to try to help resolve the conflict, and whom Indonesia would see as more neutral.[115]

A FOOTNOTE: THE 2004 BOXING DAY TSUNAMI

Australia's response to the conflict in Aceh makes for an interesting comparison with its reaction to the December 26, 2004, Indian Ocean tsunami. The tsunami was devastating for Aceh, where it killed some 170,000 people, a strong majority of its Indonesian victims.[116] In response, Australia spent $42 million on relief in Indonesia alone within the first six months, and committed $1 billion over the next five years—the country's largest international aid package.[117]

Because the scale of the disaster was too great for the Indonesian government to cope with alone, it also permitted Australia—among other countries—to send both military and civilian teams to Aceh to provide emergency relief. The ADF provided a field hospital, medical personnel, a naval amphibious transport ship carrying earth-moving equipment and other vehicles to help with reconstruction, and a 150-man contingent of army engineers. Australian soldiers played a strictly humanitarian role and were unarmed throughout their deployment.[118]

These relief efforts were extremely popular with the public, whose generosity in response to the tsunami was stunning. Over the next six months, Australians donated $330 million to relief efforts through NGOs, vastly more than they had given for East Timor in 1999.[119] Ironically enough, it was this Australian aid—including the military contribution—that, more than anything else, helped to repair relations damaged by INTERFET, and to re-establish trust between the Australian and Indonesian militaries.[120] Still, even with its extensive involvement in humanitarian aid to Aceh in 2005, Australia did not play a key role in the renewed peace process that finally ended the war later that year. Given the critical role of preexisting ties between Australians and Timorese in contributing to the deployment of INTERFET, however, it seems quite possible that Australian concern and government policy toward the conflict in Aceh might well have been different had the tsunami happened before the war.

In East Timor and Aceh, Australian policy clearly supports my expectations about the conditions that encourage different responses to complex emergencies. In line with hypothesis 1, neither case would lead us to expect an ambitions-resources gap. Instead, in Aceh the near absence of moral pressure from society or government and Australia's limited engagement with the conflict—specifically, no role in a peace operation—are consistent with hypothesis 5. Meanwhile, INTERFET vividly illustrates the dynamics of hypothesis 4 and boosts confidence in the quantitative support for it. Not only does intense domestic pressure for action together with a fairly benign operational environment help account for robust protection efforts in the aggregate, but East Timor shows how this can work not just in the absence of material incentives for action, but even in the face of countervailing strategic interests. Here, Australian officials openly acknowledged the strength of the pressure to intervene as well as the importance of the operational environment, especially as affected by the need for Indonesian consent to intervene.

This issue of Indonesian consent raises two other important points. First, as noted earlier, while INTERFET did not involve an ambitions-resources gap, many Australians initially failed to grasp the basics of their own state's force projection capacity and the significance of whether Indonesia would agree to an intervention. As a result, Howard and Downer were forced to explain repeatedly that their demands amounted to a declaration of war on a much larger country. This situation is analogous to my prediction in hypothesis 2 that concerned citizens often do not recognize the limits of ambitions-resources gaps due to limited knowledge of military operations.

Second, the Howard government's success in obtaining Habibie's consent for INTERFET demonstrates that would-be interveners may be able to alter the operational environment in a complex emergency. While many aspects of the operational environment are fixed, the consent of local parties—and especially the government—is potentially malleable, and is perhaps the single most important element in terms of expectations about the physical dangers intervening troops are likely to face. Thus, leaders who face pressure to protect civilians have strong incentives to try to bring a reluctant government around. The Bush administration recognized this point on Darfur as well, and sought unsuccessfully to secure Khartoum's agreement for a force that would not be limited to African troops. Whether such efforts are effective probably depends on idiosyncratic factors related to the leverage potential interveners and their allies can bring to bear on a target government. Indonesia in 1999 was a fairly easy target. Not only was it a fledgling democracy under extreme economic pressure, but with U.S. assistance Australia was able to threaten its access to badly needed IMF loans. In contrast, the Sudanese government was in a better position to weather Western sanctions over Darfur since it was able to continue selling oil to China.

Howard's success in convincing Habibie to accept INTERFET was, as we have seen, vital to the force's deployment and robust design. Before September 12, 1999, the operational environment in East Timor looked less auspicious, and the political dilemma the Australians faced more closely resembled the conditions that promote ambitions-resources gaps. While we cannot be sure what would have happened had Habibie not relented, my argument suggests that such a policy would have been more likely. The same logic leads to the opposite conclusion about Darfur: a successful effort to secure Khartoum's consent for Western troops should have increased the odds of more robust U.S. action. These cases thus suggest that the ability to ease the anticipated operational environment in a conflict by securing key local parties' advance consent for military action may at times make the difference between ambitions-resources gaps and robust protection efforts. I return to the significant implications of this in the final chapter.

Conclusions and Implications

> At the beginning, and despite my intense misgivings, it was stated
> unequivocally that there would be no ground troops. Without that
> statement, there would have been no air action, so I thought it worth
> agreeing to. We could work out how to unravel it later.
>
> —Tony Blair, Prime Minister of the United Kingdom,
> *A Journey: My Political Life*

The United Kingdom in Kosovo: Allied Pressure and an Ambitions–Resources Gap

I begin this chapter with a brief example of how international coalition or alliance pressures can encourage leaders to accept ambitions-resources gaps when they would not otherwise be inclined to do so: namely, the policy of the U.K. government in Kosovo in 1999.

In 1998 and 1999, the mainly ethnic Albanian population of Kosovo, a province of Serbia, was threatened by Serb security forces under the direction of president Slobodan Milosevic. In response, in March 1999 NATO launched an air campaign—Operation Allied Force—against both strategic targets in the heart of Serbia and the Serb forces in Kosovo. Although he preferred a ground operation that would have been more appropriate to the circumstances, British prime minister Tony Blair acquiesced to his allies' strong preferences for an air war while continuing to push for troop deployments after the start of the mission.

After nearly a decade of oppressive policies by Milosevic's government, by the late 1990s the Kosovar Albanian population was frustrated. Growing demands for independence from Serbia and the founding of the Kosovo Liberation Army (KLA), which was dedicated to violent resistance to Serb rule, prompted a violent crackdown by Milosevic's security forces starting in March 1998. By October some 300,000 people had been forced from their homes, with many hiding in the mountains, exposed to the elements and harsh winter weather. As of March 1999, when Allied Force began, an estimated 2,000 civilians had died. What is more, it was Milosevic and his Serb nationalists who had been responsible for much of the death and many of the worst abuses in Bosnia just a few years before. There were thus strong grounds for worry that these numbers would only keep growing without outside intervention.[1]

NATO governments began privately discussing the possibility of military action over the summer of 1998 but were reluctant even to threaten it publicly, focusing instead on mediation efforts aimed at securing a peaceful resolution to the crisis. Ultimately, however, this strategy was unsuccessful: Serbia had no intention of giving up political control of Kosovo, and the Kosovar Albanians were more committed than ever to independence. Thus, after the Serbs scuttled yet another round of talks, NATO began bombing on March 24, 1999.[2] Its core goals were to degrade Milosevic's ability to attack the Kosovar Albanians and to compel him to remove his forces from the territory, accept an international force to guarantee the population's security, and resume negotiations on Kosovo's political status. To meet these objectives NATO targeted the heart of Serbia, focusing on military installations and civilian infrastructure with possible military uses, plus leadership assets such as Milosevic's party headquarters and home. It also targeted the Serb forces in Kosovo and military installations supporting them.[3]

The limitations of relying exclusively on airpower to protect civilians quickly became apparent. As Ivo Daalder and Michael O'Hanlon explain, certain categories of targets—"notably fixed infrastructure such as fuel and ammunition facilities"—sustained serious damage, but the Serb forces in the field who were threatening the Kosovar population "went generally unscathed."[4] What is more, despite the damage caused by the airstrikes Milosevic remained determined to test NATO's resolve, ultimately holding out until June 3 before agreeing to NATO's terms. In the meantime Serb forces initiated a dramatic escalation in their attacks against the civilian population, killing an estimated 5,000 to 11,000 people and forcing almost three quarters of Kosovo's prewar population of 1.8 million ethnic Albanians from their homes in an effort to permanently change the region's ethnic composition. Some 800,000 people became refugees in neighboring countries and an estimated 500,000 were internally displaced within Kosovo. The Serbs also engaged in widespread destruction of property.[5] It was precisely such attacks that NATO's airpower strategy could not combat.

Thus, above all the decision to conduct Allied Force entirely from the air explains why it displayed an ambitions-resources gap. Both NATO as a whole and a number of member states individually contributed substantial resources, but this core aspect of military strategy limited their effectiveness for protecting civilians and made a mockery of the mission's announced protection goals.[6] The United States was by far the top contributor, deploying some 50,000 personnel and 740 aircraft. Most relevant here, the United Kingdom also made a substantial contribution of nearly 50 aircraft, the use of three air force bases, and various naval assets.[7]

NATO's reliance on airpower alone reflected two main considerations. First, its leaders largely assumed that, except to help implement a negotiated agreement between the Serbs and Albanians, the use of ground forces would be politically unacceptable to domestic audiences. Notably, their use would raise the risk of a significant number of casualties. Nowhere was this consideration more important than in the United States, but many NATO allies felt the same way. Second, most leaders both in Washington and Europe believed—or at least publicly claimed to believe—that Milosevic would quickly capitulate to their demands, probably within days but certainly within a few weeks. This expectation was based at least in part on the apparent success of earlier airstrikes in Bosnia in 1995.[8]

At least for the leaders who expected Milosevic to give up quickly, it is possible that Allied Force's ambitions-resources gap was unintentional and reflected a poor understanding of how to provide effective protection. Yet on inspection the evidence does not appear to bear this out. According to Daalder and O'Hanlon, the allies excluded the possibility of using ground troops "even though it was clear that a presence on the ground in Kosovo would offer the best way to provide some degree of protection to the Kosovar Albanians and the only sure way to defeat the Serb security forces."[9] For instance, President Clinton received several advance warnings of the limitations of an air-only campaign, but evidently decided to downplay their importance. Notably, CIA director George Tenet and chairman of the Joint Chiefs of Staff Harry Skelton separately informed him that a bombing campaign could lead to accelerated ethnic cleansing in Kosovo.[10] Thus, it seems most likely that Clinton—and probably most NATO leaders—chose to hope for the best with airstrikes because of their reluctance to accept the political risks that would come with the use of ground troops.

In stark contrast, from the earliest discussions of possible military action the British government preferred a more robust approach. Already by June 1998 Prime Minister Blair was convinced that force would be required to rein in Milosevic. Then, as Daalder and O'Hanlon explain, in August the British government decided not just that force would be needed, "but also that ground forces would have to be deployed in Kosovo—if not to end the violence then to enforce the terms of any agreement that was reached. The cabinet also agreed that Britain would play a leading role in any military action and that London would therefore be prepared to deploy ground forces in large numbers."[11]

Faced with U.S. and European reluctance, in early January of 1999 Blair began trying to forge a consensus within NATO to commit to military intervention if diplomatic negotiations failed, including the possibility of deploying ground forces. Blair spoke regularly with President Clinton throughout January and February, and ultimately Clinton agreed to pursue military action through NATO. However, as Blair recalls, "At the beginning, and despite my intense misgivings, it was stated unequivocally that there would be no ground troops. Without that statement, there would have been no air action, so I thought it worth agreeing to. We could work out how to unravel it later."[12] Thus, Blair agreed to a strategy he believed might very well fail to rescue the Kosovar population, as the price of getting the United States and other NATO allies to act.

Once Allied Force was underway, Blair quickly grew aghast at the Serbs' accelerating campaign of ethnic cleansing and decided once again to push the allies to prepare for a ground option. Throughout April and May, he repeatedly pressed the United States and the various European capitals on the issue, straining his relationship with Clinton in the process. To demonstrate Britain's own commitment, Blair told his chief of defence staff, Charles Guthrie, that the United Kingdom should prepare to send 50,000 troops. Then, at a May 27 meeting of several NATO defense ministers, the United Kingdom pressed to begin immediate planning for a ground invasion. Defence Minister George Robertson offered 54,000 troops and prepared to call up 30,000 reservists in early June to support the effort. By now France and Italy were also willing to commit smaller numbers of troops, and it appeared that Clinton had also accepted the need to prepare a ground campaign. Milosevic was aware of at least some of these developments and probably influenced by them.[13]

Before NATO made up its mind to invade, Milosevic capitulated and agreed to remove his Serb forces from Kosovo. Thereafter, some 50,000 NATO troops arrived to help guarantee the ceasefire and create a secure environment for the displaced to return. Thanks to this Kosovo Force (KFOR), almost all the ethnic Albanian refugees returned home by the end of June.[14]

For Tony Blair, the violence in Kosovo posed a classic contradiction between moral pressures to protect civilians and more material concerns. Blair himself was deeply incensed by Milosevic's treatment of the Kosovar Albanians, and his view of the situation was widely shared in the British government.[15] He also felt that he had the domestic political space to offer a major commitment of British forces to a ground effort. In contrast to the cases explored earlier, however, the source of what were ultimately decisive material pressures on the Blair government was international. Blair viewed collective action through NATO as vital to resolving the conflict in Kosovo, but Britain's allies—most importantly the United States, but also key European countries including Germany, France, and Italy—were not willing to countenance the use of ground forces until after two months of bombing had failed to achieve NATO's goals. Under the circumstances, accepting an airpower strategy and the ambitions-resources gap that it implied was a compromise that allowed the British government to do as much as it could for the Kosovar Albanians while still maintaining strong working relationships with its NATO allies. What is more, although the United Kingdom continued to press for a change in strategy behind the scenes, in publicly supporting NATO's civilian protection claims it fully participated in the organized hypocrisy they represented.

Summary of Findings

The case of British policy in Kosovo supports my contention that ambitions-resources gaps represent a compromise between competing moral and material pressures related to civilian protection, while serving as a reminder that the sources of these conflicting tensions can be international as well as domestic. In the rest of this chapter I review the book's key arguments and findings and then explore their implications for international relations and the practical challenges of deciding when and how to intervene in the world's worst conflicts.

In recent decades the challenge of protecting civilians from devastating violence has inspired numerous peace operations as well as loud and persistent hand-wringing over their frequent shortcomings. I have sought to unpack the politics behind the design of these missions, focusing on the role of the most influential Western democracies with the greatest capacity to effectively protect threatened civilians. Yet only rarely do these states design missions that reflect our best understanding of how to do so. Usually, they do not contribute to peace operations at all, or do so in limited ways that involve neither the ambitions nor the resources for meaningful civilian protection. Still, these states also regularly contribute to peace operations in ways that help create ambitions-resources gaps. Such policies are not only puzzling; they are also troubling because they can have perverse consequences, even aggravating civilian suffering.

To investigate the origins of these gaps I first developed a simple framework to distinguish them from both more limited and more robust civilian protection efforts. While these distinctions obviously gloss over certain nuances in the variation among peace operations, they allow us to zero in on the key issue of ambitions-resources gaps that has inspired so much concern among scholars and policymakers alike. In chapter 2, I elaborated on how leaders can benefit from these gaps politically and when they can be expected to create and promote them. I argued that these gaps represent a compromise between competing normative and material pressures to protect civilians but also to control associated costs and risks. Although these pressures can emerge internationally, I have focused mainly on how they arise from within democratic society and government. On one hand, democratic publics are likely to punish leaders for peace operations that go poorly or that they see as too costly in money or lives, while bureaucratic actors—perhaps especially in the defense establishment—may have various professional or policy reasons for opposing them. On the other hand, an "activist minority" within civil society or officials who are deeply concerned about a particular complex emergency can also create intense moral pressure on their leaders to protect threatened civilians.

Ambitions-resources gaps allow leaders to balance these pressures to their own political advantage. By limiting financial costs and physical risks relative to more robust missions, these gaps allow leaders to curb the threat of public backlash and bureaucratic opposition while still gesturing toward helping to protect vulnerable civilians. Activists and other concerned citizens and officials, meanwhile, are liable to accept these policies due to an incomplete understanding of their limitations, the hope that they will prove better than nothing, or organizational or psychological imperatives. Leaders, in turn, can help promote this acceptance through the rhetoric of organized hypocrisy, by portraying their policies as better-suited to address civilians' protection needs than they really are. Ultimately, I expect ambitions-resources gaps to be most appealing when leaders perceive intense moral pressure to protect civilians and strong reasons to worry about costs, such as a relatively inhospitable operational environment for intervention.

The argument also has implications for other policy choices. Notably, when pressure for civilian protection is very strong and the operational environment is quite hospitable, pursuing robust protection should be more attractive, barring other major concerns about costs and risks. Significantly, this provides a theoretical rationale for the most robust protection efforts that does not require broader geopolitical incentives for intervention, although it does not deny that such incentives may often play a major—if not the primary—role in motivating them.

The analyses in chapters 3–6 strongly support my various empirical predictions. Chapter 3 used new quantitative data to test hypotheses 1, 4, and 5 about when leaders will facilitate ambitions-resources gaps or make no, limited, or robust contributions to peace operations. In it, I used elite media coverage of complex emergencies to proxy for the normative pressure leaders perceive to respond, and the nature of the operational environment as a key indicator of material pressure related to the costs and risks of intervention. The results confirm that leaders are most likely to promote ambitions-resources gaps when concern about complex emergencies is great and when the operational environment is relatively (but not extremely) inhospitable. Yet they offer little support for the main alternative explanations for these policies. Indeed, I found that various geopolitical concerns that might plausibly create incentives to contribute to peace operations instead generally discouraged leaders from doing so, when they mattered at all. There was thus no evidence that ambitions-resources gaps are a fig leaf for other motives for action. In addition, a rough test of the possibility that these gaps are unintentional—a comparison of their frequency in the 2000s versus the 1990s—found no evidence to support it.

Interestingly, these statistical tests also indicate the empirical significance of my argument's secondary implication about robust protection efforts. While these policies do not occur only when there is extensive concern about a complex emergency and a fairly favorable operational environment, they are both most frequent and highly likely under those conditions. At the least, this suggests that these policies are about more than just pursuing interveners' geopolitical interests and that when other conditions are right such interests may be unnecessary.

The case studies in chapters 4–6 both support and extend these findings. They confirm the quantitative evidence about when leaders facilitate ambitions-resources gaps and other kinds of policies. First, for the United States in Darfur until the spring of 2004 and for Australia in Aceh, not participating in peace operations was consistent with my argument, as leaders faced no meaningful normative pressure to protect civilians and other considerations pointed away from these missions. Second, the cases of ambitions-resources gaps—Operation Turquoise and U.S. support for AMIS and then UNA-MID—both involved strong moral pressures on leaders, especially from domestic society, and serious material concerns about the costs and risks of action. The moral pressures were somewhat different in these cases. In France, advocacy pressure was important in its own right but also caused leaders to worry that NGO and media attention to France's history in Rwanda would lead to broad public criticism of inaction in the face of genocide. In the United States the emergence of a large and diverse advocacy movement devoted to "saving" Darfur led to direct, sustained pressure on the Bush administration that was more explicitly focused on using military force to protect civilians. In addition, in both cases other issues amplified concerns about a formidable operational environment: in the United States these were the wars in Iraq and Afghanistan and Sudanese counterterrorism cooperation, and in France they were the upcoming presidential election and France's recent history in Rwanda and Bosnia. Finally, Australia's leadership of INTERFET provides a detailed example to support the claim that strong moral pressure to protect civilians combined with a favorable operational environment may at times be enough to prompt robust protection efforts.

Each of these cases also shows how leaders' policy choices are affected by temporal changes in normative and material pressures related to particular conflicts. For both France in Rwanda and the United States in Darfur, the timing of decisions to contribute to peace operations coincided with the growth of moral concerns that brought the relationship between the normative and material pressures these governments perceived into line with those I expect to promote ambitions-resources gaps. For Australia in East Timor, meanwhile, Indonesia's consent to INTERFET made the operational environment the Australian government expected to face if it intervened much more manageable, thus bringing the relationship between material concerns and the acute societal pressure leaders felt to protect civilians into line with conditions that should favor robust protection. Notably, it was only at this point that Australia agreed to intervene.

Yet these cases do not just confirm when leaders tend to respond to complex emergencies in particular ways. They also provide important evidence of key causal mechanisms about how ambitions-resources gaps help leaders balance competing normative and material pressures. In line with hypothesis 2, concerned citizens and officials found ambitions-resources gaps acceptable for the reasons I would expect. In France, the public's failure to see Operation Turquoise's limits helped make it a public relations success. Yet the force also provided expressive benefits for the foreign minister and diplomatic community and gave humanitarian groups organizational incentives not to offend a broader public that did not share their objections to it. In the United States, supporting AMIS and then UNAMID balanced concerned officials' desires to do something and not to threaten other foreign policy priorities or take U.S. casualties in Darfur. For activists, too, supporting these missions partly reflected a perception that they were the best option available and a hope that they could be improved upon later.[16] Many activists also had unrealistic expectations of what the AU and UN could accomplish, or focused more on the expressive benefits of pushing for government action in any form. Meanwhile, accepting AMIS and UNAMID was consistent with NGOs' interests in showing that they could affect U.S. policy.

As anticipated in hypothesis 3, leaders who facilitated ambitions-resources gaps also sought to build public support through claims about protecting civilians that greatly exceeded what their policies were designed to do. French politicians unabashedly portrayed Operation Turquoise as a triumph despite its limitations. More subtly, while acknowledging some of AMIS's challenges, the Bush administration also regularly overstated its accomplishments as well as the outlook for and likely effects of its efforts to secure a UN replacement.

Still, although ambitions-resources gaps served very similar purposes for French and American leaders in Rwanda and Darfur, their differences in form raise the question of when leaders will deploy and constrain their own capable troops and when they will instead support foreign soldiers who cannot deliver the level of civilian protection they are asked to provide. Although my answer as highlighted in hypothesis 6 is exploratory, these two cases do support the idea that the difference reflects the availability of opportunities to assist a UN or regional mission within an acceptable timeframe. During the Rwandan genocide French leaders would have preferred to help an expanded UNAMIR II, but the rapid pace of killing combined with delays at the UN made this impossible. In contrast, in Darfur the Bush administration had already helped to lay the groundwork for an AU ceasefire monitoring force. Thus, by the time it faced substantial pressure to help protect civilians there was not only already a force on the ground, but the AU was open to expanding its size and giving it a somewhat more protection-oriented mandate. Thus, helping the AU to accomplish these goals was a readily available option.

Finally, the case studies offer more detailed evidence against the alternative explanations for ambitions-resources gaps. In both Rwanda and Darfur I investigated whether leaders facilitated these gaps because they and their military advisers were uncertain about how to offer more robust protection. Although limited, the available evidence from Operation Turquoise does not support this conclusion. On the contrary, French officials' statements about decisions concerning where to base the force and about the arrest and disarmament of the génocidaires suggest a clear understanding that they were sacrificing some of their potential effectiveness in exchange for greater control over the risks to their troops. Similarly, the Bush administration understood that the AU was not up to the civilian protection challenges Darfur presented and that any follow-on UN force would share many of its limitations, although U.S. policymakers were at times surprised at some of the obstacles to replacing AMIS.

Kosovo further supports these findings. Early on, the British government made clear that it understood the importance of ground troops to guaranteeing the security of Kosovar Albanians. In the United States, too, Bill Clinton received multiple warnings about the risks of air power and his administration's public confidence in this strategy is best seen as wishful thinking brought on by an intense desire to avoid ground troops for political reasons.[17]

I also looked for, but did not find, evidence that leaders' claims of assisting civilians are just a cover for other motives for intervention. This was important since leaders' perceptions of their states' geopolitical interests may not be easily captured through the kinds of quantitative measures used in chapter 3, as we saw in the U.S. and Australian cases. Operation Turquoise poses a hard test for this argument because skeptics have so often claimed that its purpose was to support France's former allies. Nevertheless, on close inspection it is clear that while some in the Elysée and the French military harbored this hope, their preferences had no effect on the design of Turquoise. For the United States in Darfur the Bush administration's perception of American interests pointed away from jeopardizing its relationship with Khartoum by pushing for civilian protection. Similarly in Kosovo, while intervening may have been consistent with the U.K. and NATO countries' interests in regional stability, it threatened vital relationships with Russia and critics have offered no firm evidence to refute NATO leaders' claimed humanitarian motives.[18]

Contributions and Implications

This book furthers our understanding of the related phenomena of peace-keeping, civilian protection, and humanitarian intervention in several ways. It affirms the importance of the design of peace operations for their effects on vulnerable civilians. It is also the first major study of the politics behind the key decisions that determine what these missions look like, at least where the physical protection of civilians is concerned. Most notably, it fills a prominent hole in the literature by offering and testing a unique explanation for the much-lamented phenomenon of ambitions-resources gaps. The concept of organized hypocrisy, in particular, offers a useful framework for highlighting the various sources of pressure that can encourage these policies and for explaining how leaders can benefit from them despite their inherent inconsistencies. While my focus on the role of the most influential and militarily capable democracies limits my conclusions to some degree, it has also made it possible to explore the relevant political debates at the state level where so much of the action occurs.

My argument also enhances our understanding of society's role in democratic foreign policy by bringing together ideas from diverse literatures on the impact of public opinion and advocacy activity on foreign policy decisions. In particular, numerous studies see public opinion as a mainly constraining influence on decisions about the use of force and foreign policy more generally.[19] Meanwhile, a largely separate set of arguments emphasize that societal activism can also play a motivating role in pushing governments to undertake policy initiatives they might otherwise avoid.[20] This book contributes theoretically to these literatures by emphasizing the importance of bringing them together and pointing out what we can learn by doing so. In particular, it is clear that at least in certain foreign policy arenas democratic society can put simultaneous constraining and motivating pressures on leaders, and the interaction between these pressures can influence leaders' policy decisions in ways not predictable by considering them individually. Much as intragovernmental bargaining can lead to policies that differ from what anyone would choose, efforts to balance competing pressures from society can have the same effect and may even reinforce similar pressures within government. What is more, the effects of these conflicting pressures may be most evident at the micro-level, in decisions about the specifics of policy design rather than about whether or not to take some kind of action.

The book further adds to our knowledge of democracies' foreign policy vulnerabilities, especially as they relate to humanitarian norms. My emphasis on the competing moral and material pressures that encourage ambitions-resources gaps aligns with several studies that touch on the intersection of hypocrisy, norms, and the management of costs and risks, especially regarding the use of military force. According to Gil Merom, democracies often lose small wars because they cannot manage the contradictions between the liberal democratic norms their governments publicly espouse and that domestic audiences expect them to uphold, on one hand, and the brutal military tactics required to defeat committed insurgencies, on the other. By compromising on socially acceptable military tactics, they tie their hands in ways that hamper their military effectiveness.[21]

In a related argument, Alexander Downes finds that when involved in high-cost, must-win conflicts democracies are prone to targeting noncombatants in an effort to ensure victory and limit casualties on their own side. Yet while breaking norms that they believe their publics hold dear, leaders responsible for these policies continue to uphold them in public. As Downes puts it, "All that remains of prewar liberal rhetoric is the way that politicians describe their actions to their domestic audience. Rarely do leaders admit outright that they have adopted a strategy designed or intended to murder enemy noncombatants."[22]

Further, Kelly Greenhill explains that democracies are vulnerable to coercive threats from foreign leaders who aim to affect their behavior through the use of refugee flows. According to Greenhill, democracies are susceptible to charges of hypocrisy if they do not live up to domestic liberal norms on the treatment of refugees who arrive at their shores. Yet they also face domestic opposition from those who do not want to bear the costs of accepting many foreign migrants. Thus, threats by foreign leaders to send refugees can prompt undesired political controversy in liberal democracies and convince their leaders to give in to the coercers' demands.[23]

In each of these studies, as in this book, normative humanitarian values compete with material cost-related pressures to lead democracies to commit policy compromise, hypocrisy, or both. Yet I show how similar dynamics exist even when leaders initiate policies whose core purpose is to assist vulnerable civilians, and when they explicitly claim to be acting for moral reasons. Unlike in these other studies, moreover, in my argument hypocrisy and compromise play an explicitly helpful political role for leaders. In part this is because hypocrisy is not always easy for domestic audiences to recognize, and in part it is because those who push for moral policies may have psychological or even instrumental reasons to acquiesce when it becomes clear that more robust action is unlikely. In contrast, the ethical implications are troubling. Because ambitions-resources gaps risk worsening civilians' plight, their effects may actually contradict the intent of the moral pressure that helps promote them in the first place. Pressuring leaders to protect vulnerable civilians can have unexpected and undesirable consequences by encouraging the adoption of policy compromises that pose risks to these same people.

These insights also have important practical implications for governments faced with the challenge of responding to devastating conflicts abroad and for citizens and officials concerned about the fate of threatened civilians. The regular eruption of new complex emergencies that produce clear needs and explicit demands for foreign intervention to protect civilians—most recently in places like Libya, Syria, and South Sudan—highlight the enduring nature of this problem, despite growing attention to the development of strategies for prevention.

First, my argument and findings underscore the need for explicit consideration of the ethical dilemmas involved in decisions to intervene in these conflicts. In particular, while unexpected consequences are always a possibility for peace operations, the problem of ambitions-resources gaps should encourage leaders and concerned citizens alike to reflect on whether the well-known principle of medical ethics summarized in the dictum "primum non nocere" ("first, do no harm") applies to these missions. Though there is clearly a risk that ambitions-resources gaps may increase civilian suffering, this is not an easy question. As we saw in the introduction, a number of observers have concluded that it is better not to act at all than to take these risks.[24] Yet others may see things differently. After all, there is no guarantee that ambitions-resources gaps will do more harm than good, and the opposite could occur. What is more, even if a peace operation leads to more suffering or death for some civilians, other lives may be spared that would have been lost in its absence. Those who benefit, even from flawed operations, are unlikely to agree that it would be better to do nothing. This is apparent, for instance, from Kosovar Albanians' overwhelmingly positive view of Operation Allied Force.[25]

Different answers to this question thus lead to distinct conclusions about how to address the problem of ambitions-resources gaps. If the injunction of "first, do no harm" applies, then leaders have a clear obligation to avoid policies that create or promote these gaps. At times—often in the face of inhospitable operational environments—this will mean ruling out military action entirely because the political conditions for robust protection are absent.

This restriction, in turn, implies clear limits on the moral obligations enshrined in the Responsibility to Protect (R2P), the notion that the international community should step in when a state abrogates its sovereign obligation to protect its citizens from grave harm. As the International Commission on Intervention and State Sovereignty noted in developing R2P, a key criterion for the use of force is whether there are reasonable prospects of successfully meeting the threat to civilians without making the situation worse than if there is no intervention at all.[26] While the Commission was concerned mainly with conditions on the ground that might cause intervention to prompt a wider conflict, the basic principle should also apply to domestic constraints that make robust protection politically impractical for potential interveners.[27] That is, the responsibility to protect (at least militarily) is superseded by a responsibility not to intervene unless capable states are willing to align resources and ambitions with both each other and the needs on the ground. In practice, this conclusion also roughly coincides with Robert Pape's advice to initiate humanitarian interventions only when costs are low, but for a different reason.[28] Whereas Pape emphasizes states' moral responsibility for their soldiers' lives, I find that in practice robust action is unlikely unless leaders can anticipate a relatively low-cost operation.

In contrast, if "first, do no harm" does not apply, then ambitions-resources gaps may at times be a tolerable—if flawed—alternative to more robust protection efforts. Yet leaders and concerned citizens who take this view should do so with their eyes open about the risks and moral tradeoffs, and acknowledge that these policies should be pursued sparingly and in exceptional circumstances. Notably, leaders should avoid overselling what such missions are designed to accomplish. Only by recognizing their limitations is it possible to have a reasoned debate about when and why ambitions-resources gaps might be the least bad policy available.

Finally, with all this in mind, my findings also suggest some ways to make ambitions-resources gaps less likely. In the main, they represent possible strategies concerned citizens and officials might use to change the incentives that encourage leaders to promote these gaps.

One approach would be for advocacy groups to focus on improving their ability to identify ambitions-resources gaps and commit to pointing them out when they occur. As we have seen, one reason that concerned citizens accept these policies is that they do not perceive the gaps or understand their limitations. This problem does not plague all advocacy groups, and elite human rights groups and humanitarian NGOs are often exceptions. Still, more might be done to familiarize the broader mass of citizens and activists focused on any given complex emergency with these concerns. In essence this is a matter of finding ways to popularize complicated concepts and make more informed advocacy feasible for a wider audience, a challenge some U.S. groups have taken on in recent years at least partly in response to the Darfur experience. As Enough Project co-founder John Prendergast and actor-activist Don Cheadle describe,

> The Enough Project and other groups are attempting to create foreign policy literacy and trying to move the discussion beyond just getting involved to actual participation in tactics and strategy. . . . The objective is to not just shed light on the big policy solutions but to also help people understand why, and give people the tools for participating in an informed way. We want a smarter movement because compassion and dedication have exponentially more impact when they are applied strategically.[29]

By focusing on the design of peace operations and publicly opposing ambitions-resources gaps, advocacy movements could make these policies less attractive to leaders. While no one wants to increase civilian suffering, hard-pressed leaders may feel they have little choice but to take this risk (whether they acknowledge it or not) when they face strong concerns about costs alongside intense moral pressure to show that they are acting to protect vulnerable civilians. Yet if leaders cannot expect domestic audiences to see ambitions-resources gaps as a reasonable or acceptable compromise in the face of these pressures, this calculus may change.

Another tactic for activists and concerned officials would be to focus on identifying sources of leverage that could be used to pressure reluctant governments into consenting to the deployment of peace operations. As we have seen, the consent of local actors—but especially governments—is a key element of the operational environment that may go further than any other toward affecting potential interveners' expectations about the costs and risks they will face in a possible intervention. Thus, working where possible to make the operational environment more hospitable might help to alleviate some of the material pressures that encourage ambitions-resources gaps, and thus increase the likelihood of robust protection efforts.

Typically civil society focuses on creating moral pressure for action, but this strategy highlights instead the other half of the equation, the goal of reducing obstacles to civilian protection rooted in material concerns about costs and risks. It is also an approach that demands creativity and flexibility. As the comparison of Darfur and East Timor illustrates, some countries will be easier to sway than others. A powerful democracy may have carrots or sticks it can use to shape outcomes of importance to a target government, but it may not. In the latter case other actors may have greater leverage, and the challenge then is to identify them and to convince them to use their influence. The Darfur advocacy movement in the United States had some success with this through its Genocide Olympics campaign, but ultimately the Chinese government did not exert the kind of sustained pressure on Khartoum that might have convinced the Sudanese leadership to permit the deployment of non-African troops with UNAMID. As that case shows, the prospects for using leverage to alter the operational environment in this way are likely to be idiosyncratic and highly contingent on circumstances. Still, the evidence from this book highlights the importance for both activists and concerned bureaucrats of at least exploring potential opportunities to do so.

Although it might seem callous, NGOs and activists could also adopt a sort of triage strategy, focusing calls for military action to protect civilians on complex emergencies where the operational environment for intervention is relatively favorable. While this might appear unfair to victims of some of the worst conflicts, it would help concentrate crucial moral pressures for civilian protection on those cases where robust protection efforts are most possible. As we have seen, theory and evidence support the idea that these moral pressures can help create a path to robust protection even in the absence of strategic motives to provide it. Relatedly, Samantha Power has argued that the mobilization of mass constituencies for humanitarian action is necessary to motivate states to accept the risks of such missions.[30] Yet a key insight from this book is that such pressures alone are not enough to ensure robust protection. In particular, absent favorable political conditions—including a fairly hospitable operational environment—they are more likely to promote ambitions-resources gaps instead, as in Rwanda and Darfur. Still, this does not mean concerned citizens need ignore other complex emergencies. On the contrary, they could still push their leaders to send humanitarian aid or vigorously pursue diplomatic solutions. While these policies would not solve all of the immediate protection threats civilians face, they could still save many lives.[31]

A final suggestion is for regional organizations like the AU and ECOWAS. As in Darfur, great power democracies sometimes offer financial and logistical support to peace operations conducted by these organizations as a way to show that they are helping address civilian protection challenges without deploying their own troops. Yet the greater the normative pressure their leaders are under, the more these states may push regional organizations into pursuing protection goals and strategies they are ill equipped to execute. Actors like the AU and ECOWAS might be able to limit this kind of pressure and avoid being pressed into leading operations defined by ambitions-resources gaps by establishing and sticking to clear, publicized criteria for intervention that accurately reflect their member states' capabilities.

In the end, the utility of these strategies to discourage ambitions-resources gaps depends on whether we believe that states ought to avoid these missions entirely or treat them as an occasional, least-bad option. Nor will all of these approaches necessarily make robust protection more common, since inhospitable operational environments and other cost-related concerns will not always be malleable. Instead, the result might be to discourage great power democracies from contributing to peace operations at all in some cases, an outcome that at least involves a lower risk of causing unintended harm.

The Data

Table A.1 Post–Cold War complex humanitarian emergencies and peace operations

Complex emergency name	Start year	End year	Certainty	Associated peace operations*
Afghanistan I / Soviets	1978	1992	3	UNGOMAP
Afghanistan II / Civil War	1992	2001	3	
Afghanistan III / OEF and after	2001	Ongoing 2009	3	*Excluded from analysis for all potential interveners*
Cambodia	1979	1990	3	UNAMIC; UNTAC (1992)
India I / Kashmir	1990	2004	2	
India II / Northeast	1993	1998	2	
Indonesia I / Aceh	1999	2004	3	
Indonesia II / East Timor	1999	1999	3	INTERFET; UNTAET (2000)
Indonesia III / Moluccas and Sulawesi	1999	2002	3	
Myanmar / Burma	1988	Ongoing 2009	3	
Pakistan	2004	Ongoing 2009	3	*Excluded from analysis for USA only*
Philippines I / Govt. vs. NPA	1986	1992	3	
Philippines II / Govt. vs. Muslim insurgents	1996	2009	3	
Sri Lanka I	1983	2001	3	
Sri Lanka II	2006	2009	2	
Azerbaijan-Armenia (USSR)	1988	1991	3	
Azerbaijan / Nagorno-Karabakh	1992	1994	3	
Bosnia	1992	1995	3	UNPROFOR/NATO support; Deliberate Force
Croatia	1991	1995	3	UNPROFOR/UNCRO; UNTAES & UNMOP (1996)
Russia / Chechnya I	1995	1996	3	
Russia / Chechnya II	1999	2004	3	

(continued)

Complex emergency name	Start year	End year	Certainty	Associated peace operations*
Tajikistan	1992	1993	3	UNMOT (1994)
Turkey	1992	1998	3	
Yugoslavia / Kosovo	1998	2000	3	Allied Force; KFOR
Algeria	1992	2003	3	
Angola I	1975	1991	3	UNAVEM I; UNAVEM II
Angola II	1992	1994	3	UNAVEM II; UNAVEM III (1995)
Angola III	1998	2002	3	MONUA
Burundi	1993	2004	3	AMIB; ONUB
Congo-Brazzaville	1997	1999	3	
Cote d'Ivoire	2002	2004	3	ECOMICI; MINUCI; UNOCI; Op. Licorne (Fr)
DRC (Zaire) I	1992	1996	3	
DRC (Zaire) II	1996	1997	3	
DRC (Zaire) III	1998	Ongoing 2009	3	MONUC; Artemis (EU); EUFOR RD-Congo
Eritrea / War with Ethiopia	1998	2000	3	UNMEE
Ethiopia / Civil war	1988	1992	3	
Kenya	2008	2008	1	
Liberia I	1990	1996	3	ECOMOG; UNOMIL
Liberia II	1999	2003	3	UNMIL; ECOMIL; JTF Liberia (US)
Mozambique	1982	1992	3	ONUMOZ
Nigeria	1997	2006	3	
Rwanda	1990	1999	3	UNOMUR; UNAMIR; Op. Turquoise (Fr); Support Hope (US)
Sierra Leone	1991	2001	3	ECOMOG; UNOMSIL; UNAMSIL; Op. Palliser (UK)
Somalia	1988	Ongoing 2009	3	UNOSOM I; Provide Relief; UNITAF; UNOSOM II; AMISOM; Various anti-piracy efforts (Allied Provider, Atalanta, Allied Protector, Ocean Shield)
South Africa	1986	1995	2	
Sudan I / North–South civil war	1983	2004	3	UNMIS (2005)
Sudan II / Darfur	2003	Ongoing 2009	3	AMIS; UNAMID; EUFOR TCHAD/RCA; MINURCAT
Sudan III / Southern violence	2008	Ongoing 2009	2	UNMIS
Uganda I	1987	1991	3	
Uganda II / LRA	1996	2006	3	
Zimbabwe	2005	2008	3	
Colombia	1985	Ongoing 2009	3	
El Salvador	1980	1990	3	ONUSAL (1991)
Peru	1983	1994	2	
Iraq / Kurds I	1987	1989	3	

Iraq / Kurds II	1991	1993	3	Provide Comfort; UNGCI
Iraq / Shiites	1991	1998	2	Southern Watch
Iraq / US-led coalition	2003	Ongoing 2009	3	*Excluded from analysis for USA and UK*
Kuwait	1990	1990	1	*Excluded from analysis for all potential interveners*
Lebanon I / Civil war	1975	1991	3	MNF; UNIFIL
Lebanon II / Israeli air attacks	2006	2006	1	UNIFIL

*Peace operations with dates in parentheses began the year after the end of the complex emergency. All others began during the complex emergency. Peace operations not involving a great power democracy are excluded, but listed in part 2 of the web appendix. Emergency-potential intervener pairs excluded from the analysis in chapter 3, as described there, are listed in italics.

Table A.2 Components of *operational environment*

Variable	Description	Source
Army	Size of the army in the state where the complex emergency occurs (logged). I use the earliest available estimate during the complex emergency, which is typically in the first year.	International Institute for Strategic Studies (multiple years)
Russia/China contiguity	Dichotomous variable coded 1 if the state with the complex emergency is either in or directly contiguous to Russia (USSR before 1991) or China	Correlates of War Project, Stinnett et al. (2002)
Strong and motivated rebellion	Dichotomous variable coded 1 if the conflict was either a guerrilla or revolutionary war	Guerrilla war: as coded by Valentino et al. (2004), with missing observations filled in by the author using their guidelines Revolutionary war: Marshall et al. (2014)
Number of violent parties	Coded 0 if there is only 1 violent party (complex emergencies that are 1-sided violence); .5 if there are 2–3 violent parties; and 1 if there are 4 or more violent parties	Uppsala Conflict Data Program (n.d.)
Mountains	Proportion of territory in the state with the complex emergency that is mountainous (logged)	Fearon and Laitin (2003)
Paved roads	Proportion of roads in the country with the complex emergency that are paved (logged); since it is measured intermittently I use the figure closest to the start of the complex emergency	The World Bank (n.d.)
Area	Area affected by complex emergency (square kilometers, logged)	Central Intelligence Agency (n.d.) (+ various sources to identify the relevant area for subnational complex emergencies)
Population	Average population in the area (state or subnational region) with the complex emergency while it is going on (logged)	The World Bank (n.d.) (+ various sources to estimate the relevant population for subnational complex emergencies)
Distance	Distance between the capital cities of the state with the complex emergency and the potential intervener (kilometers, logged)	Gleditsch (n.d.)

Table A.3 Control variables

Variable	Description	Source
Former colony	Dichotomous variable coded 1 if the country where the complex emergency occurs received its independence from the potential intervener	Hensel (2006)
Region	Dichotomous variable coded 1 if a complex emergency occurs in the same region as the potential intervener. The UN considers Asia and Oceania separate continents, which puts Australia outside the region of several nearby complex emergencies. In contrast, given Australia's immediate proximity to much of SE Asia and historical treatment of the region as its strategic "backyard," I code Australia as in the same region as these complex emergencies.	UN Department of Economic and Social Affairs (n.d.)
Alliance	Dichotomous variable coded 1 if there is a direct alliance tie (defense, neutrality, or nonaggression pact) between the potential intervener and the state where the complex emergency occurs, during the conflict itself. It is excluded from the regressions because it never equals 1 in any case of a gap or robust contribution.	Correlates of War Project: Gibler (2009)
Contiguous ally	Dichotomous variable coded 1 if the potential intervener has an ally (defense, neutrality, or nonaggression pact) contiguous to the complex emergency while it is ongoing	Gibler (2009) for alliances; Stinnett et al. (2002) for contiguity
Pre-1989	Dichotomous variable coded 1 for complex emergencies that began before 1989	Coded by the author
Affinity	Reflects the similarity of the potential intervener's and complex emergency state's voting positions at the UN General Assembly the year before the complex emergency begins; serves as a general measure of political ties between them	Gartzke (2010)
Trade	The combined value of trade imports and exports between the potential intervener and the state where the complex emergency occurs, as a % of the potential intervener's total trade (logged). Data are averaged over the 2 years before the CE starts. Where one or more of these is missing I use the nearest available years.	Organisation for Economic Cooperation and Development (n.d.); constructed by the author from "Trade in Value by Partner Countries" in "Monthly Statistics in International Trade"

Democracy	Seven-point scale ranging from least to most democratic. Constructed from Freedom House's *Freedom in the World* series, using data from the year before the complex emergency begins (in a few instances the scores were not available until the first year of the complex emergency). I averaged the country's scores on political rights and civil liberties and then inverted the scale so that a higher score is more democratic.	Freedom House (2014)
Mass killing	Dichotomous variable coded 1 if the complex emergency saw at least 50,000 civilians intentionally killed in a 5-year period or less	Valentino (2004); missing observations filled in using his guidelines
Civil conflict	Indicator for conflicts that involve the state and at least one organized opposition group, without external military intervention	Coded by the author using data from Gleditsch et al. (2002) and other sources. Each complex emergency was first coded as one of 5 types. These distinctions draw on the variable "type" in UCDP/PRIO's Armed Conflict Dataset, but with added categories for communal and one-sided violence. While not all complex emergencies are in the Armed Conflict Dataset, where relevant and sensible I used UCDP/PRIO's coding. For more information see Everett (2016). Here I collapse international, communal, and one-sided violence into a single category because there was insufficient variation to include them in the regressions separately.
Internationalized internal conflict	Indicator for conflicts that are based in one state, but where there is international military intervention in a non–peace operation capacity	
Non-civil conflict	Non-civil conflict is a composite category coded 1 if the complex emergency is best understood as one of three conflict types: 1) Interntional conflict: the violence is either interstate war, or a dispute between two actors in different states in which at least one is not a government 2) Communal conflict: the primary fault line reflects intercommunal tension. Here, a) government is not a primary party to the violence, b) victims are chosen based on their perceived membership in a religious, ethnic, or kinship group, and c) members of at least two communities participate. 3) One-sided violence: large-scale violence against civilians occurs without sustained concurrent hostilities between at least two organized parties	

Note: The separate web appendix, available at www.andreaeverett.com, contains detailed information about coding procedures and sources used for the data coded by me. These are the dataset of complex humanitarian emergencies, the coding of the dependent variable *contribution type*, and the coding of *CE news coverage*.

References: Tables A.2 and A.3

Central Intelligence Agency. "The World Factbook." https://www.cia.gov/library/publications/the-world-factbook/, accessed December 10, 2014.

Everett, Andrea. 2016. "Post-Cold War Complex Humanitarian Emergencies: Introducing a New Dataset." *Conflict Management and Peace Science* 33 (3): 311–39.

Fearon, James D., and David D. Laitin. 2003. "Ethnicity, Insurgency, and Civil War." *The American Political Science Review* 97 (1): 75–90.

Freedom House. 2014. "Freedom in the World Country Ratings and Status, 1973–2013." An updated version can be found at https://freedomhouse.org/report-types/freedom-world.

Gartzke, Eric. 2010. "The Affinity of Nations: Similarity of State Voting Positions in the UNGA." http://dss.ucsd.edu/~egartzke/htmlpages/data.html.

Gibler, Douglas M. 2009. *International Military Alliances, 1648–2008*. Washington, DC: CQ Press.

Gleditsch, Kristian Skrede. "Distance Between Capital Cities." http://privatewww.essex.ac.uk/~ksg/data-5.html, accessed December 11, 2014.

Gleditsch, Nils Petter, Peter Wallensteen, Mikael Eriksson, Margareta Sollenberg, and Håvard Strand. 2002. "Armed Conflict 1946-2001: A New Dataset." *Journal of Peace Research* 39 (5): 615–37.

Hensel, Paul. 2006. ICOW Colonial History Data Set (Version 0.4). An updated version can be found at http://www.paulhensel.org/icowdata.html#colonies.

International Institute for Strategic Studies. 1975–2010. *The Military Balance* vols. 75–110.

Marshall, Monty G., Ted Robert Gurr, and Barbara Harff. 2014. "Political Instability Task Force—State Failure Problem Set: Revolutionary Wars, 1955–2013." Vienna, VA: Societal-Systems Research, Inc., http://www.systemicpeace.org/inscr/PITFProbSetCodebook2015.pdf.

Organisation for Economic Cooperation and Development, OECD Stat. "Monthly Statistics of International Trade." Data on "Trade in Value by Partner Countries" are available at https://stats.oecd.org/Index.aspx?DataSetCode=PARTNER, accessed December 13, 2012.

Stinnett, Douglas M., Jaroslav Tir, Philip Schafer, Paul F. Diehl, and Charles Gochman. 2002. "The Correlates of War Project Direct Contiguity Data, Version 3." *Conflict Mangagement and Peace Science* 19 (2): 58–66.

The World Bank. "World Development Indicators." http://data.worldbank.org/data-catalog/world-development-indicators, accessed December 11, 2014.

United Nations Department of Economic and Social Affairs, Statistics Division. "Standard Country or Area Codes for Statistical Use." The data are available and regularly updated under "Geographic Regions" at http://unstats.un.org/unsd/methods/m49/m49regin.htm.

Uppsala Conflict Data Program. "UCDP Conflict Encyclopedia." http://www.ucdp.uu.se/gpdatabase/search.php, accessed December 12, 2014.

Valentino, Benjamin, Paul Huth, and Dylan Balch-Lindsay. 2004. "'Draining the Sea': Mass Killing and Guerrilla Warfare." *International Organization* 58 (2): 375–407.

Statistical Tests

Tables B.1 and B.3 present the coefficients and standard errors for the multi-nomial logistic regressions discussed in chapter 3, while table B.2 provides summary statistics for the covariates. In models 1–3 there are four possible outcomes: no contribution, limited, gap, and robust. Table B.1 thus presents individual coefficients for limited, gap, and robust contributions, which are calculated as compared with no contribution. In model 4, in contrast, there are only three outcomes: limited, gap, and robust contributions to peace operations. As a result table B.3 presents only two sets of coefficients, for gap and robust contributions. These are each calculated as compared with limited contributions.

Table B.1 Multinomial logits, *contribution type*

	Model 1			Model 2			Model 3		
	Limited	*Gap*	*Robust*	*Limited*	*Gap*	*Robust*	*Limited*	*Gap*	*Robust*
CE news coverage	-6.173 (5.702)	9.533** (4.560)	20.304*** (5.852)	-4.508 (9.666)	21.695*** (6.710)	42.901*** (15.194)	-1.663 (5.877)	22.571** (8.959)	33.808*** (9.917)
Operational environment	-8.898* (5.182)	-2.665 (5.807)	12.061** (5.034)	-12.927 (9.083)	2.259 (8.996)	22.417* (11.941)	-11.087* (6.250)	2.658 (15.729)	21.651** (9.569)
CE news coverage* operational environment	12.530 (9.704)	-3.865 (7.650)	-34.888*** (10.427)	11.788 (15.117)	-18.614 (11.873)	-66.866*** (24.884)	7.789 (10.014)	-24.808 (22.219)	-63.095*** (19.638)
Former colony				-0.711 (0.595)	1.327 (0.887)	-0.778 (1.538)			
Contiguous ally				-1.629** (0.792)	-1.185 (1.064)	-1.815 (1.421)	-1.776** (0.834)	-1.855 (1.300)	-2.016* (1.133)
Region				-1.984 (1.243)	-0.087 (0.967)	-4.082*** (1.430)	-1.431 (1.264)	-1.260 (0.979)	-4.679*** (1.370)
Trade				-0.630*** (0.236)	-1.013*** (0.258)	-0.512 (0.314)	-0.605*** (0.232)	-0.952*** (0.286)	-0.143 (0.581)
Affinity				0.315 (0.617)	-0.765 (0.979)	1.691* (0.960)			
Democracy				0.139 (0.336)	-0.093 (0.404)	-0.507 (0.478)			
Pre-1989 complex emergency				-0.311 (0.872)	-0.049 (1.172)	4.635* (2.515)	-0.717 (0.963)	-0.926 (1.347)	1.540 (1.639)

	(1)	(2)	(3)	(4)	(5)	(6)	(7)	(8)	(9)
Mass killing				4.056***	1.334	1.658	4.232***	2.133*	3.274***
				(0.912)	(1.125)	(1.045)	(0.994)	(1.278)	(1.208)
Internationalized civil conflict							1.398	2.615	1.513
							(1.348)	(1.687)	(1.641)
Non-civil conflict							1.703	1.891*	1.392
							(1.282)	(1.147)	(1.710)
Constant	3.721	-4.207	-10.342***	2.517	-11.839***	-21.170**	0.364	-12.656**	-17.854**
	(3.024)	(3.140)	(3.729)	(5.290)	(3.859)	(9.181)	(3.330)	(5.571)	(6.939)
Observations	181	181	181	181	181	181	181	181	181
Pseudo R-squared	0.214	0.214	0.214	0.498	0.498	0.498	0.482	0.482	0.482

Robust standard errors clustered on complex emergencies in parentheses. *** $p < .01$, ** $p < .05$, * $p < .10$

Table B.2 Summary statistics

	Observations	Mean	St. dev.	Minimum	Maximum
CE news coverage	181	0.526	0.164	0	1
Operational environment	181	0.520	0.228	0	1
CE news coverage*operational environment	181	0.265	0.141	0	0.817
Operational environment (model 3)	181	0.452	0.236	0	1
CE news coverage*operational environment (model 3)	181	0.229	0.139	0	0.796
Contiguous ally	181	0.320	0.468	0	1
Former colony	181	0.160	0.368	0	1
Region	181	0.110	0.314	0	1
Affinity	181	0.0376	0.345	−0.779	0.667
Trade (logged)	181	−1.995	2.048	−7.885	1.881
Democracy	181	2.881	1.437	1	6
Mass killing	181	0.348	0.478	0	1
Pre-1989 complex emergency	181	0.315	0.466	0	1
Civil conflict	181	0.613	0.488	0	1
Internationalized civil conflict	181	0.177	0.383	0	1
Non-civil conflict	181	0.210	0.408	0	1

Table B.3 Multinomial logit, *contribution type* (restricted sample)

	Model 4	
	Gap	Robust
CE news coverage	16.493***	32.046***
	(6.194)	(9.630)
Operational environment	5.222	31.679***
	(6.535)	(12.188)
CE news coverage*operational environment	−12.758	−63.370***
	(9.172)	(19.738)
Contribution decade	1.175	−1.361
	(0.765)	(1.294)
Constant	−11.555**	−15.498***
	(5.407)	(5.869)
Observations	86	86
Pseudo R-squared	0.331	0.331

Robust standard errors in parentheses.*** $p < 0.01$, ** $p < 0.05$, * $p < 0.1$

Notes

Introduction

1. Initial news accounts were unclear about the date and identity of the attackers. See Opheera McDoom, "New Darfur Fighting Kills up to 105, Thousands Flee," *Reuters*, January 26, 2005; Jasper Mortimer, "Sudanese Air Force Bombs People in Darfur, NGO Reports Casualties," *Associated Press*, January 26, 2005. However, later reports placed the blame squarely on Sudanese Army aircraft and government-backed militia. See Nicholas D. Kristof, "The Secret Genocide Archive," *New York Times*, February 23, 2005; Human Rights Watch, *Entrenching Impunity: Government Responsibility for International Crimes in Darfur* (December 8, 2005), 55.

2. For a summary of these estimates see Olivier Degomme and Debarati Guha-Sapir, "Patterns of Mortality Rates," *Lancet* 375, no. 9711 (2010): 294–300, at 295.

3. International Crisis Group, *The AU's Mission in Darfur: Bridging the Gaps*, (Nairobi/Brussels: July 6, 2005), 6–8; William G. O'Neill and Violette Cassis, *Protecting Two Million Internally Displaced: The Successes and Shortcomings of the African Union in Darfur* (Washington, DC: Brookings-Bern Project on Internal Displacement, 2005), 50–58.

4. United States Committee for Refugees, *World Refugee Survey 1996* (New York: United States Committee for Refugees 1996), 129.

5. The best estimates include a 2010 figure collected for the International Criminal Tribunal for the Former Yugoslavia of 42,106 war-related civilian deaths and a 2007 figure from the Research and Documentation Center in Sarajevo of 39,684 civilian deaths due directly to military activity. See Taylor Seybolt, "Significant Numbers: Civilian Casualties and Strategic Peacebuilding," in *Counting Civilian Casualties: An Introduction to Recording and Estimating Civilian Deaths in Conflict*, ed. Taylor B. Seybolt, Jay D. Aronson, and Baruch Fischhoff (Oxford: Oxford University Press, 2013), 14; Jan Zwierzchowski and Ewa Tabeau, "The 1992–95 War in Bosnia and Herzegovina: Census-Based Multiple System Estimation of Casualties' Undercount" (paper presented at the International Research Workshop on "The Global Costs of Conflict," Berlin, Germany, 2010), 14–16.

6. Various sources cite similar figures. See Ewa Tabeau and Jakub Bijak, "War-Related Deaths in the 1992–1995 Armed Conflicts in Bosnia and Herzegovina: A Critique of Previous Estimates and Recent Results," *European Journal of Population* 21, no. 2/3 (2005): 187–215, at 198; Nicholas J. Wheeler, *Saving Strangers: Humanitarian Intervention in International Society* (Oxford: Oxford University Press, 2000), 255.

7. James Dunn, "Genocide in East Timor," in *Century of Genocide: Critical Essays and Eyewitness Accounts*, ed. Samuel Totten and William S. Parsons (New York: Routledge, 2009), 280.

8. For an account of these events see Peter Cosgrove, *My Story* (Sydney: Harper Collins, 2007), 212–13. For related news reports see also "INTERFET Troops Seize Largest Weapons Cache Yet in East Timor," *Agence France-Presse*, September 29, 1999; Max Blenkin, "Aussies Raid Another Timor Militia Base," *Australian Associated Press*, September 28, 1999.

9. This is an intentionally broad definition of peace operations. It includes missions that provide no physical protection to civilians (e.g., traditional peacekeeping) and those where physical protection is the main goal. While some scholars look at such missions separately, I examine them together since they are at times used (inappropriately) as substitutes for one another in the worst conflicts.

10. The international humanitarian community uses the term "complex emergencies" to describe conflicts that are especially devastating for civilians. In this book I adopt this concept and use it to designate the conflicts that represent the best candidates, on humanitarian grounds, for direct physical protection of civilians and aid workers.

11. The UN has used a similar term, "commitment gap," for missions without the resources to carry out their goals. See United Nations General Assembly/Security Council, *Report of the Panel on United Nations Peace Operations*, A/55/305, S/2000/809, August 21, 2000, 11. My notion of ambitions-resources gaps is broader, and includes both these operations and those that restrict the activities of an otherwise high-capacity force.

12. For details see chapter 3 and table A.1 in appendix A.

13. Michael O'Hanlon, *Expanding Global Military Capacity for Humanitarian Intervention* (Washington, DC: Brookings Institution Press, 2003), 76–78. Beginning in 1993, Russia led a force in Tajikistan that helped protect humanitarian convoys, but it is debatable whether this qualifies as a peace operation given Russia's direct involvement in the Tajik civil war. For an assessment of the capabilities and limitations of various other states, see O'Hanlon, *Expanding Global Military Capacity*, chap. 3.

14. On African force projection broadly see Victoria K. Holt and Tobias C. Berkman, *The Impossible Mandate? Military Preparedness, the Responsibility to Protect and Modern Peace Operations* (Washington, DC: Henry L. Stimson Center, 2006), 74; O'Hanlon, *Expanding Global Military Capacity*, 71. On the AU see Paul Williams, "Military Responses to Mass Killing: The African Union Mission in Sudan," *International Peacekeeping* 13, no. 2 (2006): 168–83; Arvid Ekengard, *The African Union Mission in SUDAN (AMIS): Experiences and Lessons Learned* (Stockholm: FOI/Swedish Defence Research Agency, 2008), especially 40–49; Emma Svensson, *The African Mission in Burundi: Lessons Learned from the African Union's First Peace Operation* (Stockholm: FOI/Swedish Defence Research Agency, 2008), 15–20. On ECOWAS see Eric G. Berman and Melissa T. Labonte, "Sierra Leone," in *Twenty-First Century Peace Operations*, ed. William J. Durch (Washington, DC: United States Institute of Peace, 2006), 141–227; John M. Kabia, *Humanitarian Intervention and Conflict Resolution in West Africa: From ECOMOG to ECOMIL* (Burlington, VT: Ashgate Publishing, 2009), chaps. 4–5.

15. On the first point see International Commission on Intervention and State Sovereignty (ICISS), *The Responsibility to Protect* (Ottawa: International Development Research Centre, 2001), 57; United Nations Security Council, *Report of the Secretary-General to the Security Council on the Protection of Civilians in Armed Conflict*, S/1999/957, September 8, 1999. On the second see Holt and Berkman, *Impossible Mandate?*, 62–64, 75; Victoria Holt, Glyn Taylor, and Max Kelly, *Protecting Civilians in the Context of UN Peacekeeping Operations: Successes, Setbacks and Remaining Challenges* (New York: United Nations Department of Peacekeeping Operations/Office for the Coordination of Humanitarian Affairs, 2009), 100; Alex J. Bellamy and Paul D. Williams, "The West and Contemporary Peace Operations," *Journal of Peace Research* 46, no. 1 (2009): 39–57.

16. United Nations Organization Mission in the Democratic Republic of the Congo (MONUC; MONUSCO since 2010) is the exception that proves the rule. In 2008 it was tasked with making civilian protection in Eastern DRC its top priority, but was widely criticized for failing to do so. In 2013 the UN deployed a first-ever combat brigade of 3,000 troops with an offensive mandate to protect civilians and "neutralize" those who threaten them, and with the advanced equipment needed for this job. Only time will tell if this force offers a model for the

future, but the Security Council has stressed that it is not intended as a general precedent. See Courtney Brooks, "UN Tests Combat Brigade in Democratic Republic of Congo," *AlJazeera America*, September 6, 2013.

17. On civilians' expectations see Holt, Taylor, and Kelly, "Protecting Civilians," 3; Alan J. Kuperman, *The Limits of Humanitarian Intervention: Genocide in Rwanda* (Washington, DC: Brookings Institution Press, 2001), 117.

18. Holt and Berkman, *Impossible Mandate?*, 186. See also Kuperman, *Limits of Humanitarian Intervention*, 117.

19. Olivier Lanotte, *La France au Rwanda (1990-1994): Entre abstention impossible et engagement ambivalent* (Brussels: PIE Peter Lang, 2007), 461–77; Linda Melvern, *A People Betrayed: The Role of the West in Rwanda's Genocide*, 2nd ed. (London: Zed Books, 2009), 239–40; Jean-Claude Lafourcade and Guillaume Riffaud, *Opération Turquoise: Rwanda 1994* (Paris: Perrin, 2010), 87–89, 104–16.

20. Alan J. Kuperman, "The Moral Hazard of Humanitarian Intervention: Lessons from the Balkans," *International Studies Quarterly* 52, no. 1 (2008): 49–80.

21. Benjamin Valentino, "The Perils of Limited Humanitarian Intervention: Lessons from the 1990s," *Wisconsin International Law Journal* 24, no. 3 (2006): 723–40, quotation on 737. See also Kuperman, "Moral Hazard," 74.

22. Thomas G. Weiss, "Intervention: Whither the United Nations?," *Washington Quarterly* 17, no. 1 (1994): 109–28, at 122; see also Michael Walzer, "The Politics of Rescue," *Social Research* 62, no. 1 (1995): 53–66; Andrew Natsios, "Food Through Force: Humanitarian Intervention and U.S. Policy," *Washington Quarterly* 17, no. 1 (1994): 129–44, at 139–40; Valentino, "Perils of Limited Intervention."

23. On humanitarian intervention see Martha Finnemore, *The Purpose of Intervention: Changing Beliefs about The Use of Force* (Ithaca: Cornell University Press, 2003); Gary Jonathan Bass, *Freedom's Battle: The Origins of Humanitarian Intervention* (New York: Alfred A. Knopf, 2008). On peacekeeping generally see Virginia Page Fortna, *Does Peacekeeping Work? Shaping Belligerents' Choices After Civil War* (Princeton: Princeton University Press, 2008), chaps. 2–3; Mark J. Mullenbach, "Deciding to Keep Peace: An Analysis of International Influences on the Establishment of Third-Party Peacekeeping Missions," *International Studies Quarterly* 49, no. 3 (2005): 529–55. On state contributions see Richard Perkins and Eric Neumayer, "Extra-territorial Interventions in Conflict Spaces: Explaining the Geographies of Post-Cold War Peacekeeping," *Political Geography* 27, no. 8 (2008): 895–914; Bellamy and Williams, "West and Contemporary Peace Operations"; Vincenzo Bove and Leandro Elia, "Supplying Peace: Participation in and Troop Contribution to Peacekeeping Missions," *Journal of Peace Research* 48, no. 6 (2011): 699–714. Bove and Elia is a partial exception since it examines how many troops states send.

24. Officials often initiate relatively easy operations that are inappropriate to the situation on the ground, for instance, because they "do not want to incur the risks and costs associated with more difficult interventions." Taylor B. Seybolt, *Humanitarian Military Intervention: The Conditions for Success and Failure* (Oxford: Oxford University Press, 2008), 44. See also James Gow, *Triumph of the Lack of Will: International Diplomacy and the Yugoslav War* (New York: Columbia University Press, 1997); Kuperman, *Limits of Humanitarian Intervention*, 116.

25. See, e.g., Gareth J. Evans, *The Responsibility to Protect: Ending Mass Atrocity Crimes Once and for All* (Washington, DC: Brookings Institution Press, 2008), 224.

26. Weiss, "Intervention," 123.

27. On peacekeeping see Paul F. Diehl, *International Peacekeeping* (Baltimore: Johns Hopkins University Press, 1993); William J. Durch, *The Evolution of UN Peacekeeping: Case Studies and Comparative Analysis* (New York: St. Martin's Press, 1993); Laura Neack, "UN Peace-Keeping: In the Interest of Community or Self?," *Journal of Peace Research* 32, no. 2 (1995): 181–206; Khusrav Gaibulloev, Todd Sandler, and Hirofumi Shimizu, "Demands for UN and Non-UN Peacekeeping," *Journal of Conflict Resolution* 53, no. 6 (2009): 827–52; Perkins and Neumayer, "Extra-territorial Interventions"; Bellamy and Williams, "West and Contemporary Peace Operations." On humanitarian intervention see Andrew Natsios, "Illusions of Influence: The CNN Effect in Complex Emergencies," in *From Massacres to Genocide: The Media, Public Policy, and Humanitarian Crises*, ed. Robert I. Rotberg and Thomas G. Weiss (Cambridge, MA: World Peace

Foundation, 1996), 149–68; Jack Snyder, "Realism, Refugees, and Strategies of Humanitarianism," in *Refugees in International Relations*, ed. Alexander Betts and Gil Loescher (Oxford: Oxford University Press, 2011), 29–52.

28. This logic is rooted in realism's assertion that states typically act to promote their strategic interests. Yet realists also recognize that states may pursue moral foreign policy goals that are not directly related to their own material interests as long as these policies do not seriously threaten their security. While this second perspective does not necessarily contradict the argument about ambitions-resources gaps I build in this book, it also does not explain them since simply recognizing that states may indulge normative impulses if the strategic costs are low does not tell us when they will do so or how they go about designing such policies. As John Mearsheimer notes, realism "has little to say" about when or how states pursue non-security goals. *The Tragedy of Great Power Politics* (New York: W.W. Norton and Company, 2001), 46.

29. Bass, *Freedom's Battle*; Peter Viggo Jakobsen, "National Interest, Humanitarianism or CNN: What Triggers UN Peace Enforcement after the Cold War?," *Journal of Peace Research* 33, no. 2 (1996): 205–15; Peter Viggo Jakobsen, "The Transformation of United Nations Peace Operations in the 1990s," *Cooperation and Conflict* 37, no. 3 (2002): 267–82. In a similar vein, see Chaim D. Kaufmann and Robert A. Pape, "Explaining Costly International Moral Action: Britain's Sixty-Year Campaign against the Atlantic Slave Trade," *International Organization* 53, no. 4 (1999): 631–68.

30. Richard C. Eichenberg, "Victory Has Many Friends: U.S. Public Opinion and the Use of Military Force, 1981–2005," *International Security* 30, no. 1 (2005): 140–77; Peter Feaver and Christopher Gelpi, *Choosing Your Battles: American Civil-Military Relations and the Use of Force* (Princeton: Princeton University Press, 2004); Christopher Gelpi, Peter Feaver, and Jason Reifler, *Paying the Human Costs of War: American Public Opinion and Casualties in Military Conflicts* (Princeton: Princeton University Press, 2009); Christopher Gelpi, Peter D. Feaver, and Jason Reifler, "Success Matters: Casualty Sensitivity and the War in Iraq," *International Security* 30, no. 3 (2006): 7–46.

31. See, e.g., Evans, *Responsibility to Protect*, 229–30; Bove and Elia, "Supplying Peace."

32. ICISS, *Responsibility to Protect*, 71.

33. Michael Lipson, "Peacekeeping: Organized Hypocrisy?," *European Journal of International Relations* 13, no. 1 (2007): 5–34, quotation on 6.

34. Nils Brunsson, *The Organization of Hypocrisy: Talk, Decisions and Actions in Organizations* (New York: John Wiley & Sons, 1989); Stephen D. Krasner, *Sovereignty: Organized Hypocrisy* (Princeton: Princeton University Press, 1999); Lipson, "Peacekeeping: Organized Hypocrisy?"

35. Lipson, "Peacekeeping: Organized Hypocrisy?"

36. See e.g., Graham T. Allison, "Conceptual Models and the Cuban Missile Crisis," *American Political Science Review* 63, no. 3 (1969): 689–718.

37. United Nations General Assembly/Security Council, *Report of the Panel on United Nations Peace Operations*, especially paras. 48–64.

38. Quoted in Samantha Power, *A Problem from Hell: America and the Age of Genocide* (New York: Basic Books, 2002), 386.

39. Sarah Sewall, Dwight Raymond, and Sally Chin, "Mass Atrocity Response Operations: A Military Planning Handbook," (Cambridge, MA: Harvard College, 2010), 5. See also Dwight Raymond et al., *Mass Atrocity Prevention and Response Options (MAPRO): A Policy Planning Handbook* (Carlisle, PA: U.S. Army Peacekeeping and Stability Operations Institute, 2012).

40. Hans J. Morgenthau, *Politics Among Nations: The Struggle for Power and Peace*, 2nd ed. (New York: Knopf, 1954), 10.

41. See e.g., David N. Gibbs, "Power Politics, NATO, and the Libyan Intervention," *Counterpunch*, September 15, 2011.

42. Harry Eckstein, "Case Study and Theory in Political Science," in *Handbook of Political Science, Volume 7: Strategies of Inquiry*, ed. Fred I. Greenstein and Nelson W. Polsby (Reading: Addison-Wesley Publishing Company, 1975), 79–138.

43. Gil Merom, *How Democracies Lose Small Wars: State, Society, and the Failures of France in Algeria, Israel in Lebanon, and the United States in Vietnam* (Cambridge: Cambridge University

Press, 2003); Kelly M. Greenhill, *Weapons of Mass Migration: Forced Displacement, Coercion, and Foreign Policy* (Ithaca: Cornell University Press, 2010).

1. Devil in the Details

1. See also Andrea Everett, "Post-Cold War Complex Humanitarian Emergencies: Introducing a New Dataset," *Conflict Management and Peace Science* 33, no. 3 (2016): 311–39. For other definitions, see Centre for Research on the Epidemiology of Disasters, "Complex Emergencies Database (CE-DAT)," Université catholique de Louvain, accessed April 2, 2013, http://cedat.be/glossary; United Nations Office for the Coordination of Humanitarian Affairs, *OCHA Orientation Handbook on Complex Emergencies* (August 31, 1999), p. 4, accessed January 28, 2015, http://reliefweb.int/report/world/ocha-orientation-handbook-complex-emergencies. A longer discussion is also included in the web appendix, available at www.andreaeverett.com.

2. "Mass atrocity crimes" refers collectively to various patterns of large-scale rights abuses that can include genocide, mass killing, ethnic cleansing, war crimes, and crimes against humanity. See, e.g., Evans, *Responsibility to Protect*, 11–12.

3. Indeed, these indirect causes of mortality usually account for most deaths even where war is combined with atrocity crimes. See Frederick M. Burkle Jr., "The Epidemiology of War and Conflict," in *Handbook of Bioterrorism and Disaster Medicine*, ed. Robert E. Antosia and John D. Cahill (New York: Springer, 2006), 91.

4. See, e.g., Walzer, "Politics of Rescue," 55; Wheeler, *Saving Strangers*, 34; ICISS, *Responsibility to Protect*, 32.

5. In contrast, most prominent quantitative investigations of traditional peacekeeping and its ability to protect civilians examine responses only to wars—Michael W. Doyle and Nicholas Sambanis, "International Peacebuilding: A Theoretical and Quantitative Analysis," *American Political Science Review* 94, no. 4 (2000): 779–801; Michael Gilligan and Stephen John Stedman, "Where Do the Peacekeepers Go?," *International Studies Review* 5, no. 4 (2003): 37–54; Michael W. Doyle and Nicholas Sambanis, *Making War and Building Peace: United Nations Peace Operations* (Princeton: Princeton University Press, 2006); Fortna, *Does Peacekeeping Work*; Lisa Hultman, Jacob Kathman, and Megan Shannon, "United Nations Peacekeeping and Civilian Protection in Civil War," *American Journal of Political Science* 57, no. 4 (2013): 875–91. Meanwhile, studies of humanitarian intervention and failures to initiate it often focus only on the very worst cases of mass atrocities—Wheeler, *Saving Strangers*; Power, *Problem from Hell*; Matthew Krain, "International Intervention and the Severity of Genocides and Politicides," *International Studies Quarterly* 49, no. 3 (2005): 363–88; Bass, *Freedom's Battle*. While the former exclude both atrocities and serious communal conflicts, the latter exclude even the most debilitating wars in which civilians are not the main targets of atrocities.

6. These figures are based on data on aid worker attacks from the Aid Worker Security Database, accessed August 20, 2013, https://aidworkersecurity.org, and on a dataset of complex emergencies I present in chapter 3. Occasionally it is not clear if an attack took place in the context of a complex emergency, and in that case I exclude it from the count. Thus, 77% is a minimum estimate.

7. For an excellent summary see the overview of protection concepts in Holt and Berkman, *Impossible Mandate?*, 37–42.

8. ICISS, *Responsibility to Protect*, vii.

9. See for instance the UN's six *Aides Mémoire for the Consideration of Issues Pertaining to the Protection of Civilians in Armed Conflict*. For the latest see United Nations Security Council, *Aide Memoire for the Consideration of Issues Pertaining to the Protection of Civilians in Armed Conflict*, S/PRST/2015/23, November 25, 2015.

10. These tasks appear in individual mandates and the *Aides Mémoire*. See also Holt, Taylor, and Kelly, "Protecting Civilians," chap. 2.

11. Holt and Berkman, *Impossible Mandate?*, 3.

12. The terms "humanitarian intervention" and "coercive protection missions" both refer to operations that aim primarily to protect civilians from grave harm. The former is older and

better known, but recently consensus in the policy community seems to be settling around "coercive protection." See *Impossible Mandate?*, 5–6; Evans, *Responsibility to Protect*, 214. More recently, the term "Mass Atrocity Response Operation" has also developed a following. See Raymond et al., "Mass Atrocity Prevention and Response Options"; Sewall, Raymond, and Chin, "Mass Atrocity Response Operations."

13. On peacekeeping incidence see Diehl, *International Peacekeeping*; Durch, *Evolution of UN Peacekeeping*; Chantal de Jonge Oudraat, "The United Nations and International Conflict," in *The International Dimensions of Internal Conflict*, ed. Michael E. Brown (Cambridge: MIT Press, 1996), 489–536; David N. Gibbs, "Is Peacekeeping a New Form of Imperialism?," *International Peacekeeping* 4, no. 1 (1997): 122–28; Gilligan and Stedman, "Where Do the Peacekeepers Go?"; Mullenbach, "Deciding to Keep Peace." For exceptions that address protection themes see Jakobsen, "National Interest, Humanitarianism or CNN"; Jakobsen, "Transformation of UN Peace Operations"; Hultman, Kathman, and Shannon, "United Nations Peacekeeping and Civilian Protection." On state contributions see Neack, "UN Peace-Keeping"; Jyoti Khanna, Todd Sandler, and Hirofumi Shimizu, "Sharing the Financial Burden for UN and NATO Peacekeeping, 1976–1996," *Journal of Conflict Resolution* 42, no. 2 (1998): 176–95; Andreas Andersson, "Democracies and UN Peacekeeping Operations, 1990–1996," *International Peacekeeping* 7, no. 2 (2000): 1–22; Perkins and Neumayer, "Extra-territorial Interventions"; Bellamy and Williams, "West and Contemporary Peace Operations"; Gaibulloev, Sandler, and Shimizu, "Demands for UN and Non-UN Peacekeeping." On building peace after war see Doyle and Sambanis, "International Peacebuilding"; Doyle and Sambanis, *Making War and Building Peace*; Fortna, *Does Peacekeeping Work?*

14. For definitions of humanitarian intervention see Anthony C. Arend and Robert J. Beck, *International Law and the Use of Force: Beyond the UN Charter Paradigm* (London: Routledge, 1993), 113; J. L. Holzgrefe, "The Humanitarian Intervention Debate," in *Humanitarian Intervention: Ethical, Legal and Political Dilemmas*, ed. J. L. Holzgrefe and Robert O. Keohane (Cambridge: Cambridge University Press, 2003), 18. Two exceptions to this pattern are Finnemore, *Purpose of Intervention*, 53; and Seybolt, *Humanitarian Military Intervention*, 5–6.

15. Occasionally force commanders seek to do more for civilians than their mandate officially permits. In general, however, an operation's goals indicate the most that soldiers are asked to do to protect civilians.

16. Walzer, "Politics of Rescue," 66.

17. See e.g., Holt and Berkman, *Impossible Mandate?*, 48; Seybolt, *Humanitarian Military Intervention*, 43, 228.

18. Melvern, *A People Betrayed*, 249; Seybolt, *Humanitarian Military Intervention*, 76–77.

19. See, e.g., Michael O'Hanlon, *Saving Lives with Force: Military Criteria for Humanitarian Intervention* (Washington, DC: Brookings Institution Press, 1997), 5.

20. Seybolt, *Humanitarian Military Intervention*, 149–159.

21. Holt and Berkman, *Impossible Mandate?*, 41–42.

22. Ibid., 90.

23. Ibid., 42, 50–51.

24. On assisting aid delivery see Seybolt, *Humanitarian Military Intervention*, chap. 4, esp. p. 98.

25. On the requirements of protection for aid operations, see Seybolt, *Humanitarian Military Intervention*, chap. 5.

26. Seybolt, *Humanitarian Military Intervention*, 180. For details of Provide Comfort, see 191–94.

27. Ibid., 163, 198 (UNPROFOR), 151 (UNOSOM I).

28. See, e.g., Micah Zenko, "Say No to a Darfur No-Fly Zone," *Guardian*, March 12, 2009.

29. On defeating the perpetrators of violence see Seybolt, *Humanitarian Military Intervention*, chap. 7.

30. Still, individual national contingents in a multilateral operation may be subject to "caveats" that limit their activities and involve more restrictive ROE. In INTERFET, troops from several Asian countries deployed to relatively safe parts of the territory and declined to participate in offensive action.

31. See, e.g., Micah Zenko, "Saving Lives with Speed: Using Rapidly Deployable Forces for Genocide Prevention," *Defense and Security Analysis* 20, no. 1 (2004): 3–19, at 8.

32. As we will see, all these problems plagued Operation Allied Force in Kosovo. See also Seybolt, *Humanitarian Military Intervention*, 248–49.

33. This discussion suggests that in addition to the broader concept of an ambitions-resources gap, a peace operation may also experience a secondary gap between goals and military strategies. Military strategies, however, have little meaning except in relation to the goals they are used to pursue, and alone provide little if any information about the protection a mission can hope to offer. For this reason I bundle goals and strategies together under the banner of ambitions.

34. Holt and Berkman, *Impossible Mandate?*, 8.

35. O'Hanlon, *Expanding Global Military Capacity*, 31–32.

36. For the DRC estimate see O'Hanlon, *Expanding Global Military Capacity*, 42. For Darfur see Rebecca Hamilton, *Fighting for Darfur: Public Action and the Struggle to Stop Genocide* (New York: Palgrave Macmillan, 2011), 76. This latter Pentagon estimate was based on a ratio of 3:1 intervening to opposing forces.

37. See, e.g., Holt and Berkman, *Impossible Mandate?*, 75–76; Roméo Dallaire and Brent Beardsley, *Shake Hands With the Devil: The Failure of Humanity in Rwanda* (Toronto: Random House Canada, 2003). Dallaire and Beardsley suggest that the Rwandan genocide could have been stopped in its early stages with a modest force of about 5,000 troops; see for example pp. 356, 514.

38. Seybolt, *Humanitarian Military Intervention*, 22.

39. Holt and Berkman, *Impossible Mandate?*, 192–93.

40. O'Hanlon, *Saving Lives with Force*, 39.

41. See e.g., Zenko, "Saving Lives with Speed," 9.

42. UNITAF preceded the ill-fated UNOSOM II, which led to the deaths of eighteen U.S. Rangers and hundreds of Somalis in October 1993. Its goal of providing security for relief operations was appropriate since there was not large-scale violence against civilians at the time. On its military strategies and troop contingent see Seybolt, *Humanitarian Military Intervention*, 151–55.

43. See the Information Technology Section/Department of Public Information, United Nations, "United Nations Observer Mission in El Salvador: ONUSAL (July 1991–April 1995)," 2003, http://www.un.org/en/peacekeeping/missions/past/onusal.htm; and Information Technology Section/Department of Public Information, United Nations, "Sierra Leone—UNOMOSIL: Facts and Figures," accessed January 20, 2012, http://www.un.org/en/peacekeeping/missions/past/unomsil/UnomsilF.html.

44. Svensson, "African Mission in Burundi," 11–13.

45. Seybolt, *Humanitarian Military Intervention*, 120–22; Melvern, *A People Betrayed*, 245.

46. Kuperman, *Limits of Humanitarian Intervention*, 117.

47. As O'Hanlon has pointed out, troops from "at least one top-notch western military" are typically needed. See O'Hanlon, *Saving Lives with Force*, 44–45; see also Zenko, "Saving Lives with Speed," 11.

48. Holt and Berkman, *Impossible Mandate?*, 74; O'Hanlon, *Saving Lives with Force*, 43; Zenko, "Saving Lives with Speed," 15. This may change with EU efforts to acquire greater shared strategic airlift capacity, but at this time there is little evidence to suggest it has significantly increased the leadership capacity of states other than France and the United Kingdom.

49. For a detailed account, and for various examples related to the Rwandan genocide, see Michael Barnett, *Eyewitness to a Genocide: The United Nations and Rwanda* (Ithaca: Cornell University Press, 2003).

50. For example, in April 1994 Secretary-General Boutros-Ghali recommended giving UNAMIR an additional forty-five civilian police to help carry out its mandate. The United States was the only Security Council member to oppose this minor infusion of resources, but it held firm and refused to approve the additional personnel. See Barnett, *Eyewitness*, 96. Similarly, after the Rwandan genocide the Security Council refused to approve a Secretariat plan for a UN force to provide security in the refugee camps across the border in Zaire. See Melvern, *A People Betrayed*, 249–50.

51. On Bosnia see Barnett, *Eyewitness*, 32. On Darfur see Hamilton, *Fighting for Darfur*, 111.

52. See, e.g., United Nations General Assembly/Security Council, *Report of the Panel on United Nations Peace Operations*, 10, 22.

53. For example, when France pushed for UNAMIR in 1993, "If the United States put up a fuss and objected . . . then it could anticipate that France would return the favor sometime in the near future." Barnett, *Eyewitness*, 69.

54. On the use of side payments see Marina Henke, "The International Security Cooperation Market" (Ph.D. diss., Princeton University, 2012). Henke looks at how lead states, who place a high priority on a particular operation, recruit participants who do not care as much in order to increase their missions' legitimacy and share operational burdens. The same principle applies here: even if powerful states do not want to contribute their own troops to a mission they may be able to recruit others instead.

55. For specifics and sources on contributions to peace operations in these conflicts see part 2A of the web appendix.

56. See, e.g., Bob Breen, "Towards Regional Neighbourhood Watch," in *Australian Peacekeeping: Sixty Years in the Field*, ed. David Horner, Peter Londey, and Jean Bou (Cambridge: Cambridge University Press, 2009), 96–97.

57. Of course, capabilities vary and no state can deploy so large a force as the United States. Still, each of the four I examine has maintained the capacity to deploy a sizeable peace operation of at least several thousand troops. See e.g., O'Hanlon, *Expanding Global Military Capacity*, chap. 3.

58. Support for missions led by other great power democracies are key exceptions, which I address in chapter 3. In such cases, sending one's own troops may enhance the prospects for effective protection, but failing to do so does not necessarily limit them. Still, generally leaders choose between sending their own troops and supporting less capable ones, and I assume this except where noted.

59. Bellamy and Williams, "West and Contemporary Peace Operations," especially pp. 51–52 on reasons for avoiding direct UN involvement.

60. Ibid., 44.

61. Kuperman, *Limits of Humanitarian Intervention*, 64.

62. Sewall, Raymond, and Chin, "Mass Atrocity Response Operations," 65.

2. Political Will, Organized Hypocrisy, and Ambitions-Resources Gaps

1. For a thorough overview of their similarities and differences see Lipson, "Peacekeeping: Organized Hypocrisy?," especially 6–10.

2. Brunsson, *Organization of Hypocrisy* (1st ed.); Brunsson, *The Organization of Hypocrisy: Talk, Decisions and Actions in Organizations*, trans. Nancy Adler, 2nd ed. (Herndon: Copenhagen Business School Press, 2002).

3. The term counter-coupling comes from Lipson, "Peacekeeping: Organized Hypocrisy?." See page 10 for a discussion of the distinction between it and the better-known decoupling. On compensatory rhetoric see also the reference in Brunsson, *Organization of Hypocrisy* (2nd ed.), xiv.

4. Krasner, *Sovereignty*.

5. Lipson, "Peacekeeping: Organized Hypocrisy?," 13.

6. In this sense, my distinction between normative and material pressures is not simply equivalent to Krasner's "logics of appropriateness" and "logics of consequences." Rather, I argue that moral pressure from various domestic and international sources can and does have political consequences for leaders, but that the normative nature of this pressure is central to the divergence between talk and action that defines organized hypocrisy.

7. See, e.g., John H. Aldrich, John L. Sullivan, and Eugene Borgida, "Foreign Affairs and Issue Voting: Do Presidential Candidates 'Waltz Before A Blind Audience'?," *American Political Science Review* 83, no. 1 (1989): 123–41; Sowmya Anand and Jon A. Krosnick, "The Impact of Attitudes Toward Foreign Policy Goals on Public Preferences Among Presidential Candidates:

A Study of Issue Publics and the Attentive Public in the 2000 US Presidential Election," *Presidential Studies Quarterly* (2003): 31–71; Christopher Gelpi, Jason Reifler, and Peter Feaver, "Iraq the Vote: Retrospective and Prospective Foreign Policy Judgments on Candidate Choice and Casualty Tolerance," *Political Behavior* 29, no. 2 (2007): 151–74.

8. For evidence from the United States see, e.g., Robin F. Marra, Charles W. Ostrom Jr., and Dennis M. Simon, "Foreign Policy and Presidential Popularity: Creating Windows of Opportunity in the Perpetual Election," *Journal of Conflict Resolution* 34, no. 4 (1990): 588–623; Michael Nickelsburg and Helmut Norpoth, "Commander-in-Chief or Chief Economist?: The President in the Eye of the Public," *Electoral Studies* 19, no. 2 (2000): 313–32. For France see Richard S. Conley, "From Elysian Fields to the Guillotine?: The Dynamics of Presidential and Prime Ministerial Approval in Fifth Republic France," *Comparative Political Studies* 39, no. 5 (2006): 570–98. For the United Kingdom see Helmut Norpoth, "Guns and Butter and Government Popularity in Britain," *American Political Science Review* 81, no. 3 (1987): 949–59.

9. See David P. Auerswald, *Disarmed Democracies: Domestic Institutions and the Use of Force* (Ann Arbor: University of Michigan Press, 2000), 38–39; Bruce M. Russett, *Controlling the Sword: The Democratic Governance of National Security* (Cambridge: Harvard University Press, 1990), 30; Kurt Taylor Gaubatz, "Election Cycles and War," *Journal of Conflict Resolution* 35, no. 2 (1991): 212–44; Kurt Taylor Gaubatz, *Elections and War: The Electoral Incentive in the Democratic Politics of War and Peace* (Stanford: Stanford University Press, 1999).

10. Russett, *Controlling the Sword*, 15; Auerswald, *Disarmed Democracies*, 40. This is with good reason, since in the United States evaluations of presidential performance influence everything from citizens' vote choices to the success of the president's policy agendas in Congress. See Charles W. Ostrom Jr. and Dennis M. Simon, "Promise and Performance: A Dynamic Model of Presidential Popularity," *American Political Science Review* 79, no. 2 (1985): 334–58; Dennis M. Simon and Charles W. Ostrom Jr, "The Politics of Prestige: Popular Support and the Modern Presidency," *Presidential Studies Quarterly* (1988): 741–59; Marra, Ostrom, and Simon, "Foreign Policy and Presidential Popularity," 589–90.

11. On these differences across democratic systems see Auerswald, *Disarmed Democracies*, 40–41; Thomas Risse-Kappen, "Public Opinion, Domestic Structure, and Foreign Policy in Liberal Democracies," *World Politics* 43, no. 4 (1991): 479–512.

12. Russett, *Controlling the Sword*, 30–31.

13. For example, George H. W. Bush's legacy was an important factor in his decision to intervene in Somalia in 1992. Jon Western, "Sources of Humanitarian Intervention: Beliefs, Information, and Advocacy in the US Decisions on Somalia and Bosnia," *International Security* 26, no. 4 (2002): 112–42, see 137.

14. Matthew A. Baum, "How Public Opinion Constrains the Use of Force: The Case of Operation Restore Hope," *Presidential Studies Quarterly* 34, no. 2 (2004): 187–226; Merom, *How Democracies Lose Small Wars*; Douglas C. Foyle, *Counting the Public In: Presidents, Public Opinion, and Foreign Policy* (New York: Columbia University Press, 1999); Ronald H. Hinckley, *People, Polls, and Policymakers: American Public Opinion and National Security* (Toronto: Lexington Books, 1992); Philip J. Powlick, "The Attitudinal Bases for Responsiveness to Public Opinion among American Foreign Policy Officials," *Journal of Conflict Resolution* 35, no. 4 (1991): 611–41; Richard Sobel, *The Impact of Public Opinion on U.S. Foreign Policy Since Vietnam: Constraining the Colossus* (Oxford: Oxford University Press, 2001).

15. Council on Foreign Relations, "Public Opinion on Global Issues: U.S. Opinion on Violent Conflict" (New York: Council on Foreign Relations, August 28, 2012), 22. For similar results from the 1990s see Bruce W. Jentleson and Rebecca L. Britton, "Still Pretty Prudent: Post-Cold War American Public Opinion on the Use of Military Force," *Journal of Conflict Resolution* 42, no. 4 (1998): 395–417; Steven Kull and I. M. Destler, *Misreading the Public: The Myth of a New Isolationism* (Washington, DC: Brookings Institution Press, 1999), chaps. 2 and 4 (especially pp. 104–5).

16. Natalie La Balme, "The French and the Use of Force: Public Perceptions and Their Impact on the Policy-making Process," in *Public Opinion and the International Use of Force*, ed. Philip P. Everts and Pierangelo Isernia (London: Routledge, 2001), 186–204, quotation on 184. The survey series is the "Baromètre Les Français et la Défense nationale."

17. Délégation à l'information et à la communication de la Défense (DICoD), "Les Français et La Défense: 15 Ans de Sondages (1991–2006)," (Paris: Ministère de la Défense, 2007), 16.

18. Council on Foreign Relations, "Public Opinion on Global Issues." See 17, 22–23 for relevant results.

19. Unfortunately, this question was not asked in other Australian Election Study polls. Data are available from the Australian Social Science Data Archive, accessed January 7, 2010, http://assda-nesstar.anu.edu.au/webview/index.jsp.

20. Ivan Cook, "Australians Speak 2005: Public Opinion and Foreign Policy," (Sydney: Lowy Institute for International Policy, 2005), 14–15.

21. For instance, after the deaths of eighteen U.S. Rangers in Somalia in October 1993, several surveys found that fewer than half of respondents wanted to withdraw U.S. troops immediately. In contrast, a poll that explicitly raised the specter of casualties found 60% agreeing that, "nothing the U.S. could accomplish in Somalia is worth the death of even one more soldier." See, respectively, Steven Kull and Clay Ramsay, "The Myth of the Reactive Public: American Public Attitudes on Military Fatalities in the Post-Cold War Period," in *Public Opinion and the International Use of Force*, ed. Philip P. Everts and Pierangelo Isernia (New York: Routledge, 2001), 205–28, at 213–14; Valentino, "Perils of Limited Intervention," 731.

22. Eichenberg, "Victory Has Many Friends"; Feaver and Gelpi, *Choosing Your Battles*; Gelpi, Feaver, and Reifler, *Paying the Human Costs of War*; Bruce W. Jentleson, "The Pretty Prudent Public: Post Post-Vietnam American Opinion on the Use of Military Force," *International Studies Quarterly* 36, no. 1 (1992): 49–73; Jentleson and Britton, "Still Pretty Prudent"; Kull and Ramsay, "Myth of the Reactive Public."

23. John Connor, "Intervention and Domestic Politics," in *Australian Peacekeeping: Sixty Years in the Field*, ed. David Horner, Peter Londey, and Jean Bou (Port Melbourne: Cambridge University Press, 2009), 60.

24. Russett, *Controlling the Sword*, 54.

25. Ibid., 46.

26. Benny Geys, "Wars, Presidents, and Popularity: The Political Cost(s) of War Re-Examined," *Public Opinion Quarterly* 74, no. 2 (2010): 357–74.

27. John E. Mueller, *War, Presidents, and Public Opinion* (New York: Wiley, 1973); John E. Mueller, *Policy and Opinion in the Gulf War* (Chicago: University of Chicago Press, 1994); Scott Sigmund Gartner and Gary M. Segura, "War, Casualties, and Public Opinion," *Journal of Conflict Resolution* 42, no. 3 (1998): 278–300; Eric V. Larson, *Casualties and Consensus: The Historical Role of Casualties in Domestic Support for U.S. Military Operations* (Santa Monica: RAND, 1996).

28. On war initiation see Dan Reiter and Allan C. Stam, *Democracies at War* (Princeton: Princeton University Press, 2002); Bruce Bueno de Mesquita et al., "An Institutional Explanation of the Democratic Peace," *American Political Science Review* 93, no. 4 (1999): 791–807. On civilian targeting see Alexander B. Downes, "Restraint or Propellant? Democracy and Civilian Fatalities in Interstate Wars," *Journal of Conflict Resolution* 51, no. 6 (2007): 872–904.

29. On misreading the public see Kull and Destler, *Misreading the Public*; Kull and Ramsay, "Myth of the Reactive Public"; Gelpi, Feaver, and Reifler, "Success Matters."

30. See, e.g., Bueno de Mesquita et al., "An Institutional Explanation of the Democratic Peace"; Bruce Bueno de Mesquita et al., *The Logic of Political Survival* (Cambridge: MIT Press, 2003).

31. Kaufmann and Pape, "Explaining Costly International Moral Action." See p. 646 for the cited percentages.

32. Richard Cockett, *Sudan: Darfur and the Failure of an African State* (New Haven: Yale University Press, 2010), 156–62, 198–99.

33. Quoted in Hamilton, *Fighting for Darfur*, 147.

34. See John Prendergast and Don Cheadle, *The Enough Moment: Fighting to End Africa's Worst Human Rights Crimes* (New York: Three Rivers Press, 2010), 122. See 56–57 for a similar statement by former senator Russell Feingold.

35. Alexander Downer (Foreign Minister of Australia, 1996–2007), interview with the author, Adelaide, Australia, August 26, 2009.

36. This argument does not extend to limitations that restrict soldiers' ability to use force in self-defense, which can increase their vulnerability. In practice, however, and for this reason, such restrictions are far less common.

37. Jon W. Western, *Selling Intervention and War: The Presidency, the Media, and the American Public* (Baltimore: Johns Hopkins University Press, 2005), 19. Western argues that unless opposition groups and members of the public have independent information about conditions in a state where their government wishes to intervene militarily, they "are seriously hindered in their ability to refute the ruling group's position." The same logic applies here, but with the preferences of the government and activist minority reversed.

38. Holt and Berkman, *Impossible Mandate?*, 92.

39. Ibid., 192.

40. Ibid., 6, 50.

41. Robert H. Salisbury, "An Exchange Theory of Interest Groups," *Midwest Journal of Political Science* 13, no. 1 (1969): 1–32, at 16. See also Peter Blau, *Exchange and Power in Social Life* (New York: John Wiley and Sons, Inc., 1964), especially 236–39.

42. Alexander Cooley and James Ron, "The NGO Scramble: Organizational Insecurity and the Political Economy of Transnational Action," *International Security* 27, no. 1 (2002): 5–39; Michael Barnett, "Humanitarianism Transformed," *Perspectives on Politics* 3, no. 4 (2005): 723–40; James Ron, Howard Ramos, and Kathleen Rodgers, "Transnational Information Politics: NGO Human Rights Reporting, 1986–2000," *International Studies Quarterly* 49, no. 3 (2005): 557–88; Aseem Prakash and Mary Kay Gugerty, eds., *Advocacy Organizations and Collective Action* (Cambridge: Cambridge University Press, 2010); Sarah Sunn Bush, *The Taming of Democracy Assistance: Why Democracy Promotion Does Not Confront Dictators* (Cambridge: Cambridge University Press, 2015). In the Prakash and Gugerty volume, see Aseem Prakash and Mary Kay Gugerty, "Advocacy Organizations and Collective Action: An Introduction"; Clifford Bob, "The Market for Human Rights"; Alexander Cooley and James Ron, "The Political Economy of Transnational Action among International NGOs"; Sarah L. Henderson, "Shaping Civic Advocacy: International and Domestic Policies Towards Russia's NGO Sector."

43. Aseem Prakash and Mary Kay Gugerty, "Advocacy Organizations and Collective Action: An Introduction," in Prakash and Gugerty, *Advocacy Organizations and Collective Action*, 1–28, quotation on p. 11.

44. Hamilton, *Fighting for Darfur*, 194.

45. Allison, "Conceptual Models," 707.

46. On hierarchy and persuasive skills see Allison, "Conceptual Models," 710. For more on power and influence in bargaining see Peter B. Evans, Harold Karan Jacobson, and Robert D. Putnam, eds., *Double-Edged Diplomacy: International Bargaining and Domestic Politics* (Berkeley and Los Angeles: University of California Press, 1993). On the importance of the right arguments see Evans, *Responsibility to Protect*, 228.

47. Power, *Problem from Hell*, 508. See also Western, "Sources of Humanitarian Intervention."

48. Western, "Sources of Humanitarian Intervention," 117.

49. Evans, *Responsibility to Protect*, 232. Similarly, in 1992 the U.S. military opposed UN intervention in Somalia, largely out of fear that it would "inevitably necessitate greater U.S. military involvement." Western, "Sources of Humanitarian Intervention," 123.

50. On the importance of players who are key to policy implementation in bargaining scenarios, see the discussion by Evans in Evans, Jacobson, and Putnam, *Double-Edged Diplomacy*, especially 412–14.

51. Quoted in Power, *Problem from Hell*, 316.

52. See, e.g., Holt and Berkman, *Impossible Mandate?*, especially 74–75.

53. Quoted in Western, "Sources of Humanitarian Intervention," 121–22. By August, in the face of growing pressure to respond to atrocities in Bosnia, some commanders were claiming that at least 400,000 troops would be needed to implement a cease-fire (130).

54. Power, *Problem from Hell*, 508.

55. Bass, *Freedom's Battle*.

56. Western, "Sources of Humanitarian Intervention." The phrase "liberal humanitarianists" is first used on p. 117.

57. Allison, "Conceptual Models," 707. Similarly, Robert D. Putnam points out that negotiated compromises must fall within the "win-set" of all parties whose support is needed to reach an agreement, but differ from the ideal policy preferred by each one. "Diplomacy and Domestic Politics: The Logic of Two-Level Games," *International Organization* 42, no. 3 (1988): 427–60.

58. Power, *Problem from Hell*, 508.

59. Western, "Sources of Humanitarian Intervention," 124. In another well-known incident that September, General Colin Powell initiated a media campaign to publicize his opposition to potential U.S. intervention in Bosnia. While his attitude was consistent with the president's own preferences at the time, his actions do show the potential power of high-level officials to cause headaches for executives who may have different preferences. See Power, *Problem from Hell*, 285; Western, "Sources of Humanitarian Intervention," 132.

60. Western's study of U.S. policy on Bosnia and Somalia in 1992 offers another example. As pressure on the Bush Administration to intervene in both conflicts grew, there was strong opposition from the military to involvement in either conflict. Here, though, the eventual compromise was a decision to intervene in Somalia and not in Bosnia.

61. Allison, "Conceptual Models," 708.

62. James G. March, *A Primer on Decision Making: How Decisions Happen* (New York: Simon and Schuster, 1994), 196. Also, James G. March and Johan P. Olson, "Organizing Political Life: What Administrative Reorganization Tells Us about Government," *American Political Science Review* 77, no. 2 (1983): 281–96, at 289.

63. On legitimacy see Finnemore, *Purpose of Intervention*; Katharina P. Coleman, *International Organisations and Peace Enforcement: The Politics of International Legitimacy* (Cambridge: Cambridge University Press, 2007).

64. Kull and Destler, *Misreading the Public*; Kull and Ramsay, "Myth of the Reactive Public."

65. Caveats have also posed problems for other coalition military operations, including notably the International Security Assistance Force (ISAF) in Afghanistan. See Stephen M. Saideman and David P. Auerswald, "Comparing Caveats: Understanding the Sources of National Restrictions upon NATO's Mission in Afghanistan," *International Studies Quarterly* 56, no. 1 (2012): 67–84.

66. Michael Smith (Major General, Australian Defence Force, Retired), interview with the author, Canberra, Australia, August 7, 2009. Smith served as Director General for East Timor in the Department of Defence in 1999 and later as Deputy Commander of UNTAET.

67. As noted earlier, support for missions led by other powerful states are exceptions, which I address in chapter 3.

3. Quantitative Evidence

1. I briefly review the dataset here, but a separate article provides far more detail about the limitations of existing data sources, the process of identifying complex emergencies, the logic behind the decisions described here, and the coding rules. See Everett, "Post–Cold War Complex Humanitarian Emergencies." These issues are also covered in part 1 of the web appendix, available at www.andreaeverett.com.

2. Although my focus in this book is the post–Cold War period, some earlier conflicts persisted and inspired peace operations in the 1990s. Thus I include all conflicts that meet the other criteria and were ongoing in 1989 or later. This follows the logic laid out in Gilligan and Stedman, "Where Do the Peacekeepers Go?"

3. Benjamin A. Valentino, *Final Solutions: Mass Killing and Genocide in the Twentieth Century* (Ithaca: Cornell University Press, 2004), 10–12; Benjamin Valentino, Paul Huth, and Dylan Balch-Lindsay, "'Draining the Sea': Mass Killing and Guerrilla Warfare," *International Organization* 58, no. 2 (2004): 375–407.

4. Nicholas Sambanis, "What Is Civil War? Conceptual and Empirical Complexities of an Operational Definition," *Journal of Conflict Resolution* 48, no. 6 (2004): 814–58.

5. The World Health Organization and various humanitarian groups define a crude mortality rate of 1 per 10,000 of the affected population per day as the threshold for an emergency. For a stable displaced population (aside from these deaths), this would equate to a death rate of nearly 4% for an emergency that lasted a year. In practice, of course, displacement varies over time, and so it would be unrealistic to extrapolate further for a multi-year period. Still, recognizing that thousands of people are typically displaced each year in a complex emergency, the 4% ratio of 20,000 civilian deaths to 500,000 displaced seems broadly consistent with the standards the humanitarian community uses to recognize humanitarian emergencies.

6. I also exclude observations for Iraq's 1990 invasion of Kuwait. Although the potential interveners did not cause it, their later military response—the Persian Gulf War—does not meet my definition of a peace operation.

7. Since peace operations may sometimes deploy after the worst violence instead of addressing civilians' earlier and more pressing security needs, I include operations launched both during and shortly after complex emergencies. I use a one-year cutoff, with one exception for UNTAC in Cambodia, which began in February 1992 but was planned in October 1991 alongside an advance mission known as UNAMIC.

8. On requirements for these most ambitious strategies, see Seybolt, *Humanitarian Military Intervention*, chaps. 6–7. Also, the distinction between more or fewer than 50 observers or liaison officers may seem arbitrary, as the difference in capabilities between, say, 50 and 100 soldiers is not large. In practice, however, the distinction works well, as almost all contributions of less than 1000 personnel are still much greater than 50.

9. Part 2 of the web appendix contains detailed notes and sources for the coding decisions associated with both ambitions and resources for each contribution.

10. While a few contributions involve gaps of 2 (one component is coded 1 and the other 3), most involve gaps of 1 (one component is coded 1 and the other 2, or one is coded 2 and the other 3). Given this limited variation, I treat all gaps equally. I also treat three observations where both ambitions and resources are coded 2 as limited. However, there is also an argument to be made that they are not a clear fit for any category and should be excluded from the analysis. Dropping them rather than coding them as limited does not affect any of the findings I report below.

11. Dropping these observations instead does not substantively affect any of the findings I report below.

12. For a partial exception see Bove and Elia, "Supplying Peace."

13. See, e.g., Jonathan Mermin, "Television News and American Intervention in Somalia: The Myth of a Media-Driven Foreign Policy," *Political Science Quarterly* 112, no. 3 (1997): 385–403; Philip J. Powlick and Andrew Z. Katz, "Defining the American Public Opinion/Foreign Policy Nexus," *Mershon International Studies Review* 42, no. 1 (1998): 29–61; Western, *Selling Intervention and War*; Piers Robinson, *The CNN Effect: The Myth of News, Foreign Policy, and Intervention* (New York: Routledge, 2002). For an excellent summary and for the argument about chances for outsiders to use the media to promote alternate policy options, see Robert M. Entman, *Projections of Power: Framing News, Public Opinion, and U.S. Foreign Policy* (Chicago: University of Chicago Press, 2004).

14. Bass, *Freedom's Battle*.

15. Hamilton, *Fighting for Darfur*, 101–2.

16. Entman, *Projections of Power*, 20–21 and chap. 5.

17. On the first point see Patrick M. Regan, "Substituting Policies During U.S. Interventions in Internal Conflicts: A Little of This, a Little of That," *Journal of Conflict Resolution* 44, no. 1 (2000): 90–106.

18. La Balme, "The French and the Use of Force," 196; see also La Balme, *Partir en guerre: Décideurs et politiques face à l'opinion publique* (Paris: Editions Autrement Frontières, 2002), 85–101. On American policymakers' perceptions of media coverage as an indicator of societal opinion, see for example Entman, *Projections of Power*, 126; Powlick and Katz, "Defining the American Public Opinion/Foreign Policy Nexus," 45; Steven Kull and Clay Ramsay, "Elite Misperceptions of U.S. Public Opinion and Foreign Policy," in *Decisionmaking in a Glass House: Mass Media, Public Opinion, and American and European Foreign Policy*

in the 21st Century, ed. B. L. Nacos, R. Y. Shapiro, and P. Isernia (Oxford: Rowman and Littlefield, 2000), 95–110, at 105–6.

19. Part 3 of the web appendix contains a much more detailed discussion of *CE news coverage*. The newspapers I use are the *New York Times*, the *London Times*, *Le Monde*, and the *Sydney Morning Herald*. As discussed in the web appendix, there are a few exceptions where for reasons of full-text search availability or unusual dramatic events the denominator is calculated with fewer than five years of coverage. Further, to partly adjust for the ratio format's failure to distinguish between large and small volumes of coverage I add a small constant to the annual average number of hits in the denominator. This avoids recording unrealistically large increases in concern about places that received little coverage either before or during a complex emergency. For the primary version of *CE news coverage* this constant is fifteen, but other numbers yield similar results. Finally, I also created a version of this variable using headline rather than full-text news searches. Again my results were consistent when using this version.

20. Part 3 of the web appendix also shows the full distribution of values for each potential intervener and discusses the search terms used and dates covered for each observation. In Bosnia, public attention to and concern about the war continued to rise later in 1992 and in subsequent years. Thus, if anything this cautious approach to calculating the increase in media coverage only through May 1992 likely understates the true extent of moral pressure.

21. O'Hanlon, *Saving Lives with Force*, 12–13, 51.

22. See e.g., ibid., 12, 51.

23. Doyle and Sambanis, "International Peacebuilding," 785. See also O'Hanlon, *Saving Lives with Force*, 51.

24. O'Hanlon, *Saving Lives with Force*, 51; Perkins and Neumayer, "Extra-territorial Interventions."

25. Fortna, *Does Peacekeeping Work?*; Gilligan and Stedman, "Where Do the Peacekeepers Go?"; Mullenbach, "Deciding to Keep Peace."

26. Except for the proportion of paved roads, larger values imply a more difficult operational environment.

27. Very similar results, including in the patterns of statistically significant differences in means, are obtained when using the various alternative measures of *CE news coverage* referred to in note 19 of this chapter.

28. The pattern shown here also looks very similar for the alternative versions of *operational environment* mentioned above, although not all of the statistically significant differences in means persist in every case.

29. These models treat the dependent variable as a set of unordered choices, which is appropriate here. In some sense *contribution type* is ordered in that each move from no contribution to a limited one; from a limited contribution to an ambitions-resources gap; and from a gap to a robust contribution involves an increase in effort and commitment. Yet I do not expect the key covariates to have the same magnitude or even direction of effect across the different values of *contribution type*. For this reason it is preferable to treat the data as unordered. See, e.g., J. Scott Long, *Regression Models for Categorical and Limited Dependent Variables* (Thousand Oaks: Sage Publications, Inc., 1997), 148–49.

30. Still, this suggests that alliance ties do not drive ambitions-resources gaps. Further, including *alliance* does not alter any of my conclusions related to the relationship between *CE news coverage* and *operational environment*.

31. Andersson, "Democracies and UN Peacekeeping"; Fortna, *Does Peacekeeping Work?*

32. Michael Wesley, *Casualties of the New World Order: The Causes of Failure of UN Missions to Civil Wars* (New York: St. Martin's Press, 1997), 5.

33. It is worth noting that conflicts involving mass killing may well generate greater moral pressure for civilian protection. If so, accounting for mass killing could suppress the effect of *CE news coverage*. As shown below, however, the data are consistent with my expectations whether or not *mass killing* is included in the regressions.

34. Hausman-based tests of the independence of irrelevant alternatives (IIA) assumption that is central to multinomial logistic regression reveal that the null hypothesis cannot be rejected and that this model is appropriate for the data.

35. First, for each model, Wald tests of the hypothesis that all coefficients for *CE news coverage, operational environment* and their interaction equal zero were clearly rejected at p < .01 in all cases. Second, I compared each model to an alternative that was identical except for the exclusion of the interaction term. In each case these comparisons revealed a better fit when the interaction term is included: McFadden's R2 (and several alternatives) is larger, while Akaike's information criterion (AIC) and the Bayesian information criterion (BIC) are smaller.

36. On the particular challenges of interpreting interaction effects in non-linear models such as the multinomial logit and on the use of graphical presentation for this purpose, see Chunrong Ai and Edward C. Norton, "Interaction Terms in Logit and Probit Models," *Economics Letters* 80, no. 1 (2003): 123–29; William Greene, "Testing Hypotheses about Interaction Terms in Nonlinear Models," *Economics Letters* 107, no. 2 (2010): 291–96.

37. All predicted probabilities were calculated using Clarify. See Michael Tomz, Jason Wittenberg, and Gary King, "CLARIFY: Software for Interpreting and Presenting Statistical Results," *Journal of Statistical Software* 8, no. 1 (2003): 1–30.

38. This is not simply an effect of setting *CE news coverage* and *operational environment* to their mean values, where gap and robust contributions are relatively unlikely. I also tried several combinations of *CE news coverage* and *operational environment* where these outcomes are more common, but in no case did this yield a significant effect of mass killing on either gap or robust contributions, in either direction.

39. I also ran a number of similar models that included various pairs of up to two of the controls from models 2–3. In some cases the significant result for *contribution decade* shown here held. In others it did not, although the direction and size of the change in predicted probabilities was quite consistent across different specifications.

40. Because many of the observations that saw no contribution to a peace operation fall at the high end of *operational environment*, excluding them yields only a few observations in this restricted sample that take on high values on this variable. Within the restricted sample, the 20th percentile takes the same value as the 10th percentile in the full sample, and thus again reflects quite favorable conditions for intervention. Meanwhile, the 80th percentile in the restricted sample is greater than the 50th percentile in the full sample but less than the 90th percentile. It thus represents a somewhat more formidable operational environment than the mid-level values from models 1–3, but still not one that would qualify as extremely inhospitable.

41. I provide a brief overview of these specification tests here, but a more in-depth discussion as well as results for some of them are available in the supplementary web appendix.

42. Christopher H. Achen, "Let's Put Garbage-Can Regressions and Garbage-Can Probits Where They Belong," *Conflict Management and Peace Science* 22, no. 4 (2005): 327–39.

43. I separately dropped three observations for which both resources and ambitions were coded as 2, but which I coded as limited contributions in the main analysis; and eight observations in which a state's contribution to a peace operation was in support of a robust contribution by another great power democracy. For more information see notes 10 and 11 in this chapter.

4. France in Rwanda

1. On cohabitation and the use of force see Samy Cohen, "Cohabiter en diplomatie: atout ou handicap?," *Annuaire français des relations internationales* 4 (2003): 344–58, at 354–55.

2. In English, see Gérard Prunier, *The Rwanda Crisis: History of a Genocide* (New York: Columbia University Press, 1995); Alison Des Forges, *Leave None to Tell the Story: Genocide in Rwanda*, (New York: Human Rights Watch, 1999); African Rights, *Rwanda: Death, Despair and Defiance*, rev. ed. (London: African Rights, 1995); Melvern, *A People Betrayed*.

3. Estimates on the scale of this exodus vary from about 200,000 to 336,000 as of the mid-1960s. See Prunier, *Rwanda Crisis*, 61–62; Melvern, *A People Betrayed*, 23; Kuperman, *Limits of Humanitarian Intervention*, 7.

4. See, e.g., Prunier, *Rwanda Crisis*, 135–44; Melvern, *A People Betrayed*, 63.

5. On the formation of these militias see Melvern, *A People Betrayed*, 51–53, and, more broadly, chaps. 3–4; Prunier, *Rwanda Crisis*, chap. 4.

6. On the details of the accords see Prunier, *Rwanda Crisis*, 192–93; Kuperman, *Limits of Humanitarian Intervention*, 11; Melvern, *A People Betrayed*, chap. 5.

7. Melvern, *A People Betrayed*, chap. 9, especially pp. 99–100.

8. Barnett, *Eyewitness*, chap. 3; Melvern, *A People Betrayed*, chaps. 9–10.

9. Responsibility for the crash remains contested to this day. Two French investigations—from 2006 and 2012—came to opposite conclusions as to whether it was orchestrated by Hutu hardliners as an excuse to begin the killing, or by the RPF. Experts likewise disagree. For a summary of the ongoing debate see Filip Reyntjens, "The Struggle Over Truth—Rwanda and the BBC," *African Affairs* 114, no. 457 (2015): 637–48.

10. Prunier, *Rwanda Crisis*, 246.

11. See, e.g., ibid., 253–54; Kuperman, *Limits of Humanitarian Intervention*, 15–16.

12. Prunier, *Rwanda Crisis*, 261.

13. Ibid., 233–37, 268–69.

14. See, e.g., ibid., 265; Filip Reyntjens, "Estimation du nombre de personnes tuées au Rwanda en 1994," in *L'Afrique des grands lacs: annuaire 1996/1997*, ed. Filip Reyntjens and Marysse Stefaan (Paris: L'Harmattan, 1997), 179–86; Des Forges, "Leave None," 15; Christian Davenport and Allan Stam, "Rwandan Political Violence in Space and Time," (unpublished manuscript, 2009), PDF, p.5, http://genodynamics.weebly.com/uploads/1/8/3/5/18359923/rwanda031708c.pdf.

15. Estimates of Tutsi victims range from 200,000 to 800,000. For the low end see the work of Davenport and Stam as reported on their website, "Genodynamics," accessed March 7, 2016, http://genodynamics.weebly.com. For the high end see Prunier, *Rwanda Crisis*, 265; Marijke Verpoorten, "The Death Toll of the Rwandan Genocide: A Detailed Analysis for Gikongoro Province," *Population (English Edition)* 60, no. 4 (2005): 331–67, at 357. For further estimates of at least 500,000 see Des Forges, "Leave None," 15; Reyntjens, "Estimation du nombre de personnes tuées."

16. Prunier, *Rwanda Crisis*, 295, 299.

17. Ibid., 312; Melvern, *A People Betrayed*, 243.

18. Prunier, *Rwanda Crisis*, 302–3, 314–16.

19. On French support for the Habyarimana regime see especially Lanotte, *France au Rwanda*, chap. 3; also, Pierre Favier and Michel Martin-Roland, *La Décennie Mitterrand*, vol. 4: *Les déchirements (1991–1995)* (Paris: Éditions du Seuil, 1999), 471–73; Melvern, *A People Betrayed*, 56–58. One controversial issue is whether French troops participated directly in combat. Despite official denials, there is considerable evidence of at least some limited participation by French troops in combat alongside the FAR. See Lanotte, *France au Rwanda*, 186–93. It is also likely that the French—perhaps unwittingly—provided some military training to the Interahamwe. On this see Lanotte, *France au Rwanda*, 163–69; and Prunier, *Rwanda Crisis*, 165.

20. Lanotte, *France au Rwanda*, 145–50; Prunier, *Rwanda Crisis*, 164; Melvern, *A People Betrayed*, 57.

21. Lanotte, *France au Rwanda*, 257–63; see also Favier and Martin-Roland, *Décennie Mitterrand*, 472–74; Barnett, *Eyewitness*, 69.

22. Favier and Martin-Roland, *Décennie Mitterrand*, 475; Lafourcade and Riffaud, *Opération Turquoise*, 29–30.

23. See, e.g., Kuperman, *Limits of Humanitarian Intervention*, 101–6; Barnett, *Eyewitness*, 102–3. In France's case, after Habyarimana's death some military officials quickly foresaw large-scale massacres but not their scope or organization by Hutu extremists. For instance, General Christian Quesnot, head of Mitterrand's military staff, and General Huchon, head of military cooperation, warned on April 7 and again soon after that without immediate military intervention there would be tens of thousands or even 100,000 deaths. Lanotte, *France au Rwanda*, 344, 352. Yet even the French may have missed the extent of the Hutu extremists' plans because their intelligence efforts focused mainly on the RPF and because their military had no reliable sources of intelligence outside Kigali after 1993 and struggled to obtain information about conditions on the ground. See Kuperman, *Limits of Humanitarian Intervention*, 101; Lafourcade and Riffaud, *Opération Turquoise*, 30.

24. Lanotte, *France au Rwanda*, 351.

25. See, e.g., Lanotte, *France au Rwanda*, 344–50, 361–62; Prunier, *Rwanda Crisis*, 234–35; Melvern, *A People Betrayed*, 161–63.

26. On these dynamics see Barnett, *Eyewitness*, chap. 4; see also United Nations Security Council, *Security Council Resolution 912*, S/RES/912, April 21, 1994.

27. Barnett, *Eyewitness*, 133–36.

28. Lanotte, *France au Rwanda*, 375–82.

29. United Nations Security Council, *Security Council Resolution 918*, S/RES/918, May 17, 1994.

30. Barnett, *Eyewitness*, 142. See also Melvern, *A People Betrayed*, 220–21.

31. Lanotte, *France au Rwanda*, 386.

32. Quoted in Lanotte, *France au Rwanda*, 380; Favier and Martin-Roland, *Décennie Mitterrand*, 479; François-Xavier Verschave, *Complicité de Génocide? La politique de la France au Rwanda* (Paris: Éditions La Découverte, 1994), 121.

33. Favier and Martin-Roland, *Décennie Mitterrand*, 480.

34. Quoted in François Soudan, "Pourquoi la France s'en mêle," *Jeune Afrique*, June 30, 1994, 12.

35. Prunier, *Rwanda Crisis*, 281–82; Gérard Prunier, "Opération Turquoise: A Humanitarian Escape from a Political Dead End," in *The Path of a Genocide: The Rwanda Crisis from Uganda to Zaire*, ed. Howard Adelman and Astri Suhrke (New Brunswick: Transaction Publishers, 1999), 284–85; Soudan, "Pourquoi," 15. See also Lanotte, *France au Rwanda*, 384.

36. Lanotte, *France au Rwanda*, 386, 389. See also Howard Adelman, Astri Suhrke, and Bruce Jones, "Study 2: Early Warning and Conflict Management," in *The International Response to Conflict and Genocide: Lessons from the Rwanda Experience*, ed. David Millwood (Copenhagen: Steering Committee of the Joint Evaluation of Emergency Assistance to Rwanda, 1996), 55.

37. Lanotte, *France au Rwanda*, 390–91; Favier and Martin-Roland, *Décennie Mitterrand*, 480.

38. United Nations Security Council, *Security Council Resolution 925*, S/RES/925, June 8, 1994; see also United Nations Security Council, *Security Council Resolution 929*, S/RES/929, June 22, 1994; United Nations Security Council, *Letter from the Permanent Representative of France to the United Nations Addressed to the Secretary-General*, S/1994/734, June 20, 1994.

39. R. M. Connaughton, "Military Support and Protection for Humanitarian Assistance: Rwanda, April–December 1994," (United Kingdom: Strategic and Combat Studies Institute, 1996), 47; Lafourcade and Riffaud, *Opération Turquoise*, 52. See also Lafourcade, "Order of Operation No. 1," June 25, 1994, in Lafourcade and Riffaud, *Opération Turquoise*, annex (n.p.).

40. Lafourcade, "Order of Operation No.1," annex (n.p.).

41. Lafourcade and Riffaud, *Opération Turquoise*, 52. See also Lafourcade, "Order of Operation No.1," annex (n.p.).

42. Various sources offer slightly different figures on these numbers, putting the French contingent at 2,500 to 2,555 and the Africans at either 350 or about 500. See Jacques Lanxade, "L'opération Turquoise," *Défense Nationale* 51, no. 2 (1995): 7–15, at 10; Connaughton, "Military Support," 46; John Borton, Emery Brusset, and Alistair Hallam, "Study 3: Humanitarian Aid and Effects," in *The International Response to Conflict and Genocide: Lessons from the Rwanda Experience*, ed. David Millwood (Copenhagen: Steering Committee of the Joint Evaluation of Emergency Assistance to Rwanda, 1996), 42; Bernard Lugan, *François Mitterrand, L'Armée Française et le Rwanda* (Paris: Éditions du Rocher, 2005), 214; Lanotte, *France au Rwanda*, 429; Lafourcade and Riffaud, *Opération Turquoise*, 59.

43. Lanxade, "L'opération Turquoise," 9–10; Lanotte, *France au Rwanda*, 428–29.

44. This contingent may have been 150 or 222 men. See *France au Rwanda*, 431; Lafourcade and Riffaud, *Opération Turquoise*, 66.

45. *Opération Turquoise*, 66–67; Lanotte, *France au Rwanda*, 431, 434–35; Lanxade, "L'opération Turquoise," 11.

46. Prunier, *Rwanda Crisis*, 291; Borton, Brusset, and Hallam, "Study 3," 42; Connaughton, "Military Support," 46; Kuperman, *Limits of Humanitarian Intervention*, 45; Seybolt, *Humanitarian Military Intervention*, 213; Melvern, *A People Betrayed*, 237. See also Lanotte, *France au Rwanda*, 427.

47. Lafourcade and Riffaud, *Opération Turquoise*, 59.

48. Ibid., 58; Connaughton, "Military Support," 46–48.

49. Lanotte, *France au Rwanda*, 436; Lafourcade and Riffaud, *Opération Turquoise*, 67.

50. Lanotte, *France au Rwanda*, 437; see also Seybolt, *Humanitarian Military Intervention*, 166. Seybolt cites a slightly larger figure of 5000 square kilometers.

51. Lanxade, "L'opération Turquoise," 12; Lanotte, *France au Rwanda*, 437–46; Lafourcade and Riffaud, *Opération Turquoise*, chaps. 10 and 12.

52. These include but are not limited to the French military leaders most closely involved. See Lanxade, "L'opération Turquoise," 171–72; Borton, Brusset, and Hallam, "Study 3," 54; Connaughton, "Military Support," 54; Lafourcade and Riffaud, *Opération Turquoise*, 172.

53. Estimates of both survivors at Nyarushishi and Tutsi saved by Turquoise vary, but appear to be in this range. See Borton, Brusset, and Hallam, "Study 3," 51, 55; Adelman, Suhrke, and Jones, "Study 2," 54–55; Prunier, "Opération Turquoise," 303; Kuperman, *Limits of Humanitarian Intervention*, 49–50; Lanotte, *France au Rwanda*, 435, 483; Seybolt, *Humanitarian Military Intervention*, 210; Lafourcade and Riffaud, *Opération Turquoise*, 159.

54. Over the long run its humanitarian consequences are less clear, since for many people any respite the French provided was only temporary. See Lanotte, *France au Rwanda*, 484–85; Prunier, *Rwanda Crisis*, 311.

55. Lanotte, *France au Rwanda*, 482–83.

56. Lafourcade and Riffaud, *Opération Turquoise*, 146–49; Borton, Brusset, and Hallam, "Study 3," 55.

57. Lanotte, *France au Rwanda*, 482–83; Seybolt, *Humanitarian Military Intervention*, 167, 210; Borton, Brusset, and Hallam, "Study 3," 54–55; Adelman, Suhrke, and Jones, "Study 2," 56; Kuperman, *Limits of Humanitarian Intervention*, 50.

58. See Lafourcade and Riffaud, *Opération Turquoise*, 156–59; Connaughton, "Military Support," 52–53; Lanotte, *France au Rwanda*, 483–85; Prunier, *Rwanda Crisis*, 309–11; Lanxade, "L'opération Turquoise," 12–13. Prunier is more skeptical of the effects of the French efforts than the other authors. On the other hand, Lanotte points out that the French force may well have achieved more than it is usually credited with by helping limit the scope and extent of RPF abuses against the Hutu population.

59. Lanotte, *France au Rwanda*, 405; Seybolt, *Humanitarian Military Intervention*, 210.

60. Seybolt, *Humanitarian Military Intervention*, chap. 6.

61. Lanotte, *France au Rwanda*, 485.

62. Ibid.

63. See also ibid., 444–45; Seybolt, *Humanitarian Military Intervention*, 214.

64. Seybolt, *Humanitarian Military Intervention*, 168 (see also 166–67).

65. Lafourcade and Riffaud, *Opération Turquoise*, 147; Connaughton, "Military Support," 46.

66. Prunier, *Rwanda Crisis*, 293. See also Borton, Brusset, and Hallam, "Study 3," 55.

67. For a serious investigation of this controversial incident see Lanotte, *France au Rwanda*, 461–77. For the force commander's account see Lafourcade and Riffaud, *Opération Turquoise*, 87–89, 104–16.

68. Quoted in Connaughton, "Military Support," 49. See also Lafourcade and Riffaud, *Opération Turquoise*, 92, 138–39.

69. Adelman, Suhrke, and Jones, "Study 2," 56; Lanotte, *France au Rwanda*, 485.

70. Quoted in Lanotte, *France au Rwanda*, 441.

71. On the issues of disarmament and arrest see, e.g., Verschave, *Complicité de Génocide?*, 131; African Rights, *Rwanda*, 1150–52; Adelman, Suhrke, and Jones, "Study 2," 56; Connaughton, "Military Support," 47–49; Lanotte, *France au Rwanda*, 440–42; Seybolt, *Humanitarian Military Intervention*, 211.

72. Lanotte, *France au Rwanda*, 444.

73. Lafourcade and Riffaud, *Opération Turquoise*, 67. See also Borton, Brusset, and Hallam, "Study 3," 43; Seybolt, *Humanitarian Military Intervention*, 209.

74. Lanotte, *France au Rwanda*, 403; see also Prunier, *Rwanda Crisis*, 287–88.

75. Connaughton, "Military Support," 46; Kuperman, *Limits of Humanitarian Intervention*, 47; Seybolt, *Humanitarian Military Intervention*, 214.

76. This figure is from a July 11 speech by Balladur. See Lanotte, *France au Rwanda*, 402; also, Kuperman, *Limits of Humanitarian Intervention*, 49–50.

77. Laurence Binet, *Genocide of Rwandan Tutsi 1994* (Médecins Sans Frontières International Movement, 2014), 16–29; Corine Lesnes, "Rwanda: La plupart des organisations humanitaires ont quitté le pays," *Le Monde*, April 14, 1994; "Rwanda: Le retour de Médecins du Monde," *Le Monde*, April 28, 1994. Though founded in France, MSF has individual national chapters that can take different stances on issues and communicate independently with the media. This happened repeatedly in Rwanda.

78. Verschave, *Complicité de Génocide?*, 140–44; Danielle Birck, "La télévision et le Rwanda ou le génocide déprogrammé," *Les Temps Modernes* 583 (July–August 1995): 181–97, at 184–89; Philippe Boisserie and Danielle Birck, "Retour sur images," *Les Temps Modernes* 583 (July–August 1995): 198–216, at 201–3; Laure Coret and François-Xavier Verschave, *L'horreur qui nous prend au visage: L'État français et le génocide* (Paris: Éditions Karthala, 2005), 271–72, 279–84, 311–34; Anne Chaon, "Who Failed in Rwanda, Journalists or the Media?," in *The Media and the Rwanda Genocide*, ed. Allan Thompson (Ann Arbor: Pluto Press, 2007), 160–66, at 162–63. In many of these respects, moreover, the French press mirrored the media in other countries. See for instance Thompson, ed., *The Media and the Rwanda Genocide*, chaps. 12–24.

79. Binet, "Genocide of Rwandan Tutsi," 32–34.

80. Quoted in ibid., 34. See also African Rights, *Rwanda*, 1108.

81. Binet, "Genocide of Rwandan Tutsi," 36–37; Alain Frilet, "MSF: 'Une gesticulation tardive de l'ONU,'" *Libération*, May 18, 1994.

82. Binet, "Genocide of Rwandan Tutsi," 35–36; "Lettre ouverte de Médecins Sans Frontières à François Mitterrand," *Le Monde*, May 18, 1994.

83. On this appeal see Binet, "Genocide of Rwandan Tutsi," 40–52.

84. Sources disagree on the dates of these meetings. MSF places the encounter with Mitterrand on June 14, while Journalist Géraldine Faes puts all three meetings on June 15 and 16. However, Bradol and MSF-France General Director Bernard Pécoul recall that Mitterrand informed them about Turquoise before the official announcement. Thus the meeting with Mitterrand was probably the evening of June 14 or perhaps June 15. See Binet, "Genocide of Rwandan Tutsi," 45–46; Géraldine Faes, "Paris, faute de mieux," *Jeune Afrique*, June 30, 1994, 14; Soudan, "Pourquoi," 13.

85. Quoted in Binet, "Genocide of Rwandan Tutsi," 49.

86. Lindsey Hilsum, "Reporting Rwanda: The Media and the Aid Agencies," in *The Media and the Rwanda Genocide*, ed. Allan Thompson (Ann Arbor: Pluto Press, 2007), 167–87, at 174.

87. See, e.g., Jean-Fabrice Pietri, "Le témoignage d'un volontaire de l'AICF: Une gigantesque chasse à l'homme au Rwanda," *Le Monde*, April 27, 1994; Xavier Anglaret, Claire Gazile, and Valériane Leroy, "Courrier des lecteurs," *Libération*, June 14, 1994; African Rights, *Rwanda*, 1143.

88. Comité National de Solidarité France-Rwanda, "Urgence Rwanda: Ne laissons pas la faim achever le genocide," *Libération*, June 15, 1994. See also Binet, "Genocide of Rwandan Tutsi," 46.

89. La Balme, *Partir en guerre*, 85–96; see also La Balme, "The French and the Use of Force," 196.

90. Full-text archives for the other major dailies—*Le Figaro*, *La Croix*, and *Libération*—do not go back to 1994.

91. Chaon, "Who Failed in Rwanda?," 163; Coret and Verschave, *L'horreur*, 283.

92. Coret and Verschave, *L'horreur*, 272–76, 285–93, 301–7, 314–16, 320.

93. Birck, "La télévision et le Rwanda," 189.

94. Favier and Martin-Roland, *Décennie Mitterrand*, 479.

95. Quoted in Coret and Verschave, *L'horreur*, 273.

96. For examples from April in *Libération* and *La Croix*, see Coret and Verschave, *L'horreur*, 304, 312–14.

97. Quoted in Binet, "Genocide of Rwandan Tutsi," 33.

98. Jean-François Alesandrini as quoted in Binet, "Genocide of Rwandan Tutsi," 38.

99. Alain Frilet and Sylvie Coma, "Paris, terre d'asile de luxe pour dignitaires hutus," *Libération*, May 18, 1994; Coret and Verschave, *L'horreur*, 301.

100. Pierre Lainé, "Rwanda: Pour un pays brisé," *Le Monde*, May 20, 1994; Coret and Verschave, *L'horreur*, 286.

101. Coret and Verschave, *L'horreur*, 326–27.

102. For details except for *l'Humanité* see Coret and Verschave, *L'horreur*, 273, 315, 320–21, 329–30. See also Verschave, *Complicité de Génocide?*, 140–41; Christophe Deroubaix, "Les responsabilités françaises dans le drame rwandais," *l'Humanité* May 20, 1994.

103. For examples from *Le Figaro, Le Monde,* and *Libération* see Coret and Verschave, *L'horreur*, 274, 289–90, 305–6.

104. Birck, "La télévision et le Rwanda," 192.

105. Quoted in Soudan, "Pourquoi," 15, see also 12–13; Lanotte, *France au Rwanda*, 386–88; La Balme, *Partir en guerre*, 56; Jean Chatain, "Rwanda: massacre à l'orphelinat," *l'Humanité*, June 13, 1994.

106. Quoted in Lanotte, *France au Rwanda*, 392.

107. Mel McNulty, "France's Role in Rwanda and External Military Intervention: A Double Discrediting," *International Peacekeeping* 4, no. 3 (1997): 24–44, at 37; La Balme, *Partir en guerre*, 57.

108. African Rights, *Rwanda*, 1139.

109. Ibid.

110. Prunier, *Rwanda Crisis*, 286; see also Soudan, "Pourquoi," 15; Lanotte, *France au Rwanda*, 478.

111. Quoted in Binet, "Genocide of Rwandan Tutsi," 37. See the same page for a similar quote from Biberson.

112. The two Musitelli quotes are respectively from La Balme, *Partir en guerre*, 56; and La Balme, "The French and the Use of Force," 198.

113. Quoted in La Balme, *Partir en guerre*, 56; see also La Balme, "The French and the Use of Force," 198.

114. Soudan, "Pourquoi," 15; see also Lanotte, *France au Rwanda*, 393.

115. Lanotte, *France au Rwanda*, 383; see also Binet, "Genocide of Rwandan Tutsi," 36.

116. Soudan, "Pourquoi," 15.

117. Quoted in Lanotte, *France au Rwanda*, 389; see also Soudan, "Pourquoi," 13.

118. Soudan, "Pourquoi," 15; Lanotte, *France au Rwanda*, 386.

119. Lanotte, *France au Rwanda*, 394.

120. Quoted in Soudan, "Pourquoi," 15; Lanotte, *France au Rwanda*, 392. See also African Rights, *Rwanda*, 1139.

121. "L'intervention du premier ministre sur France 2," *Le Monde*, June 29, 1994.

122. Before the genocide the country's entire population was close to 7.8 million, and since most of the estimated 800,000 genocide victims had been killed by the time France intervened, the population can be estimated at about 7 million at this time. Prunier, *Rwanda Crisis*, 263–64.

123. Lanotte, *France au Rwanda*, 428; see also Kuperman, *Limits of Humanitarian Intervention*, 109.

124. Lafourcade and Riffaud, *Opération Turquoise*, 94.

125. Lafourcade, "Operation Turquoise Order of Operation No.1," annex (n.p.).

126. Quoted in Lanotte, *France au Rwanda*, 406.

127. Lanxade, "L'opération Turquoise," 9; Lanotte, *France au Rwanda*, 425; Lafourcade and Riffaud, *Opération Turquoise*, 58.

128. Lafourcade, "Operation Turquoise Order of Operation No.1," annex (n.p.).

129. Kuperman, *Limits of Humanitarian Intervention*, 38–39.

130. See e.g., Lanotte, *France au Rwanda*, 405; Patrick de Saint-Exupéry, *Complices de l'inavouable: la France au Rwanda*, revised and augmented ed. (Paris: Arènes, 2009), 51–52.

131. Lafourcade and Riffaud, *Opération Turquoise*, 80, 108.

132. Borton, Brusset, and Hallam, "Study 3," 43. See also Lanotte, *France au Rwanda*, 444.

133. Quoted in Favier and Martin-Roland, *Décennie Mitterrand*, 481. Similarly, the French army opposed intervention as well, "seeing no military rationale and considerable risk." African Rights, *Rwanda*, 1139.

134. Quoted in Lanotte, *France au Rwanda*, 400.

135. Indeed, according to then-adviser to Léotard Jean-Christophe Rufin, the intent was to strive for "the goal of zero deaths," a sentiment more often attributed to the U.S. government. Quoted in Lanotte, *France au Rwanda*, 426.

136. Quoted in Favier and Martin-Roland, *Décennie Mitterrand*, 482. See also Lanotte, *France au Rwanda*, 398–399.

137. Prunier, *Rwanda Crisis*, 283.

138. Ibid.

139. Lanotte, *France au Rwanda*, 426. During Operation Amaryllis, France had also rejected a Belgian proposal that they work to halt the killing out of concern for the safety of French paratroopers. See also Prunier, *Rwanda Crisis*, 234–35.

140. Lanotte, *France au Rwanda*, 426. See also Coret and Verschave, *L'horreur*, 401; Prunier, *Rwanda Crisis*, 289.

141. Prunier, *Rwanda Crisis*, 287; Lanotte, *France au Rwanda*, 416–17; Coret and Verschave, *L'horreur*, 275, 292–94, 307, 317, 320–22; Birck, "La télévision et le Rwanda," 193; Dominique Bari, "Des organisations de solidarité dénoncent l'intervention," *l'Humanité*, June 25, 1994.

142. Binet, "Genocide of Rwandan Tutsi," 53–58; Lanotte, *France au Rwanda*, 418; Stephen Smith, "Pour les ONG, la France n'est pas la mieux placée—Sauf MSF," *Libération*, June 23, 1994.

143. Favier and Martin-Roland, *Décennie Mitterrand*, 480–82; Lanotte, *France au Rwanda*, 399–400.

144. Lafourcade and Riffaud, *Opération Turquoise*, 71.

145. African Rights, *Rwanda*, 1138.

146. Melvern, *A People Betrayed*, 241.

147. Soudan, "Pourquoi," 16; see also Lanotte, *France au Rwanda*, 398–99.

148. Prunier, *Rwanda Crisis*, 290.

149. Indeed, it was not until the refugee exodus to Goma in mid-July that the Léotard-Balladur team began to consider the possibility of staying past July 31, despite their longer mandate. Favier and Martin-Roland, *Décennie Mitterrand*, 483–84.

150. Soudan, "Pourquoi," 16; Prunier, *Rwanda Crisis*, 282–85, 288–90; Connaughton, "Military Support," 45, 77; Favier and Martin-Roland, *Décennie Mitterrand*, 482–83; Lanotte, *France au Rwanda*, 407–8, 427; Lafourcade and Riffaud, *Opération Turquoise*, 62–63.

151. Quoted in Favier and Martin-Roland, *Décennie Mitterrand*, 482. See also Lanxade as quoted in Favier and Martin-Roland, *Décennie Mitterrand*, 481. The French initially looked at basing Turquoise either in Burundi or Zaire, but the Burundian government was uncooperative. See Prunier, *Rwanda Crisis*, 285; Lafourcade and Riffaud, *Opération Turquoise*, 65.

152. For all conditions imposed by Balladur see Prunier, *Rwanda Crisis*, 287; Favier and Martin-Roland, *Décennie Mitterrand*, 482; Lanotte, *France au Rwanda*, 399–401.

153. Quoted in Lanotte, *France au Rwanda*, 442.

154. Ibid., 443.

155. Prunier, *Rwanda Crisis*, 289; Prunier, "Opération Turquoise," 290; Lanotte, *France au Rwanda*, 426.

156. Lafourcade and Riffaud, *Opération Turquoise*, 138; see also Lanotte, *France au Rwanda*, 427, 438; Lugan, *François Mitterrand*, 245.

157. Favier and Martin-Roland, *Décennie Mitterrand*, 480; Lanotte, *France au Rwanda*, 386.

158. Lanotte, *France au Rwanda*, 478. See also Soudan, "Pourquoi," 15; La Balme, "The French and the Use of Force," 198–99.

159. Prunier, *Rwanda Crisis*, 282. See also Lanotte, *France au Rwanda*, 393–95; Soudan, "Pourquoi," 15. Prunier and Soudan suggest that Juppé may also have hoped to promote Chirac's presidential ambitions by seizing the initiative and denying Balladur any credit for the mission while forcing him to share the blame if it went wrong. Indeed, as we saw above, Balladur did worry about this. Yet according to Lanotte this claim is without merit: Juppé "knew how to put aside internal rivalries when they are totally exceeded by the gravity of the questions at hand" (394).

160. Soudan, "Pourquoi," 16; Coret and Verschave, *L'horreur*, 310; Lanotte, *France au Rwanda*, 418–19; Hilsum, "Reporting Rwanda," 175; Marie-Pierre Subtil, "Les critiques contre l'opération Turquoise se sont tues," *Le Monde*, August 21, 1994.

161. Rony Brauman, "L'esprit humanitaire contre le devoir d'humanité," *Le Monde*, June 30, 1994; Lanotte, *France au Rwanda*, 485.

162. Melvern, *A People Betrayed*, 144; see also Birck, "La télévision et le Rwanda," 196; Prunier, *Rwanda Crisis*, 302–3; Coret and Verschave, *L'horreur*, 277–78.

163. Favier and Martin-Roland, *Décennie Mitterrand*, 485.

164. Lanotte, *France au Rwanda*, 445; Prunier, *Rwanda Crisis*, 307; Subtil, "Les critiques se sont tues."

165. "L'intervention télévisée du président de la République à l'occasion du 14 juillet," *Le Monde*, July 16, 1994.

166. Lanotte, *France au Rwanda*, 398.

167. Quoted in *France au Rwanda*, 401–2. Balladur further boasted of the "almost complete end of the massacres where France is present," without noting the continued problems in areas outside immediate French supervision.

168. François Léotard, "La France doit garder la tête haute," *Libération*, July 22, 1994; Prunier, *Rwanda Crisis*, 302.

169. Connaughton, "Military Support," 77; Verschave, *Complicité de Génocide?*, 172; Lanotte, *France au Rwanda*, 478.

170. Prunier, *Rwanda Crisis*, 297.

171. Quoted in Hilsum, "Reporting Rwanda," 175.

172. The series is typically released early in the month, based on polling conducted shortly beforehand. Thus this period spans approximately the week that Turquoise launched to the week after it ended. For president and prime minister the poll asks if respondents are completely confident, somewhat confident, tend not to trust, or do not trust at all, the politician in question. In this same period Mitterrand went from 40 to 43% who were completely or somewhat confident while Juppé saw an increase from 31 to 35% of those who "hope to see him play an important role in the coming months and years." The data are available at "Cotes de popularités," accessed April 29, 2015, http://www.tns-sofres.com/cotes-de-popularites.

173. See, e.g., Colette Braeckman, *Rwanda: histoire d'un génocide* (Paris: Fayard, 1994); Verschave, *Complicité de Génocide*; Coret and Verschave, *L'horreur*; Saint-Exupéry, *Complices de l'inavouable*; Des Forges, "Leave None."

174. An extremely thorough investigation of all the accusations can be found in Lanotte, *France au Rwanda*, 354–75, 446–87.

175. The most serious charge against France before Turquoise is that it continued providing military assistance to the interim government and FAR during the genocide. It appears that despite official denials, France retained about ten to twenty military and/or intelligence personnel in Rwanda after Operation Amaryllis and may also have funneled weapons to the Rwandan regime, though the details of this latter charge are contested. Yet even beyond their timing before Turquoise, there are reasons to think these policies do not speak directly to the motives behind Operation Turquoise. Notably, the arms shipments likely occurred without the knowledge or agreement of France's top political authorities, as it was mainly the Ministry of Cooperation and the foreign intelligence service that supported the Rwandan government during the genocide. Alternatively, they may have been the work of arms smugglers rather than the French government. On military assistance generally, see Lanotte, *France au Rwanda*, 362–75. On the arms deliveries see also Prunier, *Rwanda Crisis*, 278; Des Forges, "Leave None," 655–57, 661–66; African Rights, *Rwanda*, 1107.

176. Favier and Martin-Roland, *Décennie Mitterrand*, 486.

177. Lanotte, *France au Rwanda*, 449.

178. Lafourcade and Riffaud, *Opération Turquoise*, 57–58.

179. Prunier, *Rwanda Crisis*, 393.

180. Borton, Brusset, and Hallam, "Study 3," 42; Connaughton, "Military Support," 49–50; Lanotte, *France au Rwanda*, 438, 454; Verschave, *Complicité de Génocide?*, 125–26.

181. See Verschave, *Complicité de Génocide?*, 122; African Rights, *Rwanda*, 1147–48; Connaughton, "Military Support," 45–46; Des Forges, "Leave None," 781; Lanotte, *France au Rwanda*, 453–54.

182. Lanotte, *France au Rwanda*, 395–98. See also Soudan, "Pourquoi," 16; Favier and Martin-Roland, *Décennie Mitterrand*, 481.

183. Quoted in Lanotte, *France au Rwanda*, 451. One of the COS troops' tasks in the first days of the mission was to exfiltrate the few French personnel who were still in Rwanda after the

departure of Operation Amaryllis in mid-April. This also supports the idea that the French did not intend to support the FAR at this point, since they chose to remove the people who were best informed on the military situation. See *France au Rwanda*, 458–59.

184. Verschave, *Complicité de Génocide?*, 127.

185. Binet, "Genocide of Rwandan Tutsi," 46; Lanotte, *France au Rwanda*, 457.

186. For Mitterrand it appears the decision on arrest also reflected a desire not to pursue punitive action against those he had recently seen as allies. Yet this sentiment was by no means necessary, since the other authorities' low risk tolerance was adequate to bring this decision about. See Lanotte, *France au Rwanda*, 443.

187. Connaughton, "Military Support," 49; Lanotte, *France au Rwanda*, 437; Lafourcade and Riffaud, *Opération Turquoise*, 131.

188. Lugan, *François Mitterrand*, 246–51; Lanotte, *France au Rwanda*, 439; Lafourcade and Riffaud, *Opération Turquoise*, 131–33; Kuperman, *Limits of Humanitarian Intervention*, 47–48.

189. Lanotte, *France au Rwanda*, 481. This view was also shared by MSF's Bradol, as cited in Lugan, *François Mitterrand*, 239.

190. Lanotte, *France au Rwanda*, 481–82.

191. Favier and Martin-Roland, *Décennie Mitterrand*, 484; Lafourcade and Riffaud, *Opération Turquoise*, 108; Lanotte, *France au Rwanda*, 403.

192. Prunier, *Rwanda Crisis*, 266; Adelman, Suhrke, and Jones, "Study 2," 63–64; Lanotte, *France au Rwanda*, 456; Binet, "Genocide of Rwandan Tutsi," 41–42. Death estimates at Kibeho varied widely, but the UN settled on a figure of 2,000.

193. Prunier, *Rwanda Crisis*, 267; Connaughton, "Military Support," 36–37, 50; Lafourcade and Riffaud, *Opération Turquoise*, 124–25, 134–35.

194. Soudan, "Pourquoi," 12; Verschave, *Complicité de Génocide?*, 127; African Rights, *Rwanda*, 1105–6; Prunier, *Rwanda Crisis*, 290; Lanotte, *France au Rwanda*, 388, 478–79.

195. Prunier, *Rwanda Crisis*, 281; Lanotte, *France au Rwanda*, 389, 479–80.

196. Prunier, *Rwanda Crisis*, 283.

197. Sections 1.1 and 2 in Lafourcade, "Operation Turquoise Order of Operation No.1," annex (n.p.).

5. The United States in Darfur

1. On British and French policy, respectively, see Paul D. Williams, "The United Kingdom," 195–212, and Bruno Charbonneau, "France," 213–31, both in *The International Politics of Mass Atrocities: The Case of Darfur*, ed. David R. Black and Paul D. Williams (New York: Routledge, 2010). I have not found any evidence of bilateral French financial support for AMIS, but it did contribute through both the EU and NATO. Beginning in 2008, France also led a third peace operation under the auspices of the EU (EUFOR Chad/CAR) in neighboring Chad and the Central African Republic that included providing protection for Darfuri refugees in those countries.

2. Alex de Waal, *Famine that Kills: Darfur, Sudan*, rev. ed., Oxford Studies in African Affairs (Oxford: Oxford University Press, 2005); Julie Flint and Alex de Waal, *Darfur: A New History of a Long War*, revised and updated ed. (London: Zed Books, 2008); Gérard Prunier, *Darfur: A 21st Century Genocide*, 3rd ed. (Ithaca: Cornell University Press, 2008).

3. Cockett, *Sudan*, 181–83.

4. Quoted in Hamilton, *Fighting for Darfur*, 23.

5. Prunier, *Darfur*, 133–34; Hugo Slim, "Dithering over Darfur? A Preliminary Review of the International Response," *International Affairs* 80, no. 5 (2004): 811–28, at 818.

6. Prunier, *Darfur*, 131.

7. United Nations Security Council, *Report of the Secretary-General on the Sudan Pursuant to Paragraph 15 of Security Council Resolution 1564 (2004) and Paragraphs 6, 13 and 16 of Security Council Resolution 1556 (2004)*, S/2004/787, October 4, 2004, 8.

8. For a summary of available estimates see Degomme and Guha-Sapir, "Patterns of Mortality Rates," 295. Other sources have also cited figures in this range: see Flint and de Waal,

Darfur, 173; International Crisis Group, *The AU's Mission in Darfur,* 3; United Nations Security Council, *Report of the Secretary-General on the Sudan Pursuant to Paragraphs 6, 13 and 16 of Security Council Resolution 1556 (2004), Paragraph 15 of Security Council Resolution 1564 (2004) and Paragraph 17 of Security Council Resolution 1574 (2004),* S/2005/68, February 4, 2005, 6.

9. Prunier, *Darfur,* 148–52.

10. Degomme and Guha-Sapir, "Patterns of Mortality Rates," 298.

11. Flint and de Waal, *Darfur,* 162–66, 187; United Nations Security Council, *Report of the Secretary-General on the Sudan, 2004,* 9.

12. Degomme and Guha-Sapir, "Patterns of Mortality Rates," 298.

13. Flint and de Waal, *Darfur,* 187.

14. United Nations Security Council, *Report of the Secretary-General on the Sudan, 2004,* 8–9.

15. Degomme and Guha-Sapir, "Patterns of Mortality Rates," 296. New displacement in the few remaining intact villages continued through at least 2007 and also contributed. See Prunier, *Darfur,* 159; United Nations Security Council, *Report of the Secretary-General on the Sudan, 2004,* 8.

16. United Nations Security Council, *Report of the Secretary-General on the Sudan, 2005,* 6. One effect of these higher estimates was that, despite the expansion of relief operations, during the second half of 2004 "the proportions of IDPs and war-affected persons who could be reached by humanitarian help regularly declined, thereby leading to a steady increase in estimated mortality rates." Prunier, *Darfur,* 138; see also United Nations Security Council, *Report of the Secretary-General on the Sudan, 2004,* 8.

17. Degomme and Guha-Sapir, "Patterns of Mortality Rates," 294; Flint and de Waal, *Darfur,* 187.

18. Flint and de Waal, *Darfur,* 205–7.

19. Ibid., 188, 259–62.

20. United Nations Security Council, *Monthly Report of the Secretary-General on Darfur,* S/2006/870, November 8, 2006, 5.

21. Degomme and Guha-Sapir, "Patterns of Mortality Rates," 294, 298. The high number of deaths primarily reflects the growth of the conflict-affected population, not an increase in the crude mortality rate. Yet there are differences in interpretation of the mortality trends. According to Degomme and Guha-Sapir, the relatively consistent overall mortality rate "masks a divergent pattern in cause-specific mortality," in which deaths continued to fall but the rate of non-violent, disease-related deaths grew (298). By contrast, Flint and de Waal claim that hunger and disease-related mortality did not rise from mid-2006 to mid-2007. *Darfur,* 191.

22. Flint and de Waal, *Darfur,* 168–70; U.S. Government Accountability Office, *Darfur Crisis: Progress in Aid and Peace Monitoring Threatened by Ongoing Violence and Operational Challenges,* GAO-07-9 (Washington, DC), November 9, 2006, 3.

23. Hamilton, *Fighting for Darfur,* 20. Since the United States did not maintain full diplomatic relations with Sudan there was no ambassador, and, as chargé d'affaires, Galluci was the highest-ranking diplomat in Khartoum.

24. Cockett, *Sudan,* 195.

25. Ibid., 198; see also James Traub, *The Best Intentions: Kofi Annan and the UN in the Era of American World Power,* 1st Picador ed. (New York: Picador, 2007), 244.

26. Hamilton, *Fighting for Darfur,* 31.

27. Colin L. Powell, "The Crisis in Darfur: Testimony Before the Senate Committee on Foreign Relations" (Washington, DC), September 9, 2004, http://2001-2009.state.gov/secretary/former/powell/remarks/36042.htm; The White House, "Statement By The President on Violence in Darfur, Sudan," press release (Washington, DC), September 9, 2004, http://2001-2009.state.gov/p/af/rls/prsrl/36065.htm.

28. Flint and de Waal, *Darfur,* 193.

29. Ibid., 182–83; Traub, *Best Intentions,* 347; U.S. Government Accountability Office, *Darfur Crisis,* 20–21.

30. Slim, "Dithering over Darfur?," 825; U.S. Department of State, "United States Policy in Sudan: Briefing with Andrew Natsios, Michael Ranneberger, and Roger Winter" (Washington, DC), April 27, 2004, http://2001-2009.state.gov/p/af/rls/rm/31856.htm; "Humanitarian Ceasefire Agreement on the Conflict in Darfur" (N'djamena, Chad), April 8, 2004, http://

www.usip.org/sites/default/files/file/resources/collections/peace_agreements/sudan_ceasefire_04082004.pdf; Flint and de Waal, *Darfur*, 169, 173.

31. Flint and de Waal, *Darfur*, 174.

32. U.S. Department of State, "United States Policy in Sudan"; Powell, "Crisis in Darfur."

33. African Union Peace and Security Council, *Report of the Chairperson of the Commission on the Situation in Darfur (The Sudan)*, PSC/MIN/2(XII) (Addis Ababa, Ethiopia), July 4, 2004, 2–3; *Report of the Chairperson of the Commission on the Situation in Darfur (The Sudan)*, PSC/PR/2(XVII) (Addis Ababa, Ethiopia), October 20, 2004, 4–6.

34. For the initial mandate see African Union, *Agreement with the Sudanese Parties on the Modalities for the Establishment of the Ceasefire Commission and the Deployment of Observers in the Darfur* (Addis Ababa, Ethiopia), May 28, 2004, available at http://peacemaker.un.org/sudan-darfur-ceasefire-commission2004. Beyond this, there was some confusion as to whether the troops to protect the monitors were also authorized to protect civilians within their capabilities. In July the AU Peace and Security Council affirmed that they were, but on their deployment in August the troops were told by force commander Festus Okonkwo that attempts to protect civilians were outside the mandate and ROE. Either way, such protection was clearly not a task these troops were expected to pursue, as discussed in chapter 1. See African Union Peace and Security Council, *Communiqué of the 13th Meeting of the Peace and Security Council*, PSC/PR/Comm(XIII) (Addis Ababa, Ethiopia), July 27, 2004; Stephanie Nolen, "African Union Troops Arrive in Sudan; Hostile Reception Greets Soldiers Assigned to Protect Ceasefire Observers," *Globe and Mail*, August 16, 2004.

35. U.S. Department of State, "On-The-Record Briefing: USAID Administrator Andrew S. Natsios and Principal Deputy Assistant Secretary of State for Africa Affairs Michael Ranneberger on Sudan" (Washington, DC), September 29, 2004, http://2001-2009.state.gov/p/af/rls/spbr/36615.htm; Powell, "Crisis in Darfur."

36. Powell, "Crisis in Darfur"; United Nations Security Council, *Security Council Resolution 1564*, S/RES/1564, September 18, 2004.

37. African Union Peace and Security Council, *Communiqué of the 17th Meeting of the Peace and Security Council*, PSC/PR/Comm(XVII) (Addis Ababa, Ethiopia), October 20, 2004.

38. Michael E. Ranneberger, "Sudan: Prospects for Peace," Speech to the Providence Committee on Foreign Relations (Washington, DC), December 9, 2004, http://2001-2009.state.gov/p/af/rls/rm/39751.htm.

39. African Union Peace and Security Council, *Report of the Chairperson of the Commission on the Situation in the Darfur Region of the Sudan*, PSC/PR/2(XXVIII) (Addis Ababa, Ethiopia), April 28, 2005, especially 10–11, 25–26. In contrast to the military forces, the deployment of civilian police was still well behind schedule by April 2005.

40. U.S. Department of State, "Press Briefing by Robert Zoellick, Deputy Secretary of State" (Khartoum, Sudan), April 14, 2005, http://2001-2009.state.gov/s/d/former/zoellick/rem/44656.htm.

41. African Union Peace and Security Council, *Communiqué of the 28th Meeting of the Peace and Security Council*, PSC/PR/Comm(XXVIII) (Addis Ababa, Ethiopia), April 28, 2005, especially para. 9; African Union Peace and Security Council, *Report of the Chairperson on Darfur (April 2005)*, especially paras. 106, 114, 126. No further expansions occurred until 2007, during preparations for UNAMID's deployment.

42. U.S. Department of State, "Press Briefing on Sudan by Robert Zoellick, Deputy Secretary of State" (Khartoum, Sudan), May 27, 2005, http://2001-2009.state.gov/s/d/former/zoellick/rem/46922.htm.

43. U.S. Government Accountability Office, *Darfur Crisis*, 45, 54–58; African Union Peace and Security Council, *Report of the Chairperson on Darfur (July 2004)*, 3–4; African Union Peace and Security Council, *Report of the Chairperson on Darfur (October 2004)*, 6–7; O'Neill and Cassis, *Protecting Two Million*, 63–66; Donna Miles, "Airlift Support for Darfur Continues Strong as Rice Visits Region," *American Forces Press Service*, July 21, 2005; United Nations Security Council, *Security Council Resolution 1590*, S/RES/1590, March 24, 2007. The U.S. Government Accountability Office notes that the number of U.S. military observers ranged between about 4 and 16 (55).

44. Flint and de Waal, *Darfur*, 176; O'Neill and Cassis, *Protecting Two Million*, 28–29, 35.

45. Based on two common rules of thumb for determining force requirements in a civilian protection mission, some 10,000–60,000 troops would have been required given Darfur's population of around 6 million. The first assumes 2 to 10 soldiers per 10,000 population, while the second assumes a protection force should be at least as large as the largest local force it might face. See Williams, "Military Responses to Mass Killing," 176–77. This is also in line with other estimates, including a 2004 Pentagon assessment that in a consensual environment it would take about 35,000 U.S. troops to secure the IDP camps in Darfur (or if Khartoum was opposed, 120,000). See Hamilton, *Fighting for Darfur*, 76.

46. African Union Peace and Security Council, *Report of the Chairperson of the Commission on the Status of the Implementation of the Peace and Security Council Decision of 10 March 2006 on the Situation in Darfur and the Conclusion of the Abuja Peace Talks*, PSC/MIN/2(LI) (Addis Ababa, Ethiopia), May 15, 2006, 10.

47. O'Neill and Cassis, *Protecting Two Million*, 50–58; Flint and de Waal, *Darfur*, 173–79; International Crisis Group, "The AU's Mission in Darfur."

48. I have seen various references to night attacks, including at least one detailed description of the typical pattern—see Cockett, *Sudan*, 186. On the other hand, former U.S. Marine captain and AMIS monitor Brian Steidle noted that in his experience militias typically attacked during daylight, "because they often were reinforced by [Sudanese government] troops using helicopter gunships and Antonov prop planes." Brian Steidle and Gretchen Steidle Wallace, *The Devil Came on Horseback: Bearing Witness to the Genocide in Darfur*, 1st ed. (New York: Public Affairs, 2007), 148.

49. Flint and de Waal, *Darfur*, 194.

50. Ibid., 177; see also U.S. Government Accountability Office, *Darfur Crisis*, 59–62.

51. Quoted in Hamilton, *Fighting for Darfur*, 75.

52. Omer Ismail (Darfur activist), interview with the author, phone, June 15, 2016. Ismail is a Darfuri exile who served on the Save Darfur board of directors and joined the Enough Project in 2007.

53. Joel Brinkley, "Plan to End Darfur Violence is Failing, Officials Say," *New York Times*, January 28, 2006; Colum Lynch, "Official Pushes for UN Force in Sudan; Envoy Cites Need for Peacekeepers," *Washington Post*, January 14, 2006.

54. Maggie Farley, "Envoy to Sudan Reports Threats," *Los Angeles Times*, March 1, 2006.

55. Colum Lynch, "Sudan's Bashir Rebuffs UN on Peacekeepers; US Backed Plan to Replace African Force," *Washington Post*, April 27, 2006; see also Flint and de Waal, *Darfur*, 199.

56. For detailed discussion of the Abuja negotiations and the U.S. role at this time see Flint and de Waal, *Darfur*, 200–229; Hamilton, *Fighting for Darfur*, 83–98.

57. Hamilton, *Fighting for Darfur*, 87, 98; Flint and de Waal, *Darfur*, 267.

58. Flint and de Waal, *Darfur*, 221–25, 267; Hamilton, *Fighting for Darfur*, 85, 169.

59. Flint and de Waal, *Darfur*, 205, 229.

60. Stephanie McCrummen, "Splintering of Rebel Groups Adds to Chaos in Darfur," *Washington Post*, April 1, 2007; Jeffrey Gettleman, "Darfur Rebels Kill 10 in Raid on Peace Force," *New York Times*, October 1, 2007; Ekengard, "African Union Mission in SUDAN," 24; Flint and de Waal, *Darfur*, 232–39.

61. Flint and de Waal, *Darfur*, 199; Alex de Waal, "Darfur and the Failure of the Responsibility to Protect," *International Affairs* 83, no. 6 (2007): 1039–54, at 1046.

62. Hamilton, *Fighting for Darfur*, 97.

63. Save Darfur Coalition, "Save Darfur Coalition Applauds UN Vote on Peacekeepers; Urges Swift International Action to Deploy Forces," press release (Washington, DC), August 31, 2006, http://savedarfur.org/save-darfur-coalition-applauds-un-vote-peacekeepers-urges-swift-international-action-deploy-forces/.

64. de Waal, "Darfur and the Failure of the Responsibility to Protect," 1042. See also United Nations Security Council, *Security Council Resolution 1706*, S/RES/1706, August 31, 2006.

65. Robert F. Worth, "Sudan Says It Will Accept UN-African Peace Force in Darfur," *New York Times*, November 17, 2006.

66. See, e.g., Lydia Polgreen, "Sudan and UN Reach New Peacekeeping Deal for Darfur," *New York Times*, June 18, 2007; Richard Holbrooke, "China Lends a Hand," *Washington Post*,

June 28, 2007; "The UN Blinks on Darfur," *Christian Science Monitor*, August 3, 2007; United Nations Security Council, *Security Council Resolution 1769*, S/RES/1769, July 31, 2007.

67. See, e.g., Warren Hoge, "UN Official Criticizes Sudan for Resisting Peace Force in Darfur," *New York Times*, November 28, 2007; "UN Peacekeeping Chief Says Darfur Mission is at Risk," *New York Times*, January 10, 2008; Hamilton, *Fighting for Darfur*, 173–74. For data on force size and troop contributors over time, see United Nations Peacekeeping, "Troop and Police Contributors Archive (1990–2016)," accessed July 10, 2014, http://www.un.org/en/peacekeeping/resources/statistics/contributors_archive.shtml.

68. United Nations Security Council, *Report of the Secretary-General and the Chairperson of the African Union Commission on the Hybrid Operation in Darfur*, S/2007/307/Rev.1, June 5, 2007, 12–15; United Nations Security Council, *Resolution 1769*.

69. Prunier, *Darfur*, 178. An additional difficulty was that the countries—including the United States—that had pushed so hard for UNAMID's deployment failed to provide all the resources it needed, including notably twenty-four much-discussed helicopters. See e.g., Salim Salim, "Peacekeeping on the Cheap," *International Herald Tribune*, July 30, 2008.

70. These figures are from a full-text search in LexisNexis.

71. Jerry Fowler (Darfur activist), interview with the author, Greencastle, Indiana, March 6, 2009; Prunier, *Darfur*, 126; Hamilton, *Fighting for Darfur*, 21. As director of the Committee on Conscience at the United States Holocaust Memorial Museum Fowler helped found the Save Darfur Coalition and served as its president from 2008–10.

72. Fowler, interview. See also Flint and de Waal, *Darfur*, 179; Hamilton, *Fighting for Darfur*, 31–32.

73. The White House, "President Condemns Atrocities in Sudan," press release (Washington, DC), April 7, 2004.

74. David Lanz, "Save Darfur: A Movement and Its Discontents," *African Affairs* 108, no. 433 (2009): 669–77, at 671.

75. Hamilton, *Fighting for Darfur*, 101–2.

76. Deborah Murphy, "Narrating Darfur: Darfur in the U.S. Press, March-September 2004," in *War in Darfur and the Search for Peace*, ed. Alex de Waal (Cambridge: Harvard University Press, 2007), 314–36.

77. Scott Straus, "Darfur and the Genocide Debate," *Foreign Affairs* 81, no. 4 (2005): 123–33, at 128–30; Flint and de Waal, *Darfur*, 180–81.

78. Prunier, *Darfur*, 140.

79. The few exceptions failed to gather any real momentum, and, notably, none of Save Darfur's members called directly for U.S. military action. Hamilton, *Fighting for Darfur*, 77; Lanz, "Save Darfur," 672; Colin Thomas-Jensen and Julia Spiegel, "Activism and Darfur: Slowly Driving Policy Change," *Fordham International Law Journal* 31, no. 4 (2007): 843–58, at 848.

80. See, e.g., Samantha Power and John Prendergast, "Break Through to Darfur," *Los Angeles Times*, June 2, 2004; Jon Corzine and Richard Holbrooke, "Help the African Union," *Washington Post*, September 9, 2004; Bob MacPherson, "Stop the Slaughter," *Washington Post*, August 8, 2004; "Next Steps on Darfur," *Washington Post*, September 1, 2004; "Civilians Are Still at Risk," *St. Louis Post-Dispatch*, September 2, 2004; Human Rights Watch, "Empty Promises?: Continuing Abuses in Darfur, Sudan," briefing paper, August 11, 2004.

81. Hamilton, *Fighting for Darfur*, 45–46, 73–74.

82. Mark Hanis, quoted in Nicholas D. Kristof, "Walking the Talk," *New York Times*, October 9, 2005. See also, for example, Patrick Kerkstra, "Students Take Action to Aid Sudan," *Philadelphia Inquirer*, April 11, 2005.

83. See for instance the text of the presidential debate between John Kerry and George W. Bush: "Transcript: First Presidential Debate," *Washington Post*, September 30, 2004.

84. There is some disagreement on the precise timing of this transition. Lanz suggests that replacing AMIS became the movement's highest priority by 2005, but as Hamilton demonstrates, it was not until 2006 that advocates "began putting their utmost into getting the UN deployed to Darfur." See Lanz, "Save Darfur," 673; Hamilton, *Fighting for Darfur*, 80.

85. See Save Darfur Coalition, "Faith-Based Coalition Praises Senate Committee for Passing Amendment to Add $50 Million to President's Emergency Funding Request for Darfur

Peacekeeping," press release (Washington, DC), April 05, 2006, http://savedarfur.org/faith-based-coalition-praises-senate-committee-passing-amendment-add-50-million-presidents-emergency-funding-request-darfur-peacekeeping/. Efforts to influence Congress continued to yield fruit as well: the Darfur Peace and Accountability Act of 2006 imposed sanctions on those found responsible for genocide and war crimes in Darfur, while the 2007 Sudan Accountability and Divestment Act forbade companies that do business with the U.S. government from doing so in Sudan.

86. Save Darfur Coalition, "Historic Rally in Washington, DC, Delivers Three-Quarters of a Million Postcards Demanding an End to Genocide in Darfur," press release (Washington, DC), May 1, 2006, http://savedarfur.org/historic-rally-washington-dc-delivers-three-quarters-million-postcards-demanding-end-genocide-darfur/.

87. Save Darfur Coalition, "Tens of Thousands Rally in Central Park for 'Global Day for Darfur,'" press release (Washington, DC), September 17, 2006, http://savedarfur.org/tens-thousands-rally-central-park-global-day-darfur/.

88. See, e.g., Save Darfur Coalition, "Coalition Applauds President's Call for UN Peacekeepers and Appointment of Andrew Natsios as Special Envoy," press release (Washington, DC), September 19, 2006, http://savedarfur.org/coalition-applauds-presidents-call-un-peacekeepers-appointment-andrew-natsios-special-envoy/; "Save Darfur Coalition Urges President Bush to Act Decisively in Darfur," press release (Washington, DC), February 5, 2007, http://savedarfur.org/save-darfur-coalition-urges-president-bush-act-decisively-darfur/.

89. Eric Reeves (Darfur activist), interview with the author, phone, April 29, 2016; Hamilton, *Fighting for Darfur*, chap. 10. Reeves is an independent Sudan and Darfur activist who has published and testified widely on the region. As he noted, by the spring of 2008 the advocacy movement's window of opportunity to influence Beijing had largely passed, and China was less willing to push Khartoum to fully implement Resolution 1769 or to make UNAMID a more effective force.

90. Flint and de Waal, *Darfur*, 169; Hamilton, *Fighting for Darfur*, 29–30.

91. Andrew Natsios, "Beyond Darfur: Sudan's Slide Toward Civil War," *Foreign Affairs* 87, no. 3 (2008), 77–93; Andrew S. Natsios, *Sudan, South Sudan, and Darfur: What Everyone Needs to Know* (Oxford: Oxford University Press, 2012), 158.

92. Andrew Natsios, "Personal Memo from Andrew Natsios to John Negroponte" (The National Security Archive: George Washington University, April 5, 2007), available at http://nsarchive.gwu.edu/NSAEBB/NSAEBB335/Document11.pdf. See also, Natsios, "Beyond Darfur," 87–91.

93. Hamilton, *Fighting for Darfur*, 146–47.

94. Ibid., 77–78.

95. See, e.g., Flint and de Waal, *Darfur*, 4.

96. Paul Carrel, "Sudan Warns UK, US Not to Interfere in Darfur," *Sudan Tribune*, July 22, 2004.

97. International Institute for Strategic Studies, "Sub-Saharan Africa," *Military Balance* 104 (2004): 246.

98. Michael Abramowitz, "U.S. Promises on Darfur Don't Match Actions," *Washington Post*, October 29, 2007.

99. See John Bolton, *Surrender is Not an Option: Defending America at the United Nations and Abroad*, paperback ed. (New York: Simon and Schuster, Inc., 2008), 351; Hamilton, *Fighting for Darfur*, 75–77; Ron Capps, *Seriously Not All Right: Five Wars in Ten Years* (Tucson: Schaffner Press, 2014), 215.

100. Quoted in George Gedda, "U.S. Opposes Western Troops in Darfur, Official Says," *Associated Press*, June 22, 2005.

101. Both quoted in Hamilton, *Fighting for Darfur*, 76.

102. Traub, *Best Intentions*, 239–40; Flint and de Waal, *Darfur*, 192; Hamilton, *Fighting for Darfur*, 23–24; Cockett, *Sudan*, 195. For further discussion of U.S. evangelical activism on Sudan see also *Sudan*, 146–56.

103. Guy Dinmore, "White House is Quiet as Darfur Killings Continue," *Financial Times*, March 14, 2005.

104. See e.g., Ken Silverstein, "Official Pariah Sudan Valuable to America's War on Terrorism," *Los Angeles Times*, April 29, 2005; Cockett, *Sudan*, 178–79.

105. Ken Silverstein, "Sudanese Visitor Split U.S. Officials," *Los Angeles Times*, June 17, 2005; Prunier, *Darfur*, 139.

106. Cockett, *Sudan*, 180. Other members of the Sudanese government shared this view.

107. Quoted in Cockett, *Sudan*, 199.

108. Prunier, *Darfur*, 139–40.

109. Traub, *Best Intentions*, 346.

110. For instance, as pointed out in note 45, in 2004 the Pentagon estimated that it would need 35,000 troops for a consensual operation to protect the IDP camps in Darfur. By comparison, the UNITAF deployment to Somalia peaked in March 1993 at less than 26,000 troops. Yet Department of Defense spending alone in Somalia between April 1992 and September 1993 was $885 million, or over $1.1 billion in 2005 dollars. See U.S. Government Accountability Office, *Peace Operations: Cost of DOD Operations in Somalia*, GAO/NSLAD-94-88 (Washington, DC), March 4, 1994.

111. U.S. Government Accountability Office, *Darfur Crisis*, 58.

112. Booker added that the administration was "willing to cover up genocide in favor of an intelligence collaboration" with the Sudanese regime. Salih Booker, interview by Amy Goodman, *Democracy Now*, May 3, 2005. For a similar quote by John Prendergast, then of ICG, see Silverstein, "Official Pariah Sudan Valuable to America's War on Terrorism."

113. Ismail, interview.

114. Chad Hazlett (Darfur activist), interview with the author, phone, July 21, 2016. Hazlett was a cofounder of GI-Net, where he worked through 2008. See also Hamilton, *Fighting for Darfur*, 77.

115. For Reeves's take on the AU's fundamental incapacity, see his many writings from 2005 at Eric Reeves, "Sudan: Research, Analysis, and Advocacy," www.sudanreeves.org. For the others see Africa Action, "Testimony Reveals Intelligence Relationship with Genocidal Regime; U.S. Failing to Take Urgent Action to Protect Civilians in Darfur," press release (Washington, DC), June 22, 2005, http://www.sudantribune.com/spip.php?page=imprimable&id_article=10324; International Crisis Group, "The AU's Mission in Darfur."

116. Eric Reeves, "A Darfur 'Crash-Course,'" *&c: A Daily Journal of Politics* (blog), July 21, 2005, https://web.archive.org/web/20050723005935/http://www.tnr.com/etc.mhtml. This view that many activists lacked a clear understanding of AMIS's basic inadequacies was also repeated to me in interviews with Reeves and Ismail.

117. Human Rights Watch, "Entrenching Impunity," 5.

118. Thomas-Jensen and Spiegel, "Activism and Darfur," 852. Indeed, the limited role of Darfurian perspectives in the advocacy movement inspired the founding of a group called 24 Hours for Darfur in 2007 and the launch of its signature "Darfurian Voices" project. Jonathan Loeb (Darfur activist), interview with the author, phone, June 20, 2016. Loeb was managing director at 24 Hours for Darfur from 2007 to 2010.

119. Sam Bell, quoted in Hamilton, *Fighting for Darfur*, 73–74.

120. Hamilton, *Fighting for Darfur*, 75.

121. Both quoted in Caryle Murphy, "Uniting in Prayer and Action on Darfur: Genocide Galvanizes Wide Array of Congregations to Push U.S. Response," *Washington Post*, August 7, 2005.

122. Anna Mayergoyz, quoted in Kerkstra, "Students Take Action to Aid Sudan."

123. Powell, "Crisis in Darfur." See also, e.g., U.S. Department of State, "On-The-Record Briefing: Andrew S. Natsios and Michael Ranneberger"; U.S. Department of State, "African Union To Expand Peacekeeping Mission in Sudan: Press Statement by Adam Ereli," press release (Washington, DC), April 29, 2005, http://2001-2009.state.gov/r/pa/prs/ps/2005/45444.htm.

124. See, respectively, "World Has Just Weeks to Save Darfur, Says UN High Commissioner for Refugees," *Reuters*, October 21, 2005; U.S. Department of State, "Sudan–Darfur Violence: Press Statement by Adam Ereli," press release (Washington, DC), October 10, 2005, http://2001-2009.state.gov/r/pa/prs/ps/2005/54637.htm.

125. Jendayi E. Frazer, "African Organizations and Institutions: Testimony Before the Senate Committee on Foreign Relations, Africa Subcommittee," report from U.S. Department of

State (Washington, DC), November 17, 2005, available at http://reliefweb.int/report/burundi/consolidate-africas-progress-promise-now-states-frazer-urges.

126. Abramowitz, "U.S. Promises on Darfur."

127. See, e.g., Judy Dempsey, "Pressure Rises Over NATO's Darfur Role," *International Herald Tribune*, February 20, 2006; Hamilton, *Fighting for Darfur*, 78–79.

128. Hamilton, *Fighting for Darfur*, 78.

129. Bolton, *Surrender is Not an Option*, 351.

130. Flint and de Waal, *Darfur*, 270.

131. International Crisis Group, *To Save Darfur*, (Nairobi/Brussels: March 17, 2006), ii. For the full set of recommendations and further details see i–iii, 23–25. For the earlier recommendation for a NATO force see International Crisis Group, "The AU's Mission in Darfur."

132. Ismail, interview.

133. Flint and de Waal, *Darfur*, 196. Initially, Darfuri civilians shared the activists' optimism. As they had when AMIS first deployed, Darfuris at first had high—indeed, "hopelessly exaggerated" (269)—hopes for UNAMID.

134. Sam Bell, quoted in Hamilton, *Fighting for Darfur*, 114. Still, as Bell's GI-Net colleague Chad Hazlett explained in an interview, at least in their group the consequences of the need for Khartoum's consent soon became all too clear. Once U.S. and UN officials began referring to the UN transition as a "rehatting" of AU forces, "it was almost an admission that it was a change in name more than anything else."

135. Ronny Strongin, quoted in Marc Perelman, "Jewish Organizations Plan a Big Push Against Genocide in Darfur," *Forward*, January 27, 2006.

136. Sam Bell, quoted in Hamilton, *Fighting for Darfur*, 145.

137. Quoted in Caroline Preston, "Grandson of Holocaust Survivors Rallies Support for Darfur," *Chronicle of Philanthropy*, June 29, 2006. In an interview, Jerry Fowler of the Holocaust Museum and Save Darfur expressed a related point that maintaining followers' engagement requires presenting both the problem (Darfur) and proposed solutions in simple, intuitive terms while still respecting the complexity of the situation.

138. Quoted in Katherine Albers, "Mia Farrow Speaks Out on Darfur Crisis," *Naples Daily News*, January 11, 2009.

139. Quoted in Hamilton, *Fighting for Darfur*, 122.

140. For instance, for GI-Net the policy gap the group hoped to fill was always central to the development of advocacy strategy. Hazlett, interview. Similarly, the Enough Project was founded in 2007 to combine advocacy with in-depth research and policy analysis. And, as Reeves lamented in an interview, "outrage just doesn't get the job done."

141. See, e.g., Condoleezza Rice, "Remarks Before the United Nations Security Council on Darfur, Sudan," (New York, NY), September 22, 2006, https://2001-2009.state.gov/secretary/rm/2006/73023.htm; The White House, "President Bush Appalled by Genocide in Darfur, Urges Support for Darfur Peace Agreement," press release (Washington, DC), December 10, 2006, https://georgewbush-whitehouse.archives.gov/news/releases/2006/12/20061210.html; "President Bush Discusses Genocide in Darfur, Implements Sanctions," press release (Washington, DC), May 29, 2007, https://georgewbush-whitehouse.archives.gov/news/releases/2007/05/20070529.html.

142. Reeves, interview.

143. The White House, "President Bush Appalled by Genocide."

144. The White House, "Fact Sheet: Stop the Genocide in Darfur," press release, April 18, 2007, https://georgewbush-whitehouse.archives.gov/news/releases/2007/04/20070418-7.html.

145. John Negroponte, "Informal Comments to the Media," (UN Webcast Archives: New York), September 21, 2007, http://webcast.un.org/ramgen/ondemand/stakeout/2007/so070921pm1.rm.

146. Hamilton, *Fighting for Darfur*, 76.

147. Traub, *Best Intentions*, 340.

148. Ibid., 342–46.

149. Flint and De Waal, *Darfur*, 194.

150. Quoted in Hamilton, *Fighting for Darfur*, 127.

151. Ibid., 112.

152. See Annan's comments in "Sudan's Foreign Minister Rejects U.S. Force in Darfur," *Reuters*, January 13, 2006.

153. The cable was leaked by Eric Reeves in "Security in Darfur: Donors' Conference in Brussels Fails to Take Action" (July 21, 2006), on "Sudan: Research, Analysis, and Advocacy," http://sudanreeves.org/2006/07/21/security-in-darfur-donors-conference-in-brussels-fails-to-take-action/. See also Capps, *Seriously Not All Right*, 209–10.

154. Natsios, "Personal Memo to John Negroponte." On U.S. acceptance of a mainly African force see, for example, U.S. Department of State, "Stopping Genocide in Darfur: Briefing with Jendayi Frazer, Assistant Secretary for African Affairs," (Washington, DC), August 24, 2006, http://2001-2009.state.gov/p/af/rls/rm/2006/71515.htm.

6. Australia in the Southwest Pacific

1. Department of Defence (Australia), *Defence 2000: Our Future Defence Force* (Canberra: Commonwealth of Australia), 2000, 31–33.

2. Department of Defence (Australia), *Defence 2000*, 52–53, 62. In 2000 it also liberalized the conditions under which reservists could be deployed abroad. Christopher Barrie (chief of the Australian Defence Force, 1998–2002), interview with the author, Canberra, Australia, August 19, 2008. In 1999 there was some debate about whether deploying INTERFET would stretch Australia's capabilities too far, and U.S. logistical assistance was needed to make Australian leadership possible. This contributed to these subsequent defense planning priorities. Interviews with Hugh White (deputy secretary for strategy, Department of Defence, 1995–2000), Canberra, Australia, August 15, 2008; and Kim Beazley (leader of the Australian Labor Party, 1996–2001), Canberra, Australia, July 30, 2009. Both White and Beazley have also served in other high-level posts in government. Notably, White was acting secretary in the Defence Department throughout the critical decision-making period related to INTERFET, and Beazley was minister of defence from 1984 to 1990.

3. As in the quantitative analysis, I use *SMH* primarily for its availability in LexisNexis. It is also generally seen as the most politically centrist of the three largest-circulation non-tabloid papers (*SMH*, the *Australian*, and the *Age*).

4. Technically, this is a coalition of the Liberal Party and the National Party of Australia. The Coalition is dominated by the Liberal Party, but effectively functions as a single party.

5. White, interview (2008).

6. Mark Dodd, "Ballot and Bullets," *Sydney Morning Herald*, May 1, 1999. See also James Dunn, "Again an Exit amid Tears and Rage," *Sydney Morning Herald*, September 11, 1999; Alan Ramsey, "Timor: A Debt Dishonoured," *Sydney Morning Herald*, September 25, 1999. These sources estimate the population at the time at 650,000 to 800,000.

7. Mark Dodd, "Fear Delays Timor Poll," *Sydney Morning Herald*, June 17, 1999.

8. Mark Dodd, "Indonesian Militia Cuts Off 60,000 from Outside Help," *Sydney Morning Herald*, July 10, 1999. On the denial of aid to refugees see also "Fear, Squalor and the Breach of Faith," *Sydney Morning Herald*, August 28, 1999. On threats against UN personnel see, for example, Dodd, "Ballot and Bullets."

9. Hamish McDonald, "Time Jakarta Stopped Fooling," *Sydney Morning Herald*, September 6, 1999.

10. Dunn, "Genocide in East Timor," 280.

11. For this statistic see Don Greenlees and Robert Garran, *Deliverance: The Inside Story of East Timor's Fight for Freedom* (Crowns Nest: Allen and Unwin, 2002), 276. For an in-depth account of the post-vote violence, see chap. 11.

12. Dunn, "Genocide in East Timor," 280. Others cite comparable estimates. For example, see Hugh White, "The Road to INTERFET: Reflections on Australian Strategic Decisions Concerning East Timor, December 1998-September 1999," *Security Challenges* 4, no. 1 (2008): 69–87, at 81. White estimates the number killed during these weeks was around 1500.

13. Greenlees and Garran, *Deliverance*, 232–35.

14. For a detailed account of these events see Department of Foreign Affairs and Trade (Australia), *East Timor in Transition 1998–2000: An Australian Policy Challenge* (Canberra: Commonwealth of Australia, 2001), chap. 3. For the text of Howard's letter to Habibie, see 181–82. For a shorter but comparable account see White, "Road to INTERFET," 71–73.

15. White, interview (2008). See also Greenlees and Garran, *Deliverance*, 109–11; White, "Road to INTERFET," 72–73; Fran Kelly, "Hugh White on East Timor," *The Howard Years*, documentary, ABC Television (Australia), 2008, formerly available at http://www.abc.net.au/news/howardyears, accessed August 24, 2009.

16. For an account of the government's policy adjustments see White, "Road to INTERFET," 74–76. See also Peter Cole-Adams, "Downer Denies Rift on Peacekeepers," *Sydney Morning Herald*, August 2, 1999; "Downer's Pledge for Timor Peace Force," *Sydney Morning Herald*, April 1, 1999; Greenlees and Garran, *Deliverance*, 110–11.

17. Greenlees and Garran, *Deliverance*, 164–70; White, "Road to INTERFET," 77; Fran Kelly, "Hugh White on East Timor"; White, interview (2008).

18. Craig Skehan and Peter Cole-Adams, "We Won't Give In to Thugs: Downer," *Sydney Morning Herald*, July 6, 1999; Greenlees and Garran, *Deliverance*, 111, 164–70; White, "Road to INTERFET," 77; Michael Wagner, "Terror Now a Delaying Tactic in East Timor," *Sydney Morning Herald*, June 14, 1999.

19. White, "Road to INTERFET," 78.

20. Although Howard and Downer decided not to press further for a pre-ballot peacekeeping force after this experience, in early August they did push successfully for a plan to increase the number of UN civilian police and military advisers in order to tighten security following the vote. See Mike Secoombe, "More Chamberlain than Churchill," *Sydney Morning Herald*, September 22, 1999; Mark Riley, "UN Backs Downer Plan to Beef Up Timor Force," *Sydney Morning Herald*, August 6, 1999.

21. Several other conditions proved easier to meet, including a UN Chapter VII mandate, active involvement by regional countries, and the logistical and political support of the United States. See White, "Road to INTERFET," 83; Greenlees and Garran, *Deliverance*, 239; Mark Riley, "UN to Consider Force in Territory," *Sydney Morning Herald*, September 7, 1999.

22. Peter Cole-Adams, "24 Hours to Action Stations for Peacekeeping Force," *Sydney Morning Herald*, September 9, 1999; Peter Cole-Adams and Greg Bearup, "U.S. Cuts Military Ties With Jakarta," *Sydney Morning Herald*, September 10, 1999.

23. The UN could not pull together a force fast enough, and, as one senior U.S. diplomat put it, "East Timor is Australia's Haiti." Mark Dodd, "Fears of Bloodbath Grow as Militias Stockpile Arms," *Sydney Morning Herald*, July 26, 1999; Mark Riley, "Kosovo Option is UN's Only Chance," *Sydney Morning Herald*, September 4, 1999; Greenlees and Garran, *Deliverance*, 264.

24. Interviews with Barrie and Smith.

25. See United Nations Security Council, *Security Council Resolution 1264*, S/RES/1264, September 15, 1999.

26. Quoted in John Birmingham, "A Time for War: Australia as a Military Power," *Quarterly Essay* 20 (2005): 1–64, at 46.

27. Cosgrove, *My Story*, 210; Barrie, interview.

28. The incident in Com described in the introduction was just one example of this at work.

29. Quoted in Birmingham, "Time for War," 23.

30. David Horner, Peter Londey, and Jean Bou, eds., *Australian Peacekeeping: Sixty Years in the Field* (Port Melbourne: Cambridge University Press, 2009), 279. For coalition size see also Cosgrove, *My Story*, 257.

31. For discussion of the resources available see Cosgrove, *My Story*, chaps. 7–12; Greenlees and Garran, *Deliverance*, chap. 14.

32. Birmingham, "Time for War," 23.

33. Quoted in ibid.

34. Timor-Leste Commission for Reception, Truth and Reconciliation (hereinafter CAVR), *Chega! The CAVR Report* (Dili, Timor-Leste: 2005), chap. 7.1, "Self-Determination," 113. The full report is at http://www.cavr-timorleste.org/en/chegaReport.htm.

35. Horner, Londey, and Bou, *Australian Peacekeeping*, 104, 279.

36. For one brief history of these events see Cosgrove, *My Story*, 260–61.

37. Richard Chauvel (expert on Indonesian history and politics and Australia-Indonesia relations, Victoria University), interview with the author, Melbourne, Australia, August 17, 2009.

38. Clinton Fernandes (Timor activist and expert on relations between East Timor, Indonesia, and Australia at University of New South Wales), interview with the author, Canberra, Australia, July 14, 2009; CAVR, *Chega!*, 97.

39. The importance of these ties came up repeatedly in interviews, including with Chauvel; with David Horner (historian of Australian defense and military operations at Australian National University), Canberra, Australia, August 13, 2008; and with Bu Wilson (advocate and expert on civil society activities regarding East Timor), Canberra, Australia, August 3, 2009.

40. CAVR, *Chega!*, 97.

41. Ibid., 96–97.

42. Fernandes, interview; CAVR, *Chega!*, 99–100.

43. Wilson, interview; CAVR, *Chega!*, 97.

44. CAVR, *Chega!*, 107–8.

45. Ibid., 112.

46. Ibid., 111.

47. Parliament of Australia, "Parlinfo," http://parlinfo.aph.gov.au/parlInfo/search/search.w3p, accessed March 3, 2010. Strangely, no petitions were entered in 1998–99, perhaps due to the change in government policy or political changes in Indonesia.

48. Interviews with Fernandes and with Andrew Hewett (Timor activist, at Oxfam Australia in 1999), phone, August 18, 2009.

49. CAVR, *Chega!*,"114.

50. Interviews with Beazley and with Janet Hunt (expert on Australian civil society regarding East Timor and Aceh), Canberra, Australia, August 4, 2009. According to Hunt, the executive director of ACFOA from 1995–2000, the NGOs also pushed hard on this issue both with Downer directly and in the media. See also Michael Wagner, "Army in the Way of Freedom," *Sydney Morning Herald*, April 29, 1999.

51. For Downer's comments on this see Cole-Adams, "Downer Denies Rift on Peacekeepers."

52. This diversity did not go unnoticed by Australia's top officials. Reflecting on a Melbourne demonstration that he observed with the prime minister, Howard's chief of staff Arthur Sinodinos recalled that it represented "a cross section of the population, not just university students. There were clerical people there and older people there and it was an issue that touched a lot of Australians." Interview with the author, Sydney, Australia, August 28, 2008.

53. James Dunn, "Courage to Call the Shots," *Sydney Morning Herald*, September 9, 1999.

54. In *SMH* see, e.g., "The Reality of East Timor," *Sydney Morning Herald*, September 11, 1999; Peter Cole-Adams, "Parties Demand Action in Wake of Atrocities," *Sydney Morning Herald*, September 13, 1999; Michelle Grattan, "Howard Tetchy at Ambivalent America," *Sydney Morning Herald*, September 11, 1999.

55. Even compared with other devastating conflicts in the region, this was a notably unique position for these groups to take. Wilson, interview.

56. Hamish McDonald, "Australia's Guilt Rising by the Hour," *Sydney Morning Herald*, September 7, 1999.

57. Leonie Lamont, "Nuns Compile a List of the Missing," *Sydney Morning Herald*, September 9, 1999.

58. Ellen Connolly and Greg Bearup, "Protesters Storm Sydney Airport, Block Passengers," *Sydney Morning Herald*, September 11, 1999; McDonald, "Australia's Guilt Rising."

59. Fernandes, interview.

60. Dunn, "Courage to Call the Shots."

61. "Postscript," *Sydney Morning Herald*, September 6, 1999.

62. Margo Kingston and Damien Murphy, "Angry Public Talks the Talk," *Sydney Morning Herald*, September 10, 1999.

63. Ibid.

64. Richard Glover, "Reality Still Has to Rule, OK?," *Sydney Morning Herald*, September 11, 1999.

65. Hal Hill, "With a Great Friend like Australia," *Sydney Morning Herald*, September 10, 1999.

66. The survey was conducted by Newspoll Market Research/The Australian by phone on September 10–12, 1999, among 1200 randomly selected respondents located across Australia. The data were weighted to reflect the population distribution and are available at http://polling.newspoll.com.au.tmp.anchor.net.au/image_uploads/cgi-lib.25638.1.0902timor.pdf, accessed August 26, 2009.

67. A second poll in October showed continued support for the decision to deploy the troops. Michelle Grattan, "UN Mission Lifts Howard's Popularity," *Sydney Morning Herald*, October 13, 1999.

68. "Whatever It Takes," program transcript from episode 2 of *The Howard Years*, documentary, ABC Television (Australia), 2008, formerly available at http://www.abc.net.au/news/howardyears, accessed August 24, 2009.

69. Ibid. For a statement Howard made at the time see Michelle Grattan, "PM Cool as Emotions Flare," *Sydney Morning Herald*, September 10, 1999.

70. "Whatever It Takes."

71. Quoted in Greenlees and Garran, *Deliverance*, 245. For another similar quote from Downer see also CAVR, *Chega!*, 114. In addition, a number of other Australians who were involved in or very knowledgeable about the process believe that the government's decisions were strongly driven by public opinion. As Hugh White later put it, the decision to deploy INTERFET "was to a significant extent out of the government's hands: the violence that followed the ballot had so galvanised Australian public opinion that by the time the decision was made the government seemed to feel that it simply had no choice, whatever the costs and risks." White, "Road to INTERFET," 86. This view was also expressed in interviews with Horner and with Ian McAllister (expert on Australian politics and public opinion at Australian National University), Canberra, Australia, August 11, 2008.

72. This came up in interviews with Downer, Sinodinos, and White (2008).

73. As a result, Howard and other ministers—particularly Downer—are thought to have felt, or have expressed feelings of, responsibility for the way that events played out.

74. White, "Road to INTERFET," 73.

75. Greenlees and Garran, *Deliverance*, 239.

76. Interviews with Barrie, Smith, and White (2008).

77. White, interview (2008).

78. Sinodinos, interview. See also Grattan, "PM Cool."

79. Interviews with Barrie and Smith. See also Cosgrove, *My Story*, chap. 6 (esp. 148, 154); Greenlees and Garran, *Deliverance*, 270.

80. On senior decision-makers' concerns see White, "Road to INTERFET," 84; Cosgrove, *My Story*, 176. For more on the risks and efforts to minimize them see also *My Story*, especially chaps. 7–10; and Greenlees and Garran, *Deliverance*, chap. 14.

81. For Habibie's relationship with the military at this time see Greenlees and Garran, *Deliverance*, 248–251.

82. See, e.g., Department of Defence (Australia), *Defence 2000*, 41; Department of Defence (Australia), *Defending Australia: Defence White Paper 1994* (Canberra: Australian Government Publishing Service, 1994), 86–88.

83. Clinton Fernandes, *Reluctant Saviour* (Melbourne: Scribe Publications, 2004), 20. The Keating government also regularly went against public opinion, and majority opinion within the Labour Party, to pursue cooperative relations with Indonesia. Paul Keating (prime minister of Australia, 1991–96), interview with the author, Sydney, Australia, August 20, 2009.

84. For Downer's comments on this see Cole-Adams, "Downer Denies Rift on Peacekeepers."

85. White, "Road to INTERFET," 80.

86. Ibid., 69.

87. Sinodinos, interview.

88. Greenlees and Garran, *Deliverance*, 110.

89. James Cotton, "'Peacekeeping' in East Timor: An Australian Policy Departure," *Australian Journal of International Affairs* 53, no. 3 (1999): 244.

90. Internal Displacement Monitoring Centre, *Aceh/Indonesia: IDPs and Returnees Still Face Significant Recovery and Reintegration Needs* (September 8, 2010), 3.

91. Ibid.

92. United States Committee for Refugees, *World Refugee Survey 2003* (New York: United States Committee for Refugees, 2003), 122.

93. Matthew Moore, "Aceh Rebels Still Resisting the Military," *Sydney Morning Herald*, November 5, 2003; Matthew Moore, "Aceh Downgraded to State of Emergency," *Sydney Morning Herald*, May 14, 2004; Matthew Moore and Karuni Rompies, "Dying for Peace," *Sydney Morning Herald*, November 22, 2003.

94. For a statement to this effect see Australian Broadcasting Corporation, "Downer Steers Clear of Violence in Other Parts of Indonesia," *ABC AM News*, September 29, 1999.

95. Mark Baker, "Aceh Crackdown Justified, Says Downer," *Sydney Morning Herald*, June 19, 2003.

96. Konrad Huber, *The HDC in Aceh: Promises and Pitfalls of NGO Mediation and Implementation* (Washington, DC: The East-West Center, 2004), viii. See this report for further information on the peace process and the Henry Dunant Centre's role.

97. Edward Aspinall (expert on Indonesian politics, particularly Aceh, at Australian National University), interview with the author, Canberra, Australia, August 12, 2009.

98. Huber, *HDC in Aceh*, ix.

99. Given the Indonesian government's sensitivity about foreign—and especially Australian—meddling in the wake of East Timor, however, it is very difficult to imagine a scenario in which it would have willingly consented to this.

100. Aspinall, interview.

101. Hugh White, interview with the author, Canberra, Australia, August 11, 2009.

102. Downer, interview.

103. Hunt, interview.

104. Interviews with Hunt and Aspinall.

105. Downer, interview.

106. Aspinall, interview.

107. Ibid.

108. Matthew Moore, "Foreign Journalists Held Back from Going to Aceh," *Sydney Morning Herald*, June 28, 2003; Moore, "Aceh Downgraded."

109. Matthew Moore, "Aceh War Fought in Silence," *Sydney Morning Herald*, November 26, 2003.

110. Matthew Moore, "Aceh and Papua Ruled No-Go Areas for Foreign Press," *Sydney Morning Herald*, November 11, 2004.

111. White, interview (2009). See also Hamish McDonald, "Indonesian Clouds Gather on Our Horizon," *Sydney Morning Herald*, February 14, 2001.

112. White, interview (2009). This point was also repeated in an interview with Christopher Ballard (expert on Australian and Pacific history at Australian National University), Canberra, Australia, July 29, 2009.

113. Matthew Moore, "Indonesia, Australia Exercises on Again," *Sydney Morning Herald*, August 1, 2003.

114. Hamish McDonald, "Foreign Affairs Lacking Some Voices of Dissent," *Sydney Morning Herald*, December 13, 2000.

115. Interviews with Aspinall and White (2009).

116. For the figure on Acehnese deaths see Nurdin Hasan, "Tsunami Rumors Cause Chaos in Aceh, Leaving One Dead and Others Injured," *Jakarta Globe*, March 19, 2011. More generally on the devastation, see also Australian Associated Press, "Howard to Visit Aceh," *Sydney Morning Herald*, February 2, 2005.

117. AusAID, *Australia's Response to the Indian Ocean Tsunami* (Canberra: Commonwealth of Australia, 2005), 1.

118. AusAID, *Australia's Response to the Indian Ocean Tsunami*; Robert Hill, interview by Gerald Tooth, *Australian Broadcasting Corporation (ABC) Radio National*, January 11, 2005; Australian Associated Press, "Howard to Visit Aceh."

119. AusAID, *Australia's Response to the Indian Ocean Tsunami*, 1.

120. See for example, Australian Associated Press, "Howard to Visit Aceh."

Conclusions and Implications

1. Ivo H. Daalder and Michael E. O'Hanlon, *Winning Ugly: NATO's War to Save Kosovo* (Washington, DC: Brookings Institution Press, 2000), 8–12.

2. Daalder and O'Hanlon, *Winning Ugly*, chaps. 2–3. See also Wheeler, *Saving Strangers*, 259–65.

3. Daalder and O'Hanlon, *Winning Ugly*, 102, 116–19.

4. Ibid., 120. See also Wheeler, *Saving Strangers*, 271.

5. On this campaign see Daalder and O'Hanlon, *Winning Ugly*, 108–15.

6. Other related decisions, including the selection of bombing targets and a choice to fly at an altitude of 15,000 feet to limit risks to the planes and pilots, were also controversial and led to charges that the mission was not conducted in a manner consistent with its announced humanitarian goals. See, e.g., Daalder and O'Hanlon, *Winning Ugly*, 121–24.

7. On the U.S. contribution see Daalder and O'Hanlon, *Winning Ugly*, 117. On the United Kingdom's contribution, see Ministry of Defence (United Kingdom), *Kosovo: Lessons from the Crisis*, CM 4724 (London: The Stationery Office), July 6, 2000, Annexes B, D, and F, available at http://webarchive.nationalarchives.gov.uk/20050404184736/http://www.mod.uk/publications/kosovo_lessons/contents.htm; Benjamin S. Lambeth, *NATO's Air War for Kosovo: A Strategic and Operational Assessment* (Santa Monica: RAND, 2001), 21; John E. Peters et al., *European Contributions to Operation Allied Force: Implications for Transatlantic Cooperation* (Santa Monica: RAND, 2001), 19, 22–23.

8. Daalder and O'Hanlon, *Winning Ugly*, 89–100; Wheeler, *Saving Strangers*, 268. On European opposition to ground forces see also Tony Blair, *A Journey: My Political Life* (New York: Alfred A. Knopf, 2010), 230–31.

9. Daalder and O'Hanlon, *Winning Ugly*, 96.

10. Wheeler, *Saving Strangers*, 268. Similarly, the administration's top Balkans diplomat, Richard Holbrooke, and other key Pentagon officials strongly doubted whether a limited air campaign could bring Milosevic into line. See, respectively, p. 298n88 and p. 71 of Daalder and O'Hanlon, *Winning Ugly*. More publicly, shortly before Allied Force began, the four U.S. service chiefs testified before the Senate Armed Services Committee that they doubted whether air strikes alone would succeed, with Air Force chief Michael Ryan adding shortly thereafter, "I don't know if we can do it without ground troops." See Lambeth, *NATO's Air War*, 222.

11. Daalder and O'Hanlon, *Winning Ugly*, 54. On the United Kingdom's position as of June see 36–37.

12. Blair, *A Journey*, 235. See also 228, 231. Blair's view on the use of ground troops was nuanced. While believing they would prove necessary and that NATO should be prepared to use them if that were the case, he did not advocate them as a first resort. A significant worry that restrained Blair at this time was the possibility that the United States would agree to an invasion force, but push to use as its core the small NATO force already deployed in Macedonia to protect civilian ceasefire monitors in Kosovo. The United Kingdom and other European allies wished to avoid this, since there were no U.S. troops in Macedonia and they did not want to deploy ground forces into Kosovo without U.S. participation. See Daalder and O'Hanlon, *Winning Ugly*, 96 and 300n105.

13. Blair, *A Journey*, 236–42; Daalder and O'Hanlon, *Winning Ugly*, 137, 141, 155–61. See also Wheeler, *Saving Strangers*, 273.

14. Daalder and O'Hanlon, *Winning Ugly*, 173–76.

15. See, e.g., ibid., 35–36; Blair, *A Journey*, 235–36.

16. Similarly, in Kosovo Tony Blair's decision to accept an air campaign in the hope of later securing a ground force suggests he saw this as an acceptable next-best option that might be rectified once the allies were committed.

17. It is not difficult to find similar evidence for other cases of ambitions-resources gaps not covered in depth in this book. For one example, a French military briefing paper leaked shortly after the beginning of the EU's Operation Artemis in the DRC in June 2003 reflected considerable pessimism about what the "short-lived and localised" mission could accomplish, anticipating that it would "have a negligible impact on tribal conflict." One European military planner described the document as "the most cynical military briefing I've read in my entire life." James Astill, "French Admit Their Congo Mission Will Have Little Impact on Fighting," *Guardian*, June 12, 2003.

18. Daalder and O'Hanlon, *Winning Ugly*, 126–27; Wheeler, *Saving Strangers*, 266–67; Blair, *A Journey*, 228.

19. Powlick, "Attitudinal Bases for Responsiveness to Public Opinion"; Hinckley, *People, Polls, and Policymakers*; Sobel, *Impact of Public Opinion on U.S. Foreign Policy Since Vietnam*; Merom, *How Democracies Lose Small Wars*; Baum, "How Public Opinion Constrains."

20. Relevant studies on humanitarian action and civilian protection include Jakobsen, "National Interest, Humanitarianism or CNN"; Kaufmann and Pape, "Explaining Costly International Moral Action"; Jakobsen, "Transformation of UN Peace Operations"; Finnemore, *Purpose of Intervention*; Bass, *Freedom's Battle*. The general point, though, is not limited to this policy arena.

21. Merom, *How Democracies Lose Small Wars*.

22. Alexander B. Downes, *Targeting Civilians in War* (Ithaca: Cornell University Press, 2008), 246. See also Downes, "Restraint or Propellant?."

23. Greenhill, *Weapons of Mass Migration*.

24. See, e.g., Weiss, "Intervention"; Walzer, "Politics of Rescue"; Valentino, "Perils of Limited Intervention."

25. Daalder and O'Hanlon, *Winning Ugly*, 193.

26. ICISS, *Responsibility to Protect*, 37.

27. In practice these conditions may overlap, since the circumstances where intervention seems likely to lead to wider war—notably, when a complex emergency occurs in a major power—also affect the operational environment for potential interveners in ways that will heighten leaders' concerns about the costs of action.

28. Robert A. Pape, "When Duty Calls: A Pragmatic Standard of Humanitarian Intervention," *International Security* 37, no. 1 (2012): 41–80, at 55–56.

29. Prendergast and Cheadle, *Enough Moment*, 21.

30. Power, *Problem from Hell*.

31. See, for instance, Valentino, "Perils of Limited Intervention," 734–36.

Index

Aceh, Indonesia
  Australian response to civil war in, 16, 170,
    191–92
  civil war in, 190–91
  December 2004 tsunami, 191, 196
  and expectations regarding response to
    complex emergencies, 19, 196–98
  material pressures regarding, 192–96
  operational environment in, 83
activism and advocacy. *See* societal
  pressures
affinity, 87, 96
Afghanistan
  civil war in, 79
  and U.S. policy on Darfur, 155, 159
African Union Mission in Burundi (AMIB), 34
African Union Mission in Sudan (AMIS)
  effectiveness of, 1, 137, 147, 162, 166–67
  efforts to strengthen, 151–52, 159–60
  operational goals of, 27
  U.S. support for, 16, 18, 143–46, 157–58,
    161, 165–67, 205–6
airpower, 30–31, 200–201, 202
Alesandrini, Jean-François, 120
alliance, 87
Allison, Graham, 54, 57
ambitions-resources gaps, 6–9
  addressing problem of, 209–11
  alternative explanations for, 13–15, 206–7
  benefiting from, 168
  case studies regarding, 16–19
  citizens' recognition of, 50–51, 197, 205–6,
    210–11
  in civil versus non-civil conflicts, 97

  and competing intragovernmental
    pressures, 57–59
  and competing moral and material
    pressures, 59–64, 202, 203–4, 205–6
  and competing societal pressures, 49–53
  and *contribution type*, 75, 83–84, 85–86
  great power contributions creating, 39–40
  hypotheses regarding, 64–66, 69–70
  and multilateral operations, 66–68
  negative impact of, 6–7, 34–35, 209
  as organized hypocrisy, 9–13, 42–45
  origins of, 4, 13–15, 203
  as politically appealing, 16
  probability of, 94, 95, 99, 100, 101
  restricted sample in analyzing, 97–99
  in two-dimensional ambitions-resources
    space, 34–35
American Jewish World Service, 164
Annabi, Hedi, 146
Annan, Kofi, 137, 148, 166
Arusha Accords, 106, 107, 109
Asian Financial Crisis (1997), 169, 176
atrocity crimes, 22–23, 28
Australia. *See also* International Force for
  East Timor (INTERFET)
  distribution of *contribution type* for, 76
  foreign policy making in, 171–72
  material pressures regarding Aceh,
    192–96
  multilateral operations of, 67
  normative pressures on, 178–86
  peace operations of, 16, 18–19, 169–71
  phases of involvement in East Timor,
    173–74

Australia *(continued)*
and policy design, 36, 37
preparation for East Timor referendum, 174–76
relations with Indonesia, 188–89
response to Aceh conflict, 16, 170, 191–92
and variation in civilian protection, 5–6
Australian Defense Force (ADF), 170–71, 178, 186, 187, 196

Balladur, Édouard, 110, 118, 123, 124–25, 126, 127, 129, 134
Barnett, Michael, 110
al-Bashir, Omar, 139, 146, 147, 148, 164
Bass, Gary, 56, 78
Belo, Carlos Filipe Ximenes, 180
Berkman, Tobias, 24, 27–28, 51
Biberson, Philippe, 122
Birmingham, John, 177
Blair, Tony, 19, 199, 201–2
Blanchard, Father, 121
Bolton, John, 155, 162–63
Booker, Salih, 159
Bosnia, 1–2, 6, 30, 56, 79, 125
Bradol, Jean-Hervé, 117–18, 122
Brahimi Report (2000), 13–14
Brereton, Laurie, 181
Brunsson, Nils, 42, 43, 44
Burma, 79
Bush, George H. W., 58
Bush, George W., 48–49, 143, 148–49, 152, 156–57, 162, 165, 167

Capps, Ron, 167
Catholic Church and charities, 183, 193
CE news coverage, 77–80. *See also* media coverage
by *contribution type*, 83–86
in regression analysis, 86–87, 89–95, 98–99
in robustness tests, 99, 100
Center for American Progress, 150
Cheadle, Don, 211
Chirac, Jacques, 125
civil conflict, 88, 89, 91, 97
civilian protection
and ambitions-resources gaps as compromise, 59–64
and competing moral and material pressures, 60
defined, 23–24
intragovernmental pressures regarding, 56–57
as operational goal, 27–28, 29–30
resources for, 31
societal pressures regarding, 45–49
Clinton, Bill, 14, 201, 202, 207
Cockett, Richard, 157
coercive engineered migration, 20, 208
cohabitation, 105, 109

complex humanitarian emergencies
and appropriateness of operational goals, 26
contribution types in, 72–76
defined, 22–23, 70
post-Cold War, 70–72
pre-1989, 88
Comprehensive Peace Agreement (CPA), 156
contiguous ally, 87, 101
contribution decade, 98
contribution type, 72–76. *See also*
ambitions-resources gaps; limited missions/contributions; robust missions/contributions
CE news coverage and *operational environment* by, 83–86
restricted sample in analyzing, 97–99
variables affecting, 89–97
Cornwell, Rachel, 161
Corzine, Jon, 151
Cosgrove, Peter, 2, 177
costs of civilian protection
intragovernmental pressure to limit, 54–56
societal pressure to limit, 45–47

Daalder, Ivo, 200, 201
Dallaire, Roméo, 107, 151
Darfur, Sudan, 137–39
advocacy for intervention in, 48–49, 205–6
alternate explanations for ambitions-resources gaps in, 165–67, 206, 207
AMIS's response to attack in Hamada, 1
civilian-protection needs in, 140–42
first phase of U.S. response to, 142
material pressures regarding, 154–65, 205
normative pressures regarding, 149–54, 156–65, 205
operational environment of, 154–56
origins of war in, 139–40
peace operations in, 16, 17–18
second phase of U.S. response to, 143–46
third phase of U.S. response to, 146–48
Darfur Peace Agreement (DPA, 2006), 141, 147
deadly force, 29–31. *See also* rules of engagement (ROE)
Delaye, Bruno, 122, 125
democracy, 11, 88, 97. *See also* great power democracies
de Waal, Alex, 145, 163, 164
displacement, forcible, 23, 71, 190
Downer, Alexander, 49, 175, 185, 186, 188, 191, 193, 195–96, 197
Downes, Alexander, 208
Doyle, Michael, 81
Dream for Darfur, 164

East Timor. *See also* International Force for East Timor (INTERFET); UN Transitional Administration in East Timor (UNTAET)

Australia's response to complex emergency in, 173–78
background and course of complex emergency in, 172–73
impact on Aceh, 190, 192–93
media coverage on Aceh versus, 194
operational environment in, 186–87, 197–98, 205
Economic Community of West African States (ECOWAS), 5
Egeland, Jan, 142
El Salvador, 27
Entman, Robert, 78
ethical dilemmas in intervening in complex emergencies, 209–10
Ethiopia, 83

Farrow, Mia, 164–65
Favier, Pierre, 129, 130–31
"first, do no harm," 209–10
Flint, Julie, 145, 163, 164
Forces Armées Rwandaises (FAR), 106, 108–9, 115, 124, 130, 132–33
forcible displacement, 23, 71, 190
former colony, 87, 96, 101
France. *See also* Operation Turquoise (1994)
arrival in Bisesero, Rwanda, 6–7
distribution of *contribution type* for, 76
executive power in, 105
peace operations of, 17–18
and policy design, 36, 37
political reception to media in, 78
public support for Operation Turquoise, 46, 205
role in Rwandan civil war, 108–10
and variation in civilian protection, 5–6
Frazer, Jendayi, 155, 161
Free Aceh Movement (Gerakan Aceh Merdeka, GAM), 190, 191, 194

Galluci, Gerard, 142, 152–53
Garran, Robert, 186
Genocide Intervention Network (GI-Net), 150, 151, 160, 164
Gerson, Michael, 154, 162
Girard, Renaud, 120
Gosh, Salah, 159
great power democracies. *See also* Australia; France; United Kingdom; United States
and ambitions-resources gaps, 8–9, 10
foreign policy vulnerabilities of, 208
and policy design, 35–40
pressures to protect civilians, 11–12
ulterior motives of, 15
and variation in civilian protection, 5–6
Greenhill, Kelly, 20, 208
Greenlees, Don, 186
Guéhenno, Jean-Marie, 139

Gugerty, Mary Kay, 53
Guterres, António, 161

Habibie, B. J., 172, 174, 175–76, 186, 187, 197
Habyarimana, Juvénal, 106, 107, 108, 109
Hamilton, Rebecca, 53, 160, 167
Hanis, Mark, 164
Hazlett, Chad, 159
Henry Dunant Centre for Humanitarian Dialogue, 191–92
Hockey, Joe, 185
Holbrooke, Richard, 151
Holt, Victoria, 24, 27–28, 51
Howard, John, 169, 174, 175–76, 179, 181, 185, 186, 189, 197
Huber, Konrade, 191, 192
Human Rights Watch, 151, 195
Hutu, 105–8, 112, 120
hybrid operations, 38

indigenous armed groups, 80–81
Indonesia. *See* Aceh, Indonesia; East Timor; International Force for East Timor (INTERFET)
Interahamwe, 106, 124
internally displaced person (IDP) camps, 27, 112, 141, 144, 166
International Commission on Intervention and State Sovereignty, 9, 210
International Crisis Group (ICG), 149, 159, 163
International Force for East Timor (INTERFET)
alternative explanations for, 187–90
deployment and design of, 2, 176–78
events launching, 172–73
and expectations regarding ambitions-resources gaps, 18–19, 196–98
military action in, 30
as multilateral mission, 67
normative pressures influencing, 178–86
operational environment of, 186–87, 197–98, 205
as robust mission, 169
significance of, 170
internationalized civil conflict, 88, 97
international partners, as source of competing pressures on great power democracies, 12, 13, 42, 67
intragovernmental bargaining, 54, 55, 57, 58
intragovernmental pressures, 53–59
and competing moral and material pressures, 59–64
on great power democracies, 11–12
and hypotheses regarding ambitions-resources gaps, 64–66, 69–70
in Operation Turquoise, 104
regarding Aceh, 192–93
regarding Darfur, 152–54, 157, 161–63, 168

Iraq, 14, 82–83, 155, 159
Ismail, Omer, 163

Janjaweed, 139–40
Juppé, Alain, 109–10, 118, 122–23, 126, 127–28, 129, 134
Justice and Equality Movement (JEM), 139

Kagame, Paul, 107
Kanyarengwe, Alexis, 124
Kosovo, 19, 76, 199–202, 206–7
Kosovo Force (KFOR), 76, 202
Krasner, Stephen, 43, 44
Kuperman, Alan, 35, 39

La Balme, Natalie, 78
Lafourcade, Jean-Claude, 111, 115, 123, 126, 131, 134
Lainé, Pierre, 121
Lake, Anthony, 55
Lanotte, Olivier, 113, 115, 122–23, 125, 128, 131, 133
Lanxade, Jacques, 124
Lanz, David, 150
Léotard, François, 110, 121, 123, 127, 129, 134
Limagne, Joseph, 121
limited missions/contributions
    and *contribution type*, 75, 83–84
    great power contributions to, 39
    hypothesis regarding, 65
    probability of, 95, 99, 100–101
    in two-dimensional ambitions-resources space, 4, 6, 34
Lipson, Michael, 10, 43

March, James, 58–59
Mass Atrocity Response Operations (MARO) Project, 14
Martin-Roland, Michel, 129, 130–31
mass killing, 71, 88, 97, 113
material pressures. *See* moral and material pressures
Médecins Sans Frontières (MSF), 116–19, 120, 122, 125, 128, 135
media coverage. See also *CE news coverage*
    on Aceh, 193–95
    on Darfur, 149, 150–51
    on East Timor, 181–82, 183–84
    on Operation Turquoise, 128–29
    on Rwanda, 116, 117–18, 119–23
Mercier, General, 131
Merom, Gil, 20, 208
military actors
    and ambitions-resources gaps as compromise, 58
    and competing intragovernmental pressures, 55

military strategies, suitability of, to operational goals, 29–31
Milosevic, Slobodan, 199, 200, 201, 202
Minawi, Minni, 146
Mitterrand, François, 110, 118, 122, 126, 128, 129, 132, 134
Montferrand, Bernard de, 118
moral and material pressures, 59–64
    ambitions-resources gaps as compromise between, 202, 203–4, 205–6
    creating path to robust protection, 211–12
    regarding Aceh, 192–96
    regarding Darfur, 149–65, 167–68, 205
    regarding East Timor, 178–86
    regarding Rwanda, 104, 116–29, 135, 205
Morgenthau, Hans, 15
Mouvement Révolutionnaire National pour le Développement (MRND), 106
multilateral operations, 4–5, 66–67
multinomial logistic regression, 86, 89
Musitelli, Jean, 122

Naivasha negotiations, 155–56
NATO, 5, 144, 162, 199, 200, 201, 202
Natsios, Andrew, 142, 152, 153, 167
Negroponte, John, 165
neutrality, in Operation Turquoise, 113–15
news coverage. See *CE news coverage*; media coverage
no-fly zones, 30
non-civil conflict, 88, 97
noncombatants, 208
non-governmental organizations (NGOs)
    in Aceh, 193
    and ambitions-resources gaps as compromise, 51–52
    and normative pressures on French government, 116–19, 120, 122, 135
    and Operation Turquoise, 125, 128
normative pressures. *See* moral and material pressures
norm of sovereignty, 43

offensive action, in peace operations, 30–31
O'Hanlon, Michael, 32, 80, 200, 201
operational environment
    altering, 211–12
    and competing moral and material pressures, 61–63
    by *contribution type*, 83–86
    of Darfur, 154–56
    and empirical expectations regarding peace operations, 61
    impact of, 12–13
    as independent variable, 80–83
    of East Timor, 186–87, 197–98, 205
    malleable aspects of, 197
    of Rwanda, 123–26

in regression analysis, 86–87, 89–95, 98–99
in robustness tests, 99–100
operational goals
    and addressing key threats, 26–28
    suitability of military strategies to, 29–31
Operation Allied Force, 19, 76, 199–202, 206–7
Operation Amaryllis, 109, 117
Operation Provide Comfort (1991), 14, 29
Operation Support Hope (1994), 27, 34
Operation Turquoise (1994), 103–5, 135–36. *See also* Rwanda
    alternative explanations for ambitions-resources gap in, 130–35, 206, 207
    ambitions-resources gap in, 34
    and background and course of Rwandan genocide, 105–8
    as case study, 16
    civilian support for, 205
    conspiracy theories about, 130–32
    detailed account of, 110–15
    and expectations regarding ambitions-resources gaps, 17–18
    firepower in, 111–12, 113–14, 115
    France's alleged motives for, 104
    and France's role in Rwandan civil war, 108–10
    institutional context of, 105
    normative and material pressures in, 116–23, 126–29
    operational environment and other material pressures in, 123–26
organized hypocrisy, 9–13
    ambitions-resources gaps as, 42–45, 65, 203–4
    building support through rhetoric of, 52
    and promotion of Operation Turquoise, 129, 135
    rhetoric of, regarding Darfur, 161, 165

Pape, Robert, 210
peace operation design, and variation in civilian protection, 4, 7–8
peace operations
    ambitions of, 4, 26–31, 32–35, 38–39
    defined, 24–25
    explaining variation in, 3–6
    great power democracies and design of, 35–40
    protection typology of, 4–5, 32–35, 39
    resources of, 4, 24, 31–35, 74–75, 177
    security for, 27, 29
    types of, 4–5, 32–35, 39
    variation in protection afforded by, 1–3
Pin, Dominique, 122
political will, 41–42
    and ambitions-resources gaps as organized hypocrisy, 42–45

and competing intragovernmental pressures, 53–59
and competing societal pressures, 45–53
    as continuum, 9
Post-Cold War Complex Humanitarian Emergencies Dataset, 70–72
Powell, Colin, 151, 161
Power, Samantha, 54, 56, 57–58, 151, 212
Prakash, Aseem, 53
pre-1989 complex emergency, 88, 97
Prendergast, John, 211
"primum non nocere" ("first, do no harm"), 209–10
Pronk, Jan, 147
Protection of Civilians in Armed Conflict (POC), 24
protection typology, 4–5, 32–35, 39
Prunier, Gérard, 125, 127, 129, 134, 140, 148, 151, 157

quantitative evidence, 69–70, 101–2
    data, 70–83
    first cut, 83–86
    regression analysis, 86–101
Quesnot, Christian, 127, 132, 134

Ramos-Horta, José, 180
Reeves, Eric, 159, 165
region, 87, 96
regional organizations, 8, 212
regression analysis, 86–101
Resolution 1706, 148, 164, 165
Responsibility to Protect (R2P), 24, 210
Returned Services League, 179
Robertson, George, 202
robust missions/contributions
    circumstances associated with, 16, 94, 204–5
    and competing moral and material pressures, 64
    and *contribution type*, 75, 83–84, 85–86
    creating path to, 211–12
    great power contributions to, 39
    hypothesis regarding, 65, 69–70
    INTERFET as, 169
    probability of, 96–97, 99, 100, 101
    in two-dimensional ambitions-resources space, 4, 6, 33–34
    and unintentional ambitions-resources gaps, 14
robustness tests, 99–101
Rubenstein, David, 164–65
rules of engagement (ROE), 29–31, 111, 113, 177
Rumsfeld, Donald, 155, 162–63
Russett, Bruce, 45, 46
Rwanda. *See also* Operation Turquoise (1994)

Rwanda (continued)
ambitions-resources gap in, 6–7
background and course of genocide in, 105–8
Clinton on, 14
France's role in civil war, 108–10
Operation Support Hope (1994), 27
U.S. involvement in, 55
Rwandan Patriotic Front (RPF), 106–10, 123–24, 128, 130, 132–33

Safe Humanitarian Zone (SHZ), 112, 115, 132–33
Sambanis, Nicholas, 71, 81
Santa Cruz Massacre, 179–80
Saperstein, David, 160–61
Save Darfur Coalition, 150–51, 152, 164
Save Darfur rally (April 30, 2006), 164
Scowcroft, Brent, 56
Security Council Resolution 1769, 148
Seybolt, Taylor, 114
Sierra Leone, 27, 34
Sinodinos, Arthur, 186, 189
Skelton, Harry, 201
Smith, Stephen, 129
societal pressures, 45–53
and ambitions-resources gaps as compromise, 51–53
and citizens' recognition of ambitions-resources gaps, 50–51, 197, 205–6, 210–11
and competing moral and material pressures, 59–64
and foreign policy literacy, 210–11
and hypotheses regarding ambitions-resources gaps, 64–66, 69–70
impact on foreign policy, 207–8
for intervention in East Timor, 178–85
regarding Rwanda, 104, 116–23
regarding Aceh, 192–95
regarding Darfur, 18, 149–52, 157, 158–61, 163–65, 168, 205
Somalia, 14, 27, 30, 58
sovereignty, norm of, 43
Special Operations Command (Commandement des Opérations Spéciales), 111
Spiegel, Julia, 159
Srebrenica massacre, 6
state-level policy, and variation in civilian protection, 4–5
Sudan Liberation Movement/Army (SLM/A), 139, 147
Sumbeiywo, Lazaro, 157

Tenet, George, 201
Tentara Nasional Indonesia (TNI), 172–73, 174, 175, 187
terrain, in operational environment, 81, 82

Thomas-Jensen, Colin, 159
Timor Gap oil and gas fields, 189–90
trade, 87–88, 97
Traub, James, 158
troops
and ambitions-resources gaps as compromise, 50, 58
Australian, of INTERFET, 177
and challenges faced during intervention, 80–81
and contribution type, 74–75
deploying versus supporting, 66, 168, 206
number of, 31–32
in Operation Turquoise, 111, 113, 131–32
preparation and equipment of, 32
al-Turabi, Hassan, 139
Tutsi, 105–8, 112, 114
type 1 ambitions, 73
type 2 ambitions, 73
type 3 ambitions, 73

ulterior motives, of great power democracies, 15
Unified Task Force (UNITAF, 1992), 14, 73
United Kingdom
distribution of contribution type for, 76–77
ends participation in slave trade, 48
intervention in Kosovo, 19, 200, 201–2, 206–7
news coverage on interventions of, 79
Operation Allied Force, 19
and policy design, 36, 37
and variation in civilian protection, 5–6
United Nations, 13–14, 24
United Nations–African Union Mission in Darfur (UNAMID)
effectiveness of, 137, 163–64
Negroponte on, 165
U.S. support for, 16, 18, 147–48, 162–63, 165–66, 167, 205–6
United Nations Assistance Mission for Rwanda (UNAMIR), 106–7, 109–10
United Nations Assistance Mission for Rwanda (UNAMIR) II, 110, 111
United Nations Mission in East Timor (UNAMET), 175
United Nations Observer Mission in El Salvador (ONUSAL), 27, 34
United Nations Observer Mission in Sierra Leone (UNOMSIL), 27, 34
United Nations Operation in Somalia (UNOSOM I), 30
United Nations Protection Force (UNPROFOR), 2, 30, 34, 73, 76
United States
alternative explanations for ambitions-resources gaps in Darfur, 165–67
competing intragovernmental pressures in, 54, 55

distribution of *contribution type* for, 76–77
first phase in Darfur, 142
intervention in Kosovo, 200, 206–7
material pressures regarding Darfur, 154–65, 205
news coverage during Afghan civil war, 79
normative pressures regarding Darfur, 149–54, 156–65, 205
operational environment of Darfur, 154–56
Operation Support Hope (1994), 27
peace operations in Darfur, 16, 18
and policy design, 36, 37
second phase in Darfur, 143–46
third phase in Darfur, 146–48
and variation in civilian protection, 5–6
United States Agency for International Development (USAID), 152–53
UN Mission in Sudan (UNMIS), 145
UN Secretariat, 36
UN Security Council, 5, 24, 36, 109, 110

UN Transitional Administration in East Timor (UNTAET), 177–78

Valentino, Benjamin, 7, 71
Védrine, Hubert, 110
Villepin, Dominique de, 122–23

Wahid, Abdel, 147
Walzer, Michael, 26
wars, and complex humanitarian emergencies, 22–23
Weiss, Thomas, 7, 8
Western, John, 55, 58
White, Hugh, 185–86, 189, 192–93, 195
Williamson, Richard, 48, 153–54
Winter, Roger, 142, 152
Wolf, Frank, 49
World War II, 178–79

Zaire, 108, 112, 115, 128–29, 133
Zoellick, Robert, 146–47, 155, 166–67

CPSIA information can be obtained
at www.ICGtesting.com
Printed in the USA
BVHW03*1150110218
507799BV00001B/8/P

9 781501 715471